MEMOIRS OF BARRAS

VOLUME III

THE DIRECTORATE
FROM THE 18TH FRUCTIDOR TO THE 18TH BRUMAIRE

MEMOIRS OF BARRAS

MEMBER OF THE DIRECTORATE

EDITED, WITH A GENERAL
INTRODUCTION, PREFACES
AND APPENDICES, BY
GEORGE DURUY

WITH SEVEN PORTRAITS IN PHOTOGRAVURE
TWO FAC-SIMILES, AND TWO PLANS

" Les pamphlétaires, je suis destiné à être leur pâture, mais je redoute peu d'être leur victime : ils mordront sur du granit." — NAPOLÉON

IN FOUR VOLUMES
VOL. III.—THE DIRECTORATE FROM
THE 18TH FRUCTIDOR TO
THE 18TH BRUMAIRE
TRANSLATED BY C. E. ROCHE

NEW YORK
HARPER & BROTHERS FRANKLIN SQUARE
1896

Copyright, 1896, by HARPER & BROTHERS.

All rights reserved.

CONTENTS

	PAGE
Preface	ix
Chapter I	1
Chapter II	51
Chapter III	79
Chapter IV	99
Chapter V	144
Chapter VI	193
Chapter VII	239
Chapter VIII	264
Chapter IX	315
Chapter X	359
Chapter XI	397
Chapter XII	440
Chapter XIII	505
Chapter XIV	541
Chapter XV	561

ILLUSTRATIONS

BONAPARTE . . . . *Frontispiece*
TALLEYRAND . . . . *Facing p.* 206

PREFACE

THE third volume of the Memoirs of Barras comprises the period extending from the *coup d'état* of the 18th Fructidor, Year V. (4th September, 1797), to the *coup d'état* of the 18th Brumaire, Year VIII. (9th November, 1799).

It has, like the second volume, been composed to some extent from the notes jotted down by Barras at the close of each sitting of the Directorate. These notes have been most faithfully reproduced by the editor. M. de Saint-Albin has indeed interspersed these analytical summaries with either supplementary particulars culled from Barras's dictation, fragments drawn up by the ex-Director himself, or again scraps from his recollection of the utterances made in his presence by his friend. But these addenda to the account proper of the Directorial sittings, already to be met with in the second volume, composed in the same fashion, do not change the nature of the documentary character of that portion of the Memoirs. On the contrary, they break upon the monotony and aridity which would doubtless characterize a purely analytical summary; they animate these reports with a breath of life and passion; they bring out in bolder relief all the figures of members of the Directorate, of Ministers, of political men, and of generals, who pass in turn before the reader's eyes; and if, in connection with a sitting of the Year V. or of the Year VI., the editor of the Memoirs, coming across the name of any one of the contemporaries most cordially detested by Barras, such as Talleyrand, Fouché, Sieyès, or Réal, there and then wages war against him and tells us with a certain complacency of some misdeed committed by the personage at a later date, either under the Empire or under the Restoration, this does not constitute any serious reason for complaining of this slight license taken with chronology. The rigor of the literary composition of the Memoirs suffers therefrom; innumerable digressions break the thread of the narrative; but the style is occasionally improved by a few pages stamped with a brisker gait and a more personal accent, a few portraits rather happily limned, piquant bits which enhance the interest felt by the reader without diminishing upon the whole the importance of the copious historical matter contained in this volume.

Chapter I., consecrated to the 18th Fructidor, does not perhaps, to speak the truth, satisfy the hopes we were entitled to build upon the deposition of a witness as well informed as was undoubtedly the man who for so long beforehand held in his hands all the threads of the intrigue of which this *coup d'état*, a parody, minus their greatness, of the revolutionary days, was the conclusion. What remains of the chapter is meagre enough, if one eliminates the interesting pages treating of the arrest of Pichegru, the flight of Carnot, Augereau's infatuation subsequent to the event, the curious quotations of letters or of proclamations from the pens of Bonaparte, of Bernadotte, and of Talleyrand. Barras has here once more enveloped facts in a discreet obscurity. He reckons on the studied lack of preciseness of his narrative to conceal from the readers of his Memoirs the brutal violation of the law which was perpetrated and in which he participated.

On the other hand, how interesting are the particulars given about Bonaparte at the Congress of Rastadt, about his return to Paris, the reception he meets with, the hold obtained on public opinion by him, "without whom the Directorate can no longer take any action," in connection with the preliminaries of the expedition to Egypt! And this interest maintains itself, not to say becomes still livelier, in the chapters wherein the ex-Director once more gives rein to his caustic raciness in joyous gratification of his rancor against poor Josephine, whom he has already handled so mercilessly; against Talleyrand, his hatred of whom is insatiable; against Fouché, whose intrigues and shady transactions he tells us with complacency, in the days when the former Lyons proconsul and the future Duke of Otranto was reduced, "in order to eke out his livelihood, and that of his she-wolf and whelp," to fattening and selling pigs!

All this may perhaps be viewed as suspicious tittle-tattle, to which it is in all fairness difficult to give greater credence than to that of which he is so lavish in regard to Napoleon and the Imperial family. Granted, but however unbridled his instinct of slander on this occasion again, it is neither in the most piquant anecdotes nor in the portraits—caricatures, if you will—which he lays before us of some of his most celebrated contemporaries, that lies, from my point of view, the genuine interest of Volume III. of his Memoirs. That which gives a rare value to the contribution supplied by him to history lies in the fact that it constitutes the most crushing evidence against this Directorial government, which an ironical fate has placed—as if better to overwhelm it by a comparison with its neighbors—between the tragic grandeur of the Convention and the glorious and restoring period of the Consulate.

THE DIRECTORIAL *RÉGIME*

I

DISCORD IN THE GOVERNMENT

The depth of the dissensions agitating this wretched government is laid bare to us in the very first pages. Three of the Directors—Barras, Rewbell, and Larevellière—are at war with the two others, Carnot and Barthélemy. It is an open war, assuming the form of violent altercations which break out among them at every moment, and, according to the confession of Barras himself, transform their deliberations "into the fights of gladiators in the arena."

An occult war also, carried on by means of venomous newspaper articles inspired, and injurious reports circulated, by themselves against one another. Barras has his secret police, at the head of which is a master in this line, Fouché, who acts the spy on his behalf with Directors, Ministers, deputies, and sends him a daily report of his doings. And why should he not have a police, "when each and every one had his police and counter-police, . . . when we could not trust any of our Ministers?" Carnot and Barthélemy are expelled and proscribed. Harmony will now perhaps reign among the Five. The glorious purge of the 18th Fructidor is hardly a month old when dissensions are again in full swing: " I am informed that Merlin, the new Director, is seeking my ruin; . . . Rewbell and Larevellière likewise bear me a great deal of ill-will, if I am to believe my informants."

And so it will be to the end. So much does discord constitute the essence of the *régime* that in vain does the governmental *personnel* change or renew itself either by the drawing of lots by law established, which annually renders vacant one of the Directorial seats, or by *coups d'état;* dissensions, petty conflicts inspired by ambition, vanity, and interest are immediately renewed among these five men. They hate and despise one another. It will be seen, in the course of this volume, how Barras treats his colleagues. I shall content myself with quoting these few lines on Merlin: "Just about that time I was handed a document in the handwriting of Merlin, *which might have implicated him in a hardly honorable transaction in regard to a contract for army supplies.* I owe it to truth not to make such an assertion without producing the document."

Carnot does not possess a police which procures for him —God knows by what means!—documents compromising his colleagues. But, although he is less well equipped with documents than the prudent Barras, he shows just as little indulgence: " This man (Barras) conceals the ferocity of a Caligula under an exterior of simulated thoughtlessness. . . . Rewbell was constantly the protector of men charged with thefts and peculations; Barras, that of noblemen of ill-repute and of bullies; Larevellière, that of scandalous priests. . . . There is no more hypocritical and immoral man than Larevellière; nature, when creating him deformed and stinking, seemed to have intended to put on their guard those coming in contact with him against the falseness of his character and the profound corruption of his heart."[1]

Peruse the following terrible deposition against Barras: ". . . He was excessively vulgar in society, and lacked distinction. . . . In spite of his fine figure and manly face, he could not shake off entirely the low and brazen air acquired in bad society. . . . He displays remarkable aptitude for intrigue, in the practice of which he is indefatigable. . . . Treachery and deep dissimulation, coupled with his other vices, had but become strengthened with advancing years. At the Luxemburg his *entourage* consisted of nothing but the leaders of the most crapulous anarchy, the most corrupt aristocrats, women of easy virtue, men of ruined reputation, jobbers, dabblers in shady transactions, mistresses, and minions. The most infamous debauchery was, he himself confessed it, practised in his house. . . . To him a lie is nothing, and calumny a pastime. Neither faith nor morality are his. . . . Although possessed of a soldier's bravery, he has no moral courage; in politics he is devoid of firmness and resolution. . . . Although a patriot's, not to say a real *sans-culotte's*, language was forever on his lips, he was wont to surround himself with extraordinary pomp. He had all the tastes of an opulent, generous, magnificent, and spendthrift prince. . . ."[2] It is Larevellière-Lépeaux who limns this portrait of Barras; such is the rancor possessing the soul of a theophilanthropist! The testimony of the honest Gohier, although more temperate in form, is in the main just as severe against Barras.[3] Sieyès charges Rewbell with pocketing wax-candles as he leaves the sittings of the Directorate, and goes about repeating the following petty pun: "This Monsieur Rewbell must needs

---

[1] Carnot, in his reply to Bailleul, quoted by M. Ludovic Sciout in his *Histoire du Directoire*, vol. i., pp. 422–425.

[2] *Mémoires de Larevellière-Lépeaux*, vol. i., pp. 337–340.

[3] *Mémoires de Gohier*, vol. ii., pp. 326–333.

take something for his health every morning." Thus do they speak of one another, these men who, from 1795 to 1799, were called to the honor of managing together the affairs of France. The ironical observer of the pettiness and seamy side of human nature cannot but smile at seeing the so naïvely revealed sentiments borne towards one another by these former colleagues, who display such ardor in dragging one another through the mire. The matter will be found less laughable if one only reflects what the dissensions of its rulers must have cost a country thus governed. Barras will show us that they indeed cost, not only France, but liberty and the Republic very dear.

II

THE METHODS OF THE GOVERNMENT

1.—THE "SEE-SAW POLICY"

This strange five-headed executive power possesses, moreover, only the semblance of a government. An emanation from two assemblies, the Ancients and the Five Hundred, both disturbed by deep and incurable dissensions, the Directorate is like them a prey to party spirit and blindly obedient to all its suggestions.

Itself a party, it lacks the strength to rise superior to the other parties, to sway them, to recall them to concord, to impose it on them, if necessary, by an appeal to some lofty and generous idea of national reconciliation. The Directors, it is true, studiously apply themselves to emulate the deeds and tone of their predecessors—a wretched parody which deceives no one, for they lack the afflatus of faith which gave such strength to the utterances of the great *conventionnels*. Fatherland, liberty, and the hatred of tyranny are still, it is true, words on their lips. But something has found its way into them, a corrupting leaven scarce known to the men of the heroic age to whom they have succeeded: egotistical calculations substituted for the ardent love of the public weal; dissembled thoughts of personal interests secretly influencing the trend of home or foreign policy, the selection of generals, of Ministers, and of the most petty agents; a shameless favoritism exercising a baneful reaction on the affairs of the country; every kind of misfortune, in short, of a *régime* under which the conception of the real duties of a government has weakened to such a degree that those who wield the power are the first to set the example of exploiting the State in lieu of serving it. Does not one of the first measures of the Directorate consist in securing pecuniary compensation for the member whom the annual drawing of lots is to deprive of his lucrative function?[1] This trait enables one to measure the distance separating France's new masters from the laborious and honest Committee of Public Safety.

But how could the public weal be their dearest and sole thought when an attentive and anxious watching of the political see-saw absorbs and holds them, their eyes persistently fixed on a single point, filled with joy or fright alternately as the machine oscillates and its ups and downs reassure or alarm their petty ambitions? On the one side are moderates, indiscriminately branded as Royalists; on the other, patriots or Jacobins, henceforth denominated anarchists; does not manœuvring and steering between the two parties, opposed one to the other, if need be, overwhelmed one by the other, constitute a programme, a policy?[2] A policy of rope-dancers, not of statesmen! The Ministers of the old *régime* and the tribunes of the Revo-

[1] This compensation was originally to have been created from an annual levy on the salary of all the members, but this troublesome burden was soon imposed on the finances of the State.

[2] "*It is in vain that one attempts to find the political system of France; it does not exist.* Each Minister decides matters in his department in sovereign fashion, and in such a manner that the public weal is not taken into consideration; and when a resolution is come to at a council of the Directorate in regard to affairs of the gravest import, it is not the wisest but the most violent who carry the day.... *Tossed about continually from one party to another, the Directorate pursues an uncertain course* and weakens public opinion, which constitutes the only strength of the government." (Report of the Prussian Minister, Sandoz-Rollin, quoted by M. Pallain, *Ministère de Talleyrand sous le Directoire*, p. xxxiv.).

lution had a nobler aim than to remain standing on a
tight-rope, guarding against a tumble. While its new government, unfaithful to the virile traditions of energetic
labor and devotion towards the public weal, and of the
disinterestedness with which the Convention has honored
itself, thinks much more of itself than of the great interests
intrusted to it, France suffers, and every part of the body
social is ailing; the country, ruined, exhausted, and dev-
astated, seems on the point of falling into dissolution.
But what does it matter? To direct one's efforts to the
alleviation of all these evils, to deliver the people from the
plague of jobbery, of brigandage, and of civil war, to exact
from all the servants of the State honesty, justice, and the
faithful performance of the duties of their offices, is a mere
accessary business to which one devotes himself, if perchance time remains for doing so. The essential point is
to retain hold by every possible means of the power of
which so bad a use is being made, to oppose to the plotting of one's adversaries other threads of intrigue more
adroitly and strongly woven together, to triturate with art
the electoral matter, to purchase or proscribe all who render you uneasy. Do not these traits reveal the noble
science of politics degraded and rendered injurious—such,
in short, as the politicians have made it? Now one of the
Directorate's misdeeds, perhaps the worst of all, lies precisely in the fact of its having inaugurated, by means of the
shady practices of its inner government, the ill-omened era
of politicians.

III

THE METHODS OF THE GOVERNMENT

II.—THE RESPECT FOR THE CONSTITUTION, FREEDOM, AND JUSTICE

In a proclamation made in Brumaire, Year IV., to the
French people, the Directorate had promised—*risum tene-
atis*—" that inflexible justice and the strictest observation
of the laws should be its rule." It pledged itself "to ex-

tinguish all party spirit, . . . to regenerate morality, . . . to smother jobbery. . . ." Protestations of respect for legality, fine sentimental words on the inviolability of the national representation, are likewise to be met with in a message to the Five Hundred, dated the 21st Prairial, Year IV. No government ever violated more shamelessly the promises made by it at its inauguration.

Its respect for legality is shown in its outrages upon the elected of the nation. A *coup d'état* directed against the Royalists on the 18th Fructidor, Year V. (4th September, 1797): a magnificent and fruitful occupation, since 197 deputies were expelled from the Councils by means of proscription or invalidation! A *coup d'état* a few months later, the 22d Floréal, Year VI. (11th May, 1798), against the "anarchists": sixty Republican deputies, legally elected, are on this occasion deprived of the right to exercise their mandate, and the see-saw policy reckons a fresh triumph no less sad than the former one, since, like it, it is won over the Law. It is now the turn of the Councils to emulate the Directorate. A *coup d'état* on the 30th Prairial, Year VII. (18th June, 1799): the legislative power, twice decimated, revenges itself on the executive, and compels, with the complicity of a third, two Directors to resign. In less than two years, from September, 1797, to June, 1799, three violent shocks, which shake the Constitution in its very foundations.

When not engaged in outrageously violating the national representation, the Directorate seeks to control the elections by sophisticating them. Official candidacies[1] and electoral corruption are its means: 185,000 francs are, on Barras's own admission, appropriated for the purpose of "manipulating" the elections of the Year VI. The President of the Directorate receives 36,000 francs as his share. "Larevellière, nay, Rewbell himself, thinks this *modus operandi* most immoral in itself, *especially in a republic whose*

---

[1] See *Histoire de la République Française sous le Directoire*, by M. Ernest Hamel, p. 106: "In several localities the Directorate itself designated the candidates whose election would be agreeable to it, and its commissaries brought all their influence to bear on the electoral assemblies."

principle is virtue. . . . But, *while blushing*, the Directorate has no scruples in ordering a distribution of funds among those who prepare and manipulate elections. . . ." Could *Tartufe* have surpassed this?

And I presume that it is with blushes also that this pure government, the friend of both humanity and virtue, sentences to transportation, without any trial, not only fifty-three Deputies, two Directors, one ex-Minister, three generals, and others, but also the printers, editors, and proprietors of forty-two newspapers opposed to its policy; that it resolves upon adding to the list of the *émigrés* the transported persons who have escaped from Guiana; that it rejects the petition of Siméon, in spite of the luminous juridical dissertation accompanying it; lastly, that it denies the hundred priests confined in filthy cells at Rochefort the judges claimed by these unfortunate men[1] in so dignified and touching a fashion, before being conveyed to Cayenne.

Liberty of the press, justice, toleration, humanity, respect for the law and for institutions — of all these the Directorate makes mere counters, with a combination of cynicism and hypocrisy of which no other period of our history probably furnishes as perfect an example.

IV

INHERENT IMMORALITY OF THE *RÉGIME*.

I.—VENALITY AND PECULATION AT HOME

The government presents another still more repugnant aspect.

Of its members there is one who stays, while the others merely pass and disappear—some victims to the constitu-

---

[1] It remains to be pointed out that the petition of Siméon and of the Rochefort priests was presented two years subsequent to the 18th Fructidor (Prairial, Year VII.). Nothing better illustrates the harshness of this government than the barbarous tenacity of its rancor against its political adversaries. Of the 329 persons transported on the 18th Fructidor, 11 died of privation and ill-treatment during the passage; 167 died within two years. See article in the *Revue Bleue*, 17th February, 1894.

tion which prescribes the annual and partial renewal of the executive *personnel:* others to *coups d'état* which expel them from the Directorate in spite of that same constitution. This Director who, owing to a unique privilege, exercises his functions from the first to the last day of the Directorate, is therefore in the eyes of France the incarnation of the *régime*—all the more so from the fact that, in addition to his having remained on the stage while his colleagues successively left it, he enjoys the prestige of the prominent part played by him in connection with memorable events, such as the 9th Thermidor and the 13th Vendémiaire, the recollection of which is still fresh in men's minds.

It is therefore no exaggeration to say that Barras was the soul of this government.[1] And as this soul was a profoundly corrupt one, the result was that the government as a whole, although not solely composed of dishonest men, nevertheless bore the special imprint of the man who was its moving spirit, and the Directorate, considered from the standpoint of the *ensemble* of its acts, of its administrative methods, and of its home and foreign policy, was, from the fact of the uninterrupted action of the perverse mind from which it drew inspiration, a *régime* of inherent immorality.

It was not even necessary, in order for it to become such, for certain of its members, Rewbell and Sieyès notably, to have given, as rightly or wrongly asserted, sad examples of cupidity. A government which bears and retains in its bosom during the whole of its existence a leaven of corruption equal in harmfulness to the one deposited in it by the vices of Barras, cannot, even if it so wished, be anything but a corrupting government. It cannot prevent public morals moulding themselves on those the scandalous example of which is presented to all by the most brill-

---

[1] Carnot and Sieyès alone could have outweighed the preponderating influence of Barras. But Carnot leaves the Directorate as early as the 18th Fructidor, Year V. (4th September, 1797), and Sieyès does not join it until Floreal, Year VII. (April–May, 1799), in succession to Rewbell, who retires pursuant to the drawing of lots.

iant representative of power; the theophilanthropy of the worthy Larevellière is a poor antidote for such a poison. Nor can it any more prevent, in spite of the personal honesty of Carnot and Gohier, the agents of the State, both small and great, when they see peculation shamelessly installed in the supreme power, in the person of one of the chiefs of the State, and the most remarkable one at that, from considering themselves authorized thereby to make a traffic of their function, just as this venal Director traffics in his own. Barras alone would have sufficed, even although unconsciously aided in his work by other immoralities adjacent to and imitative of his own, to exercise over society and over the governmental and administrative morals of this time, and thereby on the very conscience of the country, the dissolvent influence which may justly be laid at his door.

I do not care to say more at this juncture against the man whom M. Ernest Hamel designates a "member of the criminal classes," ever ready to sell himself to the highest bidder. I shall therefore dispense with pointing out the means whereby the ruined nobleman of the early days of the Revolution was in a position, under the Directorate, to meet the enormous expenses inherent to his ostentatious style of living both in Paris and in his princely domain of Grosbois. I shall content myself with referring the reader desirous of being fully edified on this point to the explanations given by Barras in regard to his shady relations with the Venetian envoy Quirini,[1] and with the Royalist agent M. Fauche-Borel.[2] After reading and weigh-

---

[1] See, in this connection, the overwhelming conclusions drawn against Barras by M. Ludovic Sciout in his learned work on the Directorate, vol. ii., pp. 388-392. See, also, *Histoire du Directoire Constitutionnel*, published in the Year VII. by Carnot-Feulins.

[2] See, in regard to the Fauche-Borel affair, the *Mémoires de Gohier*, vol. ii., pp. 326-331. In an article on "Les Bourbons et la Russie" (*Revue des Deux Mondes*, 1st October, 1885), M. Ernest Daudet states that he possesses unpublished documents proving that Barras was bought by Louis XVIII. during the residence of the Pretender at Mittau, in 1797 or 1798. See, lastly, in *Histoire de la République sous le Directoire*, pp. 187, 188, what M. Ernest Hamel says in regard to the source of Barras's fortune.

ing the value of the arguments invoked—somewhat cleverly, indeed—by Barras in his defence, impartial minds will deduce therefrom such conclusions as they may consider equitable.

It matters little, moreover, whether Barras pledged himself, in return for a sum of 700,000 francs, to save the Republic of Venice, threatened with total overthrow by Bonaparte, or whether, for a sum of twelve millions, he was won over to paving the way to a restoration for the pretender Louis XVIII. There remains an uncontested fact in history, and it is that the Directorial government afforded, in the person of at least one of its members, not to say in those of several of them, the saddest examples of dishonesty.

Now this leaven was not circumscribed by the limits of its place of birth; it went on spreading till it infected the very body of the nation and poisoned the whole of France. And this corrupting influence exercised by the *régime* over which presided the man "who regarded neither law nor gospel,"[1] "the most shameless among the rotten,"[2] which Barras was, is the second of the crimes committed by the Directorate and not atoned for. If I give only second rank to it, it is because of its really being nothing but a complement of the first—the creation of the detestable policy of the politicians.

Like master like man. The members of the Directorate, some of them at least, have a craving for money; so have their Ministers. "Talleyrand received from Sinking, Hamburg's envoy, 500,000 francs for the treaty; he received a like sum from Venice, and an enormous sum from Spain for the purpose of influencing the elections and causing the fleet to be withdrawn." But is not Talleyrand's protector, pending the time when he shall become his mortal enemy—the powerful Director who has thrown open to the Bishop of Autun the doors of the Ministry so ardently coveted—is not Barras engaged in a similar transaction with M. d'Araujo,[3] the Portuguese Minister?

[1] M. Ernest Hamel.   [2] Taine.
[3] See *Le Directoire*, by M. Ludovic Sciout, vol. ii., p. 392, foot-note 1.

Truguet has been expelled by the 18th Fructidor from the Ministry of Marine, "in which he had displayed the soundest and broadest views." The admiral out of favor is exiled to an embassy at Madrid. He succeeds admirably in his new position. But he refuses to favor certain shady financial transactions of Talleyrand's, who, under cover of his function as Minister of Foreign Affairs, extends even to foreign countries the network of his speculations. Merlin, on the other hand, covets the Madrid embassy for one of his creatures, the physician Guillemardet, a man of no ability, but a *conventionnel* and a regicide—a couple of titles to which the 18th Fructidor has added a new lustre. So Truguet is recalled. As he does not display too great a hurry in returning to France, this excellent patriot and tried Republican is inscribed on the list of the *émigrés*. Truguet is reduced to seek a refuge in Holland. The country is thus deprived of a good ambassador and of a good sailor, and an outrageous iniquity is perpetrated. But Talleyrand is left free peacefully to indulge in his little operations. This, unless I am mistaken, is a simple fact which throws a somewhat vivid light on the methods, spirit, and morality of that government.

Men of prey are wandering up and down the avenues of power, in quest of contracts for supplies, and in quest of bargains; such is that Hainguerlot of whom Barras outlines for us the piratical profile. They besiege the Ministries, circumvent deputies, Ministers, and Directors, purchasing the right to fatten with impunity upon the State. Bribing is the order of the day. "Merlin is furious with Scherer. The reason adduced for this is that the Minister of War *is alleged not to have given to Mme. Villars, Merlin's mistress, bribes which she had solicited.* . . . It would seem that Talleyrand was behind time in transmitting to Mme. Villars what she was expecting."

An infamous doctrine gets abroad—to wit, that each and every public office must not only feed the man, remunerate him for his work, but enrich him. How? By shady transactions, by the sedulous cultivation of every particle of power and influence temporarily held by each and every official. "The place of Bourguignon, Minister of Police, has of late been greatly coveted, *because big profits are reputed to be attached to this Ministry, especially the farming out of gambling licenses and so many other sources of profitable incomes. . . .*" In all degrees of the administration each one betrays his trust and indulges in thieving pursuant to his appetite or to the means he has of satisfying it. The high-placed officials of the State are actively engaged in peculation; the smaller ones, in petty thievery; dishonesty breathes from above over the country. "Pilfering is their motto," as Rabelais would say.

V

INHERENT IMMORALITY OF THE *RÉGIME*

2.—EXTORTIONS COMMITTED ABROAD BY THE AGENTS AND ARMIES OF THE DIRECTORATE

The whole truth has not yet been told. So great is the corrupting power of the *régime* that it crosses the frontier, instils its venom into the diplomatic agents, into the civil commissaries attached to the armies, into the administrators of conquered countries. "Italy is in a deplorable state; *cruel extortions have made the people rise in insurrection.* . . . The civil agents have fled and have returned to France *with their plunder.* . . ." Jourdan writes: "The civil administration of the agents of the Directorate in foreign lands *has everywhere caused the French name to be looked upon with horror.*" The extortions committed in Italy by several agents, in particular by Trouvé, a creature of Larevellière, are so shameless that the Directorate, yielding to a fine outburst of virtue, resolves upon setting a watch upon and punishing the peculators. Barras suggests the name of Fouché—Fouché, the friend and partner of the bandit Hainguerlot, Fouché, the contractor for supplies to the army equipped against England, Fouché, the custodian and avenger of morality! An explosion of laughter should, methinks, have greeted such a proposition. Quite the contrary! Fouché is appointed, and let loose on the Cisalpine Republic, and unfortunate Italian populations have once more to endure being looted by the citizen "agent-in-chief" of the French Republic.

Nevertheless, the glory of Fouché pales before that of another Verres—Rapinat. This agent thinks nothing of purging the Helvetic Directorate in true French fashion[1] —in other words, expelling on his own authority "worthy citizens" forming part of this body, and substituting for them "men totally unworthy of esteem." Accompanied by two secretaries, Forfait and Grugeon, whose symbolical names form a happy framework to that of their chief, Rapinat makes a systematic attack on the Helvetic finances. So great is the scandal that complaints reach Paris. The Directorate deliberates. The facts are patent: Rapinat "is not only an outrageous extortionist, but an audacious creator of *coups d'état*." But the scoundrel is the brother-in-law of Rewbell, who has given him this bone, Switzerland, to gnaw. It would be a pity to harrow Rewbell's soul. . . . So Rapinat is kept at his post, and left free to disgrace the Republic. Morality is avenged merely by an epigram:

>La pauvre Suisse qu'on ruine
>Voudrait bien que l'on décidât
>Si Rapinat vient de rapine
>Ou rapine de Rapinat.[2]

Truguet is dismissed, and his name added to the roll of the *émigrés*, while Rapinat remains high in favor: here we have the very policy of the Directorate summed up in two

---

[1] See, in regard to the Jacobinical methods frequently employed by the agents of the Directorate in foreign parts, the report of the Prussian Minister, Sandoz-Rollin, to his government (June, 1798). Treilhard said to his colleagues: "To the incapacity of your agents must be attributed the alarm which has spread throughout Europe. . . . Do we not see Garat advising the King of the Two Sicilies to become a Jacobin? Do we not see Ginguené organizing war against the King of Sardinia and against Genoa?" (Quoted by M. Pallain, *Ministère de Talleyrand*, p. xxxvi.)

[2] It will be noticed that a passage of the narrative consecrated to Rapinat would seem to indicate that M. Rousselin de Saint-Albin is the author of the quatrain.

cruelly significant acts, and the picture of the *régime* with its double profile, one of injustice and violence, the other of cynical dishonesty.

But there remains something still more painful and humiliating—another shameful sore which must needs be laid bare, and which one cannot, even after a lapse of a hundred years, reveal without feeling a gnawing pain at one's heartstrings. The army itself—the generous army wherein the better part of the pure and ardent soul of the Revolution had sought a refuge during the Terror—is, like all the rest, contaminated; hence France is rotten even to the soundest of her members with the corruption radiating from her chief. And it is Barras who is once more to show us in the present volume to what an extent the armies of the Directorate are inferior, not in the bravery of the soldiers, nor in the talents of the leaders, but in moral value, to the admirable armies of the Year II.

Let us first observe that the country is sick at heart of an endless war. These campaigns and distant conquests, the meaning of which it cannot fathom, affect it much less than the engagements formerly fought in defence of the frontier. During the last years of the Directorate, as during the last years of the Empire, and for the same reasons, France will no longer fight : " *The most inexorable methods are employed to levy the conscription.*" Witness the adventures of the unfortunate hunchback, repeatedly arrested by the gendarmerie, dragged from prison to prison as a recalcitrant, in spite of the duly authenticated dispensation because of his physical incapacity invoked by him: Are we in the Year VII. or in 1813?

Disorganization reigns in the armies, the recruiting for which is becoming a difficult matter : " Dislocation reigns supreme ; a portion of the generals are deprived of command and threatened with trial ; the soldiers are worn out with fatigue and ask to return to their homes. . . ." Too weak, too divided against itself, too changing, and too fluctuating in its views to impose itself with the sovereign authority of the Committee of Public Safety, the Directorate thinks it is displaying governmental strength when pronouncing brutal and numerous dismissals. So it is that Masséna is deprived of his command. Fortunately, the Minister of War interferes, and secures the postponement of the execution of the absurd decree which, at a most critical juncture, is about to deprive France of so great a soldier. On that day Bernadotte has well deserved of his country, for it is precisely a few weeks after this incident that Masséna wins the fine and decisive victory of Zurich (September–October, 1799).

In the most important Ministry—since the Republic is at war with a portion of Europe—the incumbents appear, pass, and vanish with the rapidity of the shadows cast by a magic lantern. The most significant example of this disastrous instability is furnished in the person of Bernadotte. Called to the Ministry under most critical circumstances, after the disaster and death of Joubert at Novi (15th August, 1799–28th Thermidor, Year VII.), Bernadotte gives proof of activity and resoluteness against both the Royalist uprisings at home and the coalition. It is he therefore who has paved the way, by his good administration, for the two great triumphs—of Brune in Holland, at Bergen (19th September, 1799), and of Masséna in Switzerland, at Zurich. Bernadotte, a prey to the hostility of Sieyès, who covets the portfolio of War for his *protégé*, Marescot, is none the less driven from office.

Still another trait, like the resistance to the conscription, recalls to memory the last days of the Empire: the generals are jealous of one another, show themselves less enterprising, and, having become too rich, do not care to incur any personal risk on the field of battle: "Discord makes strides among our best generals; ... the ardor of the military chiefs begins to cool: they have acquired wealth. ..." And by what means? Alas! by following the nefarious examples set by the men who govern France, by deriving profits from their commands just as Directors and Ministers reap profits from their functions, and, to tell the whole truth, by pillaging conquered countries.

The state of penury in which he is left by the government compels Bonaparte to feed war by war during the campaign of 1796–1797. The heavy contributions he levies in Italy are thus divided: with one half he feeds, clothes, and pays his troops; with the other he assists and maintains the government. The glorious general of the Army of Sambre-et-Meuse does likewise: Hoche also places funds at the disposal of the Directorate, and these funds do not seem to come from any other or more acknowledged source than the millions forwarded to Paris by his colleague of the Army of Italy. The most repugnant of spectacles is thus presented to us: victorious generals mercilessly ransoming the vanquished; a government encouraging these depredations, since it does not blush at receiving the tithe of them.

Let us not think that generals, coupling like Hoche and Bonaparte secret political ambition with the love of glory, are the only ones to indulge in such methods. "Haller and Berthier have not left a good name behind them in Italy, and especially in Rome; *on the occasion of their last mission they have been charged with peculation, not to say the theft, of several valuable objects from the Vatican. We have received official reports seriously inculpating them.* Masséna is accused of having ordered the demolition of the fortifications of Mannheim "in consequence of his having sold the materials." If the bloody battle of the Trebbia is lost, it is because Macdonald delayed his onward march, having been detained in Tuscany "by business interests."

Marceau and Dugommier would have to hide their faces in shame, were they to return among their successors. Extortion and plundering are henceforth current customs in the armies, as in the administration and in the government of the Republic. The Directorate communicates to all in its employ the vice of dishonesty inherent in itself.

VI

THE STATE OF MEN'S MINDS: GENERAL DISCOURAGEMENT AND WEARINESS; DECAY OF THE REPUBLICAN IDEA

Meanwhile the country daily suffers more and more.

The Terror once stricken to death with Robespierre, it was believed that the financial crisis would come to an end; and this idea was assuredly not foreign to the sensation of deliverance felt by the nation on learning of the 9th Thermidor. For, just as the Bastille had been the symbol of the ancient *régime*, Robespierre had ended by incarnating in the eyes of France the terrorist system and all its deeds of violence, including those of its fiscal methods.

Vain hopes! The power is in the hands of the men who have killed Robespierre, and still the financial crisis endures, since the duel waged between the Revolution and Europe—a duel deeply the cause of the crisis—is not at an end. Not only does it endure, but it recalls by its intensity, as well as by the character of the remedies employed to conjure it, the most sombre days of the Jacobinical *régime* of which France thought she had been delivered. The *assignats* are converted into *mandats territoriaux* (orders directly exchangeable for the national lands), soon as discredited as the *assignats* themselves; a forced loan of six hundred millions is raised; registration and stamp dues are increased; road-tolls (*droits de passe*) are established; the public debt is reduced to one-third by a kind of bankruptcy of the State; not a single social condition remains untouched in its interests by the desperate and brutal shifts of a fiscal system at bay.

So Robespierre is dead, but Jacobinical methods survive him. Nothing is changed. I am mistaken; something new there is, a spectacle which the detested Jacobins, which the Incorruptible would never have tolerated, and the shame of which they would justly have washed out in blood: the horde of infamous jobbers watch the reactions of these measures on the national credit and the convulsions of the public fortune, and, with the complicity of certain high-placed functionaries of the Republic, build up insolent fortunes on the ruin of all by means of audaciously calculated speculations. ° And so it comes about that the nation, so cruelly ground down, no longer possesses as of old the consolation of being able to say to itself in its misery that it is for the salvation of the Fatherland that it is thus reduced to distress, since it knows, since it sees that a portion of this gold torn from it sticks to the fingers of these bandits, and since it recognizes with stupor in the front rank of these bandits some of the men—deputies, Ministers, Directors—who govern it. Hearken to Mallet du Pan: "No brush could paint the picture of that capital (Paris), where bread is distributed every other day, where each one sees wither in his hands the representative sign of his wealth, where a pound of candles costs two hundred francs (in *assignats*), where the population is divided into dupes and rogues, the latter of whom rob even one another, while the government is in its turn engaged in robbing them. A fearful licentiousness reigns; sentiments of duty, morality, honor, and human respect are dead. . . . This depravation and distress constitute a pledge to the government of the submission of the people."[1]

Stofflet and Charette are dead (25th February and 29th March, 1796); peace has almost been restored in La Vendée by Hoche; and still the civil war is waged relentlessly. Exorcised in the West, the plague reappears in the South, where it secures a footing, and assumes, under various forms, the character of a kind of endemic evil. Brigandage infests the high-roads; the public coffers are plundered, the purchasers of national lands are ferociously butchered, together with functionaries and patriots, by the *Compagnons du Soleil* or the *Compagnons de Jéhu ;* the excesses of the White Terror constitute, as early as the end of 1795, a counterpart to those of the revolutionary Terror, and the

---

[1] *Correspondance avec la Cour de Vienne*, vol. i., p. 384.

crimes of the Royalist *chauffeurs*[1] one to those of the Jacobinical butchers of 1793. The disorganized gendarmerie are powerless to restrain the audacity of these bands. In the Haute-Garonne it is a whole army, 16,000 men, marching with the white flag unfurled to the cry of " Long live Louis XVIII !"[2] In Paris even there is a bloody collision between Chouans and Republicans on the occasion of the meeting of the *Société du Manége* (24th Messidor, Year VII.—12th July, 1799). In all directions reigns insecurity, violence becomes more audacious from impunity, highway robbery, murder, and a letting loose of savage passions disguised under the garb of political reprisals—a kind of return to the primitive state, two-thirds of France affording the spectacle of a town taken by storm and sacked.

To counteract these excesses, which it has neglected to forestall and restrain, the Directorate enacts a law entitled *des otages* (hostages), impregnated with the worst spirit of the Terror, and mercilessly smiting the innocent in order to reach the guilty—a law as barbarous as the deeds which its authors intend it shall repress. And on the very day of its promulgation, the Directorate issues to the French people a proclamation wherein it "takes an oath to bury itself in the ruins of the Republic, rather than suffer liberty in the slightest degree to be infringed upon."[3]

The government crushes with the weight of an oppressive and vexatious legislation this plundered and slaughtered nation. It enacts a police law subjecting to endless formalities all Frenchmen making a short stay and not domiciled in Paris; penalties against whosoever shall have recourse to bells for the purpose of calling citizens to religious worship; enforced celebration of the *décadi*, and the prohibition not only of all labor, but of the display on that day by shopkeepers of their wares on the public highway (December, 1797); the re-establishment of imprisonment for debt, "an

---

[1] *Chauffeurs*, literally "heaters," name given to bandits who made their appearance during the Directorate, and who extorted money and valuables from their victims by exposing the soles of their feet to the fire.—Translator's note.

[2] See Ernest Hamel, *Histoire de la République sous le Directoire*, p. 287.

[3] *Id., ibid.*, p. 279.

old and barbarous law which had succumbed to the blows of Robespierre and Danton;"[1] the responsibility of printers for all matter issued from their presses: not one of these measures which is not intolerably vexatious, or which has—like the greater part of the tyrannical or sanguinary measures of the Convention—the excuse of being imposed by the inexorable necessity of the public weal; not one, in short, which does not have its origin in the spirit most opposed to the broad and generous principles of 1789, to which the hypocrisy of this government lays claim.

Groaning under the weight of all these worries, the old Republican morality—that of the early days of the Revolution, so strict and so severe, and which instilled such strength into men's souls—has given way and become relaxed. Barras himself asserts it, and we can fully believe him. "The thirst for offices and embassies continues and redoubles. Our former colleagues of the National Convention remark: 'Why should we leave to the aristocrats every social advantage, all the prerogatives which we have been modest enough to cast from us for so long?' . . . The relaxation of Republican morality continues to invade all classes." And he sadly records, in support of this observation, that a certain number of members of the Five Hundred, military men on half-pay, have for all that claimed forage rations. "While recognizing that this constitutes an abuse, the Directorate grants the rations," dolefully says the austere moralist in conclusion. And it is indeed in this way—by the capitulation of the Law and the ransoming of the funds of the State—that this little incident, and many others of the same nature but still graver, of which Barras has dispensed himself from informing us, were bound to end.

The standard of men's minds has therefore become debased, and the Republican idea has lost the sovereign sway which it formerly exercised. And it is no mediocre honor for the Republic, as it was conceived by the men of the heroic and pure age, to have entered upon her decline at the very hour when the virtues of which it had been her gen-

---

[1] Ernest Hamel, *Histoire de la République sous le Directoire*, p. 108.

erous ambition to set an example to all nations entered upon theirs. A latent work of disenchantment is operating in the French conscience, disabused of the grand ideal which but a few years before had called forth from it irresistible outbursts of faith and enthusiasm. The fruit, whether bitter or rotten, which the Republic has produced on reaching its maturity, is being compared with the promises given in its flower; and it is a symptom of the approaching ruin of all political and religious dogmas when the spirit of criticism begins to draw up the balance-sheet of their promises and of their deeds. "Weariness is at its height," writes Mallet du Pan as early as 1796; "one and all have no other thought than to spend restfully the remainder of their days. *Men no longer record their votes even for the purpose of getting rid of administrators open to suspicion.* . . . Each one thinks always and ever of himself. . . . Pilfering and spending are uppermost in the minds of all; *no longer does any opinion exist; all past or future constitutions are mere butts for ridicule.* . . . All are plunged in a kind of indifference and lethargy in regard to their political differences. There is no other thought than to eat, drink, and enjoy life. . . ."

In order to "revive the public spirit," the Directorate enacts that the directors of every theatre in Paris "shall daily, before the curtain rises, make their orchestras play airs dear to the Republicans. In the interval between plays the hymn of the Marseillais shall always be sung. . . ." This *Marseillaise*, which formerly sprang so spontaneously from all hearts, has become obligatory! Two days later the Minister of Police, Merlin of Douai, reports that at the Théâtre Feydeau "*the airs beloved of the Republicans* were greeted with hooting."[1]

And it is not the *bourgeoisie* alone who have broken off with the Republic. Hearken to what Barras says of the spirit of the *faubourgs* of Paris: "This portion of the population, so animated in the early days of the Revolution, *had met with such painful disappointments* that it had for

---

[1] De Barante, *Histoire du Directoire*, vol. i., p. 64.

a long time past become altogether enamoured of quietude." Is not also strangely significant his narrative of the ceremony commemorating the execution of Louis XVI. in the Year V. (1797)? The people greet with jests and mockery the procession of the Directors and Ministers superbly draped in the theatrical pomp of their official costumes. As the chiefs of the State pass by them, bedizened and beplumed like Mamelukes, they are greeted with irreverent grimaces by the women of the populace. At Notre-Dame soil and spiders' webs are cast from the galleries of the nave on the Directors, who are even spat upon from this coign of vantage. Boys' tricks, it will be argued, and the incorrigible instinct of opposition and of mockery of the Paris population in regard to those in power. Granted. But the silence of this population is not to numbered among its habitual boys' tricks: its silence ever betokens some deep-rooted sentiment. Now "*the people remained silent at the cry of 'Long live the Republic!' repeated by the* authorities *alone*." To all appearances the Republic is already in a precarious state, since the population of Paris refuses to join in the falsehood of the cry which proclaims the health of one at death's door, and since it remains dumb, as if in the presence of death, when the Republic passes before it in the streets.

VII

THE IDEA OF A MILITARY *COUP D'ÉTAT.* THE FATAL AND IMMINENT DICTATORSHIP

Of all classes of the nation, the army has remained most faithfully attached to the Directorate. And yet, strange to say, it is the army which, without knowing or desiring it, is going to dig its grave. It must be pointed out that the Directorial government is to a great extent responsible for the event. Barras will prove it to us by grave and unexceptionable testimony.

During the "wars of liberty"—*i.e.*, as long as revolutionary France was threatened in its existence by the coalition—the army has held aloof from politics. As a matter of course, great crises—such as the proscription of the Girondins, the trial and sentence of Danton, and the downfall and death of Robespierre—spread beyond the precincts of the Convention and found an echo in the camp, even giving rise to ardent discussions; and indeed, who among the chiefs or the soldiers could have remained, even at a distance, an unmoved spectator of such a drama? But the impassioned interest which they took in the incidents of the struggle entered upon in Paris among the several parties in no wise implied the temptation for the armies of those days to interfere in these dissensions, and to play a direct and active part in them. Theirs was the task of defending the Revolution and the Fatherland against the foreign enemy. This was sufficient for them. They in no wise confounded their duty with that of the Convention and of its Committees, whose task it was to exterminate the internal enemy, such as the aristocrats, *modérantistes*, and others. These armies of '92, '93, and '94 were, so to speak, "citizen" armies, since the public weal was the object of their most ardent solicitude. They were not "politician" armies, since they confined themselves strictly to their heroic function, from which moreover no one sought to divert them.

With the Directorate matters are entirely changed. The government seeks in the army the prop which it finds the nation is pulling from under it. It calls upon the army to take sides with it against its enemies; it encourages it to approve its acts, until it shall invite it to participate in them. To put it briefly, it introduces—and this is not the slightest of the misdeeds of this *régime*—politics into the army, without an idea, so short-sighted are its views, that it is thus paving the way for its own ruin, which matters little, and for the downfall of liberty, which is of greater import.

Power has hardly been vested for a few months in the hands of the Directorate when the new spirit of the armies reveals itself in its addresses to the government. Read and meditate the following one, for example, the text of which Barras has transmitted to us:

"Citizen Directors, of all the animals produced by the caprice of nature the vilest is a king, the most cowardly is a courtier, and the worst of all a priest. . . ." This profession of faith would seem to call for naught but a smile: it is the revolutionary phraseology in all the comical sincerity of its bombast. But hearken to what follows: "If you are in dread of the Royalists, *summon to your aid the Army of Italy;* it will quickly sweep away Chouans, Royalists, and English. We shall hunt down these assassins even into the wardrobe of George III., *and the Clichy Club shall meet with the same fate at our hands as the Raincy Club."*

Here, then, is an army tendering its services, not against the Austrians or against the English, but against a party whose progress, whether legal or otherwise, alarms those in power. What business is it of these soldiers? What, then, is their mission? To fight the Clichy Club or to fight Davidovich and Würmser? Who would have dared to instil into them sufficient audacity to speak thus while under the flag, and to make such overtures to the chiefs of the State, did not the certainty exist that words and advances would be welcomed? And they are indeed. In vain do Carnot and Barthélemy propose to punish severely so flagrant a violation of discipline, and show an energetic opposition to the introduction of such conduct into the army. Rewbell and Barras openly approve of the strange step taken by the 21st brigade of the Army of Italy; Carnot's proposition is set aside, and the right of armies to interfere in home politics under the form of censure, praise, or advice is thereby implicitly recognized; henceforth the addresses despatched by these armies are received in regular succession, and become more and more imperious and threatening. Augereau's division *has drawn up so energetic an address* that Bonaparte has hesitated to circulate it; one from Masséna's division, another from Joubert's division, *the former addressed to the Directorate, the latter to the Army of the Interior, have reached us.* The petitioners number 12,000.

The ambitious chiefs at once seize upon the instrument placed within their grasp. Hoche and Bonaparte announce that a portion of the two armies of Sambre-et-Meuse "*speak of returning home* for the purpose of meting out justice to the assassins and counter-revolutionaries, *towards whom the Directorate has shown itself too indulgent.*" Even an Augereau claims the right to exercise, in the name of the troops under his command, pressure on the resolutions of the executive power. Admitted into the presence of the Directorate, "Augereau there and then, and without any mincing of words, declares that the brave warriors of the Army of Italy *will not endure* the Royalists organizing any counter-revolution, and that the 12,000 gallant men he commands are ready to march against them. . . . The Directorate lets him have his say; the Directorate approves, rejoicing at being able to place the deeds of violence it meditates under the patronage and safeguard of the conquerors of Europe. 'We have come to an understanding with General Hoche *that his army shall pronounce itself*, that it shall indite addresses to the Directorate, which will take measures to give effect to them.'" The army *shall pronounce itself*, the Army of Sambre-et-Meuse! In what country does this happen? In France or in Spain? And thus does this detestable and fatal practice, the interference of the army in party conflicts, become a system sanctioned by the government, and one of the essential mechanisms of the Directorial *régime*.

So here is the army introduced and thrust into the arena of politics. What will be its action? That of everybody else for the past ten years. The people have had their days—the 14th July, the 5th and 6th October, the 20th June, and the 10th August. The executive power and the legislative power have had theirs: the one, the 18th Fructidor and the 22d Floréal; the other, the 30th Prairial. Alone the army has so far not played an active part; its turn has come. What consideration is there to restrain it? Respect for the law? All have violated it. Respect for the government? All hold it in contempt. Thus does the idea of a military and liberating *coup d'état*

—carried out by the army for the greater good of the Revolution jeopardized by the incapables and traitors of the government and of the Councils, by the plots of the Royalists, by "the gold of Pitt," and by the Chouans—take a definite shape.

Moreover, the blinded government which is to become the victim of this *coup d'état* seems to be doing its best to prepare therefor the minds of those about to perpetrate it, to free them from all scruples, to weaken and destroy in them the salutary doctrine which in every triumph of force over law refuses to see anything but a crime.

The 18th Fructidor is accomplished with the complicity of Hoche, who places funds at the disposal of the Directorate, offers to move his troops nearer to the "constitutional line," in order to be in a better position promptly to give support in Paris itself to the triumvirs, and secretly despatches to Paris his chief of staff Chérin, who comes as early as the 2d Fructidor to assist Barras in preparing the plot against the Councils. It must be admitted that Hoche has participated in the plot. "All the steps taken by him," says M. Albert Sorel, "go to prove that he was hand and glove with Barras, and that he but awaited an order to go into action."[1] Who, then, has diverted the commander of the Army of Sambre-et-Meuse from the heroic tasks with which he was better acquainted than with the underhand doings of politics in which we blush to see him engaged? Who, then, has transformed the Pacifier of La Vendée into a general of *pronunciamiento?* Who, then, has corrupted, enticed him away from the paths of duty and glory; who, then, if not the government itself, has driven the victorious general of Neuwied to be the first to set the example of meditating an outrage upon the national representation, and to oppose the bayonets of his soldiers to the institutions of the country? Who is there so blind as not to see that if the intentions of Hoche and Bonaparte differed, the conduct of the for-

---

[1] See, in the *Revue de Paris*, 1st August, 1895, *Les Vues de Hoche*, by M. Albert Sorel.

mer in the Year V. already reveals that of the latter in the Year VIII., and that Fructidor and Brumaire are twin brothers, born of the same mother, rebellion against the law?

Hoche has at least remained foreign to the execution of the *coup d'état;* not entirely of his own free-will, however, but simply because at the last moment the Directorate preferred the services of a less important and consequently more docile and safer auxiliary. But what is to be said of the part which Augereau, the Augereau of Castiglione, played in the event? Hearken to Barras: "Augereau had drunk some little champagne in order to prepare himself. . . . On seeing Ramel, he tore his epaulets from him, and went so far as to slap his face with them. . . ." It is by the exploits of a drunken and brutal police officer that the intrepid soldier of the Army of Italy distinguishes himself on the 18th Fructidor; such is the uncommon claim he has acquired to the reward conferred upon him when "he is no longer *useful in Paris;*" for such purposes does the government reserve the most illustrious commanders of our armies! For it has had Moreau and Bonaparte as well as Hoche in its mind, and has wavered between Bernadotte and Augereau. It is with its own hands that it trains them to insurrection against the institutions of their country. Is not one of its principal cares that of always placing the command of the 17th division — in other words, the Paris command — in the hands of a safe man, prepared to render once more the services rendered by Augereau—a gendarme whom it can, according to the circumstances of its policy, let loose either against the "royalists" or the "anarchists" of the Councils?

So the army has henceforth, besides its mission proper—a national one, the defence of the soil—two new tasks, the fulfilment of both of which is equally inglorious: abroad it grinds down the vanquished populations, in order to maintain the government with the fruits of its pillage; at home it is the accomplice, not to say the executor, of the deeds of violence by means of which the government desperately retains the power it feels slipping from its weak and brutal hands. No more crushing indictment of the Directorial *régime* can, it would seem, be formulated than the simple revelation of such a conception of the army's *rôle*.

Now this army does not show any devotion, but rather contempt, and it is almost more serious for a government to be despised than to be hated. Two generals there are whose Republican convictions are above suspicion—Bernadotte and Joubert. Both have fought, not without glory, for the Revolution; in a few months Joubert will go heroically to his death for it at Novi. Barras records words spoken by these two chiefs in 1797. Joubert says: "*Too much time is being lost in idle talk;* I am prepared, whenever the word is spoken, *to put an end to it all with twenty grenadiers.*" Bernadotte approves, and, good Gascon that he is, adds, outvying his comrade: "Twenty grenadiers are too many; a corporal's guard is quite sufficient *to oust the lawyers.*"

I have elsewhere shown how the idea of the military *coup d'état* originated, and the share to be attributed to the Directorial government itself in the genesis of this idea. This idea has now attained its full and final expression, enriched by a new element—the idea of a military dictatorship, which, sooner or later, was bound to engraft itself upon that of the *coup d'état* carried out by the army. Henceforth the days of the Directorate are numbered. Whether it be Hoche or Bonaparte, or even another, who rids France of this *régime* of which she is heartily sick—for, failing Hoche and Bonaparte, another (there is no room for any doubt about the matter) would have come forward to do the work—one thing is quite certain, and that is, that as early as 1797, two years before its final downfall, the *régime* is doomed. People are disgusted with the government of the Chambers, their discussions, and the miserable intrigues in the midst of which the public weal is in danger, not to say agonizing; the sight of the impotence to which the executive power is a prey becomes painful.

After the 18th Fructidor, Barras, if we are to believe him, was advised by Augereau to seize upon the supreme power and govern France. As Barras's ambition does not soar so high, he is content to enjoy the good things of life. Supreme power for this indolent and sceptical Epicurean! Never! Feasting, an ostentatious style of living, pretty women of easy virtue, and money, are all that Barras asks for.

But here is a man of quite another mould with a fiery and proud soul, who has tasted glory without being satiated with it, who would now like to taste power, who feels worthy to exercise it, and who is indeed so. To become the Pacifier of France, is it not a fine dream for the Pacifier of La Vendée? Hoche is ready for the dictatorship[1] as he was ready for the *coup d'état*. His refusal of the command of the Army of Ireland — the acceptance of which would be tantamount to exile — his utterances as well as his deeds, the strangely personal tone which reigns throughout his correspondence during the last months of his life — everything reveals the uneasiness and pride of a mind haunted by great designs.

Hence — and this is what I have attempted to show in the foregoing pages — France and her government are completely divorced two years previous to Brumaire. The nation, which suffers from a thousand ills to which the Directorate does not know how to bring relief, accuses it of being the author of them; the army, which the Directorate has diverted from its true function, together with the military chiefs, whom it has mixed up in party conflicts, despises it; the military *coup d'état*, having as its object the deliverance of France from a *régime* which has fallen into the deepest disrepute, appears as the sole resource.

There is a thing far more serious and significantly indicative of the irretrievable harm that the Directorate has

---

[1] See, in this connection, M. Albert Sorel's already quoted article. He is of opinion that Hoche's intentions were "incontestably pure," and that, while prepared to seize upon the dictatorship, he was "determined to abdicate it as soon as the danger had been warded off."

done to the Republican idea, and of the decadence of this idea—to wit, the consideration that the logical result of this military *coup d'état* may be to re-establish a one-man power, a new form of the "tyranny" against which so many oaths of eternal hatred have been sworn; this consideration no longer alarms more than one or two, but seduces, on the contrary, a number of minds, even among the warmest partisans that the Revolution still retains throughout the country. In '92, '93, and '94 the French nation, completely won over to the new order of things, had detached itself forever from the Monarchy. The reconciliation of this nation to the idea of the supreme power vested in the hands of one man was the work of the Directorate. Never did any government dig with such blind perseverance as did this one the grave into which it was to be tossed contemptuously, like the dead thing that it was, and in which the Republic, unjustly expiating the wrong it had committed in the eyes of the nation of having identified itself with so vile and harmful a *régime*, was to be buried with it.

Barras relates that in 1797 a priest who had emigrated, and who had returned to France disguised as a courier, scoured the country in order to study the state of men's minds. And the letter, intercepted by the police and laid before the Directorate, which this priest had addressed to the bishop of the Puy-en-Velay, concluded with the words: "France is quick with a king."

This priest has well discerned the symptoms of a coming child-birth. Yes, France is laboring with child. But where the sagacious observer errs is when he announces that from this attempt to bring into the world a new and better form of government royalty will come forth. A king, no! It would be a return to the starting-point, to 1789, and however disenchanted France may be with the present, she is still very far from thinking of retrograding towards this past. The Revolution has not completed its cycle, and has not found the final form it is groping for. Suffer it to accomplish this supreme and logical metamorphosis; its virtue is not wholly exhausted; it still feels it has strength to expend, a great destiny merely outlined to fill, ideas to sow throughout the world by shaking over it the folds of France's victorious flag, and a future which fills its heart!

France will have none of a king who would jeopardize her precious equality—that bit of wreckage of the Revolution to which the country has so invincibly attached itself. As to Liberty. let her founder if she will; she is a liar who has not kept her promises!

France is indeed quick—not with a king, but with a master. Following upon the four years of the impotent government of these five men, it is a firm and lucid mind, a will, an energy, a head, a chief that the people call for—a dictator, in short, just as did the Romans!

Hoche might have been that man, and if France has mourned him so deeply, it is less perhaps in memory of the great things accomplished by him than a testimony to the vague and deep hope which vanished with him.

But now there arises far above the low horizon polluted with the miasma of Directorial putrefaction an imaginative head with the imperious profile of Cæsar, encircled by a halo gilded by the sun of Italy and of Egypt. Names of victories, resounding like the flourish of trumpets, herald this radiant apparition. This fiery and pensive general is neither the offshoot ot the old and desiccated trunk of royalty nor a suspicious heir of the past, but a son, a true son, of the Revolution. He the Glory, he the Strength, he the warlike Apostle of the Revolution among nations! Then, like Joan of Arc at the sight of the Archangel Michael in his glittering armor, dazzled France falls at the feet of the Hero and Master, exclaiming: "He has come!"

Such is, together with the conclusion, the philosophy of the foregoing study.

GEORGE DURUY.

CHAPTER I

Dissension in the Directorate—Alarmist rumors spread by its enemies—Intrigues in the armies and in the *corps législatif*—Affairs in Italy—Imprudence of the agent Malo—Guns and muskets offered to Spain—Diplomatic parleys in regard to the treaty with England—Conduct of France's allies—A categorical reply demanded of Holland—Bernadotte before the Directorate—Larevellière's energetic speech—The standards captured at Peschiera—Bernadotte in a quandary—Chérin Chief of the Guard of the Directorate—Carnot at Larevellière's—Dismissals from office—A curious letter from Bernadotte to Bonaparte—An explanation of his conduct—Assassinations planned by "honest folk"—Rovère's incendiary placard—The state of men's minds—Josephine's intrigues—Police and counter-police—Fouché's trade; his reports—Merlin de Thionville's request—He obtains employment—Liégard, *chef de brigade*—A flagrant conspiracy—Dossonville and Bretonnau—Pichegru in the *rôle* of a godfather—Tumult in the Councils—Marbot's speech—Siméon's mission to me—Bailleul denounced—A suspect—Royalist preparations—Hoche and Moreau—I create a stir in the Directorate—I prepare a *coup d'état*—Confidential communication made to Augereau—He quakes with fear—Rewbell terrified—I restore courage to him—Temporary madness—We determine upon action—Orders given to Augereau—The ambassadors Meyer and Staël kept under close watch—Our proclamations—François de Neufchâteau's lofty character—At midnight—Carnot and Barthélemy kept constantly under watch—The alarm-gun—Augereau insults Ramel—Arrest of the *inspecteurs de la salle*—General Verdière—Violent conduct of Bourdon de l'Oise—Verdière and his followers swept aside—His ultimate victory—Pichegru arrested—His struggle with General Pincot—The deputies conveyed to the Temple—An aide-de-camp as prison-registrar—Pichegru's pistols—M. Thibaudeau barely manages to escape—The glorious 18th Fructidor—Plans of my friends and enemies—Augereau's and Réal's utterances concerning the Revolution—Two Directors transported simultaneously with prominent deputies—Talleyrand will not be anything less than a Director—His protestations—Merlin and François de Neufchâteau elected Directors—A few letters having reference to the events of the 18th Fructidor—The anti-Fructidorian history concocted by Carnot—Adjutant-General Mucherez—M. Le Maire, Dean of the Faculty of Letters—Strange boasts of General Loison—Was Carnot assassinated?—My aims on the 18th Fructidor—Carnot's escape—Contrasted with Danton—I connive at Carnot's flight—His system of defence—Truguet's claim—All is quiet again—Treilhard and Bonnier plenipotentiaries at Lille—Breaking off of the negotiations—Plans for a revolution in Italy and Hungary—The secretary Botot sent on a mission to Bonaparte—Friendly dispositions of Prussia—Changes made in the civil service—General Pille in command in the South—Bernadotte vacillates—His plans in regard to India—Brigands in the departments of Var and Vaucluse—Saint-Christole—Hoche's death—His panegyric—The causes of his death—His affection for me—Bonaparte instructed to take Malta—Caillard negotiates peace with Russia—Augereau's great opinion of himself—The Directorate rids itself of him—Changes made in the chief military commands—Letourneur and Lambrecht Ministers—Services rendered by Prince de Carency—Energy shown by François de Neufchâteau and Merlin—The last-named wishes to perpetuate the *coup d'état*.

From the 2d to the 6th Fructidor, Year V.—A decree of special interest has been adopted by the Directorate on the motion of the Minister of Finance. Carnot and Barthélemy refuse to append their signatures to it. It would seem that this is done deliberately, and that henceforth the decisions of the Directorate will not bear more than three signatures. Our two colleagues have agreed to abstain from recording their votes; they cannot prevent three from constituting a majority, but they are appealing to the outside public. This pair of dissenters display, nevertheless, great circumspection in their speeches, and even in their looks; they have resolved upon a course of dissimulation, in order to carry on their occult government. The diatribes inspired by them against the three Directors constitute the order of the day in the *corps législatif*. Their agents are actively engaged in spreading alarm among the patriots. Compromise is breathed to some, division to others. They hint to Larevellière that he will be proscribed by the Jacobins, to Rewbell that he will share the same fate, to Barras that he will have cause to remember the 9th Thermidor. Never will the Robespierrists forgive him; an attempt is made to isolate him from his colleagues; he is represented to them as a dangerous party leader; the Triumvirate, it is said, is working for the Duc d'Orléans; lastly, the assassination of the three Directors is spoken of as the most natural thing in the world. The *inspecteurs de la salle* in the Chamber, nay, even certain generals, take part in all these doings. Arms are supplied to the youth of Paris; they are given signs by which they shall know one another. Several *émigrés*, inveterate poltroons, leave Paris, accustomed as they are to fly at the breaking out of the flames they have kindled. The Armies of Italy and Sambre-et-Meuse make manifest their indignation against the Royalists at home. The Army of the Rhine, although Republican in spirit, has so far not declared itself; it is held in check by the prudence of Moreau, in unison with those of its leaders who are not of the same opinion, or who, politically speaking, are of none. Happily the agitators in the *corps législatif* are divided among themselves; some of them are under instructions from England, others from Blankenburg; Thibaudeau and Tronçon-Ducoudray draw up reports against the majority in the Directorate, the Armies of Italy and Sambre-et-Meuse, and their generals; some of the agitators wish to wait until the next elections before determining upon any course; others would like to act at once; the Republicans, on the other hand, are making preparations; everything indicates that a collision is close at hand.

Despatches from Italy bring the news that the Emperor consents to a separate peace, negotiated at Medina. . . . Bonaparte is still of the opinion that the Venetian Isles are of such paramount importance that it would be advantageous to unite them to the Cisalpine Republic, or, if this is not done, to continue our occupation of them.

The Army of the Alps is at last done away with. Generals Liégard, Haquin, and Canuel are sent to various army corps.

In view of the grave state of affairs, the majority of the Directorate decides, in opposition to the will of Carnot and Barthélemy, to dismiss the members of several central and municipal administrations, which have done much harm by their want of patriotism. Malo, who has contributed towards unmasking the machinations of the Royalists, possesses no other talent than that of a police agent; hence it is impossible to allow him to retain command of a cavalry regiment. Upon his being placed on the retired list, he calls on Larevellière, whom he addresses in most insolent fashion; while at Barthélemy's he goes so far as to speak in most unbecoming terms against the three Directors who constitute the majority. The Directorate is indignant at the behavior of Malo, whom it has rewarded pecuniarily and generously for his political services. The Minister of War is instructed to draw up a report on his case. Barthélemy and Carnot vote in his favor, and against these propositions.

Carnot opposes the delivery of muskets promised to Spain. There are over 25,000 which the soldiers refuse to use, because of defects in their manufacture. Carnot will not have them sold; he would prefer giving guns to the Spaniards. Rewbell and Larevellière oppose this, upon its being shown that these muskets are utterly useless, whereas the guns are still serviceable. Besides, it is necessary to have in this connection Bonaparte's opinion as to the muskets, and that of artillery generals in regard to the guns. Adopted. Rewbell and Larevellière add: "We are not going to arm the hired assassins of Royalism. Enough muskets have already been distributed among the disloyal citizens of Paris."

In consequence of England's repeated demand to treat separately with our allies, negotiations have been begun with some of them. We do not find in them the sentiment of gratitude we have a right to expect as a result of our treatment.

The Minister of Foreign Affairs is instructed to ask the Dutch Government to declare itself in a precise and clear fashion in the matter of the various propositions made to it by England.

In consequence of the daily-increasing danger, and in view of the crisis at hand, Rewbell and Larevellière empower me to take every possible step towards resisting the machinations of the enemies of the Republic. The next day I say to them with confidence: "Colleagues, let us remain united, as men do who esteem one another. I am prepared: should the Royalists stir, they will be crushed."

The envoy of the Cisalpine Republic and General

Bernadotte are presented to the Directorate on the 30th of Thermidor. Larevellière, as its president, is instructed to receive them. He addresses them, on behalf of the Government, in such energetic terms as to make it plain to the Royalist conspirators that the majority of the Directorate is fully determined not to allow itself to be sacrificed. "Brave general," he says, addressing Bernadotte, "it is in vain that the relentless foes of liberty have, by a disgraceful pact, sold to the foreigner and the Bourbon race both honor and Fatherland; in vain that their criminal hands are daily engaged in undermining the edifice of our laws, and that their foul lips seek to tarnish the splendor of the most astounding, the most noble, and the most inspiring results of our form of government. It is in vain that they would degrade a naturally ardent and generous youth—a youth which, following the impulse of its season of life and the noble aspirations of lofty souls, shows itself so awake to the voice of freedom. A successful attempt has been made—will posterity believe it?—to prevail upon our youth to call for a master, and to ask for manacles for hands which wish to remain free! . . . The Executive Directorate will dare anything in order to insure to Frenchmen their liberty, their constitution, their peace, and their glory—the well-deserved fruits of seven years' labors, misfortunes, and of an unheard-of sequence of the most astounding successes. The Directorate will no more suffer itself to be frightened by the most alarming dangers than to be seduced by deceitful promises."

At the conclusion of this speech, delivered with a strength of voice and an amount of feeling which seemed beyond Larevellière's physical resources, tears were streaming from his eyes, tears of anger and emotion; and it was while in this state of agitation that, according to custom, he embraced General Bernadotte. The latter had presented the flags taken at Peschiera, with the modest and unassuming bearing ever characteristic of him throughout life; still he had thought best not to stray from the paths of prudence which had ever served him so well, and he was not desirous of forsaking them at a time when matters were getting more and more complicated; he was now doubly compromised and involved by the embrace of Larevellière and the necessity of expressing a positive sympathy for the Republic. When despatched on his mission by Bonaparte, Bernadotte had not expected that he would become pledged to such an extent; and nothing is more provoking to men irresolute by policy than to be brought face to face with the necessity of declaring themselves in a positive and open fashion. Bernadotte was, so to speak, driven to the wall. Rewbell invites him to dinner for the following day, while I invite him for the day after, remarking to him that "we count on his coming"; and then we enjoy a laugh at seeing how impossible it is for him to decline our invitations.

For some days I had harbored under my roof, albeit incognito, General Chérin, sent to me by Hoche on the 2d Fructidor. I move that this general be appointed to the command of the Guard of the Directorate; Carnot and Barthélemy abstain from voting. I move also that the 8th military division be united to the Army of Italy; adopted by the usual majority.

Carnot has called on Larevellière for the purpose

of handing over to him the presidential seals; he has once more denounced the anarchists to him, in particular Rossignol.

Several officers are deprived of their commands, which are given to others, pursuant to a report of the Minister of War.

Whatever Bernadotte's hesitancy of mind or his political calculations, these are the terms in which he renders an account to Bonaparte of his mission of observation:

"The Directorate has received me at a public audience. The speeches delivered have reanimated the Republicans. The Royalist party has changed its tactics. It no longer dares to tilt against the Directorate; yet, from my point of view, it should be hunted down and denounced, in order that the patriots may be free to have the management of the coming elections.

"Although the talk here is that you have concluded a peace with the Emperor, I will leave between the 20th and 25th to rejoin you. This home of intrigues, altogether repugnant to the character of a soldier whose sole aim is the prosperity of his Fatherland, is not to my taste. General, enjoy the delights of life; do not poison your existence with melancholy thoughts. The eyes of the Republicans are turned towards you; they press your image to their hearts; the Royalists look at it with respect and fear; my friendship for you remains unchanged."

Nothing in all this is indicative of any hostility towards Bonaparte. Bernadotte goes a good deal into society, and, giving free rein to his Southern vivacity, indulges in the strangest utterances, which might be considered at variance with one another, as will happen with men who talk much — so much, indeed, that they are apt to contradict themselves.

In those days he was fond of comparing the Republicans to a colt which prances and bounds after having been kept too long in the stable, and the conclusion he drew from his comparison was, that the consequences of political movements were to be dreaded; then referring to the Royalists, as if, according to his actual thoughts, he wrote to Bonaparte:

"I can plainly see that the addresses of the army have reawakened the patriotism of a class of timorous and faint-hearted men; nay, more, that the wish therein formally expressed has struck terror into the soul of the partisans of royalty, who believed they could quietly bring about the counter-revolution, and load the nation with chains. I cannot help laughing at the folly of these men; they must, indeed, know little of the men who are in command of the armies, and of the armies themselves, to hope to muzzle them so easily, and to believe that a more or less learned, or more or less hired, orator can disturb for an instant our repose. These deputies, who speak with such impertinence, are far from dreaming that we could enslave Europe were you so inclined."

This latter part of the letter to Bonaparte would indicate rather an ambitious inclination, a desire for military power, than an expression of civic sentiment. Besides, it is to be most clearly inferred from all these utterances and actions that, although Bernadotte was truly heart and soul with Bonaparte, yet he was with us in the sense of opposing an actual resistance to the enemies of the Republic. I do not deny that he may at the first moment have hesitated and felt his way, when called upon to adopt a decisive course; but this groping about was not due to any personal feeling against Bonaparte, whom he possibly might not like at heart by reason of his imperious character; rather was it due to Bernadotte's natural hesitancy in all matters, and to the political timidity displayed by him from the earliest days of the Revolution, when, between the *régime* which had made him a non-commissioned officer, and might perhaps have made him a captain at the age of sixty, and the Revolution, which was about to make him a colonel, a general, and perhaps something more in the course of time, he yet did not know what to do. For, it must be admitted, success was a matter of uncertainty; while to men belonging to the army from childhood, and accustomed to submit to strict discipline, there was in the Revolution something daring and audacious which could not be boldly faced by men whom the special tendency of their profession left in ignorance of the vicissitudes recorded in history, and who could not, therefore, understand beforehand the great possibilities which had just been opened by our Revolution. Moreover, our courage and our decision depend greatly on an acquaintance with the things to which we apply them. Bernadotte, a born soldier, and endowed with the faculties enabling him to adopt the right course in his profession, but entirely new to politics, with a mind terrified at the consequences of the Revolution, had hesitated from the very outset, and was still hesitating; he was still to hesitate for a long time to come, until really inured: the spontaneity and decision which a man derives from himself Bernadotte could not yet call his own. It is but justice to admit this, in order not to make him appear as acting a dual part in this matter, and not to present him in the light of the falsest of men in his relations with Bonaparte or with the Republic.

In the circles of so-called "honest folk" the simplest means of assassinating one or all of the Triumvirs is daily debated without disguise. In accordance with the system of muddling everything which is that of Rovère, constituting as it does his special talent, he has, in harmony with his colleagues and accomplices, the *inspecteurs de la salle*, caused to be publicly posted a diatribe of the armed force of Paris against the grenadiers of the Guard of the *corps législatif*. This was, indeed, a happy thought with which to start the civil war among the soldiery; the police, warned in time, arrest the bill-poster.

The Royalists are organizing, and are giving free rein to their insolence; the patriots are more calm, but fully resolved, together with the majority of the Directorate, to bring about the triumph of the Republic, as they have done hitherto, by every display of energy.

Bonaparte, who needs very little encouragement to indulge in intrigue, had not waited until the present moment to put in practice the principle, credit for which I have already given Talleyrand, "that it is necessary to set the women-folk in motion on important occasions." The woman who had so usefully served her husband when she was not yet united in marriage to him, after the 13th Vendémiaire, Josephine, has not ceased for a moment since her marriage to be put to use by him each and every time he has believed she could further his plans. She has ever been actively engaged in his intrigues at the approach of the crisis with which we are now brought face to face. She it is who has almost continually written to me at his bidding in regard to the most serious matters, as if the correspondence of a woman in such circumstances were not equivalent to that of her husband. In order to be able to speak more freely with me, and to keep more securely what we thought should remain secret, Mme. Bonaparte had asked me to adopt a cipher, coupling with this request, according to her usual mania, one that the cipher agreed upon should be known to us two only, and not even to her husband, and that I could thus freely express all the outpourings of my heart.

At a time when open hostilities were about to break out, and a secret war was already being waged with the most clandestine means, when each one had his police and counter-police, it was of course necessary that I should have mine—all the more that we could not depend on any of our Ministers. Without attaching too great an importance to all that is done through the medium of the police, or is said in its name, I could hardly dispense with the services of a few men who came to me with every outward appearance of devotion, patriotism, and the most obsequious demonstrations. Among those who undertook to keep us most fully informed as to what was going on, because they had access to all circles, Fouché was first and foremost. He offered us his services, invoking those very antecedents most thrown in his face in the course of the Revolution, assuring us that this his early career would enable him to procure for us the best of information about the several parties whose doings the Directorate was interested in knowing and watching. So it was that I received daily police memoranda from Fouché. In order to be able to grant their author the reward which was his aim, we

dignified these memoranda with the name of reports.
I find, amid a mass of documents of this kind, a few
of Fouché's memoranda, all in his handwriting. If
I give them here such as they are, if I even go so
far as to beg my editor to reproduce in their integrity those he sees fit to publish, and even to have
them lithographed, in proof of their genuineness, it
is not that these documents bear in my eyes any remarkable stamp; they do not seem to me any less
ignoble than they did at the time they were sent in
to me, and when my sole interest in them lay in their
ignobleness. But owing to the part since played by
the individual in question in a higher sphere, one in
which the powers with which he was invested so
grossly deceived people, and in which he succeeded
in mystifying the nation not only by a series of impostures, but by the profession of talents with which
he made people credit him, it is not here without
importance to judge the man by his works. These
memoranda serve to reveal his actual capacity; he
has since been able to claim the capacity of others as
his own. We see here the petty police agent who
is to witness the day when he is to enjoy the twofold triumph of attaining fortune, and if not consideration, at least an enormous notoriety, which the
deceived multitude sets down as the result of genuine merit, even going so far as to call it genius.

Memorandum for B.—Year V.

Bailleul has received a letter from Havre, wherein he is informed that the Royalists have suddenly altered their tactics;
they have received orders to postpone the day of revenge; and a
remarkable thing about this letter is its date. In this department, as well as in all others of the Republic, the tribunals and

the administrations exist for the benefit of the Royalists only. However seductive a full and entire *rapprochement* may appear, it will nevertheless require a powerful upheaval to bring about the many necessary changes! . . .

Courtois has positive information in regard to the rearming of the youth by Rovère; he avers that thousands of double-barrelled pistols, with bayonets attached, have been distributed during the past few days.

Jourdan . . .

Grison is distributing money in the Faubourg Antoine, he has given three louis to a cobbler, who informed Parrein of the fact.

Gouchon and Desjoy are in communication with Carnot; 'tis they who are continually representing the patriots to be anarchists.

Rossignol publicly denies the calumnies of Meiz against him. The following is his declaration of faith: "A sincere rallying to the Government and to the Constitution of the Year III."

Several individuals who have received money have asked Parrein whether it was true that it would be necessary for them to join an uprising. Parrein has replied to them: "Spend the money given to you, and, when the proper time comes, the Government will give the signal, and we will march against the Royalists."

I have seen Garat in relation to the address to be issued to Frenchmen. It lacks three things: (1) a statement of the doings of the *corps législatif* since the 1st Prairial; (2) the history of the revolution just accomplished; (3) an indication of what remains to be done in order to place the Constitution and the Government on a durable footing.

These three things are absolutely necessary; everything stated in this connection is so petty and so puerile that it reads like newspaper stuff; it is urgent that some great manifesto should at once go forth, in order to arouse the enthusiasm of Republican virtues in the departments and armies. Garat will call to-night on the Director Barras, and speak to him on behalf of an excellent citizen named Edouard Walkiers, for whom we claim justice at the hands of the Executive Directorate.

The law affecting those to be transported does not provide for dealing with persons sentenced by default. It seems to me that they should be required to proceed to a seaport indicated by the Directorate for their transportation, within a delay of . . ., under penalty of being shot to death if found on the territory of the Republic. Without such a provision we cannot obtain any complete result, and we shall see the same plots renewed and successfully seek support from amid the remaining conspirators, whom personal considerations have caused to connect themselves with the *corps législatif*.

Pichegru will not have anything incomplete: let the Executive Directorate act with the same aim in view, otherwise the Government will once more be exposed to danger, and we shall be threatened with a fresh revolution in less than three months.

Much has been said about the fortunes made by the men of the Revolution, and one of my colleagues, who had purchased the Calvaire national property, has been more calumniated than any one else in view of the notoriety of the place. The truth of his position seems to me a peremptory answer to this calumny; and it is with a desire of doing justice to him, as sincerely as he seems to me to deserve it, that I quote the following lines from a letter which Merlin de Thionville wrote to me on the 13th Fructidor: "Not knowing which way to turn, with not a penny in my pocket, without employment, possessing absolutely nothing, I have suffered many an injustice; my only resources lie in your friendship: come to my rescue by instructing the Minister of War to employ me. I no longer depend on any one but you, my dear Barras; do not cast me from you."

I succeeded in getting Merlin employed, in the teeth of Carnot's opposition. I consider that I am fulfilling one of the first of my duties when I can give a good place to a patriot. To come to the rescue of the men of the Revolution, and to procure a livelihood for them, as long as I am able so to do —such is my religion. Were it practised by the Directorate, this religion would moreover be good policy, for a new social order is not to be defended except by the support of those interested in its maintenance.

At Marseilles Liégard is giving his protection to the cutthroats; he was appointed general of brigade for having satisfactorily fulfilled that horrible mission. We decide upon dismissing him, greatly to Carnot's displeasure. On witnessing his display of temper, Rewbell says to him: "Would you, then, wish to appoint him general of division?"

From the 12*th to the* 15*th Fructidor, Year V.*— For some time past the *inspecteurs de la salle* have had their own police; Dossonville is at its head. Cards and muskets have been distributed among the conspirators. Bretonnau, one of the distributors, is arrested. It is on Pichegru that the factious individuals reckon; an extract from his speech is being scattered broadcast through the departments; he is publicly acknowledged as the chief of the conspirators. Carnot and Barthélemy vote against all the salutary measures determined upon by the majority of the Directorate; both of them seem to feel more assurance as the crisis approaches.

The Directorate busies itself with the dismissal of the members of several administrations, and substitutes others to them. These measures are demanded by the course of events. The Minister of War wishes to stand well with all parties; Pichegru has been sponsor to his child. The Royalists continue to be defiant in the *corps législatif*. Marbot, in the Council of Ancients, calls attention to the counter-revolution of the Five Hundred. The Republicans of that chamber venturing to apostrophize the friends of the priests and of royalty, the latter vociferate against the Directorate. The motion in regard to the Bas-Rhin is rejected. The *chouans* of the Councils continue playing various parts; some few of them have undertaken to amuse the Directorate. President Siméon, whether their accomplice or their dupe, is commissioned to approach me; I reply to him: "In lieu of indulging in personalities, you should pass severe laws against the *émigrés*, priests, and Royalists; you should devote your attention to the finances, the civil code, and other urgent laws: such is the way of allaying all fears, and of securing peace at home." The deputy Bailleul causes a declaration to be distributed among his constituents; he is denounced. The order of the day is adopted. The counter-revolutionary party in the *corps législatif* reckons greatly on Moreau. A man has behaved at my audience in such a way as to indicate that he had treacherous intentions; he is sent to the *bureau central*. It seems that the Royalists are determined to attack on the 18th. Their partisans are flocking into Paris from all directions.

Hoche is confirmed anew in the command of the Army of Sambre-et-Meuse. Carnot would like to have Moreau summoned to the aid of the Directorate; we do not consider this meet. He sees clearly —so he says—that we have taken "a fixed resolution." I say plainly to Carnot: "Yes, it is our fixed resolution to save the Republic, and this in spite of the nefarious plans of the valets of royalty. . . ."

For some time past I hold daily conferences with influential deputies and patriots; I utilize them in view of preparing the people for the indispensable *coup d'état* I have organized. The Treasury clogs all the services; Rewbell asks that its members be summoned before the Directorate; Carnot and Barthélemy make wry faces, and allude to my violence. I answer them: "You charge me with violence, and I reproach myself with weakness for not having repressed before this the evil you have done. Intrusted by the people with the duty of defending our new social organization, responsible for the maintenance of the Republic, not only to France but also to the human race, which we have called to liberty, I ought not to have waited so long to show to it that its enemies were among the chief authorities of the State; the blood spilled with impunity for the past eighteen months has been shed by you; we should enjoy a return to order had you not paralyzed the repressive measures of the Directorate. This innocent blood will be on your heads!"

17th Fructidor, Year V.—On the 17th I am informed that the Government is about to be attacked. I am of opinion that the time has come to take measures to ward off the blow. I lay the state of affairs before my two colleagues. I give the first orders, with a view to action. I summon Augereau, whom I had seen daily for some days past; he had seemed to me to be somewhat uncertain and timorous as to the consequences of so decisive a political act. I had indeed thought of associating with him Bernadotte, whom Bonaparte had sent to Paris with no other object in view; but, having sounded Bernadotte several times during his repeated visits to me, I had been unable to obtain from him anything but vague protestations of a boundless devotion that would stop at nothing. Among all the other generals unceasingly besetting me and filling my antechamber, I saw at last that Augereau was the one most thoroughly genuine, with the best-defined ideas, so to speak, in the matter of patriotism and devotion. On my speaking the word "to-morrow" to him, I noticed that he started, as is the wont with even the most valiant soldiers when they hear the cannon roar for the first time. The mere rumor of a political revolution was for Augereau a first sensation in this order of ideas; he had heroically gone to battle, and crossed the bridge of Arcola, but he had not smelled gunpowder in any of our civil engagements; he had not been trained to that kind of war, either on the 10th of August, the 9th Thermidor, or the 13th Vendémiaire; it was therefore necessary to harden him to it there and then. Augereau told me, with a frankness not unmingled perhaps with some little political uncertainty, that he was not altogether ready: he lacked conveyances to transport muskets from Vincennes to Paris; he sends Izarn, his aide-de-camp, to Rewbell and Larevellière, to inform them of the postponement of the *coup*. Rewbell, who had in consequence of my promise believed that he would rise only to hear of an accomplished fact, flies into a rage and exclaims, "All is lost; I leave Paris; let my horses be saddled!" Izarn comes and tells me of this. I go in all haste to see Rewbell, whom I find at Larevellière's; he is in a state of the deepest agitation, and is still bent on leaving Paris. Augereau, on the other hand, had said that he wished to return to Italy. Rewbell tells us, with as much simplicity as emotion, his dreams for the last few nights. He is in dread of being outlawed. Lastly, the weakness of mind and the lack of firmness displayed by Augereau at this juncture lead Rewbell to believe that all is lost. Larevellière and I seek to dissuade him from his plan, and to reassure him; he persists in his design of leaving: he intends to ride away within the hour; thereupon I say to him, "Whither art thou going? Dost thou not know full well that runaways are never welcome with the troops?" I entreat him to show courage, pointing out to him that his and our only salvation lies in carrying out the plan adopted against the enemies of the Republic. I declare to Rewbell that if he fails us I will have him arrested, that I am about to issue an appeal to the people, that disastrous consequences may ensue therefrom, but that I am determined to conquer without and in spite of him. " Persist, then, in your resolve to fly!" I exclaim. "Betray your trust and the people! Go, cover yourself with disgrace, Rewbell!" Larevellière looks at Rewbell, and, turning towards me, says, "Together with you will I save the Republic or share your fate: no act of cowardice shall ever be laid to my door."

After a lengthy and even threatening conversation, Rewbell, convinced that we are fully determined, recovers his senses, and says, "I will not desert you." "Well, then," say I, "we will attack to-morrow; our success does not depend on Augereau; his name is the only reason for my using him; willing or unwilling, he shall act." Rewbell then confessed that his understanding had become clouded, that he was tired out, but that he would join forces with us. I see him home, and order his relatives not to leave him alone, nor with any stranger, but to confine him to the family circle: this will tend to restore courage to him.

The friends as well as the relations of Rewbell, and Rewbell himself, have declared to me that at this critical moment he had truly been insane for several hours. It is not that Rewbell was not a man of strong mind: he had already given proof to the contrary; but there are times when the strongest mind reaches a breaking strain, and when it seems, so to speak, to collapse like a mechanism whose springs have given way. The reports that have reached us in the course of the day are enough to alarm us at the strength and determination of our enemies. They are bent on acting during the night —this very evening, perhaps. "Well, then," I remark, "there can no longer be any obstacles in the way; it would be madness to wait for any to arise; let us go forward without looking either to the right or left; we must conquer or die to-night. I am prepared for any and every event."

17th Fructidor, Year V.— The sitting of the Directorate was a most solemn one on this 17th day of Fructidor, Year V. In the evening I sent for Augereau. I said to him: "It is for midnight." Thereupon I give him in writing his principal orders and the positions he is to occupy. I am informed that the Councils are to decree on the following day that they intend to sit *en permanence.*

Taking Augereau with me, I call on my two colleagues; the Ministers are summoned; I show them the cards distributed among the counter-revolutionaries; muskets have been supplied to them; there is no time to be lost; it is necessary to act as has been agreed upon in order to deliver the Republican portion of the Councils. Merlin joins us in great haste, and seems anxious. My two colleagues, after having set forth the imminent danger threatening the Fatherland, adopt a resolution to the effect "that the soldiery shall seize the halls of the Councils. The halls shall be guarded with a view of preventing all ingress. The commandant of the guard of the *corps législatif* shall be summoned to surrender the custody of the doors and to join the Republican troops; in case of refusal or any opposition whatsoever, the General-in-chief is authorized to make use of the forces placed at his disposal."

After having seen to everything, and smoothed away every difficulty, I say to Augereau: " Depart, and be ready for midnight. I shall be on horseback at your side. The Pont-Neuf and the Pont-Royal are to be occupied with cannon; the Place de la Révolution and the Tuileries are to be surrounded with troops; a *demi-brigade*, of which I will dispose as circumstances may require, is to be stationed at the Luxembourg."

Augereau departs, after receiving the oral order of the three members of the Directorate to fulfil his important mission, on which the salvation of the Republic depends. I leave my colleagues together with the Ministers, in order to assign posts to the several unemployed officers who have flocked to my residence. The persons I find there—among others the ambassadors Meyer and Staël—are likewise detained till an hour after midnight, when indiscretions are no longer to be dreaded. I again join my colleagues, and we draft a proclamation protesting against the return of royalty and one to the Constitution of 1793. Larevellière and Rewbell desire that, in order to allay all fears, there should be added to it: "And against the return of the family of the Duc d'Orléans." This family, ever hunted down and forsaken by those whose duty it should have been to defend it, is always given up as a concession by weakness to wickedness. The father was sent to the scaffold by those who wished to show that they were not his partisans; to-day the children are sacrificed on the same principle.

But these are not the times when it is possible to speak reasonably and to maintain the claims of justice, even with those who are of the same opinion as myself; passions are muttering and seething to struggle with the passions that are attacking us; hence it is impossible for me to separate from our own party.

18th Fructidor, Year V.—Our proclamations are at last ready. I draw up, with the aid of Schèrer, the various orders to be issued to the troops. François de Neufchâteau displays a grand character. Midnight strikes; the columns move forward; the order is given that Carnot and Barthélemy shall be kept under close guard in their apartments. The former had already escaped from the Luxembourg. The day dawns; I order the alarm-gun to be fired; the grenadiers of the *corps législatif* embrace and fraternize with the soldiers of the line.

Augereau had drunk a little champagne in order to prepare himself, as on battle days: on seeing Ramel he tears his epaulets from him, and goes so far as to strike him in the face with them; he then hands them to an aide-de-camp. Daring must indeed be good in all matters, for Ramel, who is not lacking in courage, is dumfounded, and does not venture to stir: he considers himself rightfully arrested, for the sole reason that he has been grossly insulted.

Verdière, who is in command of the garrison, receives orders to arrest the *inspecteurs de la salle*. They had assembled in their quarters, in what is to-day the second Pavillon Marsan. General, aide-de-camp, grenadiers, and gendarmes ascend the stairs to carry out the behest. When, opening the door and holding in his hand the order of the Directorate, General Verdière announces that he has come to arrest the inspectors, all of them yell: " Your scoundrel of a Barras shall perish, and you too!" This yell comes loudest from one of the inspectors, Bourdon de l'Oise, a red-headed man, as violent as he is powerful. He shakes his fist menacingly at General Verdière, who tries in vain to utter the first word of the order of which he is the bearer. He beats a retreat, followed by the whole of his military escort. The inspectors throw them down to the very bottom of the staircase, close the door, leaving Verdière and his men below. What a position will his not be when he meets Augereau and the Directorate, who have placed their trust in him! " We must conquer or die, general; we must storm the place and remove the men," says to Verdière his aide-de-camp, a man who has more brains and more courage than his chief. At the appeal of his aide-de-camp, Verdière once more ascends the stairs with his men. He knocks at the door; he is compelled to break it open, as the inspectors had barricaded it. He and his men pounce on them, seize them by the collar; a scrimmage ensues, they succumb to numbers, are bound, pitched into cabs, and conveyed to the Temple.

Among the inspectors was Pichegru, who had shown fight in the first instance; but, on seeing that resistance was useless, he had submitted to the inevitable. Among the executors of the order was a General Pincot, a half-pay officer, who, without having any mission and as a mere amateur, had of his own accord gone into active service on that day. On seeing Pichegru, whose personal enemy he was, Pincot takes from one of the soldiers a musket to which was attached a bayonet; he is on the point of driving it through Pichegru's body, when the latter, grasping the weapon, wrenches the bayonet from it, bends it double with his powerful grip, after trying in vain to break it, and, having thus rendered it harmless, disdainfully hands it back to the soldier to whom it belonged.

The whole party proceeds to the Temple. The prison-registrar, on seeing this matutinal arrival of so many carriages containing members of the Legislature, in other words just so many men whose person was inviolable according to the Constitution—the prison-registrar, I say, flies, and there is no one to enter the new arrivals on the calendar. They stand about the jail-yard, waiting for a prison-registrar, when, in default of one, the aide-de-camp of Verdière is compelled to take up the pen and make the entries himself.

Pichegru expressed to this aide-de-camp how much he was touched by his gentlemanlike conduct. He begged him to accept as a souvenir all he had about him—viz., the pistols he still had in his pocket, for it had not occurred to any one to deprive him of them. They were pistols of honor from the factory at Versailles, presented to him from the Directorate itself, as a testimonial to his magnificent conduct when at the head of troops of the Republic. Pichegru next expressed a wish to know the name of the half-pay general who had attempted to kill him a few moments before; on learning it he exclaimed: "Ah, I remember now; it is the man I was compelled to place under arrest in Holland on account of some rather ugly doings."

M. Thibaudeau, who had come at early morn to join the *inspecteurs de la salle* as an amateur, was clever enough to part company with them in good time, and to glide out of the Tuileries, in order to save himself, as he had glided into them. Vipers know how to glide, since it is their nature to crawl. The incident, related by Thibaudeau himself, is one of the rare truths he has told in his Memoirs.

My apartments are filled with a large number of deputies, citizens, generals, and soldiers. The operations of Augereau are striking terror into the conspirators; they are scattering and seeking hiding-places; the Tuileries and the assembly halls of the *corps législatif* are closed, and guarded by soldiers, who prevent all ingress. The Council of Five Hundred meets at the Odéon, and the Council of Ancients at the École de Santé; they declare that the troops and the Republicans have deserved well of the country; laws popular and appropriate to the circumstance are passed; the conspiring deputies are prisoners, together with Pichegru, their leader. An account of the unmasked conspiracy is printed and placarded in the streets. The *collets noirs* are torn off and their elegant wearers disperse; not a drop of blood is shed on this memorable day, which saves the Fatherland.

19th Fructidor, Year V.—As early as the 19th Fructidor an attempt was made to stir up the Faubourg Saint-Antoine; but the loyal citizens dwelling in it made short work of the intriguers, who sought to deceive them, and to convey to them a false impression of the patriotic object of the events of the 18th.

It was quite enough that the painful necessity should have existed of making a *coup d'état*, which mutilated at once the two principal authorities of the Republic, without adding to it the misfortune—one might say the crime—of deriving personal advantage from the events of that day, and of not letting the Republic benefit by all its results. But this is not the way in which the vulgar herd understands great political acts; it is unable to comprehend that a man can make a display of authority without increasing his own, or even without usurping the sovereign, power. In the eyes of many people it was the simplest and most proper course to adopt; so was I craftily and also stupidly counselled by courtiers who believed I would not lend a deaf ear to their hints, and even by Republicans who imagined that it was quite natural that I should seize upon the dictatorship to the salvation of all. Thus it was that Augereau, who in those days enjoyed the reputation of being a shining light among patriots, did not consider he was failing in his duty when urging me on in that direction. Not content with suggesting the thing to me personally, he went about loudly proclaiming: "What is, after all, the use of what we did on the 18th Fructidor if it is to lead to nothing? What does Barras imagine? Does he think he can go on with his four colleagues? He alone must remain in power, and alone occupy the Luxembourg."

It was not to me alone that Augereau made these

suggestions; for this would have borne a close resemblance to flattery: he repeated them in the very court-yard of the Luxembourg, and proclaimed his sentiments from the house-tops. Réal, on the other hand, who worshipped me and openly avowed his feelings for me, argued that no revolution had been accomplished were I not placed at the head of affairs, and that in spite of myself; failing this, the revolution of the 18th Fructidor was not one, that it was a failure, and lacked energy. He even went so far as to express his sentiments in less decent words than those I place on record; in short, he said that the revolution of the 18th Fructidor was not of the male sex; and, although in those days the word "king" could neither be uttered nor listened to, Republicans, such as Augereau and even Réal, feared not to speak it in my very presence. As regards myself, my conscience told me only too well what I was to think of all this for me to pay any serious attention to their suggestions. It was because I was a sincere Republican, and in order to remain such, that I had acted in so decisive a fashion on the 18th Fructidor; so I politely thanked these gentlemen for all their compliments.

Talleyrand was first and foremost among those who had prayed for the 18th Fructidor; it was necessary to his new position, and consolidated it. Talleyrand was likewise among those who, in order to appear as having most largely contributed to victory, clamored most loudly for the punishment of the defeated. "The least that could be done would have been to kill them," he remarked, "if only to do homage to the principle of Barère — which is only half a truth—that only the dead do not come back."

Without seeking to make myself appear any better or more humane than my neighbor, I was far from thinking that it is only the dead who do not return; I believed, on the contrary, that the memory of the innocent dead can always recur to the living, and that, after all the painful experiences of the past, humanity might be considered good policy. Hence I was truly glad to see that the calming down of men's passions had allowed of moderation in the hour of victory, that not a drop of blood had been shed on the 18th Fructidor, that death had played no part in the measures of force it had been necessary to display. When I myself looked upon it as a victory within the victory that we should have been able to substitute transportation for the atrocious executions which stained with blood the early days of the Revolution, why did Talleyrand—whom, in his intercourse with enlightened men and from his previous opinions, one might have thought inclined towards moderation—affect to show so great a lack of it, and why did he attempt to take the lead and the most conspicuous place? I would fain believe that he did not do this out of purely gratuitous wickedness, and that in this instance, as in all the known actions of his life, he acted from an interested calculation, whereof his opinion was but the revelation.

We have to find the successors of Carnot and Barthélemy, who have been sentenced to transportation; we carry on this operation through the *corps législatif*, where several candidates are setting forth their divers claims. Among them comes Talleyrand, who thinks himself entitled to consideration in this competition for the inheritance of the transported Directors.

Mme. de Staël, when making Talleyrand a Minister, had been under the impression that she was satisfying all the aspirations and needs of his ambition; but nowadays he was not content with being a Minister. "All a Minister can do," he would say, "is to propose measures which are not always adopted, or to give effect to others which are infinitely distasteful to him. A Minister does not possess sufficient power to do good. To effect good, a man should be at least a Director." The 18th Fructidor, by creating two vacancies, had inspired Talleyrand with the wish, and even the hope, of becoming one of the new Directors. He did not scruple to unbosom himself to me on the subject, and prefaced his speech with the following remark: "You are the essential man of the Directorate, the warrior who is fit to take Carnot's place; you are the head and arms of the Directorate. Were I so fortunate as to become your colleague, I should make it my glory to obey you in everything, as a child obeys its father."

The illusion of my paternity did not go so far as to make me believe that I should find in Talleyrand either a very loving child or a man very able to fill the place of Director. Had I even desired to make him a member of the Directorate, it would have been impossible for me to succeed. Rewbell's opinion of Talleyrand had been proclaimed so loudly and so frequently in the presence of so many members of the Councils, that Talleyrand, in spite of the intrigues of all sorts which he had brought into play on this occasion, could not carry the day against public discredit coupled with a feeling of general fear of his treacherous character.

22d Fructidor, Year V.—Merlin, Minister of Justice, and François de Neufchâteau, Minister of the Interior, have little trouble in winning the day over Talleyrand. They are appointed members of the Directorate in lieu of Carnot and Barthélemy, and lose no time in taking up their quarters in the Directorial palace.

Compelled as I am, in the midst of all these crises, to encounter so many and such totally different individuals, whom I am liable to handle somewhat roughly, I think I cannot do better, in order to confirm several of my assertions, than to produce without comment, and side by side, a few letters from personages whom I have described; these will reveal their personal traits and portraits as drawn by themselves. I am laying autographs before the reader.

Talleyrand wrote to Bonaparte on the 22d Fructidor:

> You will see from the proclamations that an actual conspiracy, and one altogether to the advantage of royalty, has for some time past been hatching against the Constitution; it no longer disguised itself, and was obvious to the most indifferent eyes. The word "patriot" had become an insult; all Republican institutions were being disparaged. France's most irreconcilable foes were rapidly flocking into it, welcomed and honored. An hypocritical fanaticism had suddenly transported us into the sixteenth century; dissensions existed in the Directorate; men sat in the *corps législatif* who were really elected pursuant to instructions from the Pretender, and all whose motions breathed Royalism. The Directorate, strong in all these circumstances, caused the arrest of the conspirators. In order to stamp out the calumnies and hopes of all those who had so greatly desired, or who should still meditate the ruin of that Constitution, a prompt death was decreed from the very outset against those who should recall royalty, the Constitution of '93, or d'Orléans.

Bernadotte wrote to Bonaparte on the 24th Fructidor:

The arrested deputies have left for Rochefort, whence they are to embark, to be cast on the island of Madagascar. Paris is quiet. The populace, in the first instance, learned the arrest of the deputies with indifference. A spirit of curiosity soon caused them to flock into the streets; thereupon followed a burst of enthusiasm, and for the first time in many days the air was rent with cries of "Long live the Republic!" in all the thoroughfares. The neighboring departments have made manifest their discontent. The department of Allier has protested, it is said, and it is to receive a good trouncing. Eight thousand men are arriving in the environs of Paris; part of them are already in the suburbs, under the orders of General Lemoine. Just at present the Government has the opportunity of instilling fresh life into the public mind; but everybody feels that it is necessary to summon honest and energetic Republicans; unfortunately a number of men without talents are already believing that the movement was made for their benefit alone. The time is propitious to set everything straight again. The armies are again in a settled condition; the soldiers at home are respected, or at least feared; the *émigrés* are in flight, and the unsworn priests are in hiding.

Never was there a more favorable circumstance for the consolidation of the Republic; if the occasion is not grasped, we are threatened with the necessity of making another movement after the next elections. The *corps législatif* has granted the fullest powers to the Directorate. A few there are who think it would be better to adjourn until some period determined upon, leaving the Directorate to enforce the Constitution at some indefinite period. There is a difference of opinion on this score; still, the Directorate and the *corps législatif* are in unison; nevertheless, there remains beyond doubt in the two Councils a party which is not friendly to the Republic, and which will do everything to accomplish its ruin as soon as it has recovered from its fright. The Government is aware of this, and will doubtless adopt measures to ward off the danger and protect the patriots against fresh persecutions.

Bonaparte writes to the Directorate on the 26th Fructidor:

... Herewith a proclamation to the army in regard to the events of the 18th. I have despatched to Lyons the 45th half-brigade, commanded by General Bon, and some fifty mounted men, and General Lannes, with the 20th Light Infantry and the 9th Foot, to Marseilles. I am sending the enclosed proclamation to the southern departments. I am also going to devote my attention to a proclamation to the citizens of Lyons as soon as I have a fair knowledge of what has taken place there. As soon as I hear of the slightest disturbance in that city, I will wend my way thither in all haste: remember that you have here 100,000 men, who alone would be fully able to insure obedience to any measures you might take to establish liberty on solid foundations. What matters it that we win victories, if we are banished from our Fatherland? It may be said of Paris what Cassius said of Rome: "What matters it that she is called Queen, when she is, on the banks of the Seine, the slave of the gold of Pitt?"

General Lannes was indeed detached for a while from the Army of Italy, in order to restore quiet to the southern departments, and to put an end to the assassinations perpetrated in them. He made a beginning at Marseilles with a proclamation of laconic force, ending as follows: "If you conspire to-day, you are dead men to-morrow."

Talleyrand writes a second letter to Bonaparte on the 30th Fructidor:

... We intend to scatter broadcast publications which will clearly demonstrate that the Courts of Vienna and London were in perfect harmony with the faction which we have just stamped out at home. It will be shown to what a degree the negotiations of these two Courts and the movements at home went hand in hand. The members of the Clichy Club and the Cabinet of the Emperor has one common and manifest object in view—viz., the re-establishment of a king in France and a dishonorable peace, pursuant to which Italy was to be restored to her former masters.

Bonaparte wrote to Augereau on the 2d Vendémiaire, Year VI. (23d September, 1797):

... . The entire army has applauded the wisdom and vigor displayed by you on this all-important occasion, and has rejoiced at the success of the Fatherland with the enthusiasm and energy characteristic of it.

If there is a victim whom those who were compelled to make the 18th Fructidor must regret having included in their *coup d'état*, it is assuredly Carnot, who from the very outset of the Revolution has rendered so many services to his country, and who at heart was indeed a true friend of liberty. He has luckily escaped transportation by slipping out of the Luxembourg. Personally I was quite pleased, and grateful to those who assisted him in his flight. Had I not been an accomplice to it, could I not have prevented it at a time when all power was centred in me, and when every means of surveillance and of action had been placed at my disposal by the dictatorship conferred upon me by two of my colleagues? Was not this dictatorship more than sanctioned by all the military men under my orders, as well as by the portion of the *corps législatif* which was one with the majority of the Directorate? Carnot has experienced, since that time, so many troubles in life, that he might have believed that he had not been respected, and that, as he and others have said, it had been sought to assassinate him. It is easy to refute this assertion in the most complete fashion. Had any such intention been entertained, I can solemnly assure Carnot that it would have been easier to do it than to speak of it, taking into consideration the frame of mind of all the officers and men of action who were under my orders, and who waited only for a sign of my wish to give to their act the sequel of a most awful revenge.

Carnot's resentment may have equalled the angry feelings he bore towards the Directorate. He is more excusable on this score, which is but the result of his misfortunes, than in regard to the perpetual display of irritation in which he indulged for eighteen months—a display culminating at the point when, Carnot calling to his support all the enemies of our Fatherland, we could no longer separate him from those foes, in the necessity in which we found ourselves of saving the Fatherland and ourselves from attacks aimed at both. It would seem, moreover, that the violent and inflexible character of Carnot had been contended with not only by us, but even in the bosom of his family; previous to the 18th Fructidor he had been good-naturedly and fraternally remonstrated with by some of his relations, who loved him with their whole heart as much as they loved liberty. We found these sentiments most plainly expressed in the letters addressed at the Directorate to Carnot by one of his brothers, and intercepted in the tumult consequent upon the events of the 18th Fructidor. They were brought to me at the Directorate; we were glad to recognize in them the language of pure sentiments, which might have brought Carnot round by enlightening him, if passions could ever consent to allow themselves to be enlightened.

There is an anti-Fructidorian history of the Directorate which may at the very least be styled most fraternal as far as Carnot is concerned, since the authorship of it is confessed to by a brother of Carnot—General Carnot-Feulens, of the Engineers. It might have been written by Carnot himself, who more than once has indulged in anonymity, since in the history I refer to it is sought, by means of a double pseudonym, to make people believe that even the answer to Bailleul does not emanate from Carnot's pen. Among other hypotheses set forth in this history, it is said that an adjutant-general "called Mucherez stated publicly—under cover of the favor he claimed to enjoy at the hands of Barras, whom he called his friend, while at the same time displaying a diploma signed by him as president of a private society—that if he had not been fortunate enough to deal the first blows at Carnot, he had at least helped to dig his grave; that this adjutant-general died suddenly at Troyes, where he held a command, charging his friend Barras with his death, a well-deserved reward for similar services."

It may be possible that some worthless scamp, so many of whom come to the surface in revolutionary movements—that some wild fanatic, no more a democrat than an aristocrat, one seeking to pay his court to the triumphant power, may have attempted to attribute to himself the honor of having contributed to rid the Directorate from its most considerable adversary. Other utterances of a like kind have been retailed to us; they prove that in all times there have existed men who boasted of crimes which they had not committed, while seeking to derive benefit from them. It is, for instance, in the knowledge of several persons now living (notably M. Le Maire, Dean of the Faculty of Letters) that a general already then prominent in the Revolution and in foreign wars, General Loison, had boasted of being more of a grave-digger than Mucherez, claiming that he had been the actual assassin of Carnot; he was even in the habit of coupling his boast with nauseating particulars—to wit, that "when Carnot was killed in the Luxembourg an enormous quantity of blood had flowed from his body, drenching the ground, which had to be covered again and again with soil in order to destroy every vestige of it."

The first answer to these charges against Barras is that Carnot was not assassinated; that he survived in good health and in safety in foreign lands, giving every proof of his being alive by writing his answer to Bailleul, and likewise his history of the Directorate, of which his brother Feulens, however well-informed he might be, never was any more than a collaborateur. How, let us ask dispassionately, but not without reproach—how can he who claims to be an historian have brought himself to make, out of hatred for his adversaries, statements which he himself proves to have been drawn solely from imagination, and which can consequently recoil only on the head of the inventor of these fables? How came it that the stoic Carnot, the lover of truth, showed such a disregard for it when proclaiming that he was establishing it? Oh, the irritability of the good man! It leads him to be ignorant of himself, and to seem to be ignorant of the very things that he charges upon himself by his own assertions.

As for myself, who believe that, in view of my opinions and the needs of the period, it was impossible for me to avoid the painful duty of combating and even striking down opponents whom I might esteem secretly, and whom I was desirous of loving, like Carnot, I am able to swear that all my wish and all my efforts did not, even at the moment of my greatest exasperation, go beyond ridding ourselves of the resistance which clogged the march of government and fostered the rallying of its enemies; in my eyes the object had been completely attained when, on the 18th Fructidor, our adversaries were deprived of the faculty of doing any harm, either by forcible dismissal or voluntary retirement from public affairs. Danton had no other object during the fights between the Montagne and the Gironde, when he not only approved but brought on the removal of the Girondins from the National Convention; but there happened what frequently occurs in the impassioned combats of revolutions, that the conquerors are not always masters of the movement they have started: they see it go beyond the limits they had thought it lay in their power to assign to it; they see these movements leap, so to speak, over their heads, and end in knocking off their heads, after having in the first instance knocked off the heads of others. Danton, who had in all sincerity called for the removal of the Girondins, in order that the action of the government which had to repulse the foreign enemy should not be impeded, had never dreamed it possible that the result of the events of the 31st of May should go beyond removal. I have been told of his disappointment—nay, even of his deep-rooted grief—when it was decided that the twenty-two Girondins belonged to the Revolutionary Tribunal—*i.e.*, to the scaffold. I feel the same way in regard to my share in the events of the 18th Fructidor. I am entitled to repeat that I did not feel any happier than did Danton on the 31st of May, when I saw the 18th Fructidor not only sanctioned, but exaggerated, by the laws passed on the 19th. These recollections are even now sufficiently painful for me to consider it necessary to add a page to all those already devoted to these events. They are melancholy enough to dispense those who have penned them from indulging in exaggerations. I therefore admit fully and without restriction that the idea of removing Carnot and Barthélemy was entirely that of Rewbell, Larevellière, and myself, believing as we did that we could not escape this necessity; but at the same time I swear by heaven and earth that never did any one of us conceive the idea of depriving them of life: we ourselves were threatened in our existence by those meditating this same 18th Fructidor. We merely got the start of them by a few days, perhaps a few hours, perhaps only a few minutes, because Messieurs the *inspecteurs de la salle*, who had met together constantly for a whole month, had assembled during the course of that very night for the purpose of taking action, and they were at the utmost only forestalled. Not only did we not desire to kill Carnot, but we were truly glad at his having escaped arrest. I will even declare that we left him, or, rather, afforded him, the means of safety by intimidating him, so as to force him to leave. I knew at the very moment of it how he had left, whither he had gone; the persons he met in the Luxembourg, and whom he believed placed there to arrest him, were there with quite a different object; the proof of this lies in the very fact of Carnot's escape. Had not my heart dictated the course I followed on this occasion, my policy would have dictated it. The period no longer admitted of the *régime* of 1793. Yes, I declare it, I contributed to Carnot's escape; and—must I say it?—this action on my part, which

I will not call generosity, is perhaps what he has least forgiven me.

Over and above this, the friends of Carnot and his relations, who cannot but be his defenders, state that he was not taken by surprise; that he could, had he so wished, have got the start of his foes; but that he had not wished to do so, on the grounds that he felt that "his personal victory would have been that of the Royalist party against which he was fighting and which he abhorred," and that the re-establishment of a power destructive of the Republic, of which he was one of the founders, must have ensued.

This defence of Carnot may be considered as the strongest indictment against him from a Republican point of view, since he admits that the triumph of his plans would have brought about the upsetting of the social system with the defence of which he was intrusted.

If, in revolutions once set in motion, he who appears as their ostensible chief were really master of them, I should have been only too glad to reply in a positive manner to the following letter, which I received on the 24th Fructidor:

Truguet to his Friend Barras.

Once more do I come, my friend, to lay bare my heart to you, and to speak to you in all frankness. I have submitted with the pride of a Republican to a dismissal instigated and obtained by the counter-revolutionists. The majority of the Directorate was perhaps compelled to yield, in order to better conceal its great designs. I have likewise endured with some fortitude a thousand persecutions, a thousand insults, which my patriotism and my fidelity to Republican principles drew on me. To-day the Republicans are triumphant; the Directorate is no longer fettered; the conspirators are routed, and their victims must be reinstated with *éclat*. Several days have already gone by since the 18th Fructidor, and Charles Lacroix and Truguet are still smarting under the blows dealt at them by the counter-revolutionists. I have not seen my old colleague, and I do not know what his ideas are; but he is, like me, entitled to prompt reparation, which would cease to be worthy of the Directorate and of ourselves were it attributed to intrigues which have no existence, were it delayed on the eve of danger. I have officially tendered my services to the President Larevellière; to-day I speak to my friend only; it is for him to know the course to be pursued by the Directorate, which has once more so courageously contributed to saving the Republic. Once more drop me a line. I embrace you. TRUGUET.

It will be shown further on what prevented me from obtaining satisfaction for Truguet's first claim from the majority of the Directorate.

Everything is once more quiet, and the Government, which has recovered from its recent shock, goes on with its business. The most important is the appointment of functionaries; Republicans have to be substituted for the enemies of the Republic.

1st Complimentary Day, Year V.— The Directorate has decided upon recalling its plenipotentiaries at Lille, and giving their places to Treilhard and Bonnier, ex-members of the Convention. Pursuant to the ultimatum proposed by them, Lord Malmesbury is notified to quit the territory of the Republic unless he is empowered to consent preliminarily to the restitution of the possessions wrested by the English from France and her allies. Malmesbury, who is not invested with any such powers, returns to London. His arrival causes a fall in the funds and murmurs of discontent. Pitt thinks to still them by causing it to be published that negotiations have not been broken off. I ask that the decision of the Directorate which proves the breaking-off be printed, published, and sent to England. Adopted.

In consequence of such serious circumstances, and after a prolonged debate, it is resolved to send Botot, my secretary, to Bonaparte, to urge upon him speedily to revolutionize Italy, beginning with Tuscany. It is also resolved that if Austria continues to show herself hostile to us, all the propositions which have come to us from Hungary shall be taken into consideration, and that peoples shall be appealed to instead of kings.

Prussia shows a desire of cementing close ties with the Republic.

Several dismissals are made in the civil and military services; Republicans are substituted. Bernadotte, who has been in Paris for a month, has tendered us his services daily, except on the very days when we might have been likely to accept them. He never came near the Directorate on the 18th Fructidor, nor on the preceding or following days; he reappears in its midst now that the triumph is assured, and from all he declares to us it seems that we should have greatly depended on him, that we were even greatly in the wrong for not having sent for him; we are pleased to entertain his protestations of devotion, and without seeking to ascertain how much of boasting there may be in his talk, we consider we are giving him a proof of our sincere confidence by offering him the command of the departments of the South.

The reactions in the South had at least equalled the actions preceding them, and the lamentations of the wretched residents in those districts were unfortunately too well founded. After so many tribulations and exterminations, all felt the need of peace, or at least of a truce to slaughter. This sentiment was expressed by the inhabitants of the South with all the vivacity and candor that mark Southern passions. Witness the addresses received by the Directorate from these various districts subsequent to the 18th Fructidor. The time has come when firmness and wisdom can quiet the Republic's enemies and reconcile them to her. The mission is doubtless a most grand and important one; but Bernadotte has quickly perceived the difficulties besetting it, especially for a man of vacillating character. What, indeed, can be more formidable than the necessity of declaring himself in positive fashion for a man whose life is spent in dodging? Moreover, the ambition of Bernadotte—an ambition which is not revealed in the frankness displayed on his face and in his vigorous utterance—entertains other views than the government of this great military division. Unwilling as he is to give utterance to his thoughts, he prefers requests and lays down conditions, the object of which is to draw away attention from other ideas that might be discovered in him. The Directorate, unwilling to argue with a hesitation that is not avowed, and which a lack of good faith renders impossible to grasp, comes to the conclusion that a brilliant reputation is not indispensable to a post requiring merely political probity and wisdom, together with justice and impartiality towards the persons under jurisdiction, and so appoints to the command General Pille, former Minister of War previous to the 13th Vendémiaire.

So it is settled that Bernadotte is to return to

Italy to resume command of his division, and rejoin his brothers-in-arms, for whom, he says, he longs continually, and from whom he cannot remain separated without shedding tears; but before starting for Italy Bernadotte desires to have a few confidential conversations with me.

One who has held high positions, and has seen come to him, in order to prefer their requests, men possessed with ambition, knows that their ordinary formula is to begin by saying that they have no ambition. Sometimes they even submit distant projects, which they seek to represent as born of a disgust for grandeur and for the whole human race. And yet this assumed disgust consists in a desire to obtain a distant command — in other words, to be the first somewhere, in consequence of the chagrin they feel at their inability to be first at home. So it was that Bernadotte, before leaving Paris to rejoin the Army of Italy, suggests to us an expedition to India. Of course, the scheme has doubtless no other object than the welfare of France; also, of course, no one better than the author of the scheme can obtain this national benefit.

The victory won on the 18th Fructidor has not yet re-established order, especially in the South; but we learn that the brigands, no longer encouraged by the Government, cannot continue successful for any length of time. They have made an attack on Saint-Maximin; their intention was to carry off as hostages the members of the family of the Director Barras, so it is reported, but they have been repulsed by the Republicans of the Var.

The brigands who have gathered in the department of the Vaucluse have taken possession of

Pont-Saint-Esprit, and have shot down patriots. Saint-Christole is the leader of this band; he assumes the title of General of the Two Councils; he was arrested, and surrendered almost immediately by his partisans.

1st Vendémiaire, Year VI.—Hoche has just died almost suddenly at Wetzlar; he was unable to finish the letter he was writing to me. The Republic loses in him the general most distinguished, both by his intelligence and his military talents, France has produced, not even excepting Bonaparte and Moreau. Hoche was sincerely devoted to liberty; upon seeing it threatened he had detached, as agreed upon between us, a body of troops from the Army of Sambre-et-Meuse, in order to furnish the Directorate with the means of combating the Royalist conspiracy.

Considerations which might have proved fatal had rendered null this daring and patriotic step. "It is on me," he said to me, "that you must cast all the responsibility of the march of the troops on Paris. Save yourself, save the Republic, and sacrifice me if necessary; as to you, my dear Barras, hold out to the very last moment; call me, if you think it necessary; but be ever resolved to act, whether alone or supported." On the eve of his death he was under censure in the Directorate for an offending letter written by him to the Minister of War.

The career of this extraordinary man, which came to an end before he was thirty, is the one best filled up to the present time; it does not leave a blemish; it is a beau ideal worthy of antiquity. His almost sudden death may doubtless be regarded as supernatural; it has remained unexplained by the physicians who cared for him in his dying hours, and by the surgeons who vainly sought its cause by an autopsy. It has been suspected that he was poisoned at Rennes through Puisaye, the representative of Louis XVIII. and of the *chouannerie*, or at Chaillot, at a dinner he is said to have accepted a few days before his return to the army. Let us leave to Nature her mysteries; they are real and profound, and can dispense us from always seeking for explanations in men's wickedness.

Newspapers and even historians, or, rather, men assuming that appellation, have believed, or have sought to create the belief, that General Hoche had been deceived, and had considered himself deceived, by me during the days preceding the 18th Fructidor, and that he had expressed his displeasure at this in his letters to myself. I might, for all reply, enter a formal denial against all these calumnies, but I need not have recourse to this means. As a matter of fact, not only did General Hoche never feel displeased with me on the great occasion when I did all that lay in my power, and wherein all did not assuredly depend on me alone; but even if he had, owing to all the delays and painful annoyances he encountered, experienced a feeling of ill-temper, or even one of well-founded indignation, against those whom he believed to be the authors of his vexations, never would General Hoche, under any circumstances, and however deeply wrought up he might have been—never, I say, could General Hoche have so forgotten what was due to himself as to indulge in such an insulting sally. The last letters written and dictated by the dying Hoche, his last words, were expressive of his affectionate friendship for me; his very look, according to the assertion of those present at his death, was turned as if in my direction.

Bonaparte is instructed to take the necessary steps to seize Malta; I am requested to send him all the information I possess about that island, together with the names of the inhabitants and of the knights devoted to the cause of the Republic, and their letters.

An ordinance is passed to forestall the abuses which might creep in in the erasures from the list of *émigrés*.

Caillard negotiates a peace with Russia at Berlin.

Augereau, the chief military actor on the 18th Fructidor, has undoubtedly just rendered an imperishable service to his Fatherland, and too much gratitude cannot be shown him; but hardly has he acquired these rights to our gratitude when he seems to have conceived an idea of himself that would place him above all that the liveliest expression of this feeling could possibly grant. The introduction of military force into civic affairs gives birth to the idea of meddling with them, and of taking an active part in them. Augereau, as a soldier, would, like Talleyrand, who is not one, have liked to be a Director, forgetting that he had been only an instrument in the affair, and that his *rôle* was not to go beyond that. He does not see anything more worthy of his acceptance among all that can be said or done for him; he is in close contact with all that is aristocratic. He claims to be the representative and the teacher of patriotism; no one has the right to come near him, nor to unloose the latchet of his boots adorned with gold and diamonds. He is a child who has lost its head; he is suffering from a brain-fever of patriotism. In such a state of health Augereau becomes a truly embarrassing personage for the Directorate. He is a man whom one can no longer be exposed to meet without inconvenience, either in a drawing-room or at a public gathering. It is therefore urgent and indispensable to get him to leave Paris, and to return to his military duties, which, by absorbing his ambition, give him the reward to which he is entitled. As he is, moreover, no longer of any use in Paris, the Directorate appoints him commander-in-chief of the Armies of the Sambre-et-Meuse and of the Rhine, united under the name of Army of Germany. Beurnonville is again to take command of the Army of the North. This complete nobody peremptorily insisted on a title and emoluments. General Lemoine is appointed to the command of the 17th military division, filling the place of Augereau.

3d Vendémiaire, Year VI.—Ever since Merlin has joined the Directorate our dominant fear has been to have men prominent by their talents or patriotism as Ministers. François de Neufchâteau having vacated the Ministry of the Interior, Merlin suggests for the vacant portfolio some sort of a judge or advocate of Rennes or Nantes, who is in a general way held in high esteem, but whom nobody knows; this gives rise to an epigram ending as follows: "If unknown quantities are sought, the Republic is a problem." Fully provided with the required guarantees as to his nullity, citizen Letourneux is appointed Minister of the Interior; I abstain from voting for this citizen, who is entirely new to me.

Lambrecht, a Belgian jurisconsult, a man of honorable character, is appointed Minister of Justice.

It has been shown that the Prince de Carency had rendered good service on the 18th Fructidor. He had succeeded in getting acquainted with the plots of the counter-revolutionists, and had kept us informed as to the dangers threatening us. I owe it to his revelations that I was warned of the time fixed for the attack; he now informs me that his connections with the intriguing *émigrés* in various lands, and in particular in Spain, furnish him the means of serving us to good purpose in that country. A secret mission is given to him on my recommendation. He has left for Spain. We have agreed upon a correspondence in cipher.

5th Vendémiaire, Year VI.—The new Directors, François de Neufchâteau and Merlin, would like to pose as ardent patriots, so they urge that stringent measures be adopted against those who have brought the Republic to the brink of the abyss; assuredly it is impossible for them to exaggerate the dangers run by liberty on this occasion. There can be no doubt that if the Royalist party had not been struck as if by a thunderbolt, it would have brought back despotism without amendment, charter, or condition; but now that victory is ours, we must use it magnanimously and generously. Clemency on the part of the victor is also prudence; but we regret to see that this political maxim is not grasped by all the members of the Directorate. Merlin, in particular, joins it with his narrow and rancorous spirit; there is hardly an inspiration that can be derived from such a source with which he does not favor us. As for myself, I am of opinion that it is wrong to perpetuate a *coup d'état*, however necessary it may have been; it is a thing forever to be deplored; every effort should be made to obliterate its traces and to cause them to be forgotten, by means of a wise and just administration; it must be shown that a *coup d'état* was neither made nor accepted in the interest of any particular person's power, and that if it has been necessary to go beyond the limits of the laws, the authors of the *coup d'état* are eager to confine themselves to the laws once more, as in a sanctuary where all are again in full security.

CHAPTER II

Reflections on the 18th Fructidor—Bonaparte's three millions—His pretended disgust for power—His plans for a negotiation with Austria—His army reinforced—Threatening attitude assumed towards Austria—Bonaparte's alarms in regard to the 18th Fructidor—Documents from the baggage-wagon of Klenglin—Réal deciphers them—Suspension of the negotiations of Lille—Augereau and the Army of Germany—Bonaparte's ever-increasing irritation—Incoherence of his despatches—He tenders his resignation—Prophecy made by Rewbell, who is in favor of accepting it, as also that of Bernadotte—I oppose its acceptance—Lafayette's captivity—Mme. de Staël intercedes for him—I lay her prayer before the Directorate—It receives support—Bonaparte instructed to demand of Austria the liberty of the great citizen—He gladly accepts the mission—Regnaud de Saint-Jean d'Angély seeks to attribute to him all the credit for this step—What Mme. de Lafayette and M. de Lafayette themselves thought about it—Dumouriez begs to be allowed to return to France—Dumouriez and Lafayette contrasted—I am approached by a sister of the woman Lamotte—Kitchen-maid style—M. Giblotte de Turenne—"Milord Kinesester"—Zealous parents—M. de Sade—General Debelle—Hoche's profound thoughts in his last moments; his ideas on Bonaparte—He commends Férino to me—I get him reinstated—Sieyès's plan against the nobles—It is presented by Boulay de la Meurthe—Murmurs caused by it—The *émigré* Damecourt—General Sahuguet dismissed—The treaty of alliance with Sardinia sent to the *corps législatif*—Sardinia's pacific dispositions—Bonaparte's appeal on behalf of Clarke—Increasing ill-temper of Bonaparte—He once more threatens to resign—The Pope ill—The King of Naples wishes to enter Rome—Carnot's blunder in this connection—Treilhard ambassador at Naples—Austrian affairs—Agony of the King of Prussia—Advances made by the Swedish Cabinet—England's duplicity—The contractors Gobert and Séguy and their ten millions—Friendly reunions of the most influential members of the Councils at the residence of the President of the Directorate—Political breakfasts—Amusing scene with Sieyès in regard to his proposed law—Botot returns—Opinions manifested by Bonaparte, and plan of campaign proposed by him—Continuation of the debate against the nobles—Attentions shown me—I am denounced to my colleagues—Bonaparte's ruses—Joseph's *mot* in regard to his talents—Singular request preferred by Bonaparte to me—He wishes to purchase Malta.

My narrative of a day become famous in the annals of the Revolution, and especially of the part played in it by me, may have seemed considerably curtailed. Fuller particulars have perhaps been expected; but the reader has been able to see that, in regard to that necessary and unavoidable day, I have denied nothing of the part I took in contributing to it, and that I have fully confessed to my doings in this connection. Besides, the 18th Fructidor does not consist merely of the violent act which put an end to long and fatal discussions among the chief authorities of the Republic: it includes the antecedents so painfully developed at each one of the too long sittings of the Directorate so faithfully recorded by me. I was in the habit of jotting down all incidents daily, lest I should forget them or narrate them later incorrectly, and also with the object of establishing their natural sequence. For in all events more or less worthy of being recorded in history, to-day is the son of yesterday, and historical genealogy is always more accurate if one goes back to the furthest periods. It has therefore appeared to me that my fellow-citizens, fully informed as to all the causes of the angry feelings characterizing our debates, will have foreseen the fruit they were bound to bear, and that all this could but end in a battle, wherein some were to be victorious and the others defeated. Hence the reader who has followed the trend of events has foreseen the making of the 18th Fructidor. I venture to say that he has himself made it, and that, present at our combats, he has seen that our unavoidable victory was that of the Republic; our defeat its ruin, and the possession by absolute royalty of our lovely France. While recognizing the necessity of a *coup d'état* rendered natural by everything preceding it, the reader will have seen that the *coup d'état* of the 18th Fructidor might have been avoided had the Directorate been invested with the power of dissolving the Chambers. But still the 18th Fructidor by no means produced the same state of things that has existed since the famous ordinance of the 5th of September, 1816. Although our actions are fully justified, and the primary justification is in my eyes my own conscience, I hasten to pass over these painful circumstances of our civil troubles, and to come to the events which are in their turn a still further justification or indictment.

Previous to the 18th Fructidor Bonaparte had promised and even offered to the Directorate three millions, which he would at once forward if called upon to do so. He instructed Lavalette to continue this offer. He kept it open to the time when the *coup d'état*, which he was the first to hasten, had been consummated. On the day following he said it was no longer necessary, and no longer had any object; he sent nothing, as a matter of absolute fact. He has none the less caused to be bruited about as a fact that which was never more than a promise on his part; thus, instead of a tangible sum, it was another imposture added to so many others. In this respect there is no reckoning with Bonaparte.

If Bonaparte, previous to the 18th Fructidor, suffered unpleasantnesses which inspired him with the desire of withdrawing from public affairs, or at least with the pretext of expressing such a desire, the victory won in Paris, through our efforts and in conformity with all his wishes, ought to have calmed him sufficiently for him to be satisfied and feel assured of his position with the army. The praise given Augereau constituted an expression of absolute satisfaction regarding the event which had crippled the enemy and consolidated Bonaparte's military and political authority. And yet we find him once more a prey to the fits of melancholy he pretended to be subject to previous to the 18th Fructidor. In a letter dated the 4th Vendémiaire, Year VI., which crossed one which the Directorate was sending him, to encourage him to remain at his post and to assure him of the national gratitude, he wrote: " The state of my soul also needs that I should reinvigorate it amid the mass of my fellow-citizens. For already too long a time has a great power been intrusted to my hands. I have under all circumstances used it for the welfare of the Fatherland: *so much the worse for those who do not believe in virtue, and who may have suspected mine; my reward is in my conscience, and in the opinion of posterity.*"

Nevertheless, while pretending not to care any longer for a command, and in spite of his alleged disgust with power, Bonaparte still deigns to preserve that which he has so freely exercised up to the present time. He informs us that he is in hopes of concluding peace by ceding to the Emperor the districts lying along the opposite bank of the Adige. The Cisalpine Republic is to have the other bank of the river and Mantua. Venice is to give itself to the Emperor, as also Albania, Istria, and the adjacent countries.

The Directorate rejects this negotiation; it lays down that the Emperor shall rest content with Trieste, from which point a line shall be drawn which will separate his possessions from those of Venice and from the mainland. The Venetian Isles are to remain at the disposal of the French Republic. Such is the ultimatum which Bonaparte is to notify. Two regiments of light troops and 6000 men are detached from the Army of the Rhine, to reinforce that of Italy. If the proposals of the Directorate are not accepted, Bonaparte is to attack.

The Armies of the Rhine are also ordered to notify the Austrians that immediately upon an outbreak of hostilities in Italy all conventions relating to treaties are to lapse; twenty-four hours' notice is to be given previous to commencing hostilities.

Commissioners are to be sent into the departments in order to make tardy conscripts rejoin their corps.

The new agitation which has taken hold of Bonaparte since the 18th Fructidor seems to be still in operation. A letter we receive from him on this subject expresses a fear that this revolution may give the terrorists an injurious ascendency; he now writes to me, in an apparently confidential way, that his aide-de-camp Lavalette has orders to call on all the Directors, but not to interfere in any matter under discussion. This confidence taught us nothing we did not know, for we were fully informed as to Lavalette. Bonaparte, in the midst of all his anxiety, seems none the less tenacious of the conditions he has suggested for peace; they are undoubtedly shameful, for no freedom would exist in Italy. On the contrary, that beautiful and unfortunate country would be at the mercy of Austria, which, once mistress of the maritime trade of Venice and of the fortified towns, would reign supreme over Venice, and take possession of it in due course.

Documents bearing on the conspiracy were seized by Moreau several months ago. The deciphering of them had been begun at his headquarters, but he had kept them there; they are forwarded to us somewhat tardily, although his package, antedated in his letter to Barthélemy, is sent on the 17th Fructidor. The documents in question are those known as the documents found in the baggage-wagon of Klenglin, by a division of the Army of the Rhine. The Minister of General Police, Sotin, is instructed to go through them; he is asked if he has trustworthy men to assist him in this operation; he suggests Réal; the Directorate accepts him. Réal undertakes to find the key, and proceeds to decipher the documents.

The Directorate, despairing of ever seeing any termination of the Lille negotiations, the slightest discussions leading to a continual despatch of couriers to London—a despatch that truly seems derisive—determines upon breaking them off. Lord Malmesbury writes to the Lille plenipotentiaries, complaining of his being sent back; he persists in asserting that his Court wishes peace and is desirous of continuing the negotiations. The French Minister replies that the Directorate is equally anxious for peace, and that negotiations will be resumed should he obtain the powers required. Treilhard and Bonnier are to fill the places of Maret and Letourneur.

The Directorate causes its resolutions and the documents having reference to this negotiation to be printed; it orders its plenipotentiaries to remain in Lille until the end of the month, in order to await the return of the English negotiator, in case he should come back invested with full powers.

From the 9th to the 10th Vendémiaire, Year VI.— The Armies of the Rhine and Sambre-et-Meuse henceforth take the name of Army of Germany. General Augereau, before proceeding to his new post, is busy preferring requests that the Directorate shall supply him the funds with which to meet the needs of his large army. The Minister of Finance is instructed to furnish the funds, and to pay for the boots and overcoats required at the beginning of the winter. Augereau is instructed to notify the enemy's generals that if hostilities are renewed in Italy, the Army of Germany will justify its name, and will give battle twenty-four hours after having warned the enemy.

From the 12th to the 16th Vendémiaire, Year VI. —Special messengers from Bonaparte reach us daily. The tone of his despatches is more and more passionate, and seems on the point of becoming insolent. At times he wants the Army of Germany to be prepared to commence hostilities simultaneously with himself; at others, that the Army of Germany should be the first to act on the offensive. He still desires peace, as he claims that the enemy is superior to him in numbers. In his letters he gives vent to his fears of men who, he claims, have led the *corps législatif* ever since the 18th Fructidor; in others he inveighs against the clubs; in one place he complains that he is being treated like

Pichegru; in another he lets us see that he believes us to be terrorists. He complains that Augereau has sent an officer, alleged to have been despatched by the Government, to spy on him. The Directorate cannot account for the inconsistency of his curious despatches; we had shown Bonaparte the fullest trust, and heretofore he had seemed to appreciate our treatment of him. This respectful sentiment of an obsequious gratitude no longer exists since the victory of the 18th Fructidor. He displays not only great acrimony, but an altogether erroneous opinion on all that has happened since the 18th Fructidor. The events of that day seem to have put him out of countenance, in that it would seem to have deprived him of his pleasant relations with the conquered party—relations he had carried on on this occasion through Lavalette, just in the same way as he had done on the 13th Vendémiaire with the party of the "sections," which a moment later he was mowing down with grape-shot. But as he now saw that the Directorate wished above all to preserve the existence of the Republic, and not to suffer its invasion by any usurpation whatsoever, Bonaparte, whose ambition constituted his whole opinion, could say to himself, with some show of reason, that it would be easier for him to attain his goal through the Royalists, from whom he would have derived greater benefit. "Colleagues," said Rewbell to us, "that's what soldiers are! Let us beware! At the time of the replacing of the two expelled Directors they would dearly have liked to enter the Directorate. Even Augereau, the best citizen among all these people, conceived the idea of sitting among us: we are going to meet men harder to manage than Augereau; let us not await their coming, but head them off. I move that we purely and simply accept the resignation so insolently tendered by Bonaparte." Larevellière likewise moves that Bernadotte's resignation be accepted. I consider this opinion far too hasty, and especially most impolitic at the present juncture. It is agreed upon to wait for the return of my secretary Botot, whom the Directorate has sent to Italy in order to come to an understanding with Bonaparte in regard to all matters which we wish to treat as mere misunderstandings.

While the first days of the establishment of the Republic were thus frittered away, one of the pioneers, if not of that Republic, at least of freedom, General Lafayette, had languished since 1792 in the dungeons of Austria, eager for the finest quarry that could be seized by a government implacably opposed to liberty. On the other hand, all who were interested in liberty could not but be interested in the fate of Lafayette. The Revolution itself, having settled into sobriety, now saw in Lafayette a truly illustrious citizen. Brought violently face to face with the Republic in 1792, Lafayette had perhaps shown some opposition to it, when not yet released from his sworn allegiance to the Monarchy; but once freed from his oath by a new social order, and the possibility of a great Republic having been demonstrated by its victories abroad and its organization at home, and on its becoming as established as it was legitimate in its principle, Lafayette could not do otherwise than return to his former American and even French sentiments; he could not refuse to adhere to and to countenance the new compact which united the hopes and the opinions of all friends of humanity and liberty.

Not having lost sight of this odious captivity, which revealed the fate in store for us, had not the kings of Europe been brought to their senses by the force of our arms, I had on several occasions sought information as to the fate of Lafayette, when Mme. de Staël, who was never lacking on the side of friendship, came to me and said: " Barras, dear Barras, citizen Director, I believe I know better than any one the loftiness of your soul, the generosity of your heart. You are the one I should have appealed to above all to solicit the good deed for which I am going to invoke your aid. I have done you a wrong, and I beg your pardon for it; I had applied to General Pichegru, who had just arrived, as to an all-powerful man, and one whom it was sought to make still more powerful than he even dreamed of himself. The matter at issue was a demand for the liberty of General Lafayette, still detained in the dungeons of Austria; and I had imagined that the controlling influence of Pichegru's former intercourse with that Power might give great weight to any steps he might take. General Pichegru did not understand me, or did not feel it was in his power to accede to my request, or perhaps was not willing to undertake the great step I begged him to take. Moreover, he is a man of cold temperament, for he said nothing to me to excuse himself for saying to me with a certain amount of frankness that ' he regretted that it did not lie in his power to do what would give me such pleasure.' He is indeed a cold-blooded man, this famous General Pichegru. Oh, I cannot bear these icy men; they recall to me the *mot* of Ninon, who styled them 'pumpkin hearts fricasseed in snow.' You, my dear Barras—you who are not of ice, you who have one of the souls of Provence, such as I love—I appeal to you as citizen, as Republican, as member of the Directorate. It is as such that you must hear me, and that I trust myself to you without reserve. Austria must be approached on the subject, and the Directorate can alone do it. Look how Fox and Sheridan have recently spoken of General Lafayette in the House of Commons; they have proclaimed him 'one of the best citizens of the universe,' and have declared that the conduct of Austria was an act of infamy. In short, by all that they have said with the eloquence which the love of liberty inspires, I venture to say to you, Barras, that they have issued a draft upon the Directorate, and especially on you, dear Barras, who cannot do otherwise than honor it. Barras, we must restore Lafayette to France and to the Republic. I pledge myself that he will be her best citizen—next to you, of course."

As a general matter, it afforded me too great a pleasure to listen to Mme. de Staël for me to interrupt the course of her eloquent harangues, whatever their subject and their diffuseness. On this occasion Mme. de Staël was speaking not only to a man already converted to the cause she advocated, but to a man long ago convinced that Lafayette's unfortunate situation was one of the greatest crimes of Austria, and a cause for genuine sorrow among the French patriots, whose melancholy strifes it recalled. For if Lafayette had left France after the 10th of August, 1792, and if his inevitable flight had caused him to fall into the hands of the foreigner, when he believed he was finding a refuge in a neutral land—Flanders—it was because it had become plain to him, after the 10th of August, that if he attempted to resist any longer the party which had just upset the throne, he was running the twofold risk of jeopardizing the safety of his army and of surrendering our frontiers to the *émigrés;* his misfortune testified to his virtue, since he gave himself up rather than surrender anything of his Fatherland.

I therefore considered it a matter of course to lay his case before the Directorate at once. I pointed out that as it lay in our power to take the lead in so honorable a course, we should not suffer any one to forestall us. The English had already nobly taken the initiative, and it behooved us to recover all the time we had lost. Rewbell and Larevellière, without suffering me fully to develop my opinion in the matter, protested that nothing could be more just; they expressed regret that the cartel for the exchange of the deputies arrested together with Dumouriez for the daughter of Louis XVI. should not have included Lafayette, whose imprisonment was no less a criminal act on the part of Austria than had been that of Beurnonville, Bancal, Quinette, and Drouet. "But," remarked Rewbell, "the negotiation might perhaps not have been feasible in those days. Many Republicans, and I foremost among them, perhaps still entertained political prejudices against Lafayette. I thought there was cause for me to reproach him with many things done by him in the cause of the Bourbons. There are fruits that cannot be touched till they are ripe. Now that this one is ripe, since many of our revolutionary prejudices have disappeared, and that there is only one standpoint from which to view the misfortune of Lafayette—*i.e.*, as an unjust and even criminal act on the part of our enemies—I agree with Barras that the Directorate should ask that he be set at liberty. But we have no ambassador at Vienna, and we may perhaps not have one for a long time to come." "We have the very man," I reply; "if he is not yet at Vienna, he was at any rate very close to it a while ago; he is still on the road to it, and there is no reason why he should not pursue his onward march at any moment. Let us instruct Bonaparte to stipulate, as a condition of the treaty resulting from the preliminaries, that we demand the liberty of Lafayette, outrageously arrested on neutral territory, and in manifest violation of the right of nations."

My proposition was adopted. I wrote to Bonaparte that the Directorate, which believed that he could always find time to trouble himself about matters of honor, considered that he was better able than any other to successfully press our request that Lafayette be set free. I must state in justice to Bonaparte — he who subsequently considered Lafayette to be too Republican—that he did not on this occasion hesitate to interfere in the interests of this great citizen. He zealously accepted the mission with which we had intrusted him; he even wrote to me that he was personally grateful to me for having thought of him, and for having shown him the preference.

The step taken by the Directorate did not have immediate results. Austria displayed all the resistance of inertia generally characteristic of its policy; at last the greedy Acheron yielded up its prey.

I have given full credit to Bonaparte for his

personal share in the negotiation resulting in the restoration of Lafayette to liberty. The trumpeters of his fame (and especially M. Regnaud de Saint-Jean d'Angély, paid even in those days for such services), who, while with the Army of Italy, were engaged in drawing up servile pages in honor of the hero, saw fit to give Bonaparte all the credit for Lafayette's restoration to freedom. Mme. de Lafayette, the virtuous spouse who had for many a long day shared the imprisonment of her husband, was not deceived by this. She was not ignorant of my personal efforts to bring about the result which was the hope of her family, and she called on me repeatedly to express her gratitude thereat. She also expressed it to me in writing; and even did I not possess this testimony to my conduct, I should have the good-fortune to possess a witness who still lives, one whose vigorous health bids fair to survive the weakening of mine, which is daily succumbing to illness and to years. This witness is no other than M. de Lafayette himself, of whom I shall have occasion to speak again in the course of these Memoirs, with the esteem I am proud of feeling towards him. The enemies of the Fatherland would feel great grief to see this sentiment shared by all the friends of liberty. Our misunderstandings have too long given them cause for rejoicing. Just about the same time Dumouriez was getting friends to obtain permission for him to return to France, but we could not place him on the same footing with Lafayette. The latter, since leaving France, had, in spite of many sufferings, steadfastly declined to co-operate in any intrigue of the foreigner. Dumouriez had never ceased intriguing. I do not draw from this the conclusion that the course he adopted was dictated by treason, as is generally understood, and as has been stated since. Men repulsed by their Fatherland do not all possess the virtue of Camillus, and many of them believe themselves entitled to the rights claimed by Coriolanus. I do not mean to say that Dumouriez was, in respect to his talents, not to be regretted by France. He had, as I have already recorded, participated in the wars of the Revolution, and in the revolution of war, when a well-founded fear of the guillotine caused him to adopt a desperate course; but there was neither in the governing principles, nor even in the course of his actions, the conviction shown in the part played by Lafayette. Besides, I did not believe that public reason was ripe enough to pass an equitable judgment on his case; so we adjourned.

I have not concealed, in the beginning of my Memoirs, the temporary relations into which the circumstances of my youth had led me in Paris with the woman Lamotte—an intercourse which was far from constituting a connection with the frightful enterprise of the woman, and especially of her husband, more guilty than herself. These circumstances, altogether incident to my youth, having furnished a theme for exaggeration and calumny, I did not consider that I should make any reply other than the simple narration of the fact at its proper date. The Lamotte woman's sister, who had also come across me formerly, imagined, on learning of my prominence, that she might attempt to put the Government to some use. It was sufficient that I should be at its head for her to desire to captivate me by means of her superannuated charms, just as formerly the Lamotte woman had succeeded in getting near the Cardinal de Rohan. The fame of the victory of the 18th Fructidor, which had placed me on a pedestal, had still further fired her imagination. Anybody who cared to form an idea of the education of these people, who sought, by aid of a fable, to trace back their pedigree to kings, would be able to gather it from the style and orthography of the subjoined note. I leave people to judge whether such a specimen is not below the style of a cook, and if the official or even the mere citizen who respects himself can be suspected of having had any connection with such degraded beings.

La citoyenne de Valois Saint-Remy a lonheur de souhaiter le bonjour au citoyen Derecteur barras elle prie de vouloir bien lui a corder un moment dodiance, et en même tems lui fasiliter les moiens de parvenire jusqua'à lui Le Citoyen Derecteur saura que la citoyenne de Valois et venue de la campagne toutes exprès pour le voire. Elle atandra donc avec confiance le moment quel leuis demènde le plutôt possible.

RUE DE LA FRATERNITÉ NO. 63.
PARIS, *ce* 25 *fructidore*.

(The *citoyenne* de Valois Saint-Remy has the honor to wish good-morning to the citizen Derector barras she begs him to be good enough to grant her a moment's audience, and at the same time to facilitate to her the means of coming into his presence The Citizen Derector must know that the *citoyenne* Valois has come from the country quite expressly to see him. She will therefore await with confidence the moment she asks of him the soonest possible.

RUE DE LA FRATERNITÉ NO. 63.
PARIS, *this* 25*th fructidor*.)

At the very time when the victory of the 18th Fructidor gave me the appearance of being dictator, I was besieged with petitions; those who think they can derive benefit from the supreme power do not seek to analyze it, provided it is of use to them. One Amédée de Turenne claimed my protection, nay, kinship with me, asserting that "he had the honor of belonging to me." I had good reasons to have my doubts as to this great honor. Moreover, it was a fact established historically that there never had been anything in common between the family of the illustrious Viscount Marshal de Turenne and the individual here referred to. His real family name was Giblotte, and he had most unceremoniously assumed the name of Turenne, from an estate of his in Languedoc. M. Giblotte de Turenne, who had never served in the army, wished to join a Republican military staff. He has since then gone into the service of Bonaparte as chamberlain or orderly officer. In this new position he has distinguished himself by his unremitting stupidity, and equally unremitting gossiping propensities, which have caused those who have had to submit to the prolonged torture of listening to him to give him the punning sobriquet, which is as well known as the man who is the subject of it, "Milord Kinesester" (*Milord qui ne sait se taire*). I have since learned that M. de Turenne's taste for serfdom has not deserted him under the various governments which have followed one another, and that he has not ceased distinguishing himself in the manner I have related.

Following upon the requests and petitions of M. de Turenne came another claim of kinship— one preferred by the too famous Marquis de Sade. It is true that he was more of a relation of mine than the other. It seemed convenient to him, under cover of a political revolution of sufficient magnitude to cover a multitude of extraordinary things, to call himself a victim of the despotism overthrown together with the Bastille. M. de Sade, my beloved cousin, being outside the pale of common law by virtue of his hideous actions and writings, I consider myself dispensed from the duty of justifying myself for having shown little consideration to his kinship, and for not having allowed the ties of blood to influence my heart.

15th Vendémiaire, Year VI. — General Debelle, Hoche's brother-in-law, who has just reached Paris, again tells us that the last moments of that excellent general were those of a virtuous citizen entirely devoted to his Fatherland. The dying Hoche instructed Debelle to tell me that Bonaparte should be closely watched; that he had much money and much influence; that, without possessing any material proofs of it, he knew that he was aiming at independence, and perhaps at tyranny; he had seen enough and had sufficient data to warn me on this score. A half-finished letter, written by Hoche a few minutes before his death, is sufficient to justify my suspicions of that Bonaparte, whom I considered my friend, if only he had been that of our Fatherland.

Hoche, whose violent temper has been seen to break out on great occasions, and whose lively emotions perhaps shortened his life—Hoche possessed a kindliness and generosity equal to his hastiness; his character is perhaps of all those I have met most in sympathy with mine. With me, he had believed that the 18th Fructidor was a desperate action unavoidable if the Republic was to be saved; but he would have liked to forgive the defeated foes soon afterwards, and to cover with the mantle of indulgence those who, having been opposed to us before the 18th Fructidor, had erred, according to us, without malice and without treason. He had commissioned Debelle to speak to me on behalf of several generals who had been dismissed, and in particular Férino. I must explain the latter's position.

The forced misunderstanding existing among the members of the Directorate previous to the 18th Fructidor, and which brought about the crisis which could alone restore to the Government a common line of conduct, had brought about a veritable confusion among the Ministers and the generals-in-chief. The three members of the Directorate could not confide their secret to the Minister of War. The latter, pursuing therefore the tenor of his way according to what was evident to him, was bound to make most dangerous mistakes in the commands which had a decisive influence over the behavior of the armies. Thus the Minister Pétiet, to whom Rewbell, Larevellière, and myself had not intrusted our secret, had come into conflict with General Hoche, who possessed our secret fully. Hence the generals of division, who were not inclined, from any disposition of patriotism known to General Hoche, to join hands with him, found a pretext for disobeying him by arguing that they were obeying the Minister of War. Such was the case of General Férino, an officer held in some esteem in the army; he was compelled to furnish explanations in regard to his conduct. Férino had been dismissed; I caused him to be reinstated in consequence of the sincere explanations he gave of his conduct.

Why, when I should be so happy to heal the unavoidable but not incurable wounds resulting from our civil discords, must I see them reopened by people either of an incapable turn of mind, or ill advised by their bad temper and by hatred, the result of their bilious temperament? Sieyès, ever discontented with everything, and unwilling, according to his wont, either to do or to let anything be done —the patriot Sieyès, who has appropriately been styled the most aristocratic man in France, once more begins to argue that all the ills which threatened France before the 18th Fructidor, and which still threaten her, proceed from the influence of the nobles in society, and that such influence is inseparable from their persons; that in consequence of this, it becomes necessary to rid ourselves of the nobles by means of a measure that shall forever deliver our country from them.

There is doubtless something profound—*i.e.*, something very true—in this reflection; but is it to be entertained, considering the present state of society, if one does not wish or one cannot begin to reconstitute society in its very foundations? Who is there who would wish, after 1793, to make that experiment over again? The pupil or the rival of Sieyès, in wickedness and in his hatred of the nobles until he shall himself be ennobled, M. Boulay de la Meurthe, has lent an attentive ear to these diatribes. He has undertaken to put new life into them, and to present them to the Council of Five Hundred with all the freshness of a newly conceived idea. So Boulay de la Meurthe makes a motion for the ostracism of the nobles in the Council of Five Hundred. He is appointed a member of the committee charged with reporting on his motion, and is elected its chairman.

His motion has for its object the expulsion for life from the territory of the Republic of all those who have belonged to the civil or military household of the King, the Queen, the King's brothers, or of the other members of the royal family and princes of the blood; even the divorced wives of *émigrés*, if they have not married again; the *maîtres des requêtes*, governors, *lieutenants du Roi*, ambassadors, ministers, presidents, *procureurs-généraux*, members of the Parliament, etc. Only a few exceptions are made in favor of those who have served the Revolution.

In spite of the bad effect produced by this proposed measure, aimed at a numerous class of society, and which has produced great uproar, the committee of the *corps législatif* nowise seems to abandon the idea of transporting the nobles. Sieyès is the primary author of the proposition; he is, moreover, the unconfessed draftsman of the motion. In order to reconcile to the idea the victorious Republicans of the 13th Vendémiaire and of the 18th Fructidor, the concession is made of including in the transportation the conspirators of those two days, which is my own work.

Damecourt, an *émigré*, arrested and brought before the *bureau central*, escaped. He had plenty of money, and had paid three hundred louis for his residence, secured under a false name. The money was paid to a well-known personage, whom for that reason I abstain from naming.

General Sahuguet is dismissed; he had been employed and protected by Bonaparte; his dismissal will no doubt furnish a fresh cause for irritation to the commander-in-chief of the Army of Italy.

The treaty of alliance with Sardinia, of which

Bonaparte is urgently demanding the ratification, is sent to the *corps législatif*.

England would be inclined to conclude peace, on condition of the opening of Dutch ports in India, and also of Ostend.

17th, 18th, and 19th Vendémiaire, Year VI.—Bonaparte makes an appeal on behalf of Clarke; this is another of his *protégés*, just as are all those who offer him guarantees of servility; he does not know or wishes to forget that Clarke, in his secret correspondence, allowed himself continually to call "brigands" all the officers of the Army of Italy most worthy of commendation. Bonaparte's spleen increases daily; he once more expresses the desire that his resignation be accepted. Believing that he can be of still further use to us, and that he alone has the key of the negotiations with which he is intrusted, he abuses this position to request that these functions also be turned over to another. He informs us by despatch that the Pope is very ill; that Naples and Tuscany have formed a coalition. It has been bruited abroad that, in the event of the death of the Pope, the King of Naples will enter Rome. Bonaparte says he feels aggrieved because the Directorate had just written to him to let the King of Naples pass to Rome. The Directorate replies that Carnot, the author and director of this order, had given it unknown to his colleagues and against their will; that if he attributed such counsels to them, he did so on his own authority; that the Directorate has ever been of opinion that neither the death of the Pope nor the arrival of the King of Naples should be waited for before organizing the Roman States. At the point things have reached, the commander-in-chief of the Army of Italy is entitled, on behalf of France, to direct the movement by all means in his power. Treilhard is to be sent as ambassador to Naples. The incapable Canclaux is recalled; two French publicists are to be sent to Milan, in conformity with the wish expressed by Bonaparte.

The plenipotentiaries of the Emperor are daily making the most extravagant propositions. This time it is Bonaparte who thinks so, and he tells us so; he is authorized to take a few Swiss battalions into the service of the Cisalpine Republic.

The King of Prussia is dying; none of his Ministers dare urge him to adopt the plan of alliance with the Republic. It is the privilege of kings never to hear a single truth, not that which would be most advantageous to them, even when at the point of death.

The Swedish Cabinet makes advances for a *rapprochement* with France.

England complains of the lack of consideration shown in giving Malmesbury twenty-four hours' notice to leave the country. She protests that she desires peace, but is no longer inclined to despatch to Lille an envoy invested with the powers required.

The five millions paid by Portugal are turned over to the contractor Gobert, in violation of the proposed enactment submitted by the Minister of Finance, who desires that five more millions shall be paid to the contractor Séguy, who lent the Directorate 100,000 francs on the 18th Fructidor. The Minister encounters the same difficulties. I propose to apply a large portion of these sums to the purchase of horses, as well as to the levy of

6000 infantry, who are to be despatched at once to the Army of Italy. The Minister of War is to be consulted in regard to the latter matter.

From the 20th to the 28th Vendémiaire, Year VI.—The Directorate, desirous of cultivating harmonious relations with the Councils, has come to an arrangement with several influential members with the object of establishing a little friendly and informal reunion, to take place every four days at a breakfast to be given at the residence of the President of the Directorate, and at which are to be present all the members of the Directorate and the representatives Lamarque, Jean de Bry, Girod, Pouzoles, Sieyès, Jourdan, Marbot, Poullain-Grandprey, and others. At the first sitting of the reunion the proposed law against the nobles came up for discussion. Sieyès read a few of its clauses. The matter excited ridicule; it was then that Sieyès saw what we were made of. Struck with our silence, he puts into his pocket the paper of which he is the author and editor; he is not master enough of himself to conceal his vexation and his desire to see the transportation of all enemies of the people still further extended. There are no limits to the sacrifice he wishes to make of all the population who are guilty in his eyes.

Botot returns from Italy; he reassures the Directorate; he tells us that Bonaparte has expressed regret to him for all his hasty outbursts, and pretended that they were the remnants of the indignation so long felt by him against the men conquered on the 18th Fructidor; he has returned to better sentiments. Bonaparte has confessed that he had for a while been piqued at the Directorate, and especially against the Minister of War, for whom he has no regard. He has censured the plans of campaign sent to him before and after the 18th Fructidor. He alleges that the first one which had been sent to him by Carnot was but a mere copy of that of the Emperor of Austria; he believes that the Army of Germany was to be got together at an earlier date, that it should have received orders to act principally on the right, skirt the frontiers of Switzerland, march on the Danube, and reach Ratisbon; that from that town to Vienna there is about the same distance as from Udine. Naples is arming in every direction, says Bonaparte; he has notified its government that if on the death of the Pope a single Neapolitan soldier enters Rome, he will burn Naples; as to Turin, he will detach 10,000 men from its army, and convert them into a corps of French troops on his return to that State.

The Directorate devotes its attention to the plan of campaign proposed by Bonaparte—that of acting only on the right of the Army of Germany. If the Austrians refuse peace, Bonaparte is to draw them on towards the Piave, give battle to them, and then march on Vienna. The dispositions in regard to the Army of Germany are adopted.

The announcement of the resolution proposed against the nobles gives rise to agitation; the committee abandons ostracism, and contents itself with merely proposing the exclusion of the dangerous caste from public functions.

General Moreau protests his devotion and attachment to me; did he but possess a little more activity of character he might be suspected of having a hand in many intrigues that are taking place. It is sought to make me solely responsible for everything that happened on the 18th Fructidor; I considered that day as indispensable to the salvation of the Republic; as to the consequences of a great political act, I am aware that they are usually attributed to its authors. I have not the right to complain even of injustice. The founders of a republic implanted in the midst of monarchical Europe have ventured on a great undertaking. We have burned our ships, and can no longer look behind us. . . . Be this as it may, some wish to put me forward in order to compromise me; others flatter me by saying that I should seize upon the sovereign power, and tender me all the means to that end; nothing would be more simple, I must admit, were I treacherous enough to entertain such an ambition, but I did not engineer the 18th Fructidor to make myself dictator, but to remain a French citizen. This simple and noble title is sufficient to me now, and will suffice me on the day when I shall be able to retire from public affairs without risking the connection in which so many others have united with me in the course of the Revolution. Meanwhile, I am entitled to laugh at all the notice that is taken of my ambition as at the unjust comments which seek to worry me in my present position. The Directorate has hardly been renewed a month, and it is already attempted to sow discord among the Five. I am informed that the new Director, Merlin, is plotting my ruin while assuring me of his affectionate regard for me. According to certain informants, Rewbell and Larevellière bear me no good-will. "Why so?" I ask. "Are they not patriots and men of honor? Have we not been in a position to know one another thoroughly, and mutually to judge one another in these difficult days?"

Bonaparte is perhaps no stranger to these insinuations, the object of which is once more to divide the Directorate. I incline to this belief from the nature of the compliments he causes to be made to me in various quarters, as to the esteem and friendship he feels for me, and especially from the manner in which he seeks to remove my colleagues from his demonstrations, which he seems to reserve for me alone. It is not the first time that I have been able to catch a glimpse of, and it is unfortunately not the last that I shall be able to recognize, that ever double-faced character to which Joseph Bonaparte called attention, when he said of Napoleon, whose elder brother he was: " My brother is no doubt a great soldier; but what he is a great deal besides a general is a great contriver, a plotter—what the Italians call in their tongue a *macchinatore*."

Thus, while Bonaparte is paying me compliments, and is causing his several agents treacherously to coquet with me, I learn from various quarters that he is talking about me in an entirely different way. He speaks with little moderation about the new Directors, and frequently comments on Rewbell, saying that he is too fond of diplomacy. In order to prove to me his special confidence, Bonaparte lets me know that he would like me to send him daily a kind of official report of the negotiations which may be conducted in Paris. I reply to him, not without a tinge of irony, that I fully appreciate this mark of confidence, since he is kind enough to wish to look at everything through my eyes, but that my time and my respect for my functions do not allow of my undertaking such work.

Bonaparte informs us that he can purchase Malta for 600,000 francs. He is to be informed that the Directorate agrees to this.

CHAPTER III

Chénier and the verses of Camille Jordan—M. de la Chabeaussière—Poems appropriate to the circumstances—Contract entered into in regard to the salt-works—Competition in contracts—The general opinion as to the law affecting the nobles—Plans of Sieyès in regard to Italy—Conditional ratification of the treaty by Portugal—Firm attitude of the Directorate—Bonaparte commander-in-chief of the Army of England—Fouché's distress—Pen portrait of his wife and son — Fouché as a dealer in pigs—His lawsuit with Gérard — I bring about a reconciliation—Fouché as a contractor— He asks payment for his services—Danton's *mot* on the new order of things—Fouché alters its text to his advantage—Fouché's financial intrigues—M. Hainguerlot—The *Compagnie Dijon*—Report made by Gibert Desmolières as to the extortions of this company—Hainguerlot accused—His negotiations with Fouché — Fouché's first *écu*—His letter pleading for Hainguerlot—Talleyrand's enormous fortune—Treaty with the Emperor—Debate in the *corps législatif*—New parties formed in its bosom—Bonaparte President of the French Legation at Rastadt—Preparations for the Congress of Rastadt — Ridiculous posturing of the Minister Letourneur—Lambrecht's probity — Schérer falls into disrepute — The philanthropist Duquesnoy — What is a philanthropist ?— M. de Lameth's position— A compromise in regard to the ostracism of Sieyès—Is the Constitution of the Year III. to be changed ?—My cousin Lauragais—I am offered the supreme power.

IF the Royalists were daily gaining ground, they did not meet with as much approval as they expected from the masses. They were the object of much contempt and irony from all enlightened and literary people. Chénier was not the only one who, according to his opinions, ridiculed the halting verses of Camille Jordan; M. de la Chabeaussière and others of the same side addressed poems to me, together with information against the enemies of the Republican social order, whom it was justifiable to call Royalists, since they were attacking the Republic.

On the 18th Fructidor, as well as at all decisive periods of the Revolution, I was enabled to see that wherever power is, and wherever it triumphs over its enemies, it never fails to receive the applause of all. After the siege of Toulon, after the 9th Thermidor, after the 13th Vendémiaire, I had received, either in verse or prose, all the homage of adulation. I received a still greater quantity after the 18th Fructidor. Although I did not bind myself to discretion with those whose compliments I had not solicited, I owe it to my character, which greatly inclines to make allowance for poor humanity on many occasions, not to reveal the names of my adulators. I will content myself with giving a specimen of their poetical capabilities.

To the Executive Directorate

Enfin le grand coup est porté
Et votre pur patriotisme
Vient d'affermir la liberté
Sur les ruines du royalisme.

Nos vertueux législateurs
Purgés de leurs perturbateurs,
Désormais d'une marche sûre
Vont faire triompher les mœurs,

Abattre cette race impure
De brigands et d'agioteurs,
Et cueillant la palme civique,
Faire fleurir la République
Et confondre ses détracteurs.

O merveille ! votre prudence
Réparant les maux de la France
On n'a point vu le sang couler :
Le crime, réduit au silence
Sous le poids de votre puissance,

Pâlit et se voit accabler.
En tous lieux la publique joie
Renaît, éclate et se déploie
Par ce cri saint et répété :
Vive à jamais la liberté !

At the same time that M. de la Chabeaussière was thus addressing the Directorate collectively, he had also some little amount of flattery in reserve for me alone; I cannot say that his talent was of a high order, for the answer might be that his subject did not afford him the opportunity of displaying any; but, as M. de la Chabeaussière passed as belonging rather to the party opposed to us, if indeed it can be said that the opinion of a poet amounts to anything, I perhaps paid a little more attention to his compliments than to those of others, all the more so as they at least express some of those sentiments of peace and union which triumph properly conceived could certainly bring back.

Air—*Avec les jeux dans le village.*

Ni royauté ni dictature ;
De bonnes lois ; point de partis ;
La République auguste et pure :
Notre bonheur est à ce prix !
Français, vous n'êtes qu'à l'aurore
Des beaux jours qui vont luire sur vous :
La force les a fait éclore,
L'union doit les rendre doux. (*Bis.*)

Le plus beau ciel a ses nuages,
Le plus beau peuple eut ses erreurs :
Comme on voit passer les orages,
De même cessent les horreurs.
La vertu reprend son empire ;
Il est temps d'oublier nos maux :
Car les venger . . . Ah ! rien n'est pire !
C'est encore creuser des tombeaux. (*Bis.*)

Quand pour chefs nous avons des pères,
L'autorité ne pèse pas :
Les lois nous deviennent plus chères,
Et nos devoirs ont des appas.
Un gouvernement sage et juste.
Doit être notre point d'appui :
Pour comprimer tout acte injuste
Rallions-nous auprès de lui. (*Bis.*)

ENVOI

O toi, dont l'active prudence
Désespère les factieux :
Barras, quel plaisir pour la France ;
Le sort te conserve à nos vœux !
Tu charmes par ton air affable,
Sans perdre de ta dignité.
Quand on rend le pouvoir aimable,
On marche à l'immortalité !

6th Brumaire, Year VI.—Ramel brings up the matter of the salt-works. Rewbell speaks in favor of a company whose offers are advantageous; I demand that the matter be put to competition, and declare that I henceforth intend to reject, once for all, any contract not based on competition. The whole of the Directorate and the Minister of Finance side with me. The terms of the contract are left in the hands of the Minister, in order that he shall communicate them to the various companies desirous of bidding.

The public is persuaded that the law in regard to the nobles has been conceived principally against Bonaparte and myself. Sieyès, who has cherished the dream of giving to France a constitution of his own make, does not forgive the Constitution of the Year III. for having been preferred to his own; still less does he forgive the magistrates who have dared to become the depositaries of that constitution, and who seek to enforce it. It is generally believed that his bile and habitual misanthropy are impelling him in his furious onslaught on the aristocratic class, and that he expected the measure proposed against them would result in disturbances which would allow him to bring forward his constitution as the means of salvation. Having met with a check in France, Sieyès would like to fall back or avenge himself on Italy. There is some talk of sending him thither, or, rather, he talks of being sent. The modern Solon would there promulgate laws unappreciated and rejected by the modern Athens.

Portugal has ratified only conditionally the treaty of peace; its ambassador has accordingly not ventured to present the alleged ratification to the Directorate. It is decided to begin hostilities against that country at once, if its ratification is not definite and unconditional.

Now that the operations of the Army of Italy have been consummated, it becomes necessary to give its leader an active mission commensurate with his ambition. Bonaparte, at my suggestion, is appointed commander-in-chief of the Army of England. The Ministers of War and Marine are instructed to gather along the coast the troops which are to constitute this army. I have alluded to Fouché's police reports, and given specimens of them in connection with the movements which brought about the 18th Fructidor. On this occasion, as on so many others, except when he was at work in Nevers and Lyons, Fouché had been nothing but the fly on the wheel. In the Year III. he was still in great distress, living in a garret with his wife, the ex-nun — a woman as ill-natured as himself, and who was ironically called "the virtuous woman," owing to her frightful ugliness. With reddish hair like her husband, even to her eyebrows and eyelashes, she had a child, the worthy offspring of this hideous couple, no less red-headed than the authors of its being, an actual albino, but, as a matter of course, none the less dear to its parents. It was quite natural that they should be desirous of providing pap for their young wild-boar, and they did not possess the means therefor, in spite of what has been related of Mme. Fouché, who, according to what the reader has previously seen, was reputed not to have come back from Lyons poor, as it was allowable to believe after the crisis which had happened as she emerged from the suburbs, where her carriage had come to grief in so untoward a fashion. Fouché, in order to procure the strict necessaries of his existence, and of his she-wolf and his cub, had conceived the idea of becoming a dealer in pigs. He believed that by means of a certain process of feeding he could fatten these animals very quickly, and that after having stuffed them into a bloated state for the space of a week, he could sell them for twice the money he had paid for them. But Fouché did not possess the first penny wherewith to purchase even a small number of pigs. The funds were supplied to him by one of our former colleagues, Gérard by name. The pigs bought for these two partners had hardly been fattened, and were just on the point of being sold in order to give the first returns, when partners Gérard and Fouché quarrelled over the sharing of the profits. Gérard had supplied the funds for the acquisition of the stock. As such he was entitled to the larger share of the profits. To this Fouché demurred, alleging that the affair had originated in his brain; now, according to him, the primary claim was that of the man of genius, the other was but secondary and subordinate. An altercation having ensued between the two partners, they referred the matter to me as to a justice of the peace, remarking that they had full confidence in my honesty. They were on the point of conferring on me the office of *langueyeur de porcs* (examiner of hogs' tongues), for such an office existed formerly, and I will not say it was the meanest at Court, as it conferred the title of King's Counsellor.

I was fortunate enough to settle the dispute between the two litigants, and ward off the scandal which a lawsuit would have cast over two former members of the National Convention.

But the settlement of so trifling an affair did not bring fortune to a man who had none. Fouché, still suffering from extreme poverty, and resorting to all shifts, conceived the idea that since the installation of the Directorate, and in particular in connection with the 18th Fructidor, he had rendered valuable services because he had done police work, and put forth a claim for a salary. This salary might have been set at a very low figure, even if one chose to overlook all the doings of his life. As early as the day after the 18th Fructidor, Fouché, without waiting for the result of his claim, placed himself, together with individuals as little respectable as himself, at the head of those who were to supply provisions to the Army of England; now, as the 18th Fructidor was the victory of the patriots, the patriots, they argued, were those who should reap its fruits. Their arguments on this score were almost akin to those which Robespierre and Saint-Just had inveighed against and punished previous to the 9th Thermidor, as being the relaxed morality of the Molinists of the Republic, for which they wished to substitute the rigors of political Jansenism. But Robespierre and Saint-Just had succumbed in their too daring attempt; no longer were there any of these inexorable reformers to worry the life of patriots seeking to make a fortune. The time had therefore come for the Republicans to seize upon the good things of this world, too long possessed by the aristocrats. This was the motto of Marat: "*Ut redeat miseris abeat fortuna superbis.*" Had the patriots known enough to take this stand sooner they would have been stronger, and would not have had to suffer such humiliations since the reactions of the Thermidorians. All men are equal; their rights proceed from their needs, and has not nature imposed the same needs on all? But there is on earth but one portion of wealth; as it cannot be divided equally, it must forever fall into the hands of the cleverest, at least in turns. Now had not the turn of the patriots come? Were they to persist in the stupid policy of leaving all good things in the hands of the aristocrats? Danton had said it, and the word of this great patriot should be listened to: "It is henceforth the patriots' turn to feast on ortolans." Thus spoke Fouché and his friends.

These gentlemen were entirely mistaken, and were altering the very text of the modern tribune. Danton had not said, as they attributed to him, that the Revolution's object was "that some folks should in their turn enjoy the privilege of eating ortolans;" what he had said was: "The Revolution has been made in order that the people as a mass should be better fed and better clad." And in using the word *peuple* Danton did not mean a few individuals styling themselves patriots *par excellence:* he meant the mass of citizens, the universality of men cast upon this world to live a brief existence on it; he meant all. One day as David was sketching out the programme of a patriotic *fête*, Danton had indeed said to him in his familiar language, in order to make himself better understood: "The *fête* must be an *eating* one;" but what he had also said in a more positive and serious fashion was: "Henceforth all must be clad and have food." These are his very words. The men of whom I speak, and at whose head was Fouché, were therefore altering the text and the principle; in their case it was not a temporary application of which they wished only to make a beginning: they desired an application altogether exclusive, and did not think of any possible sharing with others, even in the future. Nevertheless, to use their own words, the movement had begun in favor of the patriots. The Minister Schérer, who had kept his portfolio after the 18th Fructidor in spite of public opposition, was seeking to defend himself, and thought the best he could do to retain his position was to fling a few sops into the maws of the Cerberus. Fouché and Company, coming forward as able "victuallers," had taken time by the forelock, and, unscrupulously making use of my name, although they had no sort of permission to do so, called on the Minister Schérer, and asked him, in the name of the patriots of France and under cover of my indorsement, to be allowed to act as purveyors to the Army of England. Schérer granted their request, in order to secure the popularity they promised him in exchange for his favors.

No sooner had Fouché obtained his wish than he found that his share was too small; so, sowing discord among his partners, he succeeded, by means of underhand intrigues, in getting several of them eliminated, and remaining sufficiently master of the business to sell it at a great profit. Yet this did not satisfy him. Increase of appetite grows by what it feeds on, and the dealer in pigs wished to go into trade on a wholesale scale. He formed connections with all the moneyed men who had a reputation for cleverness. None shone to a higher degree in this respect than Hainguerlot *l'aîné*. It is from Fouché himself that I have received the following particulars; he withheld from me the threats he had employed, considering them his secret.

Hainguerlot was one of those men of business who, having nothing to lose in a revolution, had not been slow in perceiving the chances opened for bold speculation by this species of social commotion. He was in the first rank of those who had made a dash for the *assignats*, and food and other supplies, in the confusion consequent upon the 9th Thermidor. Men of this kind, closely akin to wolves, had, since the 13th Vendémiaire, fastened upon the public fortune as upon their prey. From the committees of the Convention they had found their way into the closets of the new Ministers of the Directorate and into the very Luxembourg. The depreciation of the *assignats*, their conversion into *mandats*, had furnished the occasion for an incredible combination. It consisted not only in knowing the ideas of the Government in regard to the *mandats*, but in inspiring it with the policy which was to result in the destruction of this currency, and cause the Government to forsake it, through a combination by which the authors were the masters, because they controlled the salvation of the State. Having succeeded in submitting and in procuring to be accepted a treaty based on every species of trickery, Hainguerlot had, under the name of the *Compagnie Dijon*, acquired an immense fortune out of it. The mysterious part of this affair had been guessed and ferreted out previous to the 18th Fructidor by the deputy Gibert Desmolières, who had made several remarkable reports about the matter. But as this deputy belonged to the counter-revolutionist party, the greatest truths he might utter were looked upon with suspicion, owing to his political opinion. While the question of the *Compagnie Dijon* was being probed to the bottom, the 18th Fructidor transported Gibert Desmolières and his associates.

The affair of the *Compagnie Dijon*, after having remained in suspense for a while, was referred to the courts. This was truly giving it a kind of publicity, but not that of a deliberative assembly heard of throughout France, in which many things can be revealed that are stifled even in the public precincts of a tribunal. Hainguerlot's case was sent to the tribunal of Melun; this was already a great victory for him. The sophisms indulged in by men whose system is that all probity in this world consists in escaping the gallows are known to everybody. Some there are who argue that one may take certain small things without precisely committing theft, and in the first category of these things are those belonging to our relations and friends; others are more ambitious and say that, when it comes to stealing with any satisfactory result, governments are fair game, because the nation is, generally speaking, richer, and next, because governments, boasting as they do of but little good faith, and being the stronger, it is quite an innocent, nay, an honorable, thing to overreach them. If it is impossible to storm the positions, then it is better to turn them, say the reasoners whereof I speak; especially is it advisable to be in communication with those within the fort: hence it behooves one to bribe and secure the co-operation of head and minor officials in the administrations, men who are much more influential than the Ministers themselves, since Ministers see through their eyes only; it also behooves one to make sure, in the tribunals, of judges who can be approached and won over by every kind of pecuniary bribes or the allurements of pleasures; nor should one neglect the clerks of the courts and the messengers, in themselves most important personages in many decisive moments.

Imbued with this moral, which he has put into practice with great success before and since the days of the *Compagnie Dijon*, and down to those of the Kingdom of Westphalia and the Ourcq Canal, Hainguerlot, sent before the tribunal of Melun, no longer had to face opponents as formidable as the members of the Council of Five Hundred were before the 18th Fructidor; still, however inferior to them the judges might be, it was absolutely necessary that they should be "got at" by means with which Hainguerlot was well acquainted. For some time he had been looking in the ranks of society for some individual who could begin opening the breach, and who was acquainted with some one of the judges of the Melun tribunal; on the other hand, Fouché, seeking fortune at all costs, was resorting to every means and individual likely to assist him in his quest. At this juncture M. Hainguerlot introduces himself to Fouché, or, rather, Fouché gets himself introduced to him—for there was at that time between these two men all the distance existing between fortune and extreme poverty, the latter condition being Fouché's. All gaps are quickly bridged over when men stand in need of one another.

Among the members of the tribunal of Melun was one who was an ex-Oratorian, like Fouché—one of the ex-priests of that period best exercised in cunning, as a consequence of the apprenticeship served in that respect in religious congregations.

This individual had formerly been involved in intrigues with Fouché. Separated merely by circumstances, they had remained united in heart, and had agreed that the one who should first reach the coveted goal would assist the other with all his might and main. Hainguerlot having confided to Fouché that he wished to have the tribunal of Melun in his hand, and that, were he able to control it, he would make the greatest sacrifices, or, rather, that he would not consider he was making any when contributing to enrich a worthy patriot, Fouché exclaimed: "I am your man, and I have your man!"

One hundred thousand *écus* were, it is said, the price of a negotiation soon crowned with success. Fouché, in spite of his Lyons and *Compagnie d'Angleterre* antecedents, has himself said that this money was the foundation of his fortune. "The first *écu*," a great publicist has said, "is sometimes harder to earn than the last million." At all events, this was the first money conspicuously paraded by Fouché; it was with it that he purchased in the department of Seine-et-Marne the property to which he has since made so many additions; for his openly avowed ambition, even in those days, was to become the largest land-owner and the most important landed *seigneur* of France. This ambition has gone on increasing under all the *régimes* which he has since passed through and mystified; especially when, in the course of events, brought face to face with the colossal fortune of Talleyrand, which he saw with envy and rage superior to his own, he would frequently exclaim: "Do you see that scoundrel Talleyrand with his sixty millions?" It was during the Empire, and even in its earlier days, that Talleyrand was presumed to have amassed this sum. Calculations made after his negotiations with the Restoration and the allies have tripled this figure.

It has been seen in the memoranda with which Fouché supplied me as my police agent previous to the 18th Fructidor that he was already intensely occupied with ideas of money; for a M. Walkiers, whom he was constantly and urgently recommending to me, amid all the gossip he treated me to, was nothing but a Brussels banker, who, already possessed of a large fortune acquired in business, had still further increased it in dealings arising from the reunion of Belgium with France. There were, in those days, certain smuggling transactions on the new frontier, and Fouché had a share in them. Walkiers had also sums of money to collect from the French Government for army supplies. Fouché was forever speaking to me of these moneyed men, whom he recommended to me as excellent patriots, as if they were intimate friends of his. Although he so styled M. Hainguerlot, it does not seem that he was very well acquainted with this patriot his friend, for he could neither pronounce nor spell his name, as will be seen from the subjoined letter, which I beg my editor will give, together with others of that kind, just as it stands:

PARIS, 8 Brumaire, l'an VI.

Je t'ai parlé, mon ami, de l'affaire d'Hingrelot le ministre des finances doit faire son rapport aujourd'hui au Directoire sur cet objet. Il me semble juste que le citoyen Hingrelot obtienne le sursis provisoire qu'il demande ; c'est le seul moyen qui lui reste pour mettre ordre à ses affaires et pour payer sur le champ ce qu'il reconnait devoir au gouvernement. Tu m'obligeras mon ami de seconder le ministre des finances dans le désir qu'il a de faire rendre cette prompte justice.

Salut, estime et amitié.   FOUCHÉ.

(PARIS, 8th Brumaire, Year VI.

I have spoken to you, my friend, of the Hingrelot affair the minister of finance is to present his report on it to the Directorate to-day. It seems only fair to me that the citizen Hingrelot should obtain the temporary extension of time he begs for; it is the sole means remaining to him in order to set his affairs straight, and to pay immediately what he admits he owes to the government. You will oblige me, my friend, by seconding the minister of finance in his desire to do prompt justice in this matter.

Greeting, esteem, and friendship. FOUCHÉ.)

From the 10*th to the* 16*th Brumaire, Year VI.*—The *corps législatif* discusses and approves the treaty with the Emperor, laid before it by the Directorate. We might and doubtless should have insisted on the suppression of certain articles indecorous towards a republican government. They are so considered by Sieyès, Boulay de la Meurthe, Gay Vernon, and Garnier. We are continually being told of the anything but kindly utterances of these several deputies about us: Sieyès and Boulay, displeased at the failure of their law of ostracism, and attributing its rejection to me, attack me more particularly. To some they say that I am hindering the march of the revolution of the 18th Fructidor; to others, that I am a leader of anarchists. They are reported as saying also that Bonaparte and I have acquired too great an ascendency through the 18th Fructidor; that we should be undermined—nay, exterminated.

New parties are forming in the *corps législatif;* some are in favor of promptly filling up the vacancies in its membership: with that aim in view they would like to exclude fifteen more of their colleagues, in order to be reduced to less than a third; others wish to wait for the constitutional epoch which falls next Germinal. The first-named party is drifting away from the Government; those in harmony with the conspirators of Fructidor content themselves with watching the course of events.

Bonaparte is appointed President of the French

Legation at the Imperial congress to be held at Rastadt. Treilhard and Bonnier are sent as Ministers plenipotentiary. The representatives of the French Government are instructed to secularize as many states as possible; they will insist that the congress shall be composed of delegates of the Republic, of the Emperor, and of the King of Prussia only. The Empire shall be free to confer upon the Emperor the power of being represented by deputation; it is also agreed that the King of Prussia's possessions beyond the Rhine shall be restored to him if he makes an imperative claim for them. Nevertheless, the danger incident to his occupation of these possessions shall be pointed out to him.

The Minister of the Interior, Letourneur, is one of the most ridiculous and unfit individuals who have ever been seen in the Ministry. His provincial pretensions are equalled only by his incapacity, while his self-satisfaction passes imagination. He is a Desmazures in small-clothes and doublet. I have already stated that we are indebted for this treasure to Merlin, our new colleague, who believed he could find nothing that was too mediocre to be sufficiently servile. It is to the same Merlin that we owe Lagarde, the permanent secretary of the Directorate. The new Minister of Justice, Lambrecht, is an honest man in the fullest sense of the word.

Schérer is familiar with the administrative portion of war, but his intimacy with the party defeated on the 18th Fructidor, and the discredit cast upon him in so marked a fashion by the dying General Hoche, have brought him into disrepute, and burden the Directorate which retains him with one more responsibility added to so many others.

There is no better way of furthering one's plans than to pose as a philanthropist; it is a trade which has helped on a good many people in our day. M. Duquesnoy belongs to that astute corporation of men who pretend they are exclusively busied with the public interest—*i.e.*, who conceal their private interests under this disguise. Moreover, he enjoys the protection of François de Neufchâteau, who presents him to us, and induces the Directorate to grant him the administration of the salt-works.

The result of revolutionary times is to dictate laws which are no less revolutionary than the times themselves. The laws following upon the 18th Fructidor were doubtless very comprehensive; all the declared enemies of France were still in her bosom, and they had been on the verge of being her masters. The revolution of the 18th Fructidor did not seek to kill them, but to get them out of the way; still, many individuals whom a special trial would have saved from the effects of this measure are included in it. MM. de Lameth, for instance, during the whole of their career since the Revolution, had never had anything in common with the *émigration*, in whose eyes they were an object of horror, and were not mistaken in believing that I was able to appreciate their position, which was laid before me in most noble and truthful fashion by these gentlemen, particularly by M. Théodore de Lameth. Although I was unable to have full justice done them as promptly as they deserved, still I was in a position to soften the asperity of their fate.

The ostracism law of Sieyès having been rejected, the middle course of a decree assimilating the *ci-*

devant nobles with foreigners in the matter of exercising political rights is adopted.

When a constitution had been as unfortunately violated as was ours by the *coup d'état* of the 18th Fructidor, it was doubtless a question worthy of the most serious consideration whether it was safer to return to it purely and simply, or to begin by repairing the breaches, strengthening the weak parts, and filling up the gaps. The opportunity was undoubtedly furnished by the very circumstance of the temporary dictatorship resulting from the 18th Fructidor. It is because I was most sincerely desirous of upholding the Constitution of the Year III. that I should personally have desired that advantage should be taken of the very misfortune of our triumph to make good the deficiencies existing in the Constitution of the Year III. Suggestions were made to me from various quarters; they were rejected by my colleagues, who imagined that everything had been saved, because they had saved themselves and remained in their official positions. My cousin M. de Lauragais, a most original individual, but who has oftentimes had somewhat advanced philosophical and liberal ideas, brought me his tribute. I class his ideas among those which do not deserve to be relegated to oblivion, if only because of the generous intentions of him who has conceived them. Others there were who submitted to us ideas less liberal than those of my cousin Lauragais.

While bringing about the 18th Fructidor, because I judged it indispensable to the public welfare, I have already admitted that I could not deny its having been an actual *coup d'état*. The Constitution of the Year III. not having invested the Directorate with the power of defending itself by dissolving the Chambers, it had not been able to act except by violent means. Had it possessed the power vested in the King by the Charter, the 18th Fructidor would have been nothing more than the ordinance of the 5th September; but, having been unable to get over the difficulty by a violation alone, the result of the violation was that the compact of the Year III. was really dishonored and brought into disrepute. In order to raise us again in public estimation many people who could see no other remedy but the vesting of power in one man advised me to seize the supreme power; several wrote to me in that sense. I have already expressed the disgust I felt at such offers, and I do not think I can ever be called upon to repel the accusation of having aspired to supreme power.

CHAPTER IV

Various plans of campaign—A few great military talents—Schérer's plans—Bonaparte does not agree with him—Treaty of Campo Formio—The state of Switzerland—The tribune Ochs—Changes made among the generals-in-chief—François in correspondence with Louis XVIII.—The expedition against England is stopped—Beurnonville's zeal—Proposition in regard to the roads—Draft of a Dutch constitution drawn up by Daunou—It is considered too aristocratic—My friendly relations with Jourdan—His coquetting with me—His plans in regard to India—His style—A letter from Jourdan—Bernadotte's ill-temper—He wishes to leave the Army of Italy—Letter from Barthélemy dated from Cayenne—Intrigues of Wiscowitz and Quirini—Their calumny against the Directorate is proved—A couple of letters from Bonaparte—Reflections on the Italian campaign—Death of the King of Prussia—Arrest of his mistresses—Bonaparte's journey to Rastadt—He exceeds his powers—He meets with approval—Portugal tardily seeks to give to the treaty the ratification at first denied—Consternation of the Republic of Berne—Bonaparte comes to Paris—Alarm felt in that city—Casalti's assertions as to the plans of the anti-Fructidorians—Measures taken by Bonaparte—Clamor raised against me—Bonaparte's opinions on the men and things of Fructidor—His relations with Carnot—Lavalette's intrigues—Triumphs in store for Bonaparte—Amusing hyperbole of General Dufour—Declaration of d'Antraigues in regard to the portfolio—Bonaparte's monstrous act of perfidy—My reflections—I defend him in the Directorate—Bonaparte as a comedian—A conversation with Rewbell—Bonaparte in Paris—My orders to Talleyrand for his reception—Bonaparte introduced by Talleyrand—The oriflamme—Talleyrand flatters Bonaparte—The latter's reply—Profound utterance claimed by Talleyrand—My speech to Bonaparte—Important gap which I seek to fill—A recollection of Hoche—Bonaparte affects modesty.

At a time when the French armies have achieved such brilliant results, it is proper that I should here record a few reflections on the plans of campaign which governed their movements.

The plans of campaign issued in the name of the Directorate, just as all those issued since 1789 and in times much further back, have naturally furnished food for criticism. All operations should be arranged in due order, have a connection, and be placed in the hands of each and every general-in-chief. Every order issued should likewise be communicated to them. Moreau's conduct gives force to these remarks. He was to have formed a junction with Jourdan, in order to attack the enemy. There could not be any doubt of success. The junction did not take place; the disaster which followed was attributed to rivalry between the commanders. A sacrifice would have honored him who made it. The Armies of the Rhine and of Sambre-et-Meuse would have marched on Ratisbon. Bonaparte charges Carnot with having brought his influence to bear on what he called the counter-revolutionary plan. He bases his accusation on the position of the armies: that of Sambre-et-Meuse in the neighborhood of Coblentz, Düsseldorf, and Wetzlar; that of the Rhine in the valley of Kehl; the Austrian army stationed at Ludwigsburg, near Stuttgart, and at Willinghausen. It will be seen that the enemy's army separates the French armies, that it presents a front to both of them, and that it is free to march on one, to return and attack the other. As soon as the French armies invade Germany, the Austrians, still retaining their positions, will retreat simultaneously with the French advance, and will wait for an opportune time to pounce on both French armies, weakened by the loss of the troops with which they have garrisoned the fortified towns in their rear. As a consequence of this idea of Bonaparte, it becomes necessary to unite the two armies under one general. Matters thus disposed, the united French army shall march on Ratisbon, having Switzerland on its flank. As soon as Bonaparte is informed of its arrival at Ratisbon he will beat the enemy, and together will the two armies march on Vienna to overthrow the throne of the modern Cæsars.

The Directorate did indeed express a few general wishes in regard to the plans of campaign, but it was in the habit of interrogating the generals in the first place, and inquiring of them what were their plans; it thereupon added to or subtracted from them, sending the whole to the commanders-in-chief. Complete plans of campaign were always drawn up and submitted by the generals to the various governments. Of the men I have met most able in the preparation of this kind of work, in conceiving and drawing up general ideas, are Dubois-Crancé and Schérer, and, among the commanders-in-chief, Hoche first and foremost, and in the second rank, especially Bonaparte, Dugommier, Jourdan, Moreau, and Kléber.

The Minister of War, Schérer, adopts a large portion of the ideas of Bonaparte, in a report made to the Directorate on the 30th Fructidor, Year VI. He is of the opinion that the sole object of the negotiations at Udine was to obtain an armistice, which should be broken off as soon as the Austrian armies were recruited and provided with what they required to enter upon a campaign. An enlightened soldier, Schérer considers it important that we should forestall the enemy by breaking off the armistice as soon as all our provisioning and recruiting shall have been accomplished. He adds to his report a vast and detailed plan of military operations. In my opinion, nothing ever presented has been clearer, better, and more concise. It is the work of a man experienced in the management of war. But Bonaparte was not anxious to begin anew operations which might give his rivals opportunities of winning a glory equal to his own, and had signed his treaty of Campo Formio. I will now review the events following upon this peace.

From the 6th to the 28th Brumaire, Year VI.—The Swiss wish for a more democratic government than the one they have hitherto enjoyed. M. Ochs, the tribune of Bâle, is in Paris, whither he has come at the advice of Bonaparte. He proposes to us that we should assist him in bringing about a revolution in Switzerland, in order thereby to deprive our enemies of a centre of conspiracy against the Republic. Troops detached from the Army of Italy are to be set in motion with this aim in view. Berthier is appointed commander-in-chief of the Army of Italy. Desaix is given the temporary command of the Army of England, until such time as Bonaparte's mission as negotiator at Rastadt shall have been accomplished. One of our most mediocre generals, but a good sort of man, Hatry, gets the Army of Mayence; he is intrusted with the carrying out of the reciprocal concessions. Augereau is to have the Army of the Rhine. Bonaparte, who previously recommended him to us so warmly, would now have us believe that he is nothing more than a man inflated with pride, ignorant—brave, he still consents to admit, but the protector and dupe of all intriguers. Joubert is sent to Holland. General Moulin is to command the 17th division in lieu of Lemoine, whom his connections and utterances have rendered suspect.

François, implicated in the Le Maître conspiracies, is arrested. His correspondence with the agents of Louis XVIII. is intercepted, causing many other arrests.

The expedition against England, so far merely projected, is positively determined upon. The Minister of Marine is instructed to despatch the French and Spanish ships to Brest; in order to act, money and good sailors are required, and we have neither. The Minister of Finance is instructed to submit his views as to a loan. That charlatan Beurnonville, who would like to impress people with his importance, but who merely reveals his nullity even when seeking to conceal it, informs us of the preparations made by the English to burn the French, Dutch, and Spanish fleets, and thereupon to land on the French coast. Rewbell says this is not true.

The Directorate considers the question of issuing a proclamation calling upon the citizens to contribute towards the expenses of repairing the roads; I oppose this proposition, which, without producing the desired results, might reveal how lukewarm the public spirit is; modern peoples, at the point they have reached, no longer supply money to administrations in response to requests and proclamations; they prefer obeying laws which, while ordering them to pay, let them know to what uses is put the money they have paid.

Daunou has drawn up the draft of a constitution for Holland; it is submitted to us; several articles, among others that referring to eligibility, are considered too favorable to the aristocracy.

Bonaparte has arrived at Rastadt; he has the honor of opening the conferences of the congress.

General Jourdan, who had become the representative of the Haute-Vienne, had for some two years fulfilled his duties in conformity with his former political opinions; and, in a period when opinions furnished primary opportunities for a *rapprochement*, not to say the bonds which held society together, I was entitled to consider him as one of those bound up with me. I frequently received him with all the consideration due, it seemed to me, not only to the winner of the battle of Fleurus, but to the man whom I looked upon as a soldier-citizen. General Jourdan, to whom I had, ever since the installation of the Directorate, given my support as against Pichegru, seemed to me grateful for my treatment of him; not only did he express his gratitude respectfully—a most natural thing for soldiers in the presence of a civil authority which commands their respect through its dignified bearing—but he introduced into our relations more personal attentions than were consistent with his generally circumspect and reserved character. He would send me presents of game, even from distant parts, when his military duties called him thither; he was not so much liked by my colleagues in the Directorate, especially not by Carnot, who previous to the 18th Fructidor saw in him a resolute Jacobin. It was always to me that Jourdan applied when preferring to the Directorate some request for himself or his friends, or when he had any political or military ideas to communicate. Weary of his inaction since he had become a member of the Council of Five Hundred, as a result of those habits of command which produce astonishment and irritation among military men when they go out of their sphere, and even when they find themselves members of a collective authority, where contact with men warns them that they no longer may express an absolute will, and can only secure that of others by the ascendency of talent and truth eloquently demonstrated, General Jourdan, who, moreover, knew that I was fairly familiar with matters in India, where I had been several times in my youth, submits to me a memorandum, the object of which was to establish relations between the Republic and Tipoo-Sultan, in order to concert the measures and prepare the means for expelling the English from the East Indies. When sending this memorandum General Jourdan wrote to me:

PARIS, le 30 Brumaire, an VI de la République.
*Le Représentant du Peuple Jourdan, de la Haute-Vienne,
au Citoyen Barras, Membre du Directoire Exécutif.*

Je suis chargé, citoyen Directeur, de vous faire passer le

mémoire que vous trouverez ci-joint tendant à établir des relations entre la République et Tipoo-Sultan, pour concerter les mesures et préparer les moyens de chasser les Anglais des Indes Orientales. Je ne connais pas assez la situation de nos affaires dans les Indes pour me permettre des réflexions sur le mémoire que je vous remets. Je ne connais pas assez particulièrement son auteur pour le recommander au Directoire; mais il doit être connu de lui, puisqu'il a été le commandant de sa garde à cheval.

Je terminerai, citoyen Directeur, en vous *observant* que dans le cas où le Directoire exécutif se déciderait à ordonner une expédition un peu *conséquente* pour les Indes Orientales, je me chargerais volontiers du commandement en chef de cette expédition si le gouvernement voulait m'accorder sa confiance.

Salut et fraternité.

JOURDAN.

(PARIS, 30th Brumaire, Year VI. of the Republic.

The Representative of the People Jourdan, of the Haute-Vienne, to the Citizen Barras, Member of the Executive Directorate.

I am commissioned, citizen Director, to transmit to you the annexed memorandum, the object of which is to establish relations between the Republic and Tipoo-Sultan, for the purpose of concerting measures and preparing means for driving the English out of the East Indies. I am not sufficiently acquainted with the condition of our affairs in India to permit my making any remarks about the memorandum I send you. I do not know its author well enough to recommend him to the Directorate, but he must be known to it, since he has been the commanding officer of its mounted guard.

I will close, citizen Director, by pointing out to you that in case the Directorate should decide upon ordering an expedition of any importance to the East Indies, I would willingly undertake the chief command of such expedition, should the government repose its trust in me.

Greeting and fraternity. JOURDAN.)

If I quote literally this letter of General Jourdan, wherein are two blunders of style furnishing food perhaps for the criticism of some purists, it is not from a like sentiment; such a motive would seem to me as petty as malevolent. It is no disgrace for military men, or the Republic they have served, to admit that many of them, and even of the most distinguished, might, at the time they took up arms at the dawn of the Revolution, have been but imperfectly acquainted with grammar and even with orthography. Bonaparte, who had been educated in the *École militaire* and instructed in mathematics, destined as he was to a scientific corps, was hardly more proficient in this respect than most of the others. Those who have been in a position to notice in his writings, as in his speech, these deficiencies of education, have overlooked them, and have ascribed the honor of them, as of everything else, to his genius — to that superiority which made him disdain giving any attention to small matters.

As regards myself, to whom a greatly neglected early education almost gives the right to say, " I am 'a nobleman and cannot read," it is not for me to blame men, honorable and honored by their deeds and their patriotism, for deficiencies which are indeed very small and easily supplemented by a slight effort of attention. Thus, far from desiring to indulge in irony as unjust as it would be in bad taste at the expense of the illiterate men of the Revolution and of the wars, I will say that it is with genuine satisfaction that on perusing the letters of the generals most prominent since the beginning of the war, I find that, while they begin with the grossest mistakes of spelling and of style, they appear to improve both little by little, and to express their ideas with purity of style, not to say elegance. The only one among the military men who did not stand in need of such a progressive education was Pichegru, who was from the very first on a level with all the attainments necessary to his art, and who, moreover, writing a beautiful hand, has always written with as much clearness of character as purity of style both his letters and his plans of campaign, without erasures or corrections. As to those whom the Revolution found less advanced in matters of education, and whom she commanded to become worthy of her by acquiring the knowledge necessary to hold the social rank she gave them, and who obeyed this command so as to deserve to be at the head of their fellow-creatures, I repeat I honor these men all the more for it, and they seem to me all the more entitled to public esteem and consideration. I lay down as a primary condition of this reward that they shall not forget nor seek to forget their origin, but frankly and even proudly remember it; that they shall especially be grateful and respectful to that noble Revolution which ennobled them, taking this one from his plough, this other from his counter, to place a sword in his hand for the defence of the country; and whereas so many generous mortals have perished obscurely, she has given to some fortune and glory, a glory undoubtedly immortal, if the primary object of the Revolution had been constantly carried out both in war and in politics—the emancipation of the human race and the organization of liberty.

Military men, when not exclusively on active service, cannot resign themselves to remain quiet in their positions for a single moment. Bernadotte, having looked all about himself and us, had come to the conclusion that he could not for the time being see his wishes realized, and had, as has been shown, been compelled to return to the Army of Italy; but, again dissatisfied with the general-in-chief who, so he thought, did not sufficiently appreciate him, he wrote to me from Treviso on the 8th Frimaire, begging me to obtain permission for him at once to leave the Army of Italy. I submitted his request to the Directorate, several members of which looked upon his vacillation as a new expression of a disappointed ambition. Bernadotte, who had been the military pupil of Kléber in the Army of Sambre-et-Meuse, had perhaps unwittingly taken of him lessons in political insubordination, the foundations of which were already part of his character. The Directorate looked upon Bernadotte's request as upon that of a peevish child, or as an indirect demand for some other post. As all of us were well disposed towards him, we resolved upon attending to his petition in the future, and providing him with a position more to his liking.

A reflection which I may possibly more than once repeat in the course of these Memoirs, because it has more than once been cruelly suggested to me by the events of the Revolution, is that those who begin revolutions, and who are their leaders, are nowise, however much they may seem to be, their masters. The movement once set going, consequences result from it to which opposition can seldom be offered. During the first few days after the 18th Fructidor I made every possible effort to save Barthélemy from being transported, but it was decreed by law; hence the Directorate, even supposing that I had been the arbiter of its conduct, could not act in opposition to a decree pronounced by the *corps législatif.* If Barthélemy could know only my powerlessness and my regret for it, I am glad to be able to produce testimony from his own hand that his heart has done justice to mine.

CAYENNE, 2d *Frimaire, Year VI.*
The Ex-Director Barthélemy to the Director Barras.

You were good enough, previous to my departure from Paris, to tell my brother that I might indulge in the hope that the Directorate would spare me the torture of embarking, and would allow me to seek a refuge in Northern Europe. I am aware of all that your kindly heart attempted in order to keep your promise. To-day I have the honor of writing to the Executive Directorate. I venture to hope, citizen Director, that you will, with your well-known generosity, give your support to my petition; I appeal to your sense of justice and your kindly feelings. I shall always be truly grateful to you.

From the 1st to the 12th Frimaire, Year VI.—The envoys of the Republic of Genoa denounce the intrigues of one Wiscowitz, who, while claiming to have the support of Rewbell, did not know and had never seen him, and was actually selling Rewbell's influence to Quirini, the Venetian envoy. The latter, in his turn, sold it to the Republic—that is, he made his government believe all it pleased him to invent, according to the custom of diplomats, who are always begging for secret funds wherewith to bribe others, but who think they ought to be first bribed themselves. Quirini asked for considerable sums for the Directorate, making pretence of paying these sums to it; but on obtaining them he would appropriate them to his own use, meanwhile covering the Directorate, unknown to it, with shame by whispering into the ears of many the use he had made, to the benefit of certain Directors, of the sums furnished by his government. Princes who are the objects of such trickery long remain ignorant of it, while the rogues of diplomacy live in the enjoyment of their thefts, and laugh at the opprobrium with which calumny besmirches their victims. The Directorate had discovered enough to have the right to arrest the two honest diplomats. Their fraudulent dealings were laid bare by interrogating them separately and then bringing them face to face. Sufficient publicity was not, owing to a feeling of consideration, given to this act of justice; and it was not until several years later that I learned that such an infamous and positively contradicted calumny had not been destroyed by the honest behavior of the Directorate. This calumny constituted the means employed by Quirini to make good his accounts to those whom he had deceived. If Bonaparte has since given his support to this calumny, as to all those which may have been convenient to him, when seeking to injure those he had so deeply wronged that he could not forgive himself, he has shown himself all the more a calumniator on this occasion, as he was fully cognizant of the Directorate's innocence. Naturally, the fullest explanations had been made to him, in order that he should himself take up the matter for the honor of the Government, because the first denunciation of these two individuals had come to us from him, Bonaparte, as proved by a letter written to me by him from Montebello, with the effigies of liberty with which he in those days headed all written documents emanating from his pen. The two individuals referred to were therefore making a traffic of an imaginary influence.

Bonaparte, General-in-chief of the Army of Italy.

BARRAS,

I have appointed to a command at Marseilles General Sahuguet, who possesses the requisite firmness of character and talents to re-establish order.

All is well in Italy. I have just learned that the Pope's life is in danger owing to a stroke of apoplexy. I expect finally to consolidate within a few days the Cisalpine and Ligurian Republics.

The citizen Wiscowitz, a Venetian by nationality, who is with me, is a man who sells himself; he is a scoundrel.

He has stated that for a sum of 600,000 (*sic*) he could secure a decision such as prayed for by Quirini.

I greet thee.

BONAPARTE.

HEADQUARTERS AT MILAN, 15*th Brumaire.*

I have received several letters from thee. I was grieved to notice the little cloud, which passed away so quickly that nothing more need be said of it.

Botot behaved well while here; he has also behaved very well in Paris, so it seems to me; I am very glad to enjoy fresh opportunities of esteeming him.

I am waiting for news from Vienna. I am going to Rastadt, and thence to Paris, I hope. I am desirous that Truguet should command the ships which are to take part in the expedition to England. But money is required in order to be able to undertake it.

I will write thee more fully another time.

I greet thee.

BONAPARTE.

The Continental war is at last over, the treaty of Campo Formio is signed. Casting a backward glance over the two past years, so laboriously filled since the installation of the Directorate, it cannot be contested that if the Army of Italy has, by its usurpations and the new conditions by which it has been involved, increased the difficulties in the way of peace, it has, at any rate, shed additional glory over the arms of the Republic. Far from me to seek to detract from the share of decision, daring, and execution displayed to a far greater extent than conception (whatever may have been said or believed on this point) which appertains to Bonaparte in this prodigious campaign. It is in my eyes the most masterly and brilliant of all those ever carried out by the man who has since then carried out so many others. But when our enemies have sought to redeem their weakness by claiming that the campaign of Italy was nothing more than an act of brigandage, and that its general-in-chief had been nothing more than an actual brigand, I must confess that a portion of this assertion cannot altogether be denied. From the very moment that Bonaparte was about to set foot on Italian soil, he held up that rich country to the gaze of our soldiers as if to famished vultures; they were so truly, it will be said, and they were entitled to be so, considering that the Government had left them unprovided with all means of subsistence. This most unfortunate position was doubtless that of the Army of Italy; but was it not also that of all the armies of the Republic since the 9th Thermidor? and if it be true that war must feed the warrior, did not the generals of the other armies of the Republic prove that other means could be employed than those practised by Bonaparte? To prove that it is feasible, even in the direst extremities of war, to act with better morality than Bonaparte's, can we not produce the examples of our early military epoch? It was assuredly not the hope of pillage that incited our armies of the Year II. to cross the Rhine and conquer Holland and Belgium. Such were our first, our greatest, and most solid victories. It did not even enter the minds of the leaders of those days to offer money to their soldiers; they were beforehand only too certain of seeing their offers repulsed with horror, and of being handed over to justice; but in this system of interest presented to the Army of Italy by Bonaparte, in this incitement to cupidity, there is on his part a more remote combination than that of winning the victory; there is in it a test and a premeditated application of the system of the man who, to subjugate the Republicans, considered it was first necessary to degrade them; and that to dispose of the human race it was, so to speak, requisite to take it on its worst side.

End of Brumaire, Year VI.—The King of Prussia has just died. The Minister Talleyrand tells us, as an important bit of news, that his successor has caused the mistresses of the deceased to be arrested, as well as several French *émigrés*.

The project of extending the mandate of the deputies, and of renewing the authorities every two or three years by a fifth, is gaining favor.

The treaty of Campo Formio once signed, it was decided that Bonaparte should proceed to Rastadt. Nothing was easier than for him to start on his journey to reach that town; but it was necessary that the man who thought only of himself should map out his road in advance and should make it known to all the countries he was to pass through, in order that triumphal arches should be erected for him, and thus arrange what he styled the "Halts of Glory." Aides-de-camp and staff-officers, no longer clad with the simplicity characteristic of the armies of the Republic, but covered with golden embroidery and presenting an appearance of luxury, preceded him as forerunners, announcing everywhere that the great Bonaparte was to arrive in a couple of days; they made these proclamations with so much assurance that they were tantamount to an order to all classes of society and even to officials to welcome him with pomp.

Exercising even now the rights of general-in-chief of the Army of England, a command which does not confer the rank of generalissimo, Bonaparte has, on reaching Chambéry, issued a requisition calling upon the paymasters of the six neighboring departments to furnish him six millions, to meet the expenses of the 36,000 men of the Army of Italy who are coming home to take part in the expedition against England. This altogether eccentric action, which a general cannot take without the permission of the Government, is, in the first instance, justly censured. I inquire of the Ministers of Finance and of War whether they possess the means of immediately supplying the whole or part of this amount. Both of them reply: "Not a *sol*." So Bonaparte's requisition is approved.

Spain, terrified at the approach of the Republicans about to march against Portugal, has induced this Power to ratify the treaty to which it had refused its assent. The Directorate, on the motion of Rewbell, resolves that its previous decision in the matter shall stand unaltered, and that the Spanish ambassador shall be orally informed that Portugal cannot refer to a treaty no longer in existence, owing to that country's refusal to ratify it.

Berne has sent a deputation of oligarchs to the Directorate, which has sent them about their business. The example of La Valteline frightens them; these gentlemen would like to avoid the democratic revolution threatening them.

The Directorate decides that General Bonaparte shall come to Paris.

From the 12th to the 23d Frimaire, Year VI.— Paris is in a state of ferment; groups of malcontents are forming; the 18th Fructidor, as well as the days anterior to it, have resulted in nothing more than a passing amelioration; the enemies of the Fatherland have recovered their power, and are threatening us in every direction. The public mind is uncertain; one knows neither whither this movement is tending, nor what is desired; all are in a state of trepidation; the Royalists are once more gathering together; they live in hopes of dissensions in the *corps législatif* and in the Directorate. England is supplying funds to the agitators; each party thinks to derive advantage from its position in the *corps législatif*. The extension of power is spoken of in whispers, as is also the renewal of the authorities by one-fifth only; this idea gains favor with those who are about to retire from legislative functions. The true Republicans are alarmed; the resolution in regard to the nobles has failed to reassure anybody. There is talk of consulting the primary assemblies in regard to the violation of the constitutional act. Sieyès and Boulay de la Meurthe, who would like to revert once more to their law, allege that all it lacks is greater completeness; the belief exists that it has been proposed to reproduce it with a fuller scope.

When passing through Geneva on his way to Rastadt, Bonaparte has been told by one Casalti that "Carnot and Bornes passed through Geneva, conducted thither by Bontems; that they had conferences with Wickham's secretary, and also with the leaders of the slaughterers of Lyons; that money was paid to have Bonaparte and Barras assassinated; that Lestand, Flandrin, and others were intrusted with this mission." Casalti and another have been arrested.

It would appear from the letter of Félix Desportes, the agent of the French Republic at Geneva, that Bonaparte has himself taken action against all the individuals apparently connected with the conspiracy; while, in regard to the search made in Geneva for Carnot, it is fully established by a letter from Bonaparte to me on the 6th Frimaire, wherein he gives me an account of his journey, that it was he himself who, while in Geneva, busied himself with searching for Carnot; he states, in the letter to which I refer, that Casalti has admitted having conveyed from Paris to Geneva the representative of the people, Bornes, and another deputy named Charles, who, according to the particulars furnished by him, seems to be Carnot. It is again Bonaparte who, as is his wont, assuming every responsibility on this occasion, has caused seals to be affixed and has made arrests.

At the same time that Bonaparte is writing to me in a way that is still friendly and trusting, he has not ceased, ever since the 18th Fructidor, writing to others in an altogether different strain. Once more is the rumor abroad of an intention to get rid of the principal defenders of the Republic. Sieyès is conspiring, as is his wont, hardly parting his lips, but sealing with his approval everything likely to bring about disturbances. The party of exaggeration again hawks about the assertion that, had I been a Republican, I would not have usurped power by accepting the post of Director; that the great mass of the people did not give its consent to the Constitution of the Year III. Such are the habitual amenities of the Babeuf party, which sees in every public functionary an enemy to equality, and argues that five Directors means that number of scoundrels and tyrants.

The letters of Bonaparte, subsequent to the 18th Fructidor, are such as to make one incline to the belief that he imagines that he was strangely deceived in regard to men and things in connection with the 18th Fructidor and its consequences. As to things, it appears to him that the Constitution has been destroyed, while the Executive Directorate is no longer anything but a simulacrum of itself swayed by a Jacobin club, which oppresses it, and dictates to it laws and actions; or, that the Directorate itself is simply a club which dreams only of revolution and destruction, in lieu of seeking the prosperity of the State whose government is intrusted to it. This indeed reveals a poor acquaintance with the facts and the men composing the Directorate; but when giving utterance to these calumnies, is not Bonaparte perchance planting the landmarks which are to guide him later on a more daring march?

In regard to men, one would imagine that the ex-Director Carnot had been the only friend of the Republic, and of the General in particular. And yet the three so greatly calumniated Directors are the only ones who supported him most vigorously against his enemies, and in particular against Carnot. They made repeated, although fruitless, efforts to have the Rhine crossed a month earlier than it actually was. The three Directors constantly pointed out that Bonaparte would be attacked and overwhelmed by all the forces of the Emperor; while, contrary to the opinion of Carnot, they compelled Moreau to defend Kehl and the bridge of Huningen, in order to give relief to the Army of Italy and sustain the glory of its general. It was again these three Directors who, after many debates, carried the ratification by the Directorate of everything done in Italy by General Bonaparte, especially in the matter of Genoa and Venice. Carnot was the intimate friend of those who then attacked Bonaparte from the rostrum; he had them daily at his table, and took part in their consultations; he was in the habit of censuring bitterly the preliminaries of Leoben; he went so far as to find them too fine for France, since he reproached his colleagues with seeking to oppress the House of Austria. It was the three Directors who then and there told Carnot to his face that it was due to him that the preliminaries of Leoben had not been more advantageous; they would have been still less so if, in accordance with his wishes, Kehl and Huningen had been abandoned, and the crossing of the Rhine had been still further delayed; it was performed a month earlier than Carnot had sanctioned, and failing the crossing of the river by a French army, Bonaparte, who was fighting Austria single-handed, would have been left without support in the very heart of Germany. Finally, after persistent efforts, the three members were enabled to send to Bonaparte the grand despatch conferring on him the glorious attribute of Legislator of Northern Italy. It is unfortunately only too true that all Carnot's propositions tended to the ruin of both Hoche and Bonaparte. Daily, on leaving the sittings of the Directorate, he would repeat to Larevellière that the tone of Bonaparte's letters in regard to the Clichiens was alarming; that the man was not to be trusted; that he was at the very least a new Dumouriez, and so on. It was the three Directors who were constantly defending these two generals against the attacks made against them in the Directorate and in the two Councils. Did, perchance, professional jealousy exist between Carnot and Bonaparte? At all events, they well knew how to dissemble their sentiments in their letters. Carnot, whom I would fain believe to have been rather the dupe than the accomplice of Clichy, had, under pretence of a *rapprochement* and an amelioration of Republican institutions, decided upon the exclusion of four members of the Directorate. As he was hardly considered sincere in his apparent "modesty in the matter of power," hopes were held out to him of obtaining the presidency; but as he feared the issue of the project with which he was being lulled, he had thought it advisable to lean for support on Bonaparte's power. This was assuredly the basis of the repeated communications which took place between the two individuals in regard to events threatening the public peace. Bonaparte, who was entertaining the hope of attaining supreme power, had considered it necessary to get Carnot on his side. It was with that aim in view that he had sent his aide-de-camp Lavalette to Paris, with orders to watch all parties, and to avail himself of Carnot's influence to establish relations between him (Bonaparte) and Clichy. Lavalette, whose dual *rôle* was fully in harmony with the falseness of his character, had, pursuant to the instructions of his master, done his best to fill the two-faced mission of attaching himself both to Carnot and to the Clichiens, so as always to be on good terms with everybody, as Bonaparte had been on the 13th Vendémiaire with Menou and the "sections" of Paris. But, as I have already remarked, however clever may be the scoundrel who too frequently seeks to make fools of all others, it is difficult for one man to be cleverer than all the rest put together. From what has been seen, the Directorate was not free from anxiety in regard to the conduct of Lavalette previous to the 18th Fructidor; but, the day consummated, and victory having remained with us, we received from several quarters fresh information as to Lavalette's intrigues, so he was commanded to leave Paris and rejoin the Army of Italy. There only remained for the discovered agent, or, to use police slang, the *burnt* spy, to obey. But, compelled to leave the scene of his agency, he had waxed furious at his discomfiture, and had thought to avenge himself by fanning into flame Bonaparte's dispositions, already sufficiently excited against the Directorate, which he had for a long time deceived, but which had finally got to know him. Thus the same man who had taken a hand in the preparations of the 18th Fructidor, and who had added fuel to the flame, went back on his previous conduct in order to avenge himself of his shame; he turned the irritable character of Bonaparte in a direction opposite to the one in which he had heretofore guided him. Yet this Lavalette, who was gathering up these broken threads of intrigue, was a man of most mediocre parts, and totally unfit to be placed on the same footing as regards superior capacity with Carnot and Bonaparte; but his nullity had, with these eminent men, the ascendency which the phlegmatic has over the passionate in the chance meetings of everyday life, and still more so in those of politics, wherein passion is quickened by instinct and the danger of circumstances which fire the imagination. Time unfolds everything. Just as I am engaged upon my Memoirs I learn, through a publication distributed in the name of M. Lavalette, that he is a candidate for the Chamber of Deputies. He thinks himself entitled to state in his letter that he has rendered services; he sets forth that he is still able to render further services, and puts forward as an additional claim the aversion he alleges having felt in the Year V. to what he calls the "calamitous *coup d'état* of the 18th Fructidor." M. de Lavalette is greatly mistaken in his declaration of faith as to his sympathies or antipathies: I think I have sufficiently demonstrated that he never had any except those dictated by his interests, and never any scruples as to the nature of the means to which he had recourse. The whole history of this Lavalette would be as wretched as it is low had not a woman of heroic devotion come to the rescue of the ex-administrator of the *Cabinet noir* of Bonaparte!

I have alluded to these facts once more, not to justify the 18th Fructidor, concerning which I have expressed myself sufficiently when admitting its being a *coup d'état*, but to defend it against the imputations of its primary author, who is subsequently to become its chief accuser. Was it with the object of playing his cards in a double fashion that Bonaparte wrote to me that Botot had behaved well when with him in Italy, that he had undoubtedly behaved no less well in Paris, and that it would please him to have further occasions for esteeming him?

Pursuing towards Rastadt his journey, so craftily prepared by agents sent ahead, Bonaparte passed through Switzerland like a triumphant sovereign. When passing through Bâle, not only was he harangued by the magistrate of the country, but by General Dufour, the commander of the Huningen garrison. This French officer, who had until then signalized himself as one of our proudest Republicans, said to the august traveller, in the tone of a person possessed: "I am ignorant of the forms of oratorical style. I shall not compare you either to Turenne or to Montecuculli. I shall only say, Bonaparte is the greatest man in the universe." While agreeing with M. Dufour that he was not master of the forms of oratory, it cannot be denied that his speech was extremely simple. Whither would then have gone the author of such a hyperbole if he had been acquainted with the forms of oratorical language, his lack of which we must regret with him?

The appearance and even the display of conjugal forms was one of the artifices called into play by Bonaparte, to impose upon the vulgar herd and add to all his deceiving trickery. He was therefore accompanied by his wife, who already shared as a sovereign the homage he caused to be rendered unto himself everywhere; on arriving in Rastadt on the 27th of November, the august pair doubtless considered themselves far too modest in contenting themselves with occupying one of the wings of the château. It was indeed the Republic which had won the great battles which secured peace; hence Bonaparte thought that he should still invoke her on this occasion, in order to magnify himself in this congress of royal ambassadors. Had he simply been haughty, that would not have satisfied his desire of influencing men's minds; it was necessary for him to overstep all bounds. After having affected coldness and disdain towards all the German diplomats about him, he addressed them in a tone of indignation, and with threats on his lips. He did not seek to apologize to his government for his violence, but rather to pride himself on it. Sweden had sent plenipotentiaries to the congress, for the purpose of guranteeing the Treaty of Westphalia. The deputation was presided over by Count Fersen, famed for his connection with the Court of Louis XVI., a connection alleged to have been a personal one with Queen Marie Antoinette. When this Minister made his appearance at the head of the Swedish legation, Bonaparte asked him in a severe fashion who was at present Sweden's ambassador in Paris. On Count Fersen replying in an embarrassed way, Bonaparte added angrily that it was astonishing that Sweden should be oblivious of its former friendly relations with France; that it was difficult to explain the conduct of the Court of Stockholm; that it had seemed to make it a point to send on every occasion, whether to Paris or to meet French plenipotentiaries, persons essentially disagreeable to every French citizen. Would not the King of Sweden have the right to receive with indifference a French ambassador who should have tried to incite the population of Sweden to insurrection? Or could the French Republic endure that men only too well known from their intimacy with the former Court of France should come and set at defiance the Ministers of the first nation of the earth? Count Fersen did not expect such a welcome. Dumfounded at the insult, he withdrew, thinking to beat a happy retreat by saying that he would inform his Court, and, in the words of these gentry, "the king his master," of what he had just heard. When giving us an account of this scandalous scene himself, Bonaparte added to his insolence by boastfully remarking that it was the French Republic for which he had sought to secure respect, that he had intended to teach a lesson to a courtier of Louis XVI. and to the lover of Marie Antoinette. He had constituted himself a *conventionnel* and a regicide, he said, and prided himself on having done so.

Hardly has Bonaparte made his appearance at Rastadt, where he happens to be the highest plenipotentiary, than he can no longer remain there; he has two ambassadorial colleagues, and he considers his time is being wasted there. He tells us of his desire to come to Paris, in order to give us an account of everything of importance that has taken place in the last two years, and which he has been unable to tell us by letter or by intermediary. Moreover, the war being over, he does not believe that he requires a furlough, and so he is about to travel towards Paris. The Directorate thinks to escape the difficulty by evading the question; it decides that General Bonaparte shall proceed to Paris.

Just as Bonaparte's intrigues in Italy and on his journey to Rastadt, everywhere in fact where he has resided or passed, were giving us plenty of food for reflection, we received by way of Germany a declaration which appeared in the preceding month of September, giving the lie to everything Bonaparte had previously sent us under the name of the portfolio of d'Antraigues, wherein was contained the alleged famous conversation with Pichegru and Montgaillard. We had indeed, in the first instance, thought that this discovery seemed to have for its object the ruin of Pichegru personally; next, that the document given as the basis of all this affair was truly signed by d'Antraigues, according to the assertion of Berthier, who had sent an exact copy of it; but that nevertheless nothing proved that it was a document signed by d'Antraigues himself, because, it being actually nothing more than the handwriting of one of the clerks on Berthier's staff, it had no other authenticity than the signature of this general officer, who gave it merely as an exact copy of the original document. Where was this original document? And what was Berthier's character in the position of abject dependence in which he found himself respecting Bonaparte? What else but a cat's-paw in the grip of the master? Great is our astonishment when, after all our thoughts and alarms in regard to this matter, we receive a document from M. d'Antraigues, who declares that never did he dream of embodying in his alleged declaration the names of the men accused by Bonaparte alone; that Bonaparte has atrociously used his name in order to commit the most hideous of crimes. Wishing to give a greater appearance of reality to his outrageous fabrication, Bonaparte, at the time of the alleged seizure of the alleged portfolio containing the alleged documents, had stated that he intended to have d'Antraigues shot; it was then that our former colleague in the

National Convention, Bréval, a compatriot of d'Antraigues, had begged that I should interfere to save him. Mme. d'Antraigues had hastened to Paris and flung herself at my feet, imploring my protection. I was of opinion that the recognized diplomatic character of d'Antraigues should preserve him from the execution Bonaparte was about to consummate, and I was commissioned by the Directorate to order him to restore him to liberty. He greatly hesitated as to whether he should pay attention to the peremptory order of the Directorate. It was hard for him to let go of a prisoner whose voice his tyrant's instinct counselled him to silence—a voice which, he foresaw, would speak out some day, as it has spoken out in the subjoined declaration. This is so authentic that I should consider I was committing an act of treason towards history were I not to give the original text in its integrity.

Declaration of the Comte d'Antraigues.

On escaping from my Milan prison on the 28th of August, I sent as early as the 29th of August to Paris, and to a printer out of France, my declaration, signed by me, in regard to the plans of M. Bonaparte against the Five Hundred, and nominally M. Pichegru and the two Directors.

But now, the events of the 4th of September having happened, and the placards been printed and posted by order of the party dominating since that period, as I have learned the horrible calumnies it has been dared to employ, for the purpose of hunting down those who have succumbed in the struggle, and since, just as I had foreseen, M. Bonaparte, reckoning on my silence and my death, which would have served his plans, dares to bring me forward as a means of furnishing direct proofs against his enemies, I owe it to truth to make the following declaration:

I declare that I will maintain, not only unto death, as I have maintained it orally and in writing to M. Bonaparte when in chains, but that I will not lose a single moment, nor neglect any means to destroy all the allegations of the dominant power against their adversaries as fast as they become known, and as they are drawn from the papers found in my portfolio.

I was arrested on the 21st of May at Trieste; I was made to deliver up my papers.

I handed over a very bulky portfolio, which was sealed in my presence in two places, with my own seal and that of the commandant of the division of Trieste (General Bernadotte). I kept the key of it in my pocket, while the portfolio was intrusted to the care of M. Dars, an officer of the staff of the 4th division, who was instructed to remain with me, and not to lose sight of the portfolio.

On arriving in Milan, M. Dars took the portfolio to M. Bonaparte, and I was conveyed to the château of the citadel.

On arriving in Milan I sent to M. Bonaparte the letter written on the 26th of May from Verona, wherein I asked him for my papers.

On the 31st I wrote to him again, saying: "I request that my portfolio be returned to me. I cannot imagine, in spite of all I experience, that it will be opened; and if this second violation were indulged in, at least it should not be opened without my being summoned."

In spite of my request, I was never summoned to be present at the opening of my portfolio: the papers taken from it were never shown me.

These papers were in the hands of M. Bonaparte, who, on the 11th of June, delivered to my wife my portfolio, the lock and seals of which had been broken.

He gave her, together with the portfolio, a memorandum of the papers he had kept; the one last mentioned was *a conversation with M. le Comte de Montgaillard.*

From what M. Bonaparte had said to me from the 1st to the 2d of June, and from what he told my wife, I saw clearly that he wished to attach me to his party or to his plans, and to induce me to buy my freedom by furnishing him with the means of incriminating M. Pichegru and the deputies of the Five Hundred whom he disliked.

I had replied to his hints in so clear and precise a fashion that I thought he had renounced this his plan of calumny. Nevertheless, seeing that he ranked this alleged conversation with the documents which he kept, I thought that, come what might, I owed it to truth to write to him on the 12th of June what I had already told him orally.

Before quoting his letter I must describe the document in question. It was a document of which there were thirty-three pages written on foolscap, with a margin half the width of the page.

In the margin the words *contradictions, romances, lies, absurdities* occur repeatedly; they refer to facts quoted in this conversation which were absurd and contradictory.

This document was far from being in a complete state, but I had left it unfinished, for the reasons stated in the document I sent to Paris on the 14th of August while in prison, and which I duplicated on the 29th of August, the day following my escape.

In December, 1796, an adventurer named Royer, or Boucher, had called on me, alleging he was the Comte de Montgaillard, and asking for twenty-five *louis* for an alleged letter of exchange he had previously sent me by a roundabout way; I soon discovered the whole story to be a concoction.

This alleged Comte de Montgaillard could not have deceived me as to his *personnel* (sic) had I known the real Comte de Montgaillard, but I had never seen him.

The fellow claimed that I should supply him with funds for his needs, that I should also induce the Ministers of the Powers to give him money; and in order to persuade me to assist him he related to me the story of his negotiations and his importance. He had, he alleged, negotiated with the Emperor, the Archduke Charles, the Prince de Condé, and with Generals Pichegru, Moreau, and Bonaparte.

He claimed to have been the means whereby they had been won over to the party of the King.

He had conveyed to M. Pichegru propositions whose full particulars I am unable to call to mind, and to M. Bonaparte letters patent conferring on him the hereditary viceroyalty of Corsica, the title of duke and peer, the baton of Marshal of France, and the *cordon bleu*.[1]

And yet the result of all this was that he did not possess a single *écu*, and that he needed a few *louis*.

As I was aware that he had told the same story to several

---

[1] Order of the Holy Ghost.—Translator's note.

persons in Venice, I was desirous of making it known; and I resolved upon putting down in writing what he was telling me both in regard to M. Pichegru and to M. Bonaparte, and to make note of the constant variations in his narratives.

I was engaged in this occupation when I learned that the alleged Comte de Montgaillard had fled from Venice.

I then dropped this romance. This is what I explained to M. Bonaparte in my letter of the 12th of June, begging him to have the man arrested and brought face to face with me in Milan; I informed him that he was in that city under the name of Boyer or Boucher.

M. Bonaparte, on receiving my letter of the 12th of June, told my wife that such nonsense was not worthy of notice, nor of any steps being taken in the matter; that the document was a worthless one, and beneath consideration.

In spite of this speech, having learned to know the man with whom I had to deal, and to judge of what he was capable by the treatment I was experiencing, as well as from the offers he had made to me, I considered it was due to truth to make it known even at the peril of my life; and this is what I accordingly did on the 23d of June, 1797.

On that day I wrote to M. Boissy-d'Anglas to beg him to ask that I should be informed of the charge against me; and I sent simultaneously to a printer outside of France a copy of the list of the papers taken from me, together with a copy of the letter written by me in this connection on the 12th of June to M. Bonaparte.

I intrusted these letters to one Angelo, at that time in my employ, and I despatched him with them to Bellinzona, after his having secured for the purposes of this journey a passport issued by the municipality of Milan, and viséd by General Kilmaine.

Surrounded, in addition to a guard of ten men and an orderly officer, by spies of all kinds, it was impossible to conceal from M. Bonaparte the departure of my courier. He suffered him to start on his journey, and had him arrested as he was leaving Como; the papers were taken from him and delivered to Bonaparte.

The unfortunate man was at once loaded with chains and cast into a dungeon, where he remained for a month and seventeen days, without my being permitted to send him any kind of help.

III—9

On the 26th of June my wife called on M. Bonaparte. He informed her of the arrest of the courier, adding that he had intercepted my letter to the Five Hundred and to my printer.

And thereupon, without any spirit of humanity, he gave vent to an astounding outburst of rage and fury; he could say nothing too bad of me, alleging that I was threatening him and writing without his permission; that he had the power to have me shot there and then; that, had he so wished, it would have been done already; that I had tried to tamper with his troops. As a matter of fact, I have never in my life known a single one of the individuals composing them.

Finally, on my wife replying to him with the greatest firmness on all points, and informing him that, since I could not write, she was going to Paris, he at once placed her under arrest—*i.e.*, he told her she should be arrested were she to leave Milan.

Since that time I have never been able to obtain leave to write a single letter, nor to receive any, and it is impossible to conceive the excess of rigor with which I was deprived of all means of correspondence. Finally I found a means on the 14th of August, although the most profound terror existed throughout this district. I at once took advantage of it, because I saw, from the newspapers and from what was told me, that the plan conceived by M. Bonaparte of using me as a tool to destroy his enemies, by compelling me to silence, was beginning to develop itself.

On being so informed in a still more precise fashion on the 18th of August, after having sent him my petition on the 17th, I saw that it was necessary that I should make every effort to escape, and not allow myself to be slaughtered or destroyed when M. Bonaparte would have executed his plans, to which my silence or my death would give the certainty of success he wished for.

Such were the reasons of my escape on the 28th of August—reasons which I hastened to publish on the 29th of August.

In addition to this, I declare that I told every person I came in contact with while in Milan the facts such as I have put them in writing, and this from the 12th of June until the day of my escape, the 28th of August.

If terror does not freeze all hearts, truth will emerge some day from the bosom of those to whom I took great care to tell it in all its details.

Such are the facts.

It is now easy to explain the motives of my arrest.

The ruin of the *corps législatif* was being prepared, and it was hoped to find in my papers means for establishing a conspiracy. Balked in this respect, M. Bonaparte, after having sought by all possible means to bring me to serve his ends, seeing that I was as indifferent to him as to his allurements, that I despised death as much as his offers, adopted another course—that of depriving me of every means of correspondence, of allowing me to live, because my violent death would have done him harm: it would have been necessary to bring me before some tribunal or other, when I would surely have made known the truth. He therefore adopted the course of prolonging my captivity, and limiting himself to preventing my writing to any one. My wife, who like myself was acquainted with all the facts, and whose courage he knew, was placed under arrest.

So the plan was plain enough, and those who warned me of it were telling the truth.

The plan was, as soon as the party of the Triumvirs should be successful, to compel me, in order to obtain my freedom and my life, to admit as truths the calumnies my alleged papers had served as a pretext for; and, had I refused, to transport me to Guiana.

But had I been infamous enough to purchase my life through so base an act, it would have availed me little, for I was still to suffer and to be transported, lest, being set at liberty, I should retract the calumnies with which I should have sullied myself.

Such was the plan of which I was fully well informed on the 18th of August.

Those about M. Bonaparte, the habitual witnesses of all his perfidious deeds, abhor him; it is from the horror with which he inspires me that there springs a feeling of pity for those he persecutes; this is the feeling which saved me. Let him not seek to discover who has betrayed him; let him try and discover if there exists a human being whose tyrant and terror he is not, and then he will see how many outlets there are about him from which the truth, which he believes he is able to stifle, can escape.

I have never in my life either seen or known M. Pichegru; never have I written, spoken, or caused to be written or spoken to M. Pichegru.

Never in my life have I seen or known any of the Directors, or any member of the Five Hundred or of the Ancients.

I challenge M. Bonaparte to say the contrary, or to bring any such accusation in such a form as will allow of its being sifted.

M. Bonaparte knows it full well, and he knows also that as long as I live I will never remain silent in regard to his calumnies. He is well aware of the ridiculous rag which, he claims, contains the crimes of Pichegru. This is why all these unfortunate men are condemned without examination, without tribunals, without being given a chance to defend themselves; for there does not exist upon earth a tribunal, were one even to resurrect all those of Robespierre, before which the accusations made by him would stand discussion: they are one mass of falsehoods, calumnies, and absurdities.

This is why M. Bonaparte denied me that which it would otherwise have been his interest to grant—viz., to permit me to be present at the inventory of my portfolio, in order that I might be able to own to the documents and to the paraphs. Failing this, what proof is there of their genuineness? Failing this, what guarantee is there against forged documents having been introduced by him, against his having altered those he took, against his erasing and interpolating anything that may have suited his purpose? As early as the 1st of June I had requested of him that he should allow me to be present when the inventory of the papers was made; the laws of his country imposed upon him the duty of granting this request, which he denied me; he preferred breaking the seals affixed at Trieste and forcing the lock, in order to go through the contents of the portfolio alone, because he well knew I was not a man whom he could intimidate, and that I would compel him to verify in the presence of a witness the contents of the portfolio.

But, after all, if the romance of my alleged conversation with the alleged Comte de Montgaillard affords sufficient evidence to transport M. Pichegru, it must likewise supply enough to transport M. Bonaparte.

By virtue of what strange law does one select from a mass of evidence that which pleases, and reject everything which, coming from the same source, displeases the accuser?

If this romance proves that Pichegru was desirous of being *connétable*, and bringing back the King to Paris, it also clearly demonstrates that M. Bonaparte wished to be hereditary viceroy of Corsica, Marshal of France, duke and peer, *cordon bleu*.

If the latter fact is false, if the absurdity of the latter fact is palpable, why does absurdity become conviction where Pichegru is concerned?

This is why there was no trial; this is why extracts and not whole documents were printed! This is why I was not permitted to be present at the taking of the inventory, in order to verify it! It is because it is easier, even for the most cruel tyrants, to assassinate than to judge. Thus the alleged Councils, ever since the 4th of September, assassinate, but do not discuss. And how would they dare do so? There does not exist a being audacious enough to submit like accusations to discussion; it would have intimidated Barère and Saint-Just themselves, because, if the atrocity of the thing had not frightened them, the absurdity of it would. A man may be willing to admit that he is a tyrant, but not that he is a vile and cowardly forger who dares to put forward, as proofs against the *corps législatif* of his country, documents which would cause the most abject of men to die of shame, were he to venture upon propping up the most paltry trial on evidence so palpably absurd.

Heaven sometimes permits the greatest calamities; but it never permits the complete triumph of crime.

I can now understand how it was that so many deputies were transported, how Directors were proscribed and sentenced without trial; I can also well understand that a vast tomb should engulf their protests and their last sigh.

The same abyss was also in store for me.

But if some day villany forces me into it (and this is very likely, for I am acquainted with the means in use with these gentry), I shall at any rate have done to truth the homage I owe to it.

I declare that I possess written documents which prove all my statements, and I am going to work to that end with a persistency with which nothing shall interfere.

I have said it on the 29th of August in my first declaration, sent to Paris and to my printer at Neufchâtel: I love neither the defeated nor the victorious party. I know of no party devoted to the legitimate authority; but the worst of them all, so far as Europe is concerned, is the one which has just triumphed; and I do not wish, even were I to suffer a thousand deaths, to be instrumental in assisting these usurpers to consummate their dreadful plots.

(Signed)   LE COMTE D'ANTRAIGUES.
In the service of
His Majesty the Emperor of Russia.

14*th September*, 1797.

This document, read at a sitting of the Directorate, astounded us all; it threw me into a state of the greatest perplexity, so evident and so hideous was the fraud revealed. As a result of the explanations furnished by d'Antraigues, I was made to appear as having co-operated unjustly in the proscription of Pichegru: what had actually determined me to become the adversary of Pichegru, and had impelled me to an active opposition to him, perhaps unknown to myself, was his opposition to the Government, his persistency in attacking it—or, at any rate, his threats to attack it; it was the support which he gave with his name, honored as a citizen and as a soldier in the wars of the Revolution, to the implacable enemies of our Revolution. We were daily informed, previous to the 18th Fructidor, that Pichegru was about to take action, that he had reconnoitred the *matériel* as well as the *personnel* of the Luxembourg, and had said: "Pshaw! 'tis nothing more than a redoubt to be carried."

I also reflected that of all that had been said of his connections and intercourse with the Prince de Condé, nothing was actually proved by any document, not even by those of Fauche-Borel—a man whose mere assertion could only be looked upon as a piece of shameless effrontery, similar to the combinations of villains in a play, whose calculations rest on the assumed impossibility that the other actors can ever communicate together and explain matters. I likewise reflected over what several deputies worthy of belief told us had happened to them—Thibaudeau, for instance, being one who had told this of Pichegru: they had asked him "if he had ever held any intercourse of any kind with the Prince de Condé," and he had replied, " None, never," with a silent contempt for those who had asked him such a question. Furthermore, I remembered the precious description given by Joseph of his brother: " My brother (Napoleon) is undoubtedly a great general; he is a still greater machinator."

But in spite of all these reflections and probabilities, I could not, although familiar with the artfulness and inventive knavishness of Bonaparte, make up my mind to consider the captain of Toulon, the general of the 13th Vendémiaire, capable of so monstrous a machination; I persistently refused to see in him a thorough-paced scoundrel. I was willing to admit that he was a kind of fanatic carried away by his passions and his imagination. This is oftentimes the consequence of volcano-like brains, which seem a prey to a perpetual brain-fever. The Italian proverb says, *Ogni talento matto* (" Every talented man is a madman.") " I was present at what may be called Bonaparte's birth at Toulon," I said to my colleagues; "his was a perpetual and mad energy, akin to a hatred of sleep and rest; I used then to compare him to Marat, to whom I thought he bore a great physical resemblance; like Marat, it was a continual rush of ebullition; this flame-like life is the soul of great deeds. Bonaparte has, as you have seen, accomplished very great ones in Italy in less than two years; he has more than once encountered serious contradictions, which have irritated him to a high degree. Pichegru had reaped glory before he had, and seemed to hold him in contempt. He did more, for he was the president and actual general-in-chief of a party which was doubtless deceiving him, but with which he nevertheless went hand in hand against the fortunes of Bonaparte, as its object was to indict him, Hoche, and ourselves. Under such alarming circumstances Bonaparte, if he did not lose his head, may have at least cudgelled his brains vigorously to find a means to resist his enemies and to triumph over them; as he could not cope with Pichegru in the open field, he came to the conclusion that he must have recourse to sapping and mining. He began his novel, perhaps persuading himself subsequently that it was history. In this respect I can adduce observations made by me of old as to the character of Bonaparte; in the period intervening between the 13th Vendémiaire and the month of Ventôse, when we appointed him to the command of the Army of Italy, and when he was married, he used frequently to come to my house; I was in the habit of welcoming him as a familiar. He had for a long time been taciturn, until the moment arrived when his marriage was settled upon, and he obtained the command of the Army of Italy. Thereupon he seemed a prey to the maddest joy; and every time after dining with me he thought he could let himself go in the presence of my guests, he would ask my leave to close the door, in order to be free to play comedy. This comedy was always a genuine improvisation, the idea of which was sometimes supplied to him, and he would instantly dialogize, himself playing several parts simultaneously; he would ask my leave to take off his coat, and, taking tablecloths and table-napkins, make himself divers costumes, and, crouching behind arm-chairs, would suddenly emerge in the most grotesque disguises: although the delivery of his improvisation was not very fluent, he nevertheless adopted every inflection of voice at his command to give variety to the scenes, and he managed to do so fairly well. At other times he would begin tales *à la* Boccaccio or episodes in the style of Ariosto, without knowing, he would say, what the end would be, and yet he continued them to the end with an inexhaustible command of words; what was perhaps no less comical than all the rest, was that while at first ridiculing the thing he had just created, he would end by remarking, seriously, 'Do you know that this is actually true, that it is a true story.' He seemed inclined to get angry if his word was doubted, and more than once he spoke in the most imperious, not to say rude, fashion to those who would not take him at his word."

"All this is very well after leaving the dinner-table and with one's coffee," said Rewbell to me; "but such singular methods are not to be transported into the domain of politics, especially when it is a matter of disposing of the life and honor of others. If Bonaparte has been playing comedy when sending us documents incriminating Pichegru, taken from an alleged portfolio of d'Antraigues, who comes and contradicts Bonaparte in so positive and marked a fashion, how shall we be able to place reliance on him sufficient to intrust him with the command of the armies of the Republic and the direction of its negotiations? I admit that up to a certain point all men are frequently just as many comedians on the political stage as on other stages; still, there are certain limits not to be overstepped, under penalty of crime."

I reply to Rewbell: " Had we had no other reason for acting as we did on the 18th Fructidor than the suggestions of Bonaparte and the documents of the alleged portfolio of d'Antraigues—documents of which he has sent us alleged copies certified by Berthier—assuredly to-day, when so precious a ray of light is thrown on the matter, we might deeply regret having followed impulses all the more regrettable from the fact that the innocence of the victims would be still further established; but the 18th Fructidor was none the less necessary and forced upon us, even had Bonaparte not sent us the very suspicious materials now in question. The only difference is that we should have been compelled to have recourse to other subterfuges, and to adopt other means to reach the enemies who were strangling us, failing which we should have infallibly perished, and the Republic with us. The ambition and passion of Bonaparte have doubtless played their part in the affair; every little helps in a household; we make use of him as he made use of us; we must now appreciate at its value that which we could not properly estimate in the first instance, mitigate the sufferings we have caused—in a word, undo all that can be undone. Meanwhile I have received further letters from Rastadt. Bonaparte does not find sufficient pasturage in his position there; there is not, as the slang phrase goes, enough for one of his hollow teeth to crunch. You have

authorized him to come to Paris; he will not be
long in availing himself of your permission; he is
about to arrive; we must prepare to receive him
in a suitable fashion. If, after all he has done,
and which it was not in our power to prevent
being done, it were possible to preserve to the Republic one of her most glorious sons, to profit still
further by his immense talents, bring him back to
the paths of truth and honor by giving satisfaction
to his lofty ambition and making it thoroughly worth
his while, why should we not employ all possible
means to that end? Should we not blame ourselves
were we to neglect bringing them into play?" "You
are president," said Rewbell; "do what you think is
best; prepare the reception; we leave the matter
in your hands." My other colleagues agree to this,
saying, "We will stand by you, and afterwards together we shall watch him."

Bonaparte is at last in Paris. The several parties
are all attention, and all await something from him.
I send for Talleyrand, and say to him, "It is not the
Minister of War who is to present Bonaparte to us;
I prefer that it should be you. It is not the general, but the negotiator of peace, and especially the
citizen, whom we must try to praise and recognize
on this occasion. I commend him to you in this
connection. You have tact: let your compliments,
therefore, be appropriate to this view; my colleagues
especially are truly alarmed, and not without some
show of reason, by military glory, which ought not
to be extinguished, but enlightened and directed."
Talleyrand answers, with that smile which ever seeks
to be shrewd and respectfully ironical in regard
to military men: "I know what military men are,

citizen Director; I am going to concentrate my thoughts on the orders you have done me the honor of giving me; they shall be executed; I have fully grasped your meaning, citizen Director."

20th Frimaire, Year VI.—The ceremony took place on the 20th Frimaire, Year VI. (10th December, 1797). The Minister of War was bound to be present, because he had on that day to present Generals Joubert and Andréossy, who carried the flag given by the Directorate to the Army of Italy. It was a new oriflamme, not the one common to the other armies, but a special one for the Army of Italy, whose victories were embroidered on it in letters of gold; but it was Talleyrand who, as prearranged, presented Bonaparte, the negotiator of Campo Formio and the citizen of the French Republic, with all the precautions it was in his nature to take, with all those cunning devices he calls style, and which none the less remain devices when coming from his lips. Talleyrand spared no effort to follow my instructions, at the same time flattering and intoxicating Bonaparte; he seemed, in a slight degree, to ascribe the glory of the general not wholly to him, but to the Revolution, to the armies, to the great nation. Still, there was a goodly share left for the general of the great nation. So it was that Talleyrand, unable to confine himself to those things for which everybody had commended Bonaparte, praised his antique taste for simplicity, his love for abstract sciences, recalled his favorite author, that sublime Ossian who taught him to detach himself from the things of this earth. Talleyrand even went so far as to say, with his serious, solemn, and grave tone and demeanor, that which several spectators could not but smile at, that "the day might perhaps dawn when it would become necessary to entreat Bonaparte, in order to tear him away from his studious retirement."

Bonaparte spoke next, and his speech, characteristically abrupt and incisive, consisted in the first place of a sketch of the strides made by the human mind—a progress due to philosophy, liberty, and all the hopes men were free to conceive; he carefully avoided the use of the word "revolution," and finished his discourse as follows: "When the happiness of the French nation shall be based on better organic laws, Europe will become free." Those whose looks were intent upon Bonaparte, and whose ears drank in his words, were somewhat alarmed at this sentence; they even saw in it something more than a promise—viz., a threat, and they shuddered at this glimpse of the character of a man who was already dreaming of usurping the rights of his Fatherland under the pretence of giving it better organic laws. "Here is a glimpse of the future," were the words put into the mouth of Talleyrand, who in those days already fathered all *mots* of any import, and attributed to himself everything that might suit him.

Replying to Bonaparte as president of the Directorate, I did not consider myself called upon to be sparing in my praise; I gave it him without stint, in order to furnish myself with the right and the means of praising the Revolution, "the sublime Revolution of which his new genius was a glorious product." I thus attempted to fill up the important and deliberately calculated gap in his speech, in which he had not mentioned the name of the Revolution — the generous mother who had fed him, brought him up, and made him what he now was. With the object of glorifying, pursuant to the same principle, the conquest of Italy, I said to Bonaparte: "You have, after a lapse of eighteen centuries, avenged France of the fortune of Cæsar; he brought into our country destruction and servitude; you have carried life and liberty into his ancient Fatherland." It was easy to comprehend my idea, while I was appearing to look upon him as of good faith in all that he had just been saying. To catch rascals with their own words is not an immoral policy when there is still some hope of being able to praise them for these words, and to bind them to liberty and justice; and what made me feel confident that my parable had been taken somewhat generally, without escaping Bonaparte himself, was that a sentence wherein I said, as a matter of course, that "the Directorate is acquainted with the enemies of liberty and its own, and will crush all ambitions," was loudly applauded.

It had been impossible for me to speak for so long a time of Bonaparte, and to himself at that, without mentioning also some of those who had likewise had their share of glory in the war of the Revolution, begun and carried on so gloriously previous to Bonaparte's appearance on the scene. My heart went back to Hoche, and it was with a fully unexpected emotion that I said, in addition to my written speech: "Why is Hoche not here, to see, to fold his friend to his breast?" It was most true that Hoche had been a friend, and even a most generous friend, to Bonaparte; that he had warmly defended him, and not without peril, during the foregoing year; but there had been nothing to prove that Bonaparte had been the friend of Hoche. Bonaparte had never spoken of Hoche during his lifetime, except with a certain uneasiness and jealousy, either because of the glory he had reaped before him, or because of the feeling he knew Mme. de Beauharnais had borne him. He was aware that of all the men she had loved (and there was a goodly number of them), Hoche was the one she had most loved. Hence the words I now spoke to the memory of Hoche were scarcely more agreeable to Bonaparte than what I had said to the honor of the Revolution; but the nation still existed, and he could not do without its assent: he had still to court it until the time should come when he might throw off the mask.

The ceremony over, Bonaparte withdrew to return to his house in the Rue Chantereine, where he was about to give a few more well-studied representations of his modesty, simplicity, disgust of ambition, and taste for science and its votaries; he would say to his familiars that the homages done him at receptions constituted so much torture for him, and that he would soon be rid of them were he to fall into disgrace. He argued that all this blarney was equally applicable to all persons; it was merely necessary to change dates, titles, and names. Is it so very difficult to estimate such modesty at its full value, and not to see that what displeased him in those sincere homages was that they were still Republican? He was compelled to share them with another, and was as yet unable to have them rendered to himself alone.

CHAPTER V

Mme. de Staël and M. Necker—M. Necker's name struck off the list of *émigrés*—The two millions—Political variations of Mme. de Staël—Witty *mot* in this connection—She importunes the Directors—Talleyrand rends her—She receives orders to leave France—Her grievances—A *tête-à-tête*—She sends Benjamin Constant to me—Her affection for him—Birth of a daughter—A letter from Benjamin Constant in defence of his friend—Rewbell's prejudices against Mme. de Staël—Chamfort's *mot* on friendship—I seek to undeceive Rewbell—Men for whom money is an object, and men for whom it is a means—Rewbell's resentment—His opinion of Talleyrand—The latter's servility—Kosciuszko and Mme. de la Rochefoucauld—Pilferings of certain ambassadors—Araujo de Azevedo—Augereau's bluster—He is denounced by Bonaparte—His command is reduced—Revolution in the Cisalpine Republic—A loan of eighty millions—General seizure of English merchandise—Projects against England—The state of Europe—Arbitrary acts—Measures proposed by me—Switzerland engages our attention—Bad state of the national credit—Grave omission on the part of the Treasury—François and his treasures—Agitation on the right bank of the Rhine—General Brune on the look-out—Bonaparte's expedient—Cabarrus rejected as ambassador to Spain—Negotiation with Spain in regard to the States of Parma—General Duphot murdered in Rome—Berthier ordered to march on that city—Bonaparte's real or feigned alarms—He dreads poison—Contemptible exactions in regard to his wife—He succeeds Carnot at the Institut—A quarrel with Larevellière over precedence—He accepts Rastadt—He tenders his resignation—Rewbell offers to take him at his word—Excuses Bonaparte makes to him—Rewbell credited with having amassed wealth—Mme. Bonaparte wishes to give him Hortense—His answer—The aristocrats of the Café Carchy—Quarrels and duels—The 21st of January—Great discussion in the Directorate in regard to inviting Bonaparte to the ceremony—Talleyrand is intrusted with the matter—A change in Bonaparte's ideas in regard to the 21st of January—Will he

MME. DE STAËL AND M. NECKER

be present at the *fête?*—A middle term—Chénier's Republican tyranny—Talleyrand's variation—Thibaudeau and the *Mémorial de Sainte-Hélène*—Bonaparte quarrels with Augereau and Masséna—The new imitators of Cincinnatus—Bernadotte's petition—Sergeant Belle-Jambe—Mme. d'A.—Bernadotte's Republican energy—His plans of reform—He asks to be placed on the retired list—Captains Gérard and Maison—The Directorate promises Bernadotte the command of the Ionian Isles—Correspondence between Bernadotte and Bonaparte—Bonaparte's ruses to deprive Bernadotte of the command of the Army of Italy—He is successful in his attempt—Bernadotte ambassador at Vienna—Reciprocal resentments—Bernadotte's devotion to his former colonel—M. d'A. executed—Affairs in Europe—Hamburg protected by France— Dubayet's death in Constantinople — His panegyric—Augereau denounced—Bonaparte desirous of sending him to Turkey—Turkish diplomacy—Augereau sent to the Pyrenees— Bonaparte's incoherent opinions — His curious remarks on the 18th Fructidor—Calumnies spread by agitators against the authors of that day—Augereau submits— His patriotism—Adjutant-General Izard—Projects against the Elector of the Palatinate—Bonaparte's immense power—Affairs in Switzerland — Berthier marches on Rome — Affairs in Spain — The Queen of Spain quarrels with the Prince of the Peace—The ambassador Perrochette instructed to reconcile them—Fresh subjects of dissension in the Directorate—The Minister Sotin's place taken by Dondeau—Merlin's fury—Electoral operations—Patriots set aside— Police reports—Rome taken— The Pope's new government— Dondeau's ridiculous bluster— Perignon's behavior in Spain—Shall Truguet be a Minister?—Pléville le Pelley and his wooden leg—Truguet ambassador to Spain—Talleyrand's *mot* on the 18th Fructidor— Bonaparte's ambitions revealed—His familiarity in the bosom of the Directorate—Our behavior towards him—A scene at my residence— His inclination for absolute power—My narrative to Mme. de Staël—Review of the Army of England—Bonaparte returns to Paris—His plans in regard to Egypt—Opposition he meets with—Gigantic promises— An expedition to Egypt decided upon— Bonaparte commands it—Admiral Brueys—Merlin's proposition against the citizen Émery.

IT has been seen how Benjamin Constant was presented to me with his pamphlet in the Year IV., in the early days of the Directorate, by Mme. de Staël. She had for him then a most affectionate interest; he was about thirty years of age; but as a result of the affection uniting them, whatever its nature, Benjamin on his part was naturally also a means for the woman whom, even in the midst of her most ardent affections, I ever found something of a Genevese—*i.e.*, calculating, and never losing sight of her interests for a single moment. After having made Benjamin Constant work towards the elevation of Talleyrand to the Ministry, Mme. de Staël employed him no less usefully to have the name of M. Necker struck off the list of the *émigrés*. Immediately upon our granting this erasure—a most just one, undoubtedly, but a difficult one, owing to the opposition it encountered—Mme. de Staël, without losing any time, and acting up to Cæsar's motto, that "he did not consider he had done anything if anything remained to be done," thanked me a thousand times on behalf of her father, whom she likewise caused to thank me by a letter, wherein he deeply regretted that his extreme age did not permit of his bringing his gratitude and laying it at " my feet." Mme. de Staël, on the following day, got M. Necker, who had obtained his erasure, to write to me in regard to his fortune, with the object of getting back two millions he had lent the king in 1789, and which he believed he had lent the nation, which indeed would have left it his debtor; in consequence of which it was the duty of the Directorate to pay this national debt of two millions. These are the two millions since then constantly refused by Bonaparte, but which he was on the point of granting during the Hundred Days, and which were ultimately paid by Louis XVIII. a short time before the death of Mme. de Staël. But I must not anticipate: there is much to happen before that time.

Following upon the 18th Fructidor, Mme. de Staël, puffed with pride and strong in her co-operation to the events of that day, had shown a desire to direct, or at least to govern, its consequences, sometimes in one way, sometimes in another. At times she was more severe than ourselves, and revolutionary in the fullest acceptation of the term; at others gentle and indulgent, in proportion as she was influenced by her affections, which had caused those who had seen her a prey to all these transitions to say that "she liked to drown her enemies one day to enjoy the pleasure of fishing them out the next." Whether she was right or wrong as to her pretensions, the form she gave them was a ceaseless worry to several members of the Directorate. This fatigue had been inspired, I admit, and in a high degree, by Talleyrand, against whom Mme. de Staël had committed the crime of having made him a Minister, and of having lent him money previous to that. Could he after that forgive Mme. de Staël even her presence? Hence it was that he always had something irritating to tell about her when he came to the Directorate; this was, on the part of Talleyrand, independently of his resentment at the favors done him by Mme. de Staël, a manner of paying court to Rewbell, with whom he had always tried to be on good terms by tendering him burnt-offerings, beginning with that of his benefactress.

The majority of the Directorate, imagining that the conduct of Mme. de Staël was always bound up with some intrigue, ordered her to leave France, alleging as a reason the one previously employed, to wit, her being a foreigner: this was one of the discoveries of Merlin; failing compliance with this order, the name of Mme. de Staël was to be entered on the list of *émigrés*. Her blood boiling at the idea of being assimilated with the country's enemies, Mme. de Staël called in great haste upon me, whom she termed her protector, her father, not daring, she said, to call me her brother, because this might perhaps seem somewhat light, since we were not in the land of the Parsees, where brothers married sisters; she flung herself at my feet, and clung to my knees with all her strength, saying she wished to kiss them as the altar of all-saving gods, which in ancient times supplicants never invoked in vain. She was alone on the occasion of this interview, and whenever she thus came alone she would always begin by reproaching herself with it as if it constituted an act of thoughtlessness. "A young woman," she would say, "should really not call with so much carelessness on a young Director, who is far more dangerous than all the ecclesiastical directors put together." This was Mme. de Staëls joke, and I beg that people will not believe that I looked upon it as anything else, nor that I attributed to it the serious meaning it would have been allowable to believe she wished to be given to it, in the very manner with which she expressed her apprehension. I answered Mme. de Staël with my ordinary calmness, from which, I say it to the honor of my interlocutrix, I never departed, in so far as she was concerned; this did not prevent her, when I was taking leave of her with all the respect I bore to her, saying to me: "Come, now, I will never return here alone; I will either come with Benjamin Constant, or send him to you." True to her word, she came next day with Benjamin Constant, as if with a faithful body-guard whom she had impressed with the importance and urgency of her being accompanied by a defender. Nevertheless, Benjamin Constant seemed to me to do justice to the truth of the reciprocal positions Mme. de Staël had somewhat distorted for his sake, in order still further to over-excite his imagination, which was perhaps rather inclined to excitement at that time, when the public saw proofs that were hardly equivocal of an affection strongly shared, in the birth of a daughter whom Mme. de Staël called Albertine, and the resemblance of whose features, hair, everything, in fact, appeared to the world as the striking image of M. Benjamin Constant. M. Benjamin might still be sincerely attached to a woman whose celebrity forestalled that which he wished to attain in his turn, and which he could help on through that of his mistress. I have at any rate good grounds for believing that in spite of cold and frigid outward forms, which might be taken for those of calculation, Benjamin Constant possesses a soul which may occasionally have played a part in his *liaisons* of love and friendship; that he has been more of a dupe than a rascal, rather a Tom Jones than a Blifil. Witness the horrid ingratitude of which he was the unfortunate victim at the hands of Talleyrand; and if, out of so many confidential letters addressed to me in those days, and which I have not seen fit to publish, I except the one I insert here, it is that it seems to me a proof of the genuine feeling and deep emotion Benjamin Constant brought into his relations of love and friendship.

> CITIZEN DIRECTORS,
>
> I owe it to friendship; I owe it to justice, a still more sacred thing; lastly, I owe it perhaps to the Commonweal, which I have served with all my strength, and which I still hope to serve again—respectfully to address the Directorate on behalf of a person infamously calumniated. I do not consider I am doing a courageous act, and, were it so, that would be an additional incentive.
>
> Permit me, citizen Directors, before I plead for another, to presume to speak for a moment of myself. I am aware of the little importance attached to individuality, but in the present case what I am can alone enable a judgment to be formed in regard to what I assert.
>
> I have always held in contempt the underhand insinuations and dark plots of my personal enemies; my life, my actions, my works are my pledges; if these do not suffice, I would invoke among you, citizen Directors, both the members of the Directorate whom I have the honor of knowing personally, who have been able to form an estimate of my writings and principles, and the present president of the Directorate, with whom I shared the perils of the 18th Fructidor. I would invoke among the deputies the men who most contributed to that memorable day, and who saw me assist them in their plans with all my strength, and help them with all my zeal. I would invoke the shade of Hoche, the man whose presence here gave fresh impulse to Republicanism, and with whom I and two others swore, on the 8th Thermidor last, to die for the Government, or to assist in crushing the conspirators to earth. I would invoke General Chérin, who came to Paris to continue the carrying out of Hoche's salutary plans, and who was witness of my ardor and devotion on every occasion. I would say that Chayal and I founded the *Cercle Constitutionnel*, and that it was in my house that this needed society saw the light of day. I would recall the time when, alone among all writers, I attacked the reactionists; and I would call for the reading of the pages I wrote when Carnot was your president, when everything presaged the counter-revolution—

pages directed against all-powerful men, who had at their disposal every means, decrees, and assassinations, laws, and calumnies.

I do not pretend, citizen Directors, to claim the merit of having, in my resistance to Royalism, been in the field in advance of many a patriot. A Frenchman through the recovery of my rights as a citizen, possessing "biens nationaux"[1] only, having transported all my fortune into France, and concentrated all my hopes on liberty, I was, in defending her, merely following the aspirations of my soul and the calculations of my interest. But it would assuredly be most pusillanimous on my part to dread the tongue of calumny, in the face of so many pledges. I feel strong in truth, in your justice, citizen Directors, and lastly, in that indifference to fate which is the result of a certain philosophy of mind, of a certain firmness of principles, and of an appreciation of life, which is tolerable only with the hope of serving liberty.

I would therefore have remained silent in regard to all matters relating to myself; and I know, moreover, with deep gratitude, that the attempts of a few enemies against me have met at the hands of the depositaries of power the indifference they deserved; but to-day the attack is directed against a weaker being, one consequently more sacred. I hasten to her defence, and you yourselves, citizen Directors, will deign to applaud me for not abandoning an accused friend who is a woman—you who have at various times suffered from honorable proscriptions, and experienced the value of a faithful friend. And indeed, when one of you, citizen Directors, outlawed for his courage by the Ministers of Robespierre, owed his life to friendship only, what would he have said had his friend abandoned him? When another, proscribed for his talent, and in hiding in the seclusion afforded by the Vosges, scarcely escaped the scaffolds that were destroying every kind of distinction, what would he have said had his host cast him out of doors? When a third, destined to the daggers by the Decemvir who foresaw the coming of the 9th Thermidor, was planning that immortal day, what would he have felt had he been betrayed by his own? When a fourth, as the price of his Republican firmness while a member of a Ministry whose fate was fraught

---

[1] Land estates or properties purchased from the national government, after they had been confiscated from the *émigrés*.—Translator's note.

with peril, destined by the Royalists to be their first victim, was denounced from a sullied tribune, what would he have said had Republicans feared to defend him?

Hence do I, citizen Directors, undertake the defence of Mme. de Staël; convinced, ever since I have known her, of the purity of her principles, I have always defended her. I have tried to make her innocence shine forth to the eyes of the Directorate. I had flattered myself with success, when fresh calumnies threaten to do her injury. Once more do I implore the justice of the Directorate, and it is on my head that I call down the vengeance of the laws if Mme. de Staël is found guilty: for I have not left her for a year; not a single one of my days, hardly any of my hours, have been spent away from her; it has been impossible for me not to know her connections, her actions, her utterances, and her most intimate thoughts; and if she has conspired, if she has deserved any punishment whatsoever, I must share it with her; my life and properties are in your hands: let my life and properties answer for her. Deign to look into the whole of her conduct. Deign to free her from vague suspicions. Let her be tried with all the rigors of the law, or, if nothing that she has done calls for judgment, render her the justice due to her, and the good-will she is entitled to at your hands. I am ignorant of the nature of the charges which may be laid at her door; but if there exist any alleged charges, not one of which has ever been plainly asserted, I can vouch for their falseness. Deign to order, citizen Directors, that they be communicated to her, and listen to her reply to them. I repeat it, I constitute myself hostage and surety for her innocence; and the step I am now taking is not that of a man who would dread responsibility.

If there are no positive charges, allow me to oppose to erroneous prejudices positive facts. What has been Mme. de Staël's habitual society since her return? That of Republicans. What have been her outspoken opinions? Republican opinions. Who were her enemies? Your own, citizen Directors; and when Henri Larivière sought from the tribune to call for her expulsion from France, could she have imagined that three months later a Republican government would gratify the resentment of Henri Larivière? Deign to peruse once more the newspapers which daily insulted the Government: daily did these newspapers attack Mme. de Staël; read once more the opinions of those transported and of the *émigrés*, who calumniate both you and her, citizen Directors. No, the Directorate will not gratify the hatred of its own enemies by surrendering to them a Republican victim; proscribed by you, Mme. de Staël would nowhere find an asylum; the aristocracy would add to the punishment inflicted by your enactments, just as you will have pronounced the enactments of the aristocracy. Citizen Directors, the time is never to be renewed when Republicans expelled from France found across the frontier new enemies, and as they wandered about homeless, terrible and discouraging proofs of the persecuting fatality of the Republic.

Moreover, citizen Directors, what does Mme. de Staël ask? A trial if she is suspected; if she is not, then the repeal of an enactment which allows her neither to leave France nor to remain in it. When joining in this just request, I am fulfilling a sacred duty: I do not fear being charged with imprudence: was I imprudent when, in the thick of the reaction, I defended the Republic? True prudence lies in duty and justice, in the protecting of innocence, and in the fighting for liberty. Thanks to the 18th Fructidor, the time is not far distant when empty feelings of distrust will vanish, when Directors in their mansions, writers in their retreats, legislators in their tribune, and soldiers in the camps, will march towards the same goal in unanimous and spontaneous co-operation, and when each one of us shall, secure in his interests, his liberty, and his dearest affections, be able to consecrate, freely and undisturbed, all his faculties to the strengthening of the Republic and the prosperity of the first nation of the world!

Greeting and respect. BENJAMIN CONSTANT.

PARIS, 30*th Frimaire, Year VI.*

Rewbell, who had a large head and severe and grave manners, was at the same time a most passionate man. Trained to legal business early in life, he had more especially taken up cases occurring in a border country, such as Alsace is in regard to Germany, giving rise to discussions wherein public often joins issue with private right. Rewbell had acquired in these discussions a cleverness, a dialectic force which, while strengthening to a high degree his mind against all the sophisms and artifices of interest, had not left him with any high opinion of those who have recourse to them. He believed that, generally speaking, the majority of men, with very few exceptions, were at the very least rascals, and oftentimes wolves who call themselves civilized, spending the short moments of their appearance on this earth in fighting with every kind of weapon for that portion of the fruits spread over its bosom or buried in its bowels. Many reasonings which are freely made use of in this world were looked upon by Rewbell as just so many formulas wherewith to get a share of the good things of this earth without putting the noose round one's neck. It was inevitable that he should pronounce judgments that were often unjust, by weighing all in the same scales—by placing, for example, Mme. de Staël, M. Necker, and Benjamin Constant on the same level with Talleyrand, remarking bluntly: "These are all just so many intriguers." As to the Genevese, he could never credit them with any other aim than that of personal interest which no sentimental reason could ever make them depart from. He rigorously applied all such proverbs as

" Genevois, quand je te vois,
  Rien de bon je n'aperçois,"

or "When a Genevese flings himself out of a window, it is because he still stands a chance of making at the lowest five per cent. out of the performance," to the Necker family—in which he would ever include Benjamin Constant, by reason of his relations with Mme. de Staël, and especially on account of the relations of them all with Talleyrand. I admit that when a man is past forty it is allowable for him not to see the bright side of everything, and not to preserve too great a credulity. Chamfort, with whom I have already stated I was on a most intimate footing, thought that "an honest man could not reach the age of twenty-five without becoming a misanthrope." This man, made to know friendship, did not entertain any great faith in it when separating into three classes those whom one styles friends: those who talk ill of us, those who do us harm, and those who do us neither good nor harm.

I sought to point out to Rewbell that, while admitting as a melancholy generality the perversity of the human race ever since the Fall, there are nevertheless, in the dispute over interests which fill the life of the majority of mankind, a few noteworthy distinctions among those who pounce most eagerly upon the representative of value; to speak plainly, when it comes to those who love money, it is impossible to place on the same level those to whom it is an end and those to whom it is a means. Thus, considering the necessity in which men find themselves of satisfying their real or their factitious needs, such as society admits, it is indispensable that we should have money wherewith to meet these necessaries; men governed by this principle obey a law common to all, and are strictly adhering to it in having recourse to all measures which do not injure their fellow-creatures. They even contribute to their interest by an interchange of reciprocal services; moreover, there being limits to the needs of an individual, the aspirations towards fortune must have limits likewise. As to men to whom fortune seems the end and not the means, who sigh for money, for more money still, without any reference to their needs or caprices, and solely to accumulate more and more of it, "those people, my dear Rewbell," I said to him, " I abandon to you; no excuse can be found for them in the subtle reasoning with which they seek to justify in their own eyes their stupid cupidity. As to the other class, those to whom money is a means, and in whose case money does not rob them of every human thought—people among whom I class Mme. de Staël and M. Necker—this desire for fortune may, within reasonable limits, be inherent in the very sentiment of their independence: their desire has been not to be in the power of others; but in their efforts to amass wealth they have not forsaken the moral side of their human destiny, perhaps they have even deluded themselves into believing that they could better uphold it when rich than when less so. Moreover, the Necker family, if it can be charged with interested views, is not devoid of those lively sentiments which go to prove that it is not with them a matter of cold calculation; all of them, even including Benjamin Constant, are most impassioned creatures, and where there is passion there is hope, there is resource."

All my remarks failed to soften Rewbell in regard to the Genevese. His bitterness against Mme. de Staël was still further increased by people informing him of *mots* spoken against him, *mots* which, without being profoundly spiteful, were piquant to a degree; and what still further fanned the flame of Rewbell's irritation against Mme. de Staël was, that we owed to her Talleyrand's introduction into our affairs, for Rewbell constantly remarked that " Talleyrand was the agglomeration of all plagues, the prototype of treachery and corruption."

I must fain admit, when recalling to my mind all

I know of Talleyrand, that Rewbell was not doing him an injustice when reproaching him with unparalleled treachery and servility. To complete the picture, Rewbell would oftentimes remark: "He is a powdered lackey of the ancient *régime;* at most he could be used as a servant for purposes of parade, were he only provided with a decent pair of legs, but he has no more legs than he has heart." As to the falseness or at least the cunning of Talleyrand, I could not but discern it in his most trifling deeds, and even in his notes to me: when desirous of recommending to me some person of the ancient *régime*, he would always begin, as if seeking to obtain forgiveness for his introduction, by first mentioning the name of some one of quite different position and conduct; thus, having on several occasions begged that he might have the honor of introducing Mme. de la Rochefoucauld to me, he would begin by mentioning some other name, and referring to some other matter. Thus Mme. de la Rochefoucauld, in a two-line note, came after a reference to Kosciuszko, to whom he affected to give precedence. As for me, who was seeking to establish true dignity in the intercourse of the Directorate with individuals as with the foreign Powers, I considered that Talleyrand was going beyond all bounds in, so to speak, forcing to kneel to me persons of the ancient *régime*, especially those of the other sex, and exhibiting them to me in an attitude of humiliation which we were far from requiring; so it was that Mme. de la Rochefoucauld was made—through Talleyrand, it is true— to humbly "beg permission to have the honor of seeing me for one moment." This was more politeness than we required of Talleyrand or of any one else. We have reached only the commencement of his many genuflections.

I have already mentioned the doings of the ambassadors of foreign Powers who, under the pretence of bribing the governments to which they were accredited, obtained enormous sums of money which they were supposed to hand over to those to whom they were destined, but which, as a matter of course, they put into their own pockets. The Portuguese Minister was one of this kind of men, and for some time we had kept an eye on him.

From the 1st to the 16th Nivôse, Year VI.—Davanzo Dazavedo (*sic*) (Araujo de Azevedo) has been arrested. We are informed that 900,000 francs have been given by this Minister of Portugal to those from whom he hoped to obtain a more favorable treaty of peace than the one concluded with the Directorate. Talleyrand seeks to obtain the liberty of M. Davanzo (*sic*).

The best fortified town perhaps of France and Germany, the object of so many sieges and fights, Mayence, is at last occupied by Republican troops.

Augereau is an excellent general of division, *i.e.*, most capable in carrying out orders and acting within a given latitude. The chief command of an army has perhaps excited his imagination. He has believed that his new rank could best be upheld by bluster and luxury; but his blunders are greatly magnified by Bonaparte, who daily brings us notes hostile to Augereau, from emissaries whom he says he placed about him under various pretences when passing through Rastadt. Thus does the man act who two months previously so loudly complained that Augereau had sent to Italy an agent with instructions to spy on him, whereas in reality the agent had been sent on a financial mission. Who, then, has given Bonaparte the right to exercise supervision over a general-in-chief? Although not believing all these denunciations, we are compelled to recognize that so large an army as that of Germany was beyond Augereau's horizon, and we have reduced him to the command of the Upper Rhine. From that moment Augereau becomes more docile and toned down. Hatry, commander of the Army of Mayence, does not reveal himself as rising superior to mediocrity; he is a general of division and nothing more. Happily his post on the Lower Rhine does not give scope for any great development.

The peoples of the Cisalpine Republic are busy revolutionizing; they should receive support.

The loan of eighty millions is decreed: the simple gift has been rejected.

The Directorate orders the general seizure of English merchandise throughout the Republic. A message calls for the confiscation of such merchandise found in the possession of neutrals.

Rewbell is in favor of only threatening England; this is, I think, the wisest course. Bonaparte is of the same opinion; he assures us that it never has been his intention to employ in so uncertain a fashion the brave fellows who have so well served and who will still serve the Republic. "The best thing for it," he would say modestly of the Army of England, "is that I am its general-in-chief. This may give the English food for reflection."

The Directorate is warned from several quarters to doubt the good faith of Spain; the Prince of the Peace, who governs her, is a man of no morality and no principles. Nor do we feel quite safe about Prussia. The very equivocal conduct of Switzerland leads to a proposition to send troops into that country. Should the revolutionizing of Switzerland not rather be brought about by negotiations, for might not open operations once more involve us in a war with Austria and Prussia?

Arbitrary acts committed by the civil and military authorities are denounced from several points; it is time to substitute for the empire of men that of the law. François de Neufchâteau and I move that no person shall be arrested without a warrant, that he shall be heard within twenty-four hours after his arrest, and thereupon immediately sent before a legal tribunal. The Minister of Justice is instructed to see that the laws are enforced.

From the 16th Nivôse to the 20th Pluviôse.—Switzerland engages the attention of the Directorate; the confederation is to be counselled to adopt a representative form of government. Rewbell and Merlin urge that this view be taken by the Directorate, basing their arguments on their daily correspondence with Swiss citizens; they aver that the great majority of the Helvetian nation desires a constitutional government.

The loan is languishing; sinister rumors bruited abroad by the aristocracy alarm credit and cause the tightenings of purse-strings; the faint-hearted are frightened by alleged Jacobin plots; a most important formality prescribed by the law as to the form of the new Public Ledger has been overlooked. It is to the effect that no further opposition shall be entertained against the consolidated Third. The Directorate makes dispositions in conformity with Article 4 of the law relating to regulations: it constitutes the very foundation of public credit. A security which cannot be distrained must take the first rank among all securities in circulation; the consolidated Third cannot fail, considering all the guarantees attached to it, as soon as our affairs shall be in a settled state, to be the best of investments.

François has made fruitless attempts to escape from the Temple, where he is a prisoner. He now offers to serve the Republic by getting over from London a considerable amount of money kept there in reserve for the purpose of feeding the plots formed against the Republic. The Minister of Police, Sotin, is instructed to attend to the matter, which is happily carried out: five thousand louis are received in the first instance, and are paid into the coffers of the police; further sums are to arrive in the same way. The Minister of Police informs us of this successful issue, which, he avers, proves the sincerity of the intentions of François; he moves that he be set free, and merely placed under police supervision.

The public prosecutor of the department of Bas-Rhin writes that the spirit of liberty is manifesting itself on the right bank of the river. The circumstance, which is known to the negotiators at the congress, awakens a hope that they will infuse more celerity into their operations. The Directorate decides that no support shall be given to the agitators, and that the conclusion of a peace shall be frankly proceeded with.

Bonaparte, on the occasion of his continual visits to the Directorate, incessantly urges the revolutionizing of Switzerland. General Brune is at his request appointed commander of the divisions which are to give support to expected uprisings. He is authorized to enter Berne should he deem it necessary. "But on what grounds?" we inquire. "All that is necessary is to pick a quarrel," answers Bonaparte. "How else could I have accomplished anything in all the countries where I have had to substitute the new for the old order of things?" A constitution is drawn up for Switzerland and for Rome; that for Holland has already been despatched.

Cabarrus, Spain's ambassador, is not recognized. The refusal of the Directorate is based on the fact that he was born in France. The Minister of Foreign Affairs is instructed to negotiate with Spain for the union of the States of the Duke of Parma with the Cisalpine Republic. Sardinia is to be granted as compensation to the prince; failing the Sardinian Government's consent, some other possession.

It will be fresh in the reader's memory how our ambassador in Rome, Basseville, was murdered in 1793, and how the too generous French Republic did not avenge this crime. Bonaparte should have borne the matter in mind more than he did at the time of the Treaty of Tolentino. It was not sufficient to have obtained paintings and money; a reparation should have been demanded and solemnly carried out; it might have warded off fresh crimes. Impunity has emboldened fanaticism: a similar scene has just been enacted in the capital of the Catholic world. General Duphot has been murdered as was Basseville. General Berthier is to march on Rome at once, with orders to establish there a constitutional Republican government. This operation and the one in Switzerland are to be carried out by a few columns which were to have joined the Army of England.

Bonaparte shuns society; he seems uneasy; he is

irritated at the Jacobins, and imagines that they are seeking to assassinate him. This species of fright reveals perhaps some of his innermost sentiments; this genuine or false fear of the Jacobins has oftentimes been an indication of the plans of those who, preparing to commit treason, would protect themselves beforehand against censure or punishment. Bonaparte's fear seems to extend to many who should not inspire that sentiment. He is on his guard against what he eats in his own home; nay, when he dines at the Directorate, he partakes only of such dishes as he has seen one of us eat of, or boiled eggs into which no seasoning can have possibly entered, and drinks nothing except what is handed to him by a confidential servant, who follows him always and waits upon him at table. This is the man, so great when with the Army of Italy, who is about to shrink in many other particulars of his life! Do we not see him lay great stress on his decision that his wife shall not call on the wives of the Directors if she is not at once received by the assembled Directorate? If his pretension is not acceded to, he will consider himself insulted and will himself no longer call on the Directorate. Not satisfied with demanding such a reception, he goes the length of finding it unbecoming that the Directors and their wives do not call on him and his wife first, in order to pay their respects to him as well as to Mme. Bonaparte. The General-in-chief of the Army of Italy is beyond doubt entitled to our regard and interest in consideration of the brilliant services he has rendered at the head of one of the armies of the Republic; but, without wishing to remind him of his position previous to his holding this command, what is there to change the etiquette of the relations between the chief magistrates of the French Republic and its civil and military subordinates, whom it appoints or dismisses at will? Bonaparte needs to be in power himself in order to conceive a better idea of the proprieties of life.

The ambition of Bonaparte seemed to increase in his retreat, and not to know on what to pounce. There is a vacant membership, Carnot's, at the Institut; Bonaparte accepts it with eagerness, in spite of the regrets which have previously escaped his lips in regard to what he styles the violent consequences of the 18th Fructidor, to which he has nevertheless contributed more violently than any other individual. It would look more like a sincere expression of regrets not to accept the place of a man who has been transported; for, "Can a murderer inherit from his victim?"

Flatterers, who ever have good reasons to advance in justification of all ambitions, discover a fresh trait of modesty in this conduct of Bonaparte's. "See," they argue, "the title of Member of the Institut is the one he places above all others, and which he will assume in preference to everything." The modest member of the Institut will not be slow in justifying the good opinion held of his simplicity. He makes his appearance in the hall of the Académie, to whose bosom he has just been admitted, some time after Larevellière, our colleague in the Directorate. The latter, if only by virtue of the date of his appointment, made at the time of the creation of the Institut, is naturally seated previous to the new-comer. He has a twofold right to such preference being shown him, because of his age and perhaps of his high political position. But, forsooth, here is Bonaparte offended because he has seen Larevellière enter and take a seat ahead of him! He calls this preference scandalous. My colleague, unable to understand this outbreak of haughty temper, and believing that I still possess some influence over my former *protégé*, begs me to speak to him on the subject. I do so, employing every precaution not to offend him. I address to him a few friendly reproaches, which it would not seem he could possibly take amiss. Bonaparte, without vouchsafing any reply whatsoever in regard to the cause of his irritation, abruptly tells me that he will not go to Rastadt. I reply to him with the dignity imposed on us by duty that "the Republic will not lack negotiators." Bonaparte looks at me confused and with downcast eyes; then, after a moment's thought, recognizing that the glory of a pacificator, which he has known so well how to snatch from others, is likely to be shared with another, he corrects himself, and tells me that he accepts the Rastadt mission.

In the mind of Bonaparte, to go to Rastadt was simply to gain so much more time to remain in Paris, in order to hold dominion over the Government and impose his will on it in all matters. On one of the occasions when, seeking as usual to make us break off the bargain, Bonaparte had spoken of tendering his resignation, Rewbell, who had a moment before taught him that he had no right to sit at the Directorial table, said to him: "Step forward, general; here is a pen: the Directorate awaits your letter." François de Neufchâteau and myself put a stop to the quarrel. Bonaparte did not sign his resignation; far from it, he formally apologized to the Directorate, and to Rewbell personally.

Rewbell was credited with having a very large fortune; this was a calumny countenanced by the hatred of Sieyès, who, having dreaded being his colleague in the Directorate, had attempted to give moral scruples as a reason for this. He was in the habit of telling, in connection with Rewbell's mission to Holland, stories which might go to prove that Rewbell was economical, but not that he was a thief—which did not prevent Sieyès from saying continually: "*Rewbell a volé sans ailes au Directoire; il y vole encore.*[1] He has to *take* something every day for his health!" However this might be, Mme. Bonaparte thought that Rewbell was exceedingly wealthy, and this was quite sufficient for her; in her eyes it was not necessary that he should be equally honest. Mme. Bonaparte and her husband therefore intended that Hortense de Beauharnais should become the bride of young Rewbell, on their return from Italy. I mentioned the matter to Rewbell, who absolutely refused to entertain the idea. "We are," he said to me, "good Alsacian folk, and not fit to cope in the matter of marriage with a daughter of Mme. de Beauharnais and with a Corsican father-in-law."

And now come disturbances of another kind. A few young men with black coat-collars and wearing *cadenettes*, who have come safely out of the 13th Vendémiaire and the 18th Fructidor, thinking it an easy matter once more to indulge in the bluster and threats already so often repressed by the Republi-

---

[1] There is here a play on the word *voler*, which in French means both "to steal" and "to fly."—Translator's note.

cans, have established headquarters at the Café Carchy, where they daily muster in numbers, insulting citizens whom they suspect of patriotism. A few military men at present in Paris consider it behooves them to do police duty in this resort. Without having received this mission from any one but themselves, they proceed to the Café Carchy. The insolent *habitués* imagine that they can, as is their wont, set at defiance the citizens who enter and are suspected of Republican opinions; but toleration is a thing of the past. Sides are formed; chairs are freely used as weapons; then swords are drawn. An aide-de-camp of Augereau is wounded; he was a colonel who was in the habit of boasting of his patriotism, and even laid claim to a reward for his conduct on the 18th Fructidor. How came it, then, that he was hand in glove on this occasion with the aristocracy, which fled as fast as its legs would carry it? Men without principles are always found in bad company.

I have previously and in due course recorded Bonaparte's behavior on several occasions. At the time of the first celebration by the Directorate of the anniversary of the 21st of January in the Year IV., previous to his departure for the Army of Italy, this first anniversary since the installation of the Directorate had in a certain way been mixed up with the *fêtes* of his journey with Mme. de Beauharnais. He has now returned, after an absence of two years undoubtedly well filled. The anniversary of the 21st of January is once more approaching. Bonaparte, in spite of the glory which surrounds the conqueror of Italy, holds in Paris neither any political function nor any active military command compelling him to be present in any capacity at this new ceremony; but the high position he has assumed since his return seems to give him the right to appear at all times side by side with those in power. The Directorate has suffered itself to be so thoroughly imbued with this idea, that Merlin brings up for discussion the question " whether or not Bonaparte shall take part in the ceremony: should he be absent from it, is it not to be feared that his absence will detract from the popularity of the ceremony; while if he attends it, will he not attract greater attention than the Directorate?" Other trifling particulars, worthy of Merlin, are also put forward, and have no other result, after both sides of the question have been duly weighed, than to leave the Directorate in a state of uncertainty. Finally it is decided that policy requires the presence of General Bonaparte. Talleyrand—who in order to become a Minister, and since he is one, has sought to persuade us, individually and collectively, that he was "a *conventionnel* and a regicide at heart," and that he had shared in all our revolutionary responsibilities—is instructed to confer with Bonaparte about the matter.

At this point the scene changes, or rather the man reveals himself, and is about to unveil the new system he would still prefer to conceal, but which appears in spite of him; he who two years ago displayed so much excitement over the anniversary of the King's death, seems nowadays no longer to remember his former views, and seeks to escape from the consequences of his previous conduct. He replies with a cold and grave demeanor to the officious and yet official invitation of Talleyrand that he holds no public office; that personally the celebration does not concern him; that, without pretending to discuss whether the sentence passed on Louis XVI. was salutary or noxious, he is of opinion that it was an unfortunate incident; that it was well enough to celebrate national *fêtes* in honor of victories, but that one should mourn those whose bodies strewed the battle-field.

Talleyrand replied that the anniversary *fête* of the 21st of January was proper, inasmuch as it was politic; that it was politic because every country and every republic had always celebrated as a triumph the downfall of absolute power and the killing of tyrants: thus Athens had always celebrated the death of Pisistratus, and Rome that of the Decemvirs; moreover, it was a law which governed the country; all were bound to bow to and obey it; lastly, the influence of the General of the Army of Italy over public opinion was such that he ought to appear at the ceremony, as his absence might be harmful to the interests of the Commonweal. After much parleying, a middle term was found: the Institut was going to the *fête*, and so it was agreed that Bonaparte should attend in the capacity of a member of that body. Talleyrand, with an air of self-satisfaction, pronounced his allocution, which was really of a fairly pronounced Republican type; it united all present at the ceremony. The Republican oath of Chénier was rendered with full orchestral accompaniment; the following lines attracted attention:

> Si quelque usurpateur vient asservir la France,
> Qu'il éprouve aussitôt la publique vengeance,
> Qu'il tombe sous le fer, que ses membres sanglants
> Soient livrés dans la plaine aux vautours dévorants!

> S'il en est qui veulent un maître,
> De Rois en Rois dans l'univers,
> Qu'ils aillent mendier des fers,
> Ces Français, indignes de l'être !

Were I not as sure as I am of the facts I have daily committed to paper, my narrative would receive confirmation from the actors themselves, who have since spoken in no uncertain tones. It is in the narratives of the alleged publicists of the Court of St. Helena, writing at the dictation or under the inspiration of their master, that I find the authenticity which might be denied to what I assert from personal recollection; the same facts are again related in memoirs recently published, and which are brought to me just as I am finishing my own (Thibaudeau, *Guerres d'Italie*, vol. iii., 1828). He can certainly not be charged with hostility towards Bonaparte; he has served him religiously and rigorously from the time of his advent to power to that of his two abdications or dethronements inclusively. As to the behavior of Talleyrand on this occasion, the witnesses to it are all of my colleagues of the Directorate. I could, moreover, supply further proofs of the pronounced Republicanism of Talleyrand, as well as of the peculiar species of his sincere attachment to the dynasty and persons of the Bourbons, under circumstances when he was displaying a luxury of patriotism altogether gratuitous, and carried far beyond anything that the most exacting Republicans could have asked of him, causing us occasionally to remark jokingly in regard to the limping spurts of the former Bishop of Autun: "What, monseigneur, without being compelled to do so!"

Bonaparte and Augereau are completely at variance. Masséna is no less displeased with his former general-in-chief, who seems to regret all he has ever said to the credit of these two generals at the time they were performing heroic deeds under him in Italy. Nowadays Bonaparte looks upon Augereau and Masséna as merely a couple of thieves, one of whom is perhaps a little braver or less cowardly than the other.

Peace, coming after a war of six years, had left a large number of generals without commands; it was a most difficult thing for the Government to satisfy all these men, who had acquired habits of activity akin to perpetual motion, and who had conceived towards the close of the war a desire for wealth, for which glory could not compensate. As it is in human nature oftentimes to deceive one's self as to one's own desires, while seeking to deceive others, many of these military men, following upon all the hardships they had endured, believed themselves to be aspiring to a well-earned rest, and sought to play the *rôle* of Cincinnatus. Bernadotte, who could readily be classed in the category of both deceivers and deceived, talked of nothing else but rest; he dreamed that he would like to retire to some country-place—or rather, he publicly proclaimed that to be his dream. This is at least what he was wont to say to me with the outpouring of what he was in the habit of styling the innermost thought of his "bowels." I could see in this exordium, which preceded a request for employment, another trait of the cleverness displayed by men about to petition those who are in power. I knew, moreover, how subtle were the men of the South, especially those from the land of Bernadotte, characterized by the proverb,

Feez é cortez ("False and courteous"). Pretending not to understand the subtle Béarnais, I told him that he could not possibly think of forsaking the military career while in the flower of his age, and especially in the presence of an expedition so important as the one being prepared against England. "The Directorate reckons on you," I added, "and reserves for you the command of one of the principal divisions of the Army of England." Bernadotte thanked me with all the marks of a respectful and affectionate gratitude, allowing, however, the remark to escape that he feared the general-in-chief would not treat him with all the consideration to which he was entitled; that from the very time he had joined the Army of Italy with his division of the Army of Sambre-et-Meuse he had had cause to complain of Bonaparte's treatment of him; that he had, by way of a pastime, sought to stir a civil war in his army; that he had not found him, Bernadotte, who boasted of "being a Republican in his very bowels," Republican enough—he, Bernadotte, who prided himself on being a child of the Revolution, one of the born soldiers of liberty, of that liberty to which he owed his successive promotions on the field of battle. "And yet I must confess," he went on to say, "that I was a non-commissioned officer, and on very good terms with my colonel." "And with your colonel's wife," I remarked, with a smile. (She was a Mme. d'A——; she had become enamoured of her sergeant, who had a smart appearance, and in particular a pair of well-shaped legs: he was nicknamed "Sergeant Belle-Jambe.") Bernadotte looked down with a modesty which nowise denied Mme. d'A——, and went on to say: "I have never bowed and will never bow to any tyranny; I pride myself on being a determined Jacobin, in life and unto death." Bernadotte told me, in support of all these fine utterances, that he had not in the least absented himself or held aloof on the 18th Fructidor, as had been unjustly said of him; he was ready to serve the Directorate if a sign had been made to him: in which case, perhaps, the aristocrats, the counter-revolutionists, the Royalists—in a word, all the monsters who do not belong to the human species, would have had a harder time with him than with General Augereau. "By the living God!" exclaimed our Béarnais, in a loud voice (this was his usual form of Béarnais oath), "if I had but had in front of me all those vile slaves, those satellites of tyranny, this sword so familiar to the Austrians would have made the acquaintance of the aristocrats of my country! They shall become acquainted with it, by the living God!" he repeated, in a tone which would have been heard beyond the precincts of the Luxembourg Palace had we not been in the farthest closet of my apartment. "I am glad to meet once more such noble energy," I replied to General Bernadotte; "you are a true Republican, and none better than you can serve our country; there are still several campaigns left in you." "I have over twenty campaigns in the belly at the disposal of the Directorate," answered Bernadotte, with increased energy, and waving the big sword which we carried in those days; his black eyes were glistening, and the nostrils of his big nose were distended. This is the way General Bernadotte was quietly aspiring to retirement and rest in the country. I remarked laughingly to him: "In this way, general, you will not have rested too long; it will have been the rest of Hercules. You have hardly entered upon your military career; you have not yet begun building up your personal fortune. In order to be able to retire to a cottage and to grow vegetables, one must first have a cottage." "Perfectly true," said Bernadotte, with a deeply concerned and confused air, and pressing my hands; "'tis true, and only too true, that I own nothing, not even a cottage. I could hardly buy one with my savings. Indeed, and what do they amount to? To 50,000 francs, given me as a gratuity by General Bonaparte on the mines of Hydria, conquered by my division, and which he has appropriated to himself, while giving us a few crumbs fallen from his table. Now what do 50,000 francs amount to considering our mode of life? Both in town and in country we are compelled to spend more than formerly. When with the Army of Sambre-et-Meuse it was wool and wool alone; on joining the Army of Italy it was gold all over the uniforms, boots, horse-cloths, and the horses' bits. How different all this from the first years of our wars! In those days I used to say in all sincerity that, were I able to acquire a capital of 10,000 francs, I would consider myself the most fortunate of men; yes, in those days I would indeed have gone quietly back to the place of my birth; nowadays, with savings amounting to 50,000 francs, I have just enough to tide me over a year. It is true I get 25,000 francs when on the active list, but is that enough for a general of division to keep up appearances with?"

It will be seen from all this how little Bernadotte dreamed of rest, how little he thought of a cottage, of vegetables, and of retiring, when neither ordinary nor extraordinary gratuities and salaries any longer satisfied him; and when it is considered that the wishes just confessed to by him were much more modest than any of those which were to bud forth afterwards, this modesty will bear a close resemblance to virtue when compared with the future.

"With me you recognize," I said to Bernadotte, "that you must serve for a long time to come, and with still further honor; with this idea, worthy of you, in my mind, I take leave of you. You shall very shortly receive your letter of service."

A few days after this conference Bernadotte wrote to the Directorate, asking a command in the Islands of France and Réunion or in the Ionian Isles, an infantry inspectorship, employment in the Army of Portugal, or his retirement. In order to free himself from the quasi-bond by which he feared to be connected with the General-in-chief of the Army of England, he sent a copy of his letter to Bonaparte, begging him, in case his retirement should be granted to him, to give employment to two of his aides-de-camp in the Army of England. These two aides-de-camp were men destined to attain some day the highest rank in the French army. They were Captains Gérard and Maison, who will later be seen occupying the highest military positions. Thus was Bernadotte, in his hour of spleen, truly making a present to Bonaparte. Unfortunately for the men whom he recommended, he accompanied their introduction with a sentence likely to do them much harm with a man who, like Bonaparte, hated nothing so much in those with whom he was to come into relations as their superior as an independence of character which might at times clash with his imperious will. "Like me," wrote Bernadotte, "they will bow to talent, but never to audacity; although I have grounds for complaint against you, I shall part from them without ceasing to hold your talents in the highest esteem."

I replied officially to the foregoing request of Bernadotte, on being so empowered by my colleagues, in the following terms: "The Directorate intended that you should command one of the principal divisions of the Army of England; but if reasons which it cannot foresee cause you to prefer the military command of the Ionian Isles, the Directorate will gladly intrust you with it. It awaits your reply." Bonaparte was aware of the answer I had been instructed to make to Bernadotte, for he knew everything that took place in the Directorate; he would even have wished that nothing should be done in it except by his order or permission. The letter Bernadotte had written to him was in the nature of a challenge; Bonaparte pretended not to look at it in such a light; acting in this as a man who had the art of self-control, he replied to Bernadotte, complimenting him on the purity of his principles, the uprightness of his character, and his military talents. In another letter he told him, in the most flattering terms, that he should like to have had him by his side in England, but that it seemed that the Government believed his presence necessary in Italy; that this post was of so vital an importance that he must resign himself to occupying it. He added that he would on all occasions give him proofs of the regard in which he held him.

But at the same time that he was writing to him in this honeyed style, Bonaparte was harboring more strongly the resentment he had repressed; he was, to use a vulgar expression, "working" Bernadotte, seeking to have him looked upon as a very ordinary soldier with limited intellectual capacities, who should be nothing more than a general of division, and never command in chief; and it was precisely because he pretended to be pleased at Bernadotte's holding the command-in-chief of the Army of Italy that he tried to prove to us that it was a serious mistake, that the post required a man more broken into harness, one in fact trained by him to well understand and manage Italians. In this regard he did not so far see any one better than Berthier or certain others, Brune among the number perhaps, but above all, anybody but Bernadotte.

The Directorate had already appointed Bernadotte *in petto;* we had even instructed our secretary-general to draw up the enactment, which was done. On learning this, Bonaparte loudly raised his voice against what he called a blunder and an actual danger for France as well as for Italy. On failing to get us to chime in with his severe judgment of Bernadotte, he saw fit to follow another course—that of praising Bernadotte, doing justice to his qualities, except those required to take chief command of the Army of Italy, or the chief command of any army. "Bernadotte," he said, "is amiable, full of seductive power, shrewd, and crafty; diplomacy claims him as its own; he must be started in this career; the highest post in it should be given to him, in order doubly to overpower first our enemies, by forcing them to accept a soldier of the Republic, and next the titled enemy at home, who would like to see diplomatic posts the exclusive property of the nobility, by sending a plebeian to that Austria which is so stiff in the matter of etiquette, and demands no less than sixteen quarterings." All these intrigues and many others resulted in the command of the Army of Italy being taken from Bernadotte; and we appointed him to the Vienna embassy.

It will be seen from the foregoing particulars, which I recollect as well as the day they happened, how little sincerity existed in the minds of Bonaparte and Bernadotte in their mutual dealings, and what such resentful feelings foreboded. Considerations of policy postponed an explosion. After having revealed, perhaps somewhat severely, the weak side of Bernadotte as a public man, I should consider myself worthy of censure were I to overlook traits which reflect credit on the private individual. Bernadotte had heard of the arrest of the colonel of his old regiment of *Royal Marine*, in which he had served as a private and as a sergeant; this was the Marquis d'A——, who, proscribed pursuant to the law against the *émigrés*, had been recognized while strolling about Paris, arrested, and turned over to a military commission. It was on this occasion that Bernadotte's sincere and generous soul stood revealed to us. He promptly called on the Directorate to beg that his former colonel's offence might be condoned. " It is," he said, " the only price I ask for my services." Bernadotte had already on a former occasion, at the time of a riot in Marseilles in 1789, saved the life of M. d'A——; in those days he was nothing more than a sergeant. Bernadotte become a general was not to be so successful on this occasion. He had to deal with a Director, a former Minister of Justice, a man far more terrible than the popular fury of the early days of the Revolution. I moved that M. d'A—— be conducted to the frontier. Merlin called for his execution, which took place. M. d'A——'s wife had been and was, so it was said, the mistress of Bernadotte; even if his devotion was thus further stimulated, it was none the less an act of genuine devotion worthy of the esteem of all honest hearts.

So here is Bernadotte appointed ambassador to Vienna. Berthier has clumsily awaited orders from the Directorate before taking Rome. The government of Naples, alarmed, protests that it will not stir. England is somewhat uneasy in regard to the preparations making against her by France; it compels her to keep up a ruinous military establishment.

Hamburg solicits our protection; we ask twelve millions in exchange for it.

General Dubayet, our ambassador in Constantinople, has just died there. He was an upright and witty gentleman, somewhat giddy, perhaps, in his private life, but believing sincerely in liberty and incapable of doing anything dishonorable.

Letters received from Strasburg convey to us the information that an attempt is making to compromise Rewbell; that Augereau is at the head of the party planning this scheme; that letters are being forged against this Director, in connection with his former mission to Mayence. Bonaparte is everlastingly plaguing us in seeking to prove to us that Augereau should be deprived of the command of the Army of Germany, a portion of which has already been taken from him; in order to remove far from France all the generals with whom he has had dealings, he would like to make so many diplomatists of them. And having caused Bernadotte to be sent to Vienna, he would now like to see Augereau sent to Constantinople; only a while ago he was daily depicting him to us as a boor, and he can hardly make him an elegant personage at this juncture; but he argues that the men Turkey requires are men imposing by their physical stature and deportment; this is why he absolutely desires that Augereau should go to Turkey. The Directorate, whom Bonaparte tells daily that Augereau is a man devoid of moderation, can hardly confer upon him there and then a post requiring this quality to a high degree, even in Constantinople; although the forms of the people of Turkey are less gentle and flattering than those of Europeans, still they too have their policy, which demands no less prudence and serious thought than that of other governments. Besides, always their own masters at home, since even when they receive ambassadors they do not deign to do other governments the honor of sending ambassadors in return, the Turks have very little intercourse with the Christians; when such intercourse is granted it causes heart-burnings among all the residents of Pera, who eagerly seek it, engaged as they are in spying upon one another, in order to appear in the eyes of their respective Courts to be doing something. For many other reasons the Directorate is in no way inclined to admit that, even if General Augereau is unfit to be the commander-in-chief of an army, he should therefore be made an ambassador.

From the 10*th to the* 30*th Pluviôse, Year VI.*—Meanwhile Bonaparte continues urging us to pursue a different course. He brings us fresh letters from

Strasburg, announcing that the Jacobins, with Augereau at their head, are intriguing against the Government, and against Rewbell personally. The police agent who supplies all this information goes so far as to assert that on an occasion when he made a call on Augereau he saw on the table of that general letters affording conclusive proof of his accusations. I point out to the Directorate that if it was myself instead of Rewbell who chanced to be the object of Augereau's malevolence, I should ask that the matter be treated with supreme contempt. I should go even further than showing contempt: I should demand that the informer be proceeded against, and not the person informed upon. He may be, nay, he must be, a liar and a calumniator; for of what is a man not capable who glides furtively into the library of a citizen in order to violate the secrecy of his letters? Is he sure that they were his? Has he even seen any? "Nevertheless," says Rewbell, alarmed, with Bonaparte as his prompter, "we can no longer defer adopting a course in regard to so imprudent and insolent a general, who, if he is not checked, will get perilously near rebellion." We decide that Augereau shall be deprived of the command of the Army of Germany, and at once proceed to the Pyrenees, with instructions to organize the Army of Portugal.

It would indeed be difficult to know what Bonaparte really desires just now, if any attention is to be paid to his utterances, for they are all disconnected and incoherent: one day he is all for moderation; the next he is the champion of Jacobinism and the instigator of severe measures. His conversations do not reveal what is uppermost in his mind.

Bonaparte, when questioned in regard to the 18th Fructidor, would say: "It was a *coup d'état* against the Constitution; it will authorize others; there is for me no security except in Barras. How comes it that he did not grasp this new opportunity of seizing power? He has a strong party at his back throughout the country. Such a *coup d'état* would have been an easy matter and sure of success; even the Clichy Club would not have opposed it. When Barras became president of the Directorate I did not think he would turn over the position to another. He is a daring man only in a crisis; had he but called me to the Directorate, the *coup d'état* would have succeeded; he told me that in his eyes my youth was an objection to my entering the Directorate. I might have assisted him in this great enterprise, after driving out those who sat with him. It is a blunder which he will some day repent. Popular favor is like a storm: it passes quickly." "Why did not you who have passed through the Revolution with Barras," he said to Fouché and to Réal, "use your influence to determine him on following such a course? Another, less scrupulous, will attain the goal."

Here now are the Royalists reinforced by some hot-headed fools inveighing against the events of Thermidor and Fructidor; as a consequence of this union of homicide and liberticide, calumny is set in motion against the authors of the great deeds which have saved the Republic. England is paying the agitators, whose mission is to sow discord among the Republicans.

Augereau, aware of the reason which has caused him to be despatched to the Pyrenees, submits with resignation to his fate; although he has not been prohibited from passing through Paris on his way, he sees fit to abstain from so doing, and goes direct to Perpignan. His conduct proves what I was already fully convinced of—to wit, that if he has had little control over his tongue, and has momentarily indulged in bluster and indiscreet utterances, all this exuberance is redeemed by sincere patriotism. The man who took upon himself to execute the perilous *coup d'état* of the 18th Fructidor cannot be treated without consideration by the members of the Directorate, whom he on that day saved from ruin and from death. Moreover, we learn from several quarters that Augereau was perhaps led astray by one Izard, an ex-priest, now his first aide-de-camp. The Directorate decides that Izard shall be employed as adjutant-general in the Army of England. Izard comes to Paris.

The Elector of the Palatinate imagines that the Directorate has conceived the plan of seizing upon his dominions; in consequence of this, he calls upon England, Russia, Prussia, and Austria to come to his rescue. Rewbell moves that, as a reply to his feeling of terror, the General of the Army of Mayence be instructed immediately to occupy Mannheim. It is resolved first to confer with the Ministers of War and of Foreign Affairs, who also spoke of the matter to Bonaparte, already informed of everything before ourselves; for nothing can any longer be done by the Directorate without him.

Switzerland is in full ferment; the instructions given to Brune are that he shall enter the Vaud country, and Berne by main force, if any resistance is encountered. Two soldiers belonging to the aide-de-camp of the General-in-chief are assassinated by the Swiss. Vaud accepts the constitution proposed to it. Berthier marches on Rome. The papal government offers up prayers; commissioners are instructed to establish a constitution and a representative government.

Spain is in the toils of several parties. The Court of Madrid, with the exception of the Prince of the Peace, is bodily sold to England. The Aragonese party is said to be the most powerful; the queen is said to have quarrelled with the Prince of the Peace. This weak and incapable Minister comes to no determination; he causes secret messages to be sent to the Directorate, entreating it to come to his help. The Directorate instructs Perrochette, our envoy, to see the queen and to bring about a reconciliation between her and the prince. He is to warn the queen that she is ruining her cause, and that she will become the victim of the English. Her natural ally is the French Republic; she must rally to us and expel the English from the Spanish possessions. We consent to her and the king acting as arbitrators to put an end to the dispute with Portugal; if she succeeds in re-establishing our friendly relations by means of a suitable treaty, she will escape seeing a Republican army pass through her territory; in the contrary case, a French army will advance at the expense of the districts it will pass through and at that of Portugal. This latter Power shall be mulcted in a contribution of eighty millions.

Dissension stimulated by our enemies is beginning to invade the Directorate. The incoming of the new Third of the *corps législatif* is already looked upon as a subject of alarm, in an opposite sense to that which rendered necessary the 18th Fructidor. Two members of the Directorate seek to terrify the others with alleged sinister plots of the Jacobins. They pretend that Sotin, the Minister of Police, encourages them.

This Minister is dismissed. Merlin had immediately asked that Sotin's place be given to Dondeau; Rewbell and I, who have never heard of this individual, vote against his appointment, pending such time as we shall have information about him. But, Sotin having been dismissed, the Ministry of Police cannot remain untenanted at so awkward a juncture; hence Dondeau's appointment is at once determined upon, doubtless as a counterpart to that of Letourneur. It is to Merlin that we owe the selection of both these nullities. This Director seems to be under the impression that a Minister of Police cannot be dispensed with even for the space of twenty-four hours; besides, he is uneasy about various matters; he is particularly furious at General Beurnonville, yet another nullity, more deserving of contempt than of anger, even if he has, as alleged, spoken somewhat disrespectfully of the Director Merlin.

From the 1st to the 4th Ventôse, Year VI.—In order to give support to the elections, the Directorate considers it is its duty to send new agents to its commissioners in the departments, that the lists may be presented to them of those whom it is desired to have as deputies to the *corps législatif;* unfortunately these lists, drawn up under the influence of passions, omit in spite of me such excellent patriots as Bentabole, Dubois de Crancé (*sic*), Hardy, Guy-Vernon, Lamarque, Auguis, Chazal, and others. The last-named is the only one in whose favor I have been able to plead successfully; they will none of Jourdan, but insist on having Rivaud.

Letters received from police agents at Perpignan are full of information about Augereau. He is still looked upon as a Jacobin. The Directorate persists in retaining Schérer as Minister of War. Isos asks that the Directorate order the closing of all the clubs in Perpignan. This proposition brings up that of closing all clubs. Still, we content ourselves with the former. The only idea uppermost seems to be to govern without tolerating any opposition. Is the Government once more about to give heed to words spoken in conversation or transmitted by the press? I foresee that the course followed by the Directorate, if it once more gives way to passion, will necessarily excite serious denunciations in the *corps législatif.* The deputies whom one does not wish to see will nevertheless appear there.

Berthier has entered Rome; he has left both temporal and spiritual power in the Pope's hands. Can the maintenance of such a government offer any security to the French? It is proposed to seize the Pope and his family and convey them to Portugal.

The new Minister of Police, Dondeau, is introduced at a sitting of the Directorate; he begins by saying that he has come to enlighten us as to the state of the public mind. "It has improved," he goes on to state, "in spite of a few individuals who cling to my predecessor; nevertheless, I have many partisans, and on the whole people are glad that I have stepped into Sotin's shoes, public opinion is daily growing more favorable to me." The speech of this police Démazures would have continued in the same strain had we not interrupted his monologue, which was to us a source of as much embarrassment as mirth. As soon as this too ridiculous individual had gone his way, I inquired who was to take his place. We could not keep such a man for another three days without covering ourselves with shame.

We had, so far, not been represented in Spain by our ambassador. What was in this respect General Pérignon? Nothing but a wretched, bragging soldier, in spite of his claiming to have received a few sabre-cuts on the field of battle. He was an example of braggadocio coupled with the most absolute incapacity. Moreover, he was a man of very little delicacy in money matters. He had continually allowed himself to be duped, in order to receive presents and compliments; he had indulged in smuggling in an altogether shameless fashion—smuggling, indeed, of such a nature that it is not allowable even in an ambassador; it was therefore meet that a successor should be found to him. Men of every shade of opinion had long since called for this. Simultaneously, the best thing to have done would have been to have reinstated Truguet as Minister of Marine; he had conducted himself well while occupying the post. I was quite prepared to adopt this course, but it was sufficient that we had dismissed him, even unjustly, "and all the more so because it was done unjustly," to quote Rewbell, for us not to take him back as Minister. Rewbell said that it would be tantamount to taking a step backwards, and he was continually remarking that "a government which takes a step backward is exposing itself to ruin." If this maxim is good up to a certain point, it is in respect to reasonable persons and things. I had heard tell in my youth that the prince of a great house was in the habit of remarking that "France had shown herself poor-spirited, and that Louis XVI. had perished because he had not taken M. de Calonne back as his Minister." I have heard men of the highest merit reply to the comment of this prince, who was very young then, and who has perhaps not ceased to be so: "It was not because Calonne was dismissed, but because he was chosen for Minister a single day, a single moment, that the French monarchy perished through this very notion that no step should be taken backwards." It was decided that Truguet should be sent to Spain to take Pérignon's place. Truguet rightly considered himself more adapted to the administration of naval matters than to diplomacy; but, as has just been shown, it was impossible to come to any understanding with Rewbell, who was of a most determined character, and assuredly the strongest-minded man in the Directorate, and not to be shaken in his obstinacy, which he called *a governmental principle;* Rewbell persisted in maintaining that the taking back of a man who had once before been a Minister would constitute an actual danger; nothing was therefore left but for Truguet to go to Spain. That wooden-leg Pléville le Péley was consequently retained as Minister of Marine; he was a most obsequious man and an adept at flattery, with boorish ways generally called bluntness, or rather the coarseness tolerated in sailors: these manners often conceal craftiness; but a leg lost in the wars serves as an answer to many things, and this answer must have sufficed to Pléville to help him as Minister until he was replaced by a man shrewder than himself, and perhaps shrewder than all others, because he was their superior in morality, which much enhances the estimate of the power of a man's shrewdness.

The consequences of the 18th Fructidor would sometimes carry us back to particulars which we had not grasped at the time. "Do you know," said Talleyrand to me one day with a confidential and mysterious smile, "to what an extent you showed resolution and deserved well of the Fatherland on the 18th Fructidor, when it was announced in the evening at Rewbell's residence that Carnot had escaped? The two members of the Directorate who had joined hands with you were continually saying, in their fright: 'If Barras does not act with vigor, Carnot will place himself at the head of the Royalists.'" From this fact Talleyrand drew the conclusion that we had on the 18th Fructidor acted in self-defence, and that had Carnot been killed at the time, it would have been most legitimately, since it is better to kill the devil than to suffer one's self to be killed by him.

From the very first days of his return from Italy Bonaparte had cast on France an ambitious eye; it would have been difficult not to notice it; but in order to divert attention from his designs on his real prey, he sought to direct our attention into other channels. It was patent to us, although he naturally enough felt a desire to speak of Italy, where he had been so actively engaged for two years that many of his utterances about Italy were merely a roundabout way of censuring or complimenting France. It had been impossible not to recognize this hidden thought in many of his doings in Italy, in the phantom-like constitutions with which he had endowed several parts of that country, and even in his farewell addresses to the Italians; but Rewbell and I were all attention, and were not his dupes. We were not afraid of letting him know it. Every time that he came to pay us a call at the Directorate he seemed to quiver with suppressed agitation, and would stamp with impatience if kept waiting a few moments. We would at times mischievously enjoy the pleasure of keeping him waiting a little while; and when, having entered, he would seek to sit in Directorial fashion at our table, just as if he were a colleague, we would repulse his familiarity with excessive politeness by giving him a chair which was not one of ours. It was difficult not to notice the angry cloud overshadowing his face, but this was far from intimidating us, and almost amused us. Less ceremonious in my apartments, whither he would come of an evening, I was in the habit of doing him the honors of the sofa, although I often made other people take a seat on it beside him, in order to give him a few lessons in the equality he seemed so inclined to forget and trample upon. One fine evening, possessed with the need of forever speaking of himself, since he could no longer, as in Italy, do so by means of bulletins and proclamations, he was telling me, without anything having led up to it, but with singular animation, "of the docility of the Italian peoples, of the ascendency he had had over them:" they had been desirous of creating him "Duke of Milan, King of Italy;" from the very outset of his talk I could hardly conceal my feelings. Bonaparte, perceiving with his incomparable promptness that I saw that he was feeling his ground, checked himself, while seeming to pursue his theme, and said to me, "But I do not dream of anything of the kind in any country." "You do well not to dream of such a thing in France," was my answer, "for were the Directorate to send you to the Temple to-morrow, as the reward of such thoughts, there would not be found four persons to oppose such a course; you must remember that we live under a Republic." Whereupon the man who had until then feigned to be simply telling a story in ingenious fashion, and who had appeared to be recalling something connected with bygone days and other climes, seemed to become a prey to a feeling of irritation he could not control; he leaped up from the sofa, and at one bound rushed towards the mantel-piece, quickly recovering that kind of apparent calm which is one of the best-studied artifices practised in Italy, and is actually the height of knavery. Mme. de Staël called to see me next morning, and asked me about Bonaparte questions which seemed, as if by a species of intuition, to divine this very anecdote. I told her of the scene exactly as it had happened; Mme. de Staël has most truthfully recorded it.

The little success Bonaparte met in putting out

feelers of this kind made, as he confessed, his sojourn in Paris unbearable. He was continually remarking that it was the hot-bed of intrigue; however well-grounded such a reproach may always be when addressed to a great aggregation of men called civilized, there is good authority for believing that in all that town "of mud and smoke" there was no intriguing to be compared with that of Bonaparte. To cut it short, while still showing him some consideration, we invited him to make a general inspection of the Army of England, which was already scattered along the coast. The word "inspection" not seeming to him quite the proper one, he asked that the word "review" be substituted. "A review then," was our reply. Off he went to visit the seacoast. It was the matter of a fortnight. On his return to Paris, he affected to believe that the expedition to England was not seriously entertained; and truly the Directorate had no other intention than that of threatening this Power; but Bonaparte was in quest of an outlet for his ambition, and was going about seeking whom he might devour.

An expedition to Egypt had several times been mooted, but the idea had not found acceptance with the Directorate. With Rewbell, I was altogether opposed to it. In vain did Bonaparte, amid a mass of sophisms, the children of his lively imagination, assure us that, once master of Egypt, he would establish connection with the potentates of India, and with them attack the English in their possessions; all that I knew of India from personal experience confirmed me in the belief that the English Government was unassailable in that portion of Asia as long as it remained master of the seas. How, indeed, could it be conceived that after occupying fertile Egypt Bonaparte could lead his army to India through deserts, without provisions, and under a burning sun; that he could deliver the peoples of Hindustan from the English yoke, conclude advantageous treaties with the Indian princes, and thus procure us the exclusive trade of the peninsula of Coromandel and Malabar? All my objections were met with a plan traced on a map; we all know that no obstacles are ever to be met with in maps. But something absolutely new was wanted by the man who, after having sounded all parties since his return to Paris, was all the time trying to get into the Directorate as its fifth member, as he could not yet become sole Director; he realized that the time was not yet at hand; still he did not wish to run the risk of perishing or languishing in men's imaginations; he therefore daily became more pressing in urging the Directorate to give effect to this expedition to Egypt, which had repeatedly been discussed.

I have just stated that neither Rewbell nor I approved of the expedition to Egypt. After lengthy debates on the matter, I still persisted in my opposition; but Bonaparte had held great private conversations with Larevellière, and although only two days before he had ridiculed the theophilanthropy of our colleague, he had discovered in him an imagination which could easily be worked upon, and had given Larevellière hope that this new cult which Larevellière was destining to Europe might be carried into Africa and Asia. After having taken possession of Larevellière's mind and excited him in the above way, Bonaparte approached Merlin and François de Neufchâteau with considerations of another kind, which they deemed of the highest political importance — one of them being, for instance, the getting rid of that military surfeit of daring, enterprising men inured to war, so dangerous to France, at present overflowing with troops, which he would take away with him; he would thus be giving relief to the Directorate, and so this ambitious and armed solicitor would firmly establish the existence of the Government, compromised by the military *coup d'état* of the 18th Fructidor. These ideas were bound to suit the perverse character of men like Merlin and François de Neufchâteau; they were imparted to Rewbell. Fear is of a contagious nature; Rewbell was already inclined to such a course, owing to his dislike of the military, whom he distrusted in general, believing nowise in their patriotism, but only in their cupidity and ambition. Rewbell, conquered in his turn, ended in giving his adhesion to the plan. As a result, on the 15th Ventôse, Year VI. (5th March, 1798), corresponding to the second anniversary of Bonaparte's departure for Italy, the Directorate decided upon an expedition to Egypt. Full powers were given to the general-in-chief to assemble an army of 30,000 men at Toulon, together with a squadron to transport and protect the expedition; arsenals, money, everything, in fact, was placed at the disposal of Bonaparte. Admiral Brueys was appointed commander of the naval force. After having until then repeatedly testified to my opposition to the scheme, on seeing my colleagues, when about to take a decision, uneasy at the responsibility of one which did not enjoy the authority of unanimity, I considered it was my duty to sign in my turn, in order to mitigate the evil of the expedition. The Directorate, believing that it should persist in its threatening attitude against England, decided that the fitting out of the expedition should be so hurried forward as to enable an army to land in that island in the following October.

Merlin submits a most extraordinary proposition, which we cannot explain except by referring it to some secret causes: it is to expel from the Republic the two citizens Émery of Dunkirk; he wishes them to be considered as foreigners because they have accepted consular functions from another government than France; let their *exequatur* be recalled, if there are serious reasons for such action, but should we, can we thus expel merchants against whom no specific charges are brought, and who, moreover, furnish a livelihood to so many workmen by their fortune and undertakings? Postponed.

CHAPTER VI

Strange project of Boulay de la Meurthe and Pison du Galand—The conquest of Switzerland—The Army of Rome mutinies—Masséna charged with robbery—He saves himself from punishment—Cause alleged by him for the mutiny—Quiet restored—Energetic measures taken by the Directorate—Motion made by Pérès of the Gers in regard to the *émigrés*—Tallien's timid speech—Bonaparte's cunning—He seeks to compromise Réal—Talleyrand's flatteries—His intrigues against Rewbell—Mme. Bonaparte informs me of them—Mme. Grand—Talleyrand's amours—His letter to the Directorate on behalf of Mme. Grand—A stormy debate—Rewbell vigorously attacks Talleyrand—Merlin's attack on Talleyrand—Skirmishing attacks against Merlin—Rewbell suspects Talleyrand of being in communication with England—Distinguished character of François de Neufchâteau—He is both judge and plaintiff—Larevellière and his theophilanthropy—Matters grow warm—I put an end to it—My opinion as to the relations existing between Talleyrand and Mme. Grand—Bonaparte seeks to become a Director—Tallien on a mission to me—My answer—News furnished by the Prussian envoy—Amiability shown by the Queen of Spain towards Truguet—Preparations for the expedition to Egypt—Switzerland organized as a republic—The Jacobins denounced—The Pope leaves Rome—Disturbances in Italy—Geneva asks to become part of France—Félix Desportes—Large amount of funds sent to Toulon—Bad electoral selections in Paris—Financial negotiation with Hamburg and Bremen—Incapacity of some of the Ministers—Rewbell inveighs against Talleyrand—Trick that he plays on him—Talleyrand Bonaparte's Minister—Napoleon's piquant *mot* to Talleyrand—Talleyrand wishes to be ambassador at Constantinople—Memorandum in regard to a few superior naval officers—Bougainville—Peinier—Charrette—Girardin—Marigny—Buor—Beaumont—Granchain—Bras Puget—Medine—Montgabvier—La Lanne—Chavagnac—De Grasse du Bar—Rossilly—Grasse Briançon—Fontblanche—Tenel—Clavel

—Du Bouzet—Ramatuelle—Chabon—Bons—Blaise Delmas—Fortin—Turpin—La Villéon—Aubin—Borda—La Roque Dourdan—De Glandevès—Delort Serignan—De Broves—Isnard Chancelade—Du Rouvet—Alphiran—Bataille Manldoux—Bearge (?) Saint-Hypolite—General Moulins's project against the *émigrés*—Merlin seeks to have Julien of Toulouse arrested—Merlin fills Larevellière with fear—Preparations for the elections—Talleyrand proposes the distribution of money—How the money is distributed—My opinion as to this corrupt measure—Benjamin Constant a candidate—Commissioners sent to Rome—Installation of the Roman consuls—Excessive conditions imposed on the Cisalpine Republic—Secret coalition against France—A questionable agreement entered into by four Directors—The Prince of the Peace a Minister in spite of us—The Helvetic Republic established—Brune goes to take command in Italy—Incapacity of the Minister of the Interior and Police—The forced loan—Baudin and Le Tellier—The English commissioner Crawford—The Army of Condé in the pay of Russia—The French princes at Mittau—Bonaparte's grievances—His wife and he indulge in mutual recriminations—Mlle. Lepelletier married to M. de With—Hymen and love—The Minister Capellis—Malo makes use of my name—He is restored to liberty—Veausersin—Police pranks—Deplorable state of affairs in the bosom of the Directorate—Resignation of the Minister of Marine—Desherbières—An attempt to prevent Garat's election—Numerous divisions in the electoral assemblies—Talleyrand's shrewdness in electoral matters—Antonelle and Tissot—Geneva united to the Republic—Hamburg complies.

THE Directorate receives the visit of deputies sent by the Flore gathering (this name is given to the gathering of a few deputies considering themselves constitutional, who have for some time past been sitting in the Pavillon de Flore). These deputies are the citizens Pison du Galand and Boulay de la Meurthe; they speak in turn regarding a singular project at present engaging their attention. They argue in favor of the prolongation of the powers of the *corps législatif* and of the Directorate, which should henceforth be renewed together, but only every ten years. No one should go out during the present year; it would be enough to fill the places of the absent. The Directorate is greatly surprised at this strange proposition. Still Boulay sees fit to persist in his opinion, and bases it on what is nothing more than a supposition, but what he calls a principle—to wit, that the nation will submit to what the great powers of the State ordain. There are people whom a legal *régime* tires and worries even before they have tried it. It is not enough to have been compelled to make the 18th Fructidor; other *coups* must be made in order to prevent the Constitution of the Year III. from crumbling on its base. Pison du Galand plays merely a secondary part in the matter; it is Boulay who is the father and evidently the supporter of the idea. A few days ago he was desirous of transporting a very numerous class of society; to-day he would seek to transport the Constitution itself. Is this anything but an attempt to discredit the Directorate, with the object of destroying it later on?

Heavens! Change, renew the men if they do not properly fill their places; substitute others if they can do better, but do not attack the thing itself, do not undermine the vital principle of the Republic, do not kill the institution!

From the 12th to the 18th Ventôse, Year VI.—Letters from Switzerland bring the information that the French army has taken Fribourg by storm, and that Lucerne has opened its gates. Brune is marching on Lucerne; Switzerland is as good as conquered. The Directorate decrees that this country shall at once adopt a representative government.

The Directorate receives from Rome distressing

news in regard to the behavior of our army of occupation in that capital. The French officers and soldiers have not been paid for four months; they have mutinied against their general. This general is Masséna, who has so often led them to victory; but the new Marius seemingly possesses all the insatiable cupidity and avarice attributed to the first. These two faults are oftentimes one and the same; few people seek to acquire riches in order to share them with others. Charged with acts of robbery and pillage by his troops, he who has repeatedly faced with courage the enemy's cannon is no longer strong enough to repress the excesses of which he is on the point of becoming the victim, from the fact that he can no longer escape his accusing conscience when facing those whom he has deprived of their bread, and who have all the eloquence and "the strength imparted by hunger" which protests. Finally, Masséna seeks safety in flight. In his letters to the Directorate he seeks to ascribe as a reason for the insurrection the old discord which broke out between his division and that of General Bernadotte, when the latter arrived from the Army of Sambre-et-Meuse and the soldiers of Bernadotte, persisting in calling one another "monsieur," refused the title of "citizen." According to Masséna, the feeling of resentment engendered by the sabre-cuts formerly inflicted by his citizen soldiers on the "messieurs" of Bernadotte have brought about the present altercation. Masséna is committing an altogether voluntary mistake; his bad faith is the natural consequence of his position. In the first place, he has no right to pretend that the soldiers of the Army of Sambre-et-Meuse love liberty less than himself; they had shown what they were made of before they joined the Army of Italy; and if probity, courage, the practice of equality, and the chief virtues constitute true citizenship, they were, perhaps, in many of these respects far superior to the soldiers of Masséna's division. This general, believing that he could throw the blame of the insurrection on Bernadotte's division, would also like to throw it on a demi-brigade of his own division, which had given him cause for dissatisfaction in the Tyrol expedition, and which had sought revenge because of his having detached it from his command. Masséna is once more mistaken. The insurrection was based on the indignation felt by his soldiers at his continual and accumulated pillage under their very eyes. The general who does not see to the feeding of the unfortunate soldiers lavishly shedding their blood to his greater glory exposes himself to reprisals which are, after all, but poor justice. Berthier assumes command; Masséna flies to Ancona; order is restored. A few Frenchmen have been killed by the Italians, in the hope of making these disturbances turn to their profit. The ambassador of Naples, Pignatelli, and the ambassador of Vienna went through the streets exciting the populace. The Directorate has disbanded and incorporated the demi-brigades participating in the insurrection, and has ordered the arrest of the officers who signed the orders and declarations.

Masséna is called to Genoa, but with no command. Berthier is not undeserving of censure; he is to give up his post on the arrival of General Brune, who will assume the chief command of the Army of Italy and of the troops in the States of the

Church. The French commissioners in Rome are invested with the highest civil and political powers in the Pope's dominions. The Pope has sought an asylum in Florence. The Minister of Foreign Affairs is to notify the Court of Naples of the dissatisfaction felt by the French Government at the behavior of its ambassador Pignatelli. All the ambassadors in Rome are to be sent away, with the exception of Azara.

Pérès of the Gers, one of the deputies in the Council of Five Hundred, makes a motion favorable to the *émigrés*. Tallien, who had spoken to this motion, had done so far less vigorously than is his wont. He tells me that he was under the impression that the matter had been previously settled with me, because it had been previously agreed to at the house of Bonaparte, who had even seemed to desire that the motion should be made by his brother Joseph, now a deputy. One already sees Bonaparte, in so far as he can take a hand in public affairs, seeking to play the two *rôles* between which he hesitated on the 13th Vendémiaire. While the popular party is under the impression that he is with it, he seeks, through his followers and through himself, to establish friendly relations with the Royalist party by making advances to the *émigration*. Deputies who think they are well informed, and who are desirous of informing me of all they know, do not suspect that Bonaparte is the prime mover in this. They fondly imagine that, unknown to himself, he is an instrument which the aristocracy wishes to put forward to its own uses; while I am able to see that it is Bonaparte who seeks to make use of it, just as he seeks to make everything serve his ends. I am determined to know what to think about it. I mention the matter to Bonaparte, who seems greatly embarrassed. As he must needs, pursuant to his custom, compromise somebody, he says to me: "Why, the patriots were the first to conceive the idea: Réal was on our side."

It might have been thought that Bonaparte had renounced his secret ambition on obtaining his desires in regard to the expedition to Egypt; but while pouncing on this prey he did not renounce the other, or indeed any of the others. It would seem that he had given his confidence to Talleyrand, who always stimulated his ambition more and more—if, indeed, Bonaparte required to be stimulated. The object of Talleyrand's caressing attitude towards Bonaparte ever since the latter's return from Italy had not for its sole object that of strengthening himself with Bonaparte's support in the Directorate, where he felt he was not very strong; he also sought to use Bonaparte as an instrument wherewith to attempt something against the Directorate. He would point out to him as an odious injustice that his youth should have been the pretext for preventing him from becoming a Director. "Is there a single one of the five," he would argue, "who can vie with your genius? Nay, are the five of them together, past and present, worth your little finger? You were not asked your age when it was a question of saving our country at home, of covering it with honor and glory in Italy. Was Alexander asked his age when he avenged the Greeks of the Great King? When the son of Chatham was Prime Minister he had not the age of General Bonaparte." Talleyrand would repeat to

Bonaparte all the compliments he had paid to me personally, when, following upon the 18th Fructidor, he had imagined he was himself immediately to become a Director in the place of Carnot or Barthélemy, with this difference—that in those days he did not think it necessary to be quite as young as Bonaparte. On the contrary, he adduced his age as the most legitimate and provident guarantee of the Constitution of the Year III. In those days, he argued, young men and military men should not be allowed to take part in public affairs; they were the ones who accomplished the ruin of empires; according to him, reason and maturity were needed. But Rewbell's opposition having upset Talleyrand's pretensions, he had ever since borne a grudge against this Director, and hated him with a priestly hate. What he especially looked for from Bonaparte's machinations, which he incessantly stimulated, was that the latter should do something against Rewbell. Bonaparte was one with Talleyrand in his hatred of Rewbell, who had several times put Bonaparte in his proper place, on the occasions of his seeking to assume an arrogant tone towards the Directorate. Bonaparte had apologized, and for that reason bore him all the more ill-will; and it was this feeling of rancor upon which Talleyrand played unceasingly, saying: "Even if we do not succeed in making you a Director this time, my dear general, still it is important that Rewbell should be driven out of the Luxembourg; this is meet, necessary, indispensable, and politic." He would also add "moral," which sounded well when coming from Talleyrand, who, as we all know, attaches so great an importance to things moral.

We were informed of these intrigues of Talleyrand and of Bonaparte's conniving at them through divers reports. Mme. Bonaparte was the first to tell me of the conversation I have just recorded. She said to me: " Talleyrand is seeking to accomplish Bonaparte's ruin; he is continually inciting him against the Directorate; he bears a special grudge against Rewbell, who, he argues, must be got rid of. He says it is in order to get my husband into the Directorate; but I can clearly see that he wishes to enter it himself, for he has gone the length of telling me personally that he would work harmoniously with Bonaparte were they seated at the same table; that he guaranteed he would secure him the majority on all occasions; that as for himself, Talleyrand, he had no personal ambition; that his ambition would be complete if he could but enjoy the happiness of being Bonaparte's most humble servant, as in his eyes Bonaparte was the Republic, and much more than the Republic." These nauseating compliments were the same that Talleyrand had caused to be made to me, and had made to me himself before becoming a Minister; and he had outdone himself in this respect at the time of the 18th Fructidor, when he had hoped I was about to secure his admission to the Directorate.

While Talleyrand, pursuing the train of his ambitious aspirations, was incessantly, although so far unsuccessfully, intriguing against the Directorate which had made him its Minister, he was somewhat disturbed in his machinations by a personal affair, which, to use a vulgar expression, put a flea in his ear.

The police had arrested a woman of the name of

Grand, who was suspected, not to say convicted, so I believe, of carrying on a correspondence with England, or at least with Englishmen. Lords and gentlemen had been the lovers of this lady, whom Talleyrand, when abroad, had taken from the hands of this goodly company. On his occupying a position, Mme. Grand had followed him with the intention of sharing his newly acquired fortune, and had made him believe that feelings of love attached her to his person, just as Talleyrand had made me believe that he was attached to mine; in spite of his *blasé* heart, if ever heart beat in that breast, he had indulged in the illusion we are in general greatly inclined to receive at the hands of either sex, when one succeeds in making us suppose that we are really loved for ourselves.

But in the case of Talleyrand the persons, of whatever sex they may be, with whom one may consider him to have been on an intimate footing, never engendered in him so complete an illusion that he did not treasure up against them a certain dose of the irony he always has at the service of everybody, and doubtless at his own, since in the case of a being who can no more escape from the stings of his conscience (when conscience there is) than from the judgment of others, Talleyrand cannot, even in his own eyes, be the least ridiculous of all those whom he makes game of. While therefore begging that the lady—who he publicly confessed was his mistress, but whom he will disown later on, only when she shall have become his wife—should be restored to liberty, he talked about her in a tone of disdain almost akin to contempt; even in those days he all but said what he has said since—to wit, that "she was as stupid as she was beautiful."

CITIZEN DIRECTOR,

Mme. Grand has just been arrested as a conspirator. She is the person in all Europe the farthest from and the least capable of embarking in any business; she is a very lovely Indian, very indolent, and the most unoccupied of all the women I have ever met. I beg your influence on her behalf, for I am sure that not even the shadow of a pretext can be found against her, so that this little affair be hushed up, as it would grieve me to see it create a noise. I love her, and I affirm to you, as man to man, that never in her life did she mix up in nor is she capable of mixing up in any business. She is a genuine Indian, and you know to what a degree this species of womankind is a stranger to intrigue.

Greeting and attachment.

CH. MAUR. TALLEYRAND.

3d Germinal, Year VI.

If, on the one hand, Mme. Grand deserved to be called lovely owing to a large and robust figure, I have never been able to see that she was entitled to such praise in regard to her face; for, as I have already, at the time of my first interview with Talleyrand, pointed out how much he personally resembled Robespierre, it is quite exact to state that Mme. Grand has something of Talleyrand's physiognomy. Her rather large but lifeless eyes, her tip-tilted nose, her thin lips, and her pale, not to say pallid, face, do not allow of my admitting that Mme. Grand was, even in the full bloom of her forty years, as beautiful as Talleyrand was good enough to tell me, since her physiognomy and his constituted a kind of copy of that of Robespierre, for whom assuredly no one will claim personal attractions.

Moreover, if Talleyrand saw fit in his intellectual superiority to speak thus lightly of our fair prisoner, who was his mistress, and who was to be his wife, she, on the other hand, in her conversation and her hardly distinguished correspondence did not treat her lover and future husband with much consideration; she seemed to be discounting the disgust which was subsequently to be the cause of their marital union. Everybody knows the *mot* of Louis XV. in regard to one of his courtiers, when told that he had just married his mistress: "There is no way of parting company more decently." Pending the disgust which was to bring about the lawful union of these two individuals, vastly more interested than interesting, and subsequently to put an end to this connection, as it happened, Mme. Grand was also making sport of Talleyrand in less measured terms in letters intercepted by the police; in these she conversed about France with one of the friends she had left in England, speaking hardly more reverently of Talleyrand than Mlle. Bourgoing has done since of her lover the Minister Chaptal, whom, so they say, she called *Papa Clistorel*, for the reason that Chaptal had been an apothecary. Mme. Grand, also seeking a simile in a man's profession, styled her worshipper Talleyrand in her letters *l'Abbé Piëbot* (*pied bot*, club-foot), thus committing a double baseness towards a couple of involuntary misfortunes, both almost equally natural. Talleyrand was, in a way, born a priest and club-foot simultaneously, since it is said that he would not have been consecrated to this profession, which did not suit his character, but for the reason of his being ill-favored; for, had it not been for this accident of birth, it is he who, as the eldest son, should have been the first to enter upon a military career, which was given to his brothers Archambaud and Bozon. These two brothers, variously known in several other respects, are equally known as the most distinguished mediocrities and nonentities of our period, whom the accident of birth and Court connections alone brought to notice. In comparison with such brothers Talleyrand might be a phœnix, but a phœnix to whom was fully applicable the *mot* of Rivarol to a man as null as pretentious in more ways than one, and who had a brother: "Your brother is exceedingly common, and as mediocre as a man can possibly be; nothing but his incapacity can equal his conceit. And yet your brother is infinitely superior to you in all things."

But the nullity of Talleyrand's two brothers was no bar to their being successful at Court, for it is well known how skilful such people are in besetting those in power, and in obtaining positions both of profit and of honor, which always go together, all for the good of nations who can hardly meet the expense under an annual *milliard*.

Whatever might be the immorality of Talleyrand's connection with the lady, and the impropriety of his petition on her behalf, I nevertheless, with my usual weakness, used my influence to obtain the release of the alleged beauty. I was under the impression that her case could be treated with the kind of indifference with which Talleyrand had tried to invest it when writing to me about her as he had done; I was mistaken: the discussion following my request resulted in my experiencing one of those disappointments which have often fallen to my lot in matters of slight importance, because of my not having sufficiently taken into account the fact that these matters are precisely those which inflame passions to the highest degree. Hence it was that Rewbell intoned as usual his favorite anthem: "I can plainly see herein Talleyrand, this wretched unfrocked, or rather still frocked, priest, who, not content with being the vilest of libertines, cannot gratify his desires in France, which certainly is not lacking in loose women; he must needs go and seek one in England, and one of those to boot whom Englishmen import from India, just as they import their wines from Oporto, which would not be strong enough were they not subjected to several sea voyages. Talleyrand would not enjoy life unless spiced with a scandal proclaimed from the house-tops. There you have the priest; he thinks we are still under a monarchical *régime*, that he is the agent of the clergy, that he has livings at his disposal, and that he can play the deuce. He does not realize that he is now under a republic, that he occupies one of its Ministerial residences, and that he should have at least the decency of his position, as he cannot have its dignity.

"I demand that the appointment of this impudent priest be cancelled; otherwise the Directorate," said Rewbell, "is exposing itself to shoulder all the disrepute which Talleyrand already enjoys, and which he thinks he should perfect now that he is one of the Ministers of the Republic.

"Citizens and colleagues," Rewbell went on to say, in an animated and violent tone not without its dignity, "when the National Convention struck the name of Talleyrand from the list of the *émigrés* with whom he so proudly protested against being associated, he asserted that he had spent the days of his exile from France in the United States, and had enjoyed the friendship of the illustrious chiefs of the American Republic. Well, then, I ask him

now if the morals practised by him here in this country are those of which he has received an example from the Washingtons, the Jeffersons, and all the true patriots who have held the helm in the affairs of their country, as it is our duty to hold it in ours. I assert that a man who should have had the effrontery to parade in that country what he now parades here would there and then have been expelled from the Republic of the United States. What does he take us for that he should dare to come and make a display of his cynicism, and set at defiance our desire to observe at least better morals than those of the ancient *régime* of Talleyrand? If, moreover, when considering this wretch under a physical aspect, I could only discover in his physique something strong, constraining, and irresistible, which might be considered indicative of invincible passions wherein the individual was but the victim, like so many others, of his natural organization; but in this case nature has seen to it: he is a cripple, a man destitute of a portion of his members, who with difficulty can stand on his two fleshless bones; he is a living corpse for whom there is not the excuse which others might plead; he is a libertine without needs or means, who calls to his aid all the resources of debauchery, in accordance with the tenets of the school of de Sade."

Rewbell, although bearing me a sincere friendship by reason of that which I bore him and the similarity of our opinions in nearly all things, seemed to couple me with Talleyrand when thus reproaching him. He looked me full in the face, keeping his eyes fastened on me the whole time; yet coming a little closer to me so as not to be heard by my colleagues, he said to me: "You are too good-natured; you are giving your support to a blackguard; watch what will come of it, what will perhaps happen to you the very first."

I was not to be let off with this allocution, for it was now Merlin's turn to pronounce himself in regard to Talleyrand. Merlin said that it was to his great regret that he had nothing complimentary to say about this Minister of the Republic whom the Directorate had honored with its trust, but that the duty imposed on him by his conscience and the love of truth which constituted the ordinary rule of his judgments and his opinions compelled him to speak out with a frankness perhaps no less severe and harsh than that displayed by Rewbell; he was of the opinion that we should not among ourselves spare our agents, when such action was likely to react against the Directorate, and ultimately be fatal to its authority. "Undoubtedly the men we were compelled to send to the scaffold on the 9th Thermidor, Robespierre and Saint-Just," said Merlin, "had carried the strictness of morality too far; they had the luxury of it, a luxury which is often akin to hypocrisy; they had even the ferocity of it, since they believed that those who strayed from the paths of morality in the slightest degree should be punished with death. Pursuant to their way of viewing things—a view, indeed, in harmony with their own action—it was an easy matter at once to discover an original sin, and there was no reason why the whole of the human species should not be placed on trial, condemned, and executed. By whom then? I do not see where could have been found the executioner who would not have had to suffer the same penalty; then the judges who had commissioned the executioner, to be followed by Robespierre and Saint-Just, who had commissioned the judges, and who in their turn met with the end they had prepared for others. My dear colleagues," Merlin went on to say, " allow me to make one remark. Are we to believe that there is not between the impossible demands and the implacable severity of Robespierre and Saint-Just and the cynical laxness of Talleyrand some perceptible shade and some interval? A man who, devoid of passions and without the pretence of the means which excuse them, goes and invests himself with all the bluster of licentiousness in order to experience the sensations of scandal, seems to me to display a refinement of corruption which escaped even the most rigid puritans of the period preceding the 9th Thermidor. I fail to discover any excuse for him from the moral point of view; and, were it possible to find an excuse for him, looking at him as a private individual, it might perhaps result in aggravating his case as a political person. For after all, as said by our colleague, women are not scarce in France, supposing that our passions called for them. There are so many of them, all lovely, kind, and excellent!" Merlin seemed to utter these last words with a little air of vainglorious coquettishness, soliciting personal indulgence for peccadilloes he would have liked to parade. Rewbell, thinking he could detect this swaggering weakness, remarked to Merlin: "But you are, like ourselves, a married man; hence you do not require to be forgiven mistresses you have not. If, however, you wish to appear as a *Céladon* in order to acquire rights to indulgence, tell us what there is to be told; speak, let us hear all about your lady-killing exploits."

Merlin replied, with true ingenuousness and a more than malicious smile: "All I can say about myself is that when I have the pleasure of captivating a woman, not only do I not boast of the fact, but I do not admit it; much less do I name the lady." Could *Jocrisse* have defended himself more cleverly? Merlin resumes: "Since we all agree that France is not lacking in lovely, kind, and accommodating women, why, if one desires or needs them, should one go and seek them in British India, *i.e.*, in England? There is in this something, I must confess, which seems to me to leave the private domain and belong altogether to that of politics. Who will guarantee us that this alleged gallant *liaison* of Talleyrand with this loved woman is not a political *liaison*, of which love is only the officious screen; and that the vices of which Talleyrand is assuredly open to accusation are nothing else than the disguise of his policy? Who is there, in short, to guarantee that Mme. Grand, owing to her disrepute, was not for that very reason looked upon as the woman who could best don the appearance of a gallant *rôle* intended to conceal the *rôle* of political falseness—that, in short, Talleyrand, against whom so many patriots have long since brought the charge, is not a man sold to England, an actual agent of England, of whom Mme. Grand is only the intermediary? I ask," adds Merlin, "that instead of restoring to liberty the woman or the girl Grand, the Minister of Police be instructed to question her himself very closely; this affair should be probed to the quick; this intrigue should be sifted; we cannot close our eyes to what Talleyrand really is: he is undoubtedly more of an intriguer than a lover; simultaneously, all letters addressed to foreign parts as well as to home destinations should be intercepted; all English agents who may have a hand in this machination should be arrested. In order better to catch Talleyrand *in flagrante delicto*, we must appear to look upon the matter as one of slight importance, so that he may be less on his guard; we must also jointly resolve not to let him perceive that we think that anything is amiss; nay, we must go so far as to receive him kindly when he comes before the Directorate on Ministerial business. If, as I hope, we succeed in unearthing the plot, we will make a striking example of him, and after dismissing him as a matter of course, we will send him for trial before a military commission. Mme. Grand naturally falls under the cognizance of such a tribunal, since she is an *émigrée* who has returned to France; hence Talleyrand will be concerned in the suit, involved forcibly as he will be in the main charge. You will thus have absolute mastery over the counter-revolutionist whom you have too carelessly admitted into your midst. As to the libertine priest with more or less physical powers, that is none of our business. In that matter it is rather for women than for men to judge. It is not for us to investigate the means and the rights of all these priestly flirtations."

On hearing these last words, François de Neufchâteau, whose conscience perhaps reproached him with peccadilloes akin to those of Talleyrand, but who was not a priest, believing that it was incumbent upon him to say a word in harmony with the conclusion of Merlin, remarked: "The Directorate has undoubtedly the right to keep an eye on the political conduct of its agents, but it has no right to meddle with their private life; that is a sanctuary." Rewbell, on hearing François de Neufchâteau thus express himself, smiled as the thought came uppermost in his mind that our colleague might to a certain extent be pleading his own cause. François de Neufchâteau was just as much of a cripple as Talleyrand, and enjoyed the reputation of being a libertine of old, whom neither infirmities nor years had reformed.

It is now the turn of Larevellière to reveal himself, on this occasion when each one is laying bare his character. Larevellière would like things looked at from a loftier standpoint. He remarks: "Talleyrand is doing in this instance only what he has done all his life: he screens his intrigues with his licentiousness, or his licentiousness with his intrigues. It all amounts to the same thing. His double-faced character is, as a matter of course, open to suspicion in regard to all he does and in connection with everything. This derives its origin from the ecclesiastical education he has received." In the eyes of Larevellière this education had produced no other result than to strengthen his bad inclinations. Discovering in this instance a further argument in support of the opinion which he (Larevellière) has always held in regard to ecclesiastical depravity, he is not sorry to impart it to the Directorate, or even to make the public cognizant of it. Sacerdotal corruption can never be unmasked too much, he argues. It would all be done away with, moreover, if instead of allowing the Catholic religion to subsist, a religion based on deceit and mummery, one had the good sense to substitute for it a sensible moral cult, which, while taking possession of men's hearts, would both elevate the imagination and satisfy intelligent minds. "You would, with a form of worship based on morality and reason," says Larevellière, "long since have thrust back, blasted, and annihilated everything that directly or indirectly has its origin in modern Rome. Talleyrand is one of its products. I will admit that in the first place his natural inclinations were none of the best; but his perversity has undoubtedly been increased and refined by the priesthood and episcopate. In order to destroy all the capital vices which have filtered into the present generation—vices of which Talleyrand affords a perfect prototype—it is necessary to eradicate the evil; religion, like political society, must be made over again in its very foundation." "I could see what you were driving at," exclaimed Rewbell, "with your roundabout way of coming to it; all this would suit you perfectly, if it but furnished you the opportunity of palming off your theophilanthropy on us. Why did you not speak out the word?" "I am not afraid of doing so," replies Larevellière. "I am looking at matters from a broad standpoint. I tell you that there is in man a religious chord which you cannot ignore; there is a need of God which you cannot escape from; society calls for a God different from the God of the Catholics; if you let society delude itself with vain hopes, it will bite its tongue, bite you also and swallow you whole, as the whale swallowed Jonah, with the sole difference that the new whale will not vomit out the new Jonahs. Is there a more simple and happy lesson to be taught men than gratitude towards their Creator and love for their fellow-men?" "And is all this combined in your theophilanthropy?" "Yes, of course," replies Larevellière, with fury, his eyes starting out of their sockets. "I will prove it to you: it is for lack of a simple and natural form of worship, one in harmony with the principles of reason, that we have witnessed the growth, under the protecting shelter of absurdity and falsehood, of priestly impostors, who have imported into our country every species of vice and crime."

I could see that Larevellière was getting enraged beyond all bounds, and I could not foresee what excesses both sides might indulge in, as a result of the incident I had awkwardly brought up for discussion. It had been my intention to avoid an explosion, in conformity with the request expressed by Talleyrand in his letter to me; and, lo and behold, here was an explosion likely to resound beyond our halls, had not our doors been well closed! I rise angrily from my seat, and, interposing between Rewbell and Larevellière, exclaim, in a tone that will silence them both, "It seems to me we are all agreed upon throwing light upon this affair, in order to be able better to judge of it; hence the first thing to be done is to refer it to the Minister of Police. I make that motion." Carried.

Glad at having thus put an end to this unexpected scene, I discharged my conscience of any interest I might have taken in Talleyrand, by viewing his connection with Mme. Grand as that of a more or less exhausted profligacy. I did not consider this noble couple as otherwise guilty, and, pursuant to this view of the matter, I considered it meet to let Talleyrand know the reasons for which he should exercise precautions; I do not, of course, mean precautions having for their object the concealment of any treasonable act. In those days I did not believe Talleyrand capable of treason, and I considered that my colleagues judged him too harshly. I was of opinion that it was still a far cry from a greatly relaxed morality in private life to political treachery. I did not take into consideration that the immorality of a priest is not to be compared with any other, and that, just as Mme. de Staël had told me, this priest "combined all the vices of the ancient and the new *régime*."

Tallien calls on me to tell me confidentially that Bonaparte persists in his desire to be appointed a member of the Directorate, arguing that the Legislative Councils could decree his appointment as a reward for his eminent services. His age might seem to present a difficulty, but from what he knew of the dispositions of the Councils it was not one. He felt sure that such a motion would be carried without trouble.

Bonaparte calls on me the next day, and makes the same overture to me. I tell him it cannot be done; were the Councils to adopt such a resolution, it would be tantamount to a violation of the Constitution. Besides, the Directorate would reject such a decree. Bonaparte went away completely abashed, and returned to Tallien's. "He never should have imagined," he said to the latter, "that I would have opposed his entering the Directorate. I was acting against my own interests; no one was more interested in this appointment than myself, owing to the attachment and devotion he bore me for life."

The Prussian envoy comes to us breathless, to tell us that Russia and Austria are forming a coalition for the purpose of attacking and partitioning the Ottoman Empire.

Truguet, who has been sent as our ambassador to Spain, has been granted a private audience with the queen, who has treated him with marks of consideration, not to say special affection. Talleyrand, who does not like Truguet, thinks that there is a little of vanity or of modesty in the sensitiveness shown by the Republican ambassador to the kindly courtesy of the old queen.

The Directorate gives orders for the preparing of all things required for the expedition to Egypt and the assembling at Toulon of the troops which are to take part in it.

From the 20th to the 30th Ventôse, Year VI.—Following upon several engagements reflecting honor upon the French army, Switzerland is conquered. The whole of Helvetia throws off the yoke of the oligarchic government; the Directorate decrees that it shall be organized as a republic. It is proposed that Valais shall be united to the Republic, but no resolution is come to in the matter.

Denunciations against the Jacobins have once more come into vogue; the Directorate gives credit to them, while admitting that they are extremely vague. I and François de Neufchâteau are the least alarmed at them. Rewbell, Merlin, and Larevellière propose to take, in regard to their respective departments, measures to exclude alleged terrorists from the primary assemblies. I oppose the taking of similar measures in the departments of the South.

The Pope leaves Rome and retires to Sienna, accompanied by two French officers in command of an escort. The treaty with the Cisalpine Republic is rejected. The too harsh domination exercised by the French Directorate has stirred up the enemies of liberty, and has compelled us to have recourse to such measures as the sending of a legislator before a tribunal, and removing a number of legislators, together with two members of the Government. The general commanding the French is empowered to establish a new government, and to levy upon the republic a contribution of war equal to that stipulated in the treaties for the maintenance of 25,000 French soldiers.

Geneva asks to be united to France. The envoy Félix Desportes is empowered to deal with this proposition.

The expedition to Egypt necessitates the despatch of considerable funds to Toulon. Bonaparte prefers a request for the Berne treasury. Everything that comes from Switzerland and from everywhere else is to be placed at his disposal.

The selection of the primary assemblies in Paris is bad. Several constitutional clubs are closed. The enactments closing them are almost invariably drawn up by Merlin.

Hamburg and Bremen agree to take twelve millions' worth of Batavian scrip, and to pay twelve million *écus*. This negotiation has been effected from fear of the French Government, and in hopes of a special protection promised them.

The Batavian Assembly has at last accepted the Constitution.

Spain is not acting in good faith; she seems to be seeking the friendship of England. Portugal is the intermediary in this intrigue.

The Ministers of the Interior and of War no longer enjoy confidence. Dondeau, the Minister of Police, is nothing but a fool. Talleyrand himself, although he has received a passport for wit from Mme. de Staël, is considered by Rewbell as no less incapable than Dondeau. Rewbell was of the same opinion as Mme. de Staël in the days when she introduced Talleyrand to me and worried me to make him a Minister, and when she told me, as a thing all to the honor or at least in favor of Talleyrand, "that he had the vices of the ancient and of the new *régime;*" but Rewbell attached a less happy meaning to it, and drew therefrom an altogether different conclusion, to wit, that far from being desirable because he combined all vices in himself, Talleyrand should for that very reason be excluded from all offices at the hands of the Republic, and that no one was less fit to be one of the high functionaries of a State of which he was the most unworthy citizen. While recognizing in Talleyrand capacity in regard to his embodiment of the corruption of every *régime*, Rewbell was far from recognizing in him an equal capacity in regard to intellectual faculties. If, on the one hand, Mirabeau and so many revolutionists or counter-revolutionists showed themselves superior in immorality, they none the less shone superior by their talents. Rewbell held that Talleyrand was unable in the slightest degree to redeem his immorality by his talents. Replying to some one who said to him in familiar style that "this fellow (Talleyrand) at any rate has forgotten to be stupid," Rewbell remarked: "He has had nothing to forget in that respect." He believed he was demonstrating Talleyrand's incapacity when asking him in his Ministerial capacity questions which could hardly be classed as difficult, but to which he required an immediate answer; true it is that Talleyrand oftentimes, taken unawares and in order to get over the difficulty, would end as he had begun, saying: "Citizen Director, I am not prepared, and even had I been, I would not consider myself able enough to carry on a discussion with the citizen Director Rewbell, whom everybody knows as the cleverest man in Europe both in diplomacy and in administration. I must beg your permission to retire to my office to meditate, and to-morrow I will have the honor of bringing you a satisfactory answer to your questions. I can hardly satisfy you otherwise; even in regard to things with which I am most familiar, I require to collect my thoughts, and to be alone for a few moments." "If all that is needed to fecundate your genius is that you should be alone," replied Rewbell, one fine day, "I am going to supply you with a means which will preserve you from being disturbed in your meditations." So, taking Talleyrand by the arm, with friendly irony, Rewbell locked him in a closet adjacent to our council-room. Talleyrand struggled, but Rewbell, continuing to push him along, pretended not to understand his resistance, and locked him in; at the end of an hour of forced imprisonment Rewbell let him out. Talleyrand had been unable to write a single page, and said he had got a headache. "Go home to bed, Basilio; you look feverish," said Rewbell to him with his usual roughness. He then pushed him out of the Council, and, turning towards us, said with a laugh: "Well, gentlemen, now you have an idea what your great mountebank is made of."

In spite of the lengthy part subsequently played by Talleyrand under the government of Bonaparte, it would seem that the latter did not entertain any greater idea of his capacity than had Rewbell. This is not the place to illustrate how little necessary was the great talent of the Minister of Foreign Affairs, when victory dictated treaties to which the Minister had merely to affix his signature; but a word spoken by Napoleon to Talleyrand after the battle of Austerlitz reveals in a most precise fashion what his estimate was of this stage Minister, whom he several times ordered to follow in the rear of the baggage when he took the field. While Bonaparte, pushing onward, was preparing to fight the dicisive battle of the campaign, Talleyrand was in Vienna quaking with fear while the issue remained undecided, when the victory of Austerlitz, crowned with the interview of the three emperors, announced a peace, not only begun but concluded. Then only does Bonaparte see Talleyrand come post-haste to him; he arrives breathlessly but swaggering to sign the Treaty of Pressburg. "Well then," says Napoleon, "you are going to be a man of wit on this occasion because I have won the battle; it would have been altogether different had I lost it: you might perhaps then have looked like nothing so much as a fool."

Rewbell daily persisted in his sarcasms, and made Talleyrand's life miserable in his intercourse with us; the latter, in spite of his natural or feigned indifference (for he was wont to boast that he sent himself to sleep reading the lampoons written against him), could hardly endure them, or, rather, he foresaw that he was about to lose our support. Under the circumstances, he devoted himself to studying which party would come out victorious, and whether he had anything to hope from it. He allowed the remark to escape that he was ready to give up his portfolio, and even to leave France. He asked us for the Constantinople embassy, even getting Bonaparte to prefer his request to us, with a view to contributing diplomatically to the military expedition planned against the East. The East seemed to offer a compensation to these two disappointed ambitions; and yet neither of them dreamed of leaving the West except with extreme reluctance.

Desirous of disposing of the navy as he disposed of the army, Bonaparte asked us for a detailed report on all the able men still in the former service. He was going to make a selection from among them, he said, and compel all these fellows, who were strangely behind the times, to go forward. The Minister, and especially Admiral Kerguelin, supplied us with a list of names, which nowise satisfied Bonaparte, in spite of the accompanying statement of their many services; he found nothing worthy of him among these men, and spoke of them with profound contempt.

BOUGAINVILLE, *Vice-Admiral.*—His services are well known; has held several commands, and has commanded a division under General de Grasse.

PEINIER, *Rear-Admiral.*—His distinguished services have always made him conspicuous; has held several commands, and has served under General Suffren in India; his military and tactical talents entitle him to the command of a naval force.

CHARRETTE, *Rear-Admiral.*—Has always been in command, whatever his rank; distinguished himself particularly under General de Grasse; possesses all the talents of a general who leaves nothing to be desired.

GIRARDIN, *Vice-Admiral.*—Has commanded several rather important divisions; has been intrusted with several missions; commanded in chief the naval forces which captured Saint-Eustache. His military talents have always caused him to be considered a distinguished officer, raising great expectations.

MARIGNY, *Rear-Admiral.*—Has always commanded; an officer of the highest merit, both theoretically and practically; acted as major-general of the naval forces at Brest; has in him all the qualifications required to command an army, and has an extensive knowledge of all things pertaining to naval matters.

BUOR, *Rear-Admiral.*—Distinguished by his military acquirements and in naval evolutions; was major-general in the army of General Guichen; enjoys a well-founded reputation among the generals and the men of the navy.

BEAUMONT, *Chef de Division.*—Has held several commands; distinguished himself at the capture of the English frigate *Fox;* nothing remains to be added to his military acquirements and his talents, which entitle him to a command-in-chief.

GRANCHAIN, *Commodore.*—Has commanded on several occasions; has served as major in the squadron of General Herai, and subsequently in that of General Barras; has great military acquirements and a good knowledge of evolutions. His distinguished reputation has always caused the navy and its chiefs to consider him a man fit to command a naval force.

BRAS PUGET, *Chef de Division.*—Has commanded on several occasions; has been in command of the Leeward Islands station; his talents and his acquirements have always caused him to be looked úpon in the navy as an officer of great promise.

MEDINE, *Chef de Division.*—Has held many commands, and

has always enjoyed the confidence of the generals under whom he has served.

MONTCABRIER, *Commodore.*—Has held many commands; commanded the Islands (West India) station, and was major in the squadron of General Vaudreuil. His military and special talents have always caused him to be looked upon as an officer of distinction.

LA LANNE, *Commodore.*—Has held several commands, and was sent on a special mission to India under General Suffren; his talents and ability are fully recognized.

CHAVAGNAC, *Commodore.* — Has commanded corvettes and frigates; was second in command of the navy at Cherbourg, then *aide-major* of the navy at Brest. He is science personified, and has an extensive knowledge of everything connected with the service.

DE GRASSE DE BAR, *Commodore.*—Has commanded a number of times; has been employed on several missions; his military talents and acquirements are of the highest.

ROSSILLY, Senior.—Has commanded on many occasions, and in particular in India. This officer is replete with military talents and acquirements. Is at present employed at the depot of the journals of the navy.

ROSSILLY, Junior.—Has commanded corvettes and frigates; has always won the approval of the generals under whom he has served; has always given great promise owing to his military talents and acquirements.

GRASSE BRIANÇON, *Captain.*—Has commanded a number of times. His military acquirements have ever caused him to be looked upon as a most distinguished officer, giving the greatest promise; is highly thought of in the navy, and has many claims to the confidence of the Government.

TENEL, Junior, *Captain.*—Has commanded on several occasions; he possesses all the acquirements required of an officer of merit and distinction; he is deservedly entitled to the confidence of the Government in respect to any command or matter of detail that may be intrusted to him.

CLAVEL, *Captain.*—Has commanded several times while holding various ranks; has filled special missions; his military acquirements have drawn to him the attention of the navy and its chiefs. He is capable of filling the post of *sous-aide-major* in a naval force, or taking second command of the commissariat of an army.

DE BOUZET, *Captain.* — Has commanded repeatedly while holding various ranks; has been sent on special missions; his military acquirements have drawn the attention of the navy to him, and have won him the confidence of the officers under whom he has served. He is an officer of great promise, and deserves the confidence of the Government.

RAMATUELLE, *Lieutenant.*—Has repeatedly commanded; his special acquirements have been the cause of his reaping distinction on every occasion. He can be put to anything, and deserves the confidence of the Government.

CHABON, *Lieutenant.*—Has twice held a command. This officer possesses all the talents that can be desired; his acquirements justify his being looked upon as of great promise.

BONS, *Lieutenant at La Ciotat.*—Has served at sea with distinction in the last war; has on several occasions shown himself to be a well-grounded officer; he deserves to receive at the hands of the Government the command of a ship or frigate.

BLAISE DELMAS, *Lieutenant at La Ciotat.*—Has seen service aboard ships of the State, both in this war and in the one preceding it; he has always displayed the acquirements that qualify an officer to be intrusted with a command and to deserve the confidence of the Government.

FORTIN, *an officer of the Compagnie des Indes.*—Served in that company since 1759. General Bellecombe, Governor of Pondicherry, employed him with profit both at sea and on a political mission to Tipu-Sahib and to the Mahratta government; he subsequently held commands under the company; has sailed a squadron. Looking to his acquirements, this officer can be employed as commander of a ship, or in regard to matters of detail connected with a naval force; he knows England thoroughly, as well as everything appertaining to the East India Company in London.

TURPIN, *Captain.*—Has held many commands. His special knowledge of matters of detail has always drawn to him the attention of the navy, which considers him an officer of distinction and of great promise.

LA VILLÉON, *Captain.*—Has held several commands; has served under General Barras; subsequently flag-captain under General Grasse. His talents and his acquirements leave nothing to be desired; has always been highly spoken of by the generals under whom he served.

AUBIN, *Lieutenant at La Ciotat.*—This officer has never held a command, but has always distinguished himself when sailing a squadron; he is likewise, owing to his acquirements and activity, fit to fill every kind of post in regard to matters of detail.

BORDA, *Captain.*—Has commanded; served as major in the squadron commanded by General d'Estaing. His acquirements in matters of detail connected with a naval force leave nothing to be desired.

LA ROQUE DOURDAN, *Captain.*—Has held several commands; has been intrusted with various missions; major in the navy at Toulon and Marseilles; has been naval commander at Marseilles. His acquirements and activity recommend him to consideration as an officer of great promise.

GLANDÈVES (LE COMMANDEUR DE), *Rear-Admiral.*—After holding the naval command at Toulon, was stationed at Malta, then at Cadiz, whither he was summoned by the Government, for the purpose of being consulted and of enjoying the emoluments of his rank. This officer has commanded while holding various ranks, in all the wars and in time of peace; has been charged with several missions, and has commanded divisions. Has a consummate experience and acquirements which have on all occasions brought him distinction; his talents have caused him to be noticed as an officer entitled to take command of a naval force.

DELORT SERIGNAN, *Captain.*—Has commanded on different occasions either corvettes, frigates, or divisions; major of a division of naval troops at Toulon his acquirements and his acquaintance with matters of detail have won him an excellent reputation.

DE BROVES, *Captain.* — Distinguished himself in the late war; has commanded two men-of-war; has been intrusted with important missions, which he fulfilled with zeal and activity; his acquirements and his talents leave nothing to be desired.

ISNARD CHANCELADE, *Captain.* — Served with the greatest distinction in the last war; has commanded and held the positions of major of division and squadron commissary; has on all occasions acquired the reputation of an excellent officer.

DU ROUVET, *Captain.*— Has served with distinction in all

the wars; has commanded a number of times; possesses all the acquirements and qualities characterizing a perfect officer.

ALPHIRAN, *Captain.*—Has commanded several ships. This officer has acquirements and talents which have attracted attention to him in the various squadrons in which he has served; moreover, he enjoyed the confidence of General Barras when serving under his orders.

BATAILLE MANLDOUX, *Captain.*—Has distinguished himself on several occasions, and principally in a long-boat engagement with corsairs, brigands whom he destroyed; has been at Malta for a number of years; has repeatedly commanded while holding different ranks; has enjoyed the confidence of General Suffren and of all his chiefs capable of judging talent and merit; his distinguished services have won him the rank of captain at an unusually early age.

BEARGE (?) SAINT-HYPOLITE, *Lieutenant.*—Has held commands. Has always enjoyed in the navy the reputation of an officer of talent by his acquirements; he promises very well.

From the 1st to the 10th Germinal, Year VI.—Merlin proposes to adopt a project of General Moulins having for its object the police supervision of *émigrés* who, while being permitted to reside in Paris, seem to be serving the foreigner; in which case to arrest and arraign them before military commissions. I raise my voice against such a measure, exclaiming, "Let us fight openly, but no cowardly treachery concealing assassination!" The proposition is shelved; still, certain *émigrés* denounced by General Moulins are to be arrested.

Merlin asks for the arrest of Julien of Toulouse, denounced as professing principles contrary to those of the Directorate. Merlin remarks that he can be arrested by virtue of an indictment which has existed against him for a long time past. "It is as good as repealed," he is told. "It matters little," he replies;

"we are not supposed to know it." Larevellière and I get this proposition shelved.

A number of persons are in the habit of meeting in a tavern situated in a street of the Faubourg Marceau, which Larevellière sometimes passes on his way to the Jardin des Plantes; when they have drunk a good deal they are noisy. They may be anarchists getting ready, and keeping their hands in till the game of the elections begins, Larevellière imagines. He asks that they be arrested by the police. I oppose this. Larevellière finally agrees with me, and, in spite of Merlin, the motion to arrest these people is rejected. For some time past Merlin has been successful in deceiving the honest Larevellière, and in inspiring him with fright; Merlin, alone, plays again the former game of Carnot, Barthélemy, and Letourneur rolled into one. Still, a number of arrests are taking place. I move that all arrested shall at once be set free or arraigned before a tribunal. The Directorate restores several of them to liberty.

A list is drawn up of the deputies to be elected to represent Paris. Copies of it are given to the Ministers of Police and of the Interior; Merlin undertakes to distribute copies to the electors of his acquaintance, in pursuance of the reports he receives about Cambacérès, Gohier, and Génissieu. Merlin avers that these three are highly dangerous in connection with the elections; he thinks that all he has to do is to call them to him and pat them on the back in order to convert them; but he is vexed on seeing that they pretend not to understand him, and that they almost laugh in his face. He no longer even dares to offer them a copy of the proposed list.

He lays down as a principle that a division will occur if the individuals named in the list are not elected. I ask my colleagues to take notice that the *corps législatif*, already fallen into disrepute by the mutilation it suffered on the 18th Fructidor, will fall into still further disrepute through the influence it is sought to exercise over the elections. Rewbell has an extraordinary dread of this electoral renewal; he argues that means should be taken, and all means seem to him excellent, to lay the storm. Talleyrand, who is present at the scene, would like to patch up a peace with Rewbell by falling in with his views. He asks leave to speak, for the purpose of saying "that in all things the question at issue is success; that in England elections are influenced not only by opinion, but by all the means which money supplies; that money is the mainspring of English elections, just as it is the sinews of war. Hence the Directorate would perhaps be well advised at this critical electoral juncture to send considerable sums to trustworthy men, who should distribute them as they saw fit among all men within or without electoral colleges likely to exercise some authority over them and serve the cause of the Government." Larevellière and Rewbell himself consider such a proceeding as most immoral in itself, and especially in a republic whose principle is virtue, and which must never have recourse to such infamous methods; but passions do not practise morality as well as they preach it, and the Directorate, while blushing with shame, determines upon a distribution of money to be made as follows among those preparing and machinating the elections; in vulgar language, we are going to get our money's worth.

List of functionaries or special agents to whom money has been paid out of the secret-service fund for the purpose of manipulating the elections of the Year VI.

	FRANCS
TREILLARD,[1] Président du Directoire	36,000
BESNARD, Président de l'Admon. cle. de la Sarthe	3,000
LETELLIER (Hypolite), Secrétaire du Directeur Merlin	4,800
BODARD (Félix), Vice-Consul de la Répub. à Smyrne	4,800
FENOUILLET FLAKMAC, Com. du Dre. près l'Odéon	4,000
LETELLIER, Chef du Bureau des Com.	4,800
BOSC (Laugne. Gme.), Consul de France à New York	4,800
GAY (J.-B.), homme de loi à Paris	4,800
CAREZ (J.-Pt.), sans qualité indiquée	4,800
MATHIEU, Comre. du Dre. près l'Admon. c. de Seine-et-Marne	1,000
SARDON, sans qualité indiquée	2,000
HERWYN, de la commune de Bruges, dépt. de la Lys	1,200
PORTIER P. LEBLANC, dépt. de l'Oise	1,000
SIBOUT CORNILLON, dépt. du Gard	1,500
ORTALÉE, dépt. du Nord	7,200
BASSAGET, dépt. de Vaucluse	2,400
TARDY, Comre. cal. de l'Ain	1,000
BEAUCHANY, Comre. cal. de l'Allier	1,200
GUIEU, Comre. cal. des Basses-Alpes	1,000
BOUTOUX,[2] Comre. cal. des Hautes-Alpes	1,000
CHAUCHET, Comre. cal. des Ardennes	1,000
BOSC, Comre. cal. de l'Aube	1,000
L'ÉVÊQUE, Comre. cal. du Calvados	1,000
SAVARY, Comre. cal. de la Charente-Inférieure	1,200
MALFUSON, Comre. cal. du Cher	1,000
GAUTHIER, Comre. cal. de la Corrèze	1,200
VOLFINS, Comre. cal. de la Côte-d'Or, ex-Constituant	1,800
HAREL fils, Comre. cal. des Côtes-du-Nord	1,200

[1] An order on the paymaster of the Army of Italy.
[2] Returned 500 francs of 1000.

	Francs
Michelet, Comre. cal. de la Creuse	1,000
Beaupuy, Comre. cal. de la Dordogne	3,000
Carnier, Comre. cal. de la Drôme	1,000
Rouppe, Comre. cal. de la Dyle	1,200
Dubosc, Comre. cal. de l'Escaut	2,000
Dazard, Comre. cal. d'Eure-et-Loir	1,000
Renouard, Comre. cal. du Finistère	1,000
Imbert, Comre. cal. de l'Isère	1,200
Pradier,[1] Comre. cal. de Jemmapes	1,000
Cears, Ingénieur en Chef du dépt. du Léman	1,000
Durand, Comre. cal. de Loir-et-Cher	1,000
Legall, Prést. de l'Admon. cle. de la Loire-Inférieure	1,000
Servierès, Comre. cal. de la Lozère	2,000
Mereau, Comre. cal. de Maine-et-Loire	1,200
Frain,[2] Comre. de la Manche	1,000
Laloi,[2] Comre. cal. de la Hte.-Marne	1,000
Garnin, Comre. cal. du Mont-Blanc	1,000
L'Évêque, Comre. cal. des Deux-Nèthes	1,000
Dupin, Comre. cal. de la Nièvre	1,200
Bassange, Comre. cal. de l'Ourthe	1,000
Garnier, Comre. cal. du Pas-de-Calais	1,000
Boutarel, Comre. cal. du Puy-de Dôme	2,400
Allard, Comre. cal. du Rhône	2,000
Ricard, Comre. cal. du Var	1,000
Bruyères, Membre de l'Admon. cle. de l'Ardéche	700
Génie, Comre. cal. de l'Aude	1,000
Devars, Juge au Tribal. cil. de la Charente	1,200
Combet, Comre. cal. du Gard	1,200
Dast, Comre. cal. de la Hte.-Garonne	1,200
Dauriot, Comre. cal. du Gers	1,200
Le Hary, Comre. cal. de la Gironde	2,000
Rey,[3] Comre. cal. de l'Hérault	2,400
Turgan,[4] Comre. cal. des Landes	1,200

[1] Received 1000 francs additional.
[2] Returned the 1000 francs that he received.
[3] Returned these 2400 francs.
[4] Returned 1133 fr. 50 of 1200.

	Francs
FERRAND, Comre. cal. de la Loire	2,000
COMBES D'AMOUS, Comre. cal. du Lot	1,200
BOUVET, Comre. cal. de la Mayenne	900
SOLNIER, Comre. cal. de la Meurthe	700
TOQUOT,[1] Présidt. de l'Admon. cle. de la Meuse	600
LE MALLIAUD,[2] Comre. cal. du Morbihan	2,000
FRESNAYE, DUPRÉ, Comre. cal. de l'Orne	600
CAZENAVE, Comre. cal. des Basses-Pyrénées	800
DESCAMPS, Comre. cal. des Hautes-Pyrénées	800
SIMON, Comre. cal. du Haut-Rhin	1,000
NEUKOMME, Comre. cal. de Sambre-et-Meuse	1,000
DESSEIGNES, Comre. cal. de Saône-et-Loire	2,009
CORBIÈRES,[3] Comre. du Dirre. p. les Trib. civ. et cle. du Tarn	3,000
PERIGORD, Comre. cal. de la Haute-Vienne	2,000
POUGNY, Comre. cal. des Vosges	600
MOREL, Comre. cal. de la Marne	1,000
SAVARY, Comre. cal. de l'Eure	1,200
BARDES, Comre. cal. de l'Ariège	800
BOIZARD, Chef de Brigade de la Gendie. nle. de Tours	1,200
PRADIER, Comre. cal. de Jemmapes à Mons	1,000
SARDOU, Ingr. en Chef des Bâtiments civils de la Mne. à Toulon	2,000
ROEMERS,[4] Membre du Conseil des Cinq-Cents	1,200
LUDOT, sans qualité indiquée	600
FRANÇOIS DE NEUFCHÂTEAU,[5] Ministre de l'Intérieur	5,400
GENTIL, Comre. cal. de la Loire	1,000
EDME ROGER, sans désignation de qualité	1,800
BLINSIN MORE,[6] sans désignation de qualité	300
SIBEREL, sans désignation de qualité	1,000

[1] Returned the 600 francs that he had received.
[2] Returned the 2000 francs that he had received.
[3] Returned 1323 francs of the 3000 that he had received.
[4] To reimburse advances made by the family to the citizen Chenorre.
[5] To distribute to secret agents of the commissary department.
[6] As a recompense for extra work in the correspondence of the secret-service funds.

	FRANCS
LASSAUT ET FELLETTE, postillons de la poste de Paris	414
Aux Commissaires des Hospices civils de Lisieux, dépt. du Calvados	1,040
Total	185,281

Unable to prevent by my personal and solitary opposition this corrupting decision, I refused to let any of the money be distributed by my hands, fully convinced that the funds given to the alleged influential managers of elections would not be productive of any good; besides, I had too lofty an idea of the electors of France to believe that they could be bought. The scheme was doubly hazardous, because some of the commissioners intrusted with funds for distribution did not enjoy the confidence of the Republicans. Whenever we really intend to secure good selections, let us begin by driving away the enemies of liberty if they have fraudulently wormed their way into the elections, and let us fill their places with sound Republicans; let us make our selection from among the good citizens unjustly persecuted as anarchists; the majority of them are so many authors of and actors in the Revolution; let us give them our support, and let us not suffer malice to bring into disrepute those who with us have founded the Republic. This disrepute is the work of the nobles and priests who have not rallied to the Fatherland and who conspire against it; if excesses have afflicted the Revolution, it has been fully established nowadays that they were perpetrated by the vampires of the ancient *régime*, who went over to the *émigration* in order to stir up coalitions against us, and by the agents of the foreigner. Did not the Treaty of Pillnitz, drawn up by the Abbé Maury, proclaim the dissolution and partition of our lovely Fatherland? Let us not forget that the alleged denomination of "honest people" is often nothing more than a flimsy disguise assumed by the most implacable enemies of the Republic. Of the patriots who begged me to assist them in securing their election, Benjamin Constant was among the most able and most deserving. This young publicist had devoted himself to Talleyrand when the latter was in the deepest distress. It would have been imagined that a contract of mutual services would thus have been formed between two liberal men (I use the word "liberal" merely in its old meaning, to express an advanced education) who had promised each other help, and one of whom had so honestly kept faith with the other; and that the one who should reach the goal first would help along the one who had remained behind. Mme. de Staël had indulged in this hope in regard to the two friends. What had not been Talleyrand's protestations of sincere gratitude previous to success! How quickly had he forgotten them immediately afterwards! Nay, what skill did he not display in thrusting back Benjamin Constant, dreading lest this young and ardent citizen should make his way by his talents! Talleyrand would have wished not only to snuff him out, but to bury him alive. We bless this revolting ingratitude of Talleyrand, who in this respect is to be credited with many similar deeds; for in keeping Benjamin Constant from an administrative career he lifted him into the national tribune. Hence, from this point of view, we think we may attribute to Talleyrand's nauseating actions the development of the grand talent and of the ever-progressive intellect of Benjamin Constant. In my capacity as a private citizen I should have liked with all my heart to contribute to the election of Benjamin Constant; he wrote me the following letter:

HÉRIVAUX, *7th Germinal, Year VI.*

CITIZEN DIRECTOR,

Permit me, since business matters detain me in the country, to write to you, in order to remind you that you have often expressed to me the desire of seeing me among the friends of the Republic to be sent at the coming elections to the *corps législatif*. Appointed an elector in my canton, I may succeed in getting elected if you still show me your good-will. I little know how to solicit, and the boundless devotion I have sought to show you does not seem sufficient to justify my request. But if you believe that my conduct from the time that I attached myself to the Republic, and the manner in which I fought reaction when alone you dared to resist Carnot in the Directorate, render me worthy of such a post, I feel confident that you will give me the support of your influence. I am already indebted to you for more than I can tell; I shall be still further in your debt, for I will owe you an occasion of proving to you more efficaciously that, whether in the tribune or whenever it becomes necessary to fight side by side with you, I shall always be what I have tried to be, when on the 18th Fructidor you saved the French Republic and the liberty of the world.

Greeting, respect, inviolable attachment.

BENJAMIN CONSTANT.

Benjamin Constant had done justice to me when thus addressing me; but the electoral movement was more powerful than my recommendation. France was still to wait a long time ere she was to see one of her most eloquent defenders ascend the steps of the tribune.

Switzerland is organizing itself; Rome also; in other words, two Republics are springing up. The commissaries whom the Directorate has sent into the old capital of the world—Daunou, Faypoult, Nouge, and Florent Guyot—inform us that she is free and independent, that she has a constitution, laws, and a republican government, and that the installation of the Roman consuls was celebrated as a festal day. Since the people are showing themselves so grateful and so favorably disposed to accept our laws, the acceptance of which has been left in their hands up to a certain point, it is desirable for our honor and security that we should not impose too hard conditions upon our sisters, the new republics. That is what seems to me to threaten us already on the side of the Cisalpine Republic.

The negotiations of Rastadt are progressing. The left bank of the Rhine is ours, as the frontier of the French Republic. A fresh coalition is being secretly plotted in Europe; the expedition to Egypt will quicken it. All our military resources should have been retained at home, and scattered principally along the coast facing England; but Bonaparte must leave the country: his presence really weighs heavily on the Directorate; my colleagues think they can justify their weak conduct in the matter by remarking, "Asia will hear of us."

At the time of the first constitution of the Directorate we decided that the members remaining after the fate of the outgoing member had been determined by lot should each contribute a sum of 10,000 francs, *i.e.*, a total of 40,000 francs, towards his maintenance; now this compensation is no longer considered sufficient, and it is sought to couple an office with it; it is agreed that the outgoing member of the Directorate shall be appointed a Minister. Such an arrangement does not seem to me worthy of the chief magistrates of the Republic. I consider it my duty to enter beforehand my formal disclaimer of it.

The negotiation having for object to keep the Prince of the Peace out of the Spanish Ministry has failed, owing to the lack of skill of our agents.

After having disarmed the Swiss cantons, and laid down regulations for the establishment of the Helvetic Republic, which is to have a *corps législatif* and a Directorate, General Brune has left to take up his command in Italy.

The anarchists are not many, but they derive support from the aristocracy at home and abroad. The Ministers of the Interior and of Police are so incapable that the Directorate considers it meet that it should take the matter in hand and propose the issuing of proclamations. Speeches everywhere repeated, and attributed more especially to the Jacobins, are beginning to be a pretext for alarming good citizens. The loan has become a forced one, owing to the measures which the Directors have been compelled to take to force contractors to deliver supplies. The contractors continue stealing in the most scandalous manner, and the employés of the Republic are dying of hunger. The Directorate believes that it has traced the moving spirit of much of the agitation which is disturbing the country to the irritating and narrow administration just now intrusted to an ex-priest, one Baudin, and to one Le Tellier; these two members of the *bureau central*, who owe their appointment to Larevellière, are dismissed, and their places filled by two citizens designated by the department of the Seine.

The English commissioner Crawford informs us that the Army of Condé is no longer in the pay of England, but in that of Russia. The alleged Court of France acts in conformity: we are informed that the Pretender has arrived at Mitau, accompanied by the Duc d'Angoulême. Paul I. is good enough to place at their disposal a château, where he has had magnificent apartments prepared for them.

Bonaparte daily displays the greatest fear of the terrorists. He incessantly tells me he will travel "in the lands of the foreigner if the expedition to Egypt does not take place." He complains of his wife, and she complains of him; she tells me that he is "close and avaricious; that he leaves her with an income of only 100,000 francs during his absence." She does not find this amount sufficient.

A portion of the family of Michel Lepelletier and the Directorate consider it their duty to oppose the marriage which the adopted daughter of the nation wishes to contract with young de With, a Dutchman. Mlle. Lepelletier triumphs over this twofold opposition; the love-match is celebrated. The presidents of the two Councils are present at the wedding festivities, which are very brilliant. A short time afterwards it is learned that love has changed to antipathy; the loving couple soon separate.

From the 10th to the 20th Germinal, Year VI.—There is some talk of giving the Genevese Minister Cappellis, who opposes the union, his passport; but it stops at sending away Gosse, his secretary, whose correspondence has been intercepted.

Malo, of the camp of Grenelle, the denouncer of Berthier, La Villeheurnois, appeals to me to obtain the cancelling of a warrant issued for his arrest as a result of his sally at Larevellière's. The Directorate orders the Ministers of War and of Police to restore Malo to liberty. The Minister of Police, Dondeau, seeking to reply to the charge of incapacity which our silence as well as our complaints bring against him daily, has conceived the idea of causing the Government's posters to be torn down during the night, and of charging this operation to the mischievousness of the anarchists. He had intrusted the execution of this to one Veauversin, one of his detectives. On this man refusing to carry out the misdeed ordered by the Minister Dondeau, he is arrested for having, says the Minister who gave him the order, "betrayed and compromised" the Government by divulging the great conception of this nocturnal tearing down of official posters. I call for the setting at liberty of Veauversin and the censure of the Minister. Carried.

Whatever the dissensions among the members of the present Directorate, as well as those of the preceding one, these members are assuredly not to be looked upon as enemies of the Republic proper; neither were such enemies, I am happy to state, those of my colleagues such as Carnot and Letourneur, who, as a result of their passions, finding themselves, if not united in heart, at least amalgamated *de facto* with the Royalists, necessitated the *coup d'état* of the 18th Fructidor against themselves, without which *coup* we could not have saved the Republic. But, worried for some time past by an ill-will which seems to be on the increase, the new Directorate allows itself to be invaded by a dread of imminent dangers which, it alleges, enjoin upon it to put itself in a state of defence; and, a prey to its growing uneasiness, the Directorate listens calmly to and even favors motions to arrest citizens represented to it as dangerous, and to disperse all gatherings. Such motions are made almost daily. No longer does any confidence exist among those who co-operated to the 18th Fructidor, and they do not see the traps set for them by their primary enemies.

The Minister of Marine, Pléville Le Pelley, tenders his resignation, which is accepted; he is to be made vice-admiral.

We have given orders for an attack on the Îles Saint-Marcouf. It cannot be long before they are in our power.

From the 20th to the 30th Germinal, Year VI.—The electoral movement which the Directorate has disapproved of, by seeking to interfere in it, is reacting in a contrary direction. Guyot Desherbières and a few members of the Institut, who are trying to get themselves elected deputies, work for the rejection of patriots who, like Garat, enjoy a greater popularity than themselves. To attain their object, they provoke divisions. The electoral assemblies, which are far from being as bad as Merlin believes, or as he would have us believe, plainly see the system of dissension invented by Merlin—a system dangerous and contrary to all order, as it decides in favor of the minority; for there can no longer be any society, but dissolution only, when the majority is disregarded. This fatal system, to which all parties may in case of need have recourse in turn, is bound to have as bad an effect abroad as it has at home.

Talleyrand, who is less worried by Rewbell since the latter is engaged with the electoral movement, hopes to retain his portfolio, and no longer speaks of Constantinople; but, as he has activity to spare, he takes a lively part in the elections, and sends me hourly reports on the situation in Paris. Seeing Merlin and Rewbell alarmed at the idea of certain selections which they consider shameful—such as those of the citizens Tissot and Antonelle, whose names are proposed at the assembly of the Oratoire, and who are represented as "Medusa heads" made to terrify the nation—Talleyrand chimes in with a strange opinion put forward by Merlin, who suggests that instead of opposing the selection of Jacobins, a certain number of electors should be paid to elect them. "As soon as you shall be able to show the nation such specimens," he says, "it will be easy to prove to it that anarchy has taken possession of the national representation. Let then men like Tissot, Antonelle, and Félix Le Pelletier be elected representatives of the people! This will speak more loudly than anything else, and it will afford you the means of reinforcing yourselves with all the alarms of the nation for combating them." In spite of all the shrewdness there may be in this way of looking at things, Rewbell and Merlin prefer to have Tissot and Antonelle excluded from the national representation rather than to submit their election to the consideration of the public.

Geneva has just voted in favor of being united to the French Republic. How powerful we shall be when all peoples come to us, if we can but show them the example of concord!

Hamburg has paid an additional four millions in cash, against a like amount in Dutch scrip.

CHAPTER VII

La Peur de Poultier—Bernadotte ambassador at Vienna—Disgusted with his post—Besieged in his mansion—His energetic conduct—Bonaparte's charges against him—Perfidious story he tells us—MM. de Colloredo, de Sauran, and Degelmann—Bonaparte in correspondence with the Austrian Government—Yet another story—Rewbell's lively rejoinder—Happy transition of Talleyrand—Projected message in regard to the electoral assembly of Paris—Vague charges preferred by Merlin—Sieyès sent as ambassador to Prussia—His exacting demands—Truguet recalled—His place filled by Guillemardet—Slight outbreaks in Switzerland—Sequel to the Vienna affair—Thugut—Bernadotte at Rastadt—Quarters given to him in the palace reserved for Bonaparte—The latter's discontent—His hopes—He defers his departure for Egypt—Fresh intrigues—His secret letter to Cobentzel—A sitting of the Directorate—His haughtiness—He threatens to resign—Rewbell's firmness—Supposed object of the expedition to Egypt—Wonders worked by the Directorate—Bonaparte ordered to start—I am instructed to communicate the order to him—His embarrassment—A clever reply—Departure for Toulon—Bourrienne—Firm note sent to Naples—Alarming proposition against the newly-elected—A conference in the Directorate—Chénier and Lamarque—The see-saw—Heated discussion in the Council of Five Hundred—Jourdan opposes the proposition—A "middle term"—Financial laws—Active zeal of the deputies—Sidney Smith removed from the Temple on a forged order of the Directorate—Merlin seems to charge me with it—My reply—Bonaparte at Toulon—The title of Member of the Institut—Philosophical hypocrisy—I am once more elected to the *corps législatif*—Bailleul reports on the decree relating to electoral operations—Alarms of the deputies—Reflections on the *coup d'état*—An explosion among the Five Hundred—A word restores calm—Speakers against Bailleul's project—Rouchon's speech—Pathetic scene between Chénier and Jourdan—Apostrophe of Crassous—Grotesque horror—The project is adopted.

From the 1st to the 9th Floréal, Year VI.—Rewbell presents a work entitled *La Peur de Poultier*, and demands that it be printed and posted; it is addressed to the author of *Le Bonhomme Richard*, printed, and posted all over Paris.

Bernadotte had written to me on the 24th Germinal from Vienna, where he had not long been our ambassador, that he could not follow such a career; he expressed himself as follows: "I have put my character to the test, citizen Director, and I am convinced that I am not suited to a diplomatic career; my organization will not suffer my remaining any longer among men whom I hate." I do not wish to connect the facts which follow with the foregoing disposition of Bernadotte's mind. The circumstances connected with them justify the belief that in this matter Bonaparte's intrigues once more played an active part.

The inhabitants of Vienna celebrated the anniversary of their voluntary and spontaneous arming for the defence of their city, threatened by the French armies. Our ambassador, Bernadotte, on the same day gave a *fête* in honor of the victories of the Republic. He hoisted a tricolor flag in front of his residence. The animosity of the Viennese was aroused at the sight of it; a mob proceeded to the residence of the ambassador. Bernadotte at once armed his household, placed himself at their head, and, sword in hand, heroically defended his residence and saved his life. He would infallibly have perished had he been merely a lawyer or a literary man unable to defend himself. During the attack, which he withstood for over four hours in his residence against an unbridled populace which was invading his dwelling, he received no help from the Austrian Government, which he repeatedly notified of the attack. The ambassador has been compelled to let his tricolor flag and his armorial bearings be removed. After this most determined outrage, and others which have likewise remained unpunished, Bernadotte asked for his passport, and left Vienna, unable to remain any longer in a city the seat of a government which cannot or will not take measures to prevent such outbreaks. Information reaches us that England, Russia, and the *émigrés* are the instigators of this outrage. It is decided that Bernadotte shall proceed to Rastadt, and a public reparation be demanded of the Emperor; that His Austrian Majesty shall, moreover, be summoned to explain his intentions in regard to Rome, Naples, and Switzerland.

Talleyrand and Bonaparte, although not summoned by the Directorate, both came before it to speak of the Vienna incident, the result of which has been the withdrawal of our ambassador. They seem to have agreed beforehand to censure severely Bernadotte's behavior. "What would you have had him do?" I inquire. "Should he have died? It would truly have been a Roman act, of ancient Rome at least, if not of modern Rome. Well then, citizens, you may put such high-flown maxims into practice yourselves. Moreover," I add, addressing Bonaparte, "was it not you who worried us to make a diplomat of Bernadotte, and who had him deprived of the command of the Army of Italy?"

Bonaparte, in order to strengthen the accusation he brings against Bernadotte, declares that he knows that about this matter it is his hot-headedness which has spoiled everything. He ought to have remained in Vienna, especially after a note which he knew had been addressed to him with every mark of friendship by Count de Colloredo. The Emperor Francis, deeply grieved at these disturbances, had at once given instructions both to the commander of the garrison and to the Minister of Police, whose well-known zeal and punctuality in the performance of his duties do not admit of any doubt that they would have carried out his intentions as much as circumstances permitted; that His Imperial Majesty, desirous that Bernadotte should not persist in his demand for his passport, had appealed to him to take into consideration all the difficulties likely to result when it became noised about that a misunderstanding had arisen between the two Powers, which would certainly happen were the ambassador to take his departure; that the Emperor had commanded Count de Sauran and Baron von Degelmann to call a second time on the citizen ambassador, in order to investigate and throw light on the matter, and to remove all well-grounded complaints of the ambassador, to the mutual satisfaction of both parties; that the Emperor, when commanding Count de Colloredo to be the bearer of his sentiments to the citizen ambassador, had commissioned him to couple with them the assurance of His Majesty's unalterable intention of carefully and on every occasion preserving the harmony so happily re-established between the two Powers — a resolution which the punctual execution of the Treaty of Campo Formio by the Emperor placed absolutely beyond doubt."

Bonaparte told us all the foregoing out of the abundance of his heart, and as if it were his own speech; but, noticing that he had in his hand a somewhat large-sized sheet of paper to which he constantly referred, we asked him "whence he had obtained all these particulars which he laid before us in so positive a fashion." "It matters little," was his reply, "if it is the plain truth, as I declare it to be." Rewbell answered that it was not unimportant for us to know how General Bonaparte was and could be informed, ahead of the Directorate, of things which immediately interested the Government and should come to it directly; in case it was an official communication made to him by the Minister of Foreign Affairs, the latter ought not to have made such a communication without previously referring the matter to the Directorate.

Talleyrand protests that Bonaparte had obtained no information from him; quite on the contrary, all Talleyrand knew about the matter was what he had learned from Bonaparte. Thereupon we ask that Bonaparte should frankly, and without subterfuge, communicate any documents which he might have received from whatever source, and on which he based his opinion.

Thus brought to bay, Bonaparte disdainfully produced a very legible copy, made on a sheet of brief-paper, of a note alleged to have been delivered to Bernadotte in Vienna by Count de Colloredo, and which the *chancellerie* of Vienna had probably despatched at once to Bonaparte, thus clearly establishing the fact that the two parties communicated with each other. We all looked at one another in genuine amazement on seeing that the simple citizen of the Rue Chantereine allowed himself to entertain such an intercourse unknown to his government, thus really usurping the chief rights of the Directorate. Under the impression that he can throw off all reserve, and placing himself above all reproaches we might be about to make, Bonaparte tells us naïvely that "he possessed a further quantity of information at his service; that he was moreover not in the least surprised that the Government had not been informed earlier of such important affairs; that before long the Government would receive official information, as he knew that the Austrian Cabinet had despatched a messenger, who must in the end reach Paris."

Bonaparte adds that he had knowledge of the whole matter and of its consequences previous to Bernadotte's departure for Vienna; that this general-ambassador, although he did not altogether lack ability, had lacked the first of all qualities— that of understanding the population with which he entered into relations. Bonaparte alleged that he had warned Bernadotte, long before his departure for Vienna, that the population of that capital was not like that of Milan, which hated the House of Austria; on the contrary, the Viennese people were deeply attached to their Lotharingian dynasty. Bonaparte drew the conclusion that it was a sentiment of affection for the sovereign which had impelled the population to this demonstration against the French ambassador; moreover, he claimed to know, as authentically as everything else he had told us, that on the day following Bernadotte's sally the Emperor had caused to be published a proclamation signed by Count de Pergen and conceived in terms indicative of the sorrow of the sovereign for the incident. This proclamation read that His Imperial Majesty had learned with the liveliest displeasure that, from a mistaken sentiment of zeal, a few inhabitants of Vienna had deviated from their customary respect for public order; that His Majesty, persuaded that all right-minded citizens would from henceforth abstain from taking a direct or an indirect part in disturbances or any kind of gatherings, had ordered that the most efficacious means should be taken to preserve public peace and order; that should any one disappoint his hopes in this respect, His Majesty would cause the disturbers of the peace of their fellow-citizens to be punished with all the severity of the law.

With his inexhaustible vanity of showing himself always the best informed, Bonaparte adds that the Emperor thereupon summoned a Council of State, to which he invited all the Ministers of foreign Powers; that the official report drawn up by the French ambassador himself was laid before this council, together with all documents likely to shed light on the untoward incident; that, after mature deliberation, all the ambassadors had signed a declaration which completely exonerated the Austrian Government, and cast the blame of the troubles of the 13th of April on the imprudent conduct of the Republican Minister. According to Bonaparte's version, it was Bernadotte who was alleged to have in the first place begun the disturbance, in seeking to oppose the commemoration about to be celebrated by the volunteers of Vienna, and next, by way of a wretched reprisal and a churlish bit of teasing, in hoisting the tricolor flag. Bonaparte told us further that a declaration of the Ministers assembled in Vienna had been sent to all foreign Courts.

Pursuing his diatribe against Bernadotte, while seeking to appear as merely accusing him out of devotion to the Directorate, Bonaparte informs us that the "prank" of Bernadotte was all the more unfortunate from the fact that the enemies of the Republic sought to attribute it to the Directorate itself, by bruiting abroad that it was a feeler in the direction of an insurrection which we had tried to stir up in Vienna, just as we had already done in Geneva, Rome, Switzerland, and everywhere else. Rewbell interrupts Bonaparte, saying: "Those who repeat such rumors are the accomplices of those who first uttered them. We were no more in Vienna these last few days than we were in Venice in your time, citizen general, and certain methods of procedure in the matter of insurrection are better known to you than to us. The Directorate is able to defend itself against all comers, but it never attacks any one, especially not by underhand means; such theories and practices are Italian, but in no way French." Bonaparte thereupon adopted the course of remaining silent, remarking that all he had just said had been spoken out of devotion to the Directorate. During all this conversation Talleyrand did not open his mouth; he merely sought the eyes of Bonaparte, as if to applaud his words; but, as our gaze was fixed upon him, the subtle courtiership of the eyes was a rather difficult matter, from fear of our noticing it. He sought to come to the rescue of Bonaparte, and get out of the scrape himself by bringing up another subject. I do not know how he went to work in order to propose that we should make war on Naples, if this Power did not immediately recognize the Roman Republic.

Persisting in his idea of dividing the electoral bodies into fractions, Merlin draws up a message in regard to the electoral assembly of Paris; in it he lays down that a vast conspiracy similar save in color to that of the 18th Fructidor is being plotted in the bosom of the Republic, and threatens the Fatherland. I ask that this article be struck out. A lively discussion ensues. In his message, wherein Merlin gave vent to all his spleen and fright, he said, by way of antithesis, that the names of Robespierre and Saint-Just had been invoked in the committees, possession of which had been taken by the anarchists, just as those of Vaublanc and Mathieu Dumas had been seized upon previous to the 18th Fructidor. According to Merlin, Paris was the centre of this vast conspiracy. It had, he alleged, been proposed in one of the electoral assemblies "to tear out the heart of a Chouan;" and the framer of this motion had stated he was prepared to put his threat into execution. We call upon Merlin to name the author of such an utterance: he replies that it must be Antonelle, Tissot, or Félix Le Pelletier; that the thing had occurred at the assembly of the Oratoire, where these anarchists had been reinforced by Cambacérès, who supported and prompted them. I interrupt Merlin, saying: "You are not in the least proving a fact in denouncing an utterance as vague as it is shameless, which you indiscriminately attribute to three persons, without actually specifying any one of them; why, having named Antonelle, Tissot, and Félix Le Pelletier, do you not add Rewbell, or Barras, or even yourself?" I enjoy for the time being witnessing the various expressions which overcast in turns the timorous physiognomy of Merlin.

This habitual frame of his soul furnishes his intellect with dangerously subtle resources; it would even lead his conscience astray, were he possessed of one.

When casting a look on the inner state of France, and especially on the legislative councils, we daily find additional motives for uneasiness. The dissembled discontent of Sieyès increases since the rejection of the law on the transportation of the nobles. The Directorate is importuned by the murmuring he incites. One of his friends comes and tells us that Sieyès would accept the Prussian embassy; we do not delay giving it to him; he indeed accepts it, but subject to the condition that he shall receive emoluments superior to those already established; he asks also for an additional 60,000 francs for household expenses, as he is absolutely without table-linen and silver plate. Granted.

Truguet is recalled; his successor in Madrid is to be the ex-deputy Guillemardet.

There have been a few slight outbreaks in Switzerland, instantly repressed.

Bernadotte is at Rastadt; we knew that he was young, ardent, and that it was impossible for him to possess the calm of deceit known as diplomatic experience, when Bonaparte urged and almost compelled us to send him as an ambassador; but Bonaparte shows himself guilty of a far greater wrong in bringing accusations at such a juncture against one who has only defended himself against fanatical assassins, led on by other paid murderers. The wickedness and perfidy of the Austrian Minister Thugut should be held responsible for the Vienna outrage. Bernadotte accused him alone, and did not blame the Emperor for it; he even spoke of him with consideration and respect for his intentions, while doing justice to his nonentity.

Bernadotte had been welcomed at Rastadt with every mark of respect on the part of the diplomats there assembled. It was also reported that the palace destined for General Bonaparte had been given to him as a residence; this circumstance was looked upon as a breach of decorum by the man who wished that his person, whether present or absent, should be treated with well-defined attentions and privileges, which could not be misunderstood. "It was," said Bonaparte, "a violation of all forms to have quartered a dismissed and retired ambassador in the apartment reserved for the president of the congress"—for such he was, had he but chosen to fill the post. Bonaparte came daily to the Directorate, now saying that we had exposed ourselves to disturbing the peace "which he had given to Europe," and then, that we should show a spirit of decision and break off from Austria. The Directorate was far from desirous of adopting this course; it had always been in favor of peace, and wished nothing more sincerely than to maintain it. All our thoughts were centred in perpetuating the harmony existing between the two nations by means of explanations satisfactory to both.

But such were not Bonaparte's ideas; his love of agitation made him sigh for events under cover of which he could glide into power. The 13th Vendémiaire had obtained for him the command of the Army of Italy; he was surprised and indignant at the fact that its triumphs had not, immediately upon his return, given him at the very least a seat in the

Directorate. A few days previous to the Vienna incident it might have been believed that his thoughts were wholly concentrated on the great expedition he was to lead; but since the Vienna incident he saw with pleasure the recurring chance of a fresh European war. The day for his departure had been fixed; he postponed it; in spite of all the foregoing discussions and of the pacific intentions manifested by the Directorate, so clearly that he could make no mistake about them, in spite of our plainly informing him that his talents were devoted to the expedition in the East, and that there was consequently nothing left for him to do but to proceed to Egypt, he persisted in offering us his services for a war against Austria, a war of which he had been the first to manifest a fear, in order to lay the blame of it at Bernadotte's door. Were the necessary powers given to him, he would say, he would undo the blunders committed by Bernadotte.

From this time forth Bonaparte, without the Directorate in any way acquiescing, attributed to himself all the powers it pleased him to assume, and seemed to consider himself the arbiter of France's fate. He continued to keep up his secret correspondences with foreign Cabinets. A letter from Bonaparte to Cobentzel was given to the Directorate, wherein, revealing some of his designs, he pointed out the necessity of a political change which might finally put an end to all the difficulties to which the Treaty of Campo Formio might have given birth. Enlightened by this warning, coupled with so many others, we realized all the dangers to which the Republic was exposed, and, with one common accord, we resolved upon hastening his departure for Toulon.

Bonaparte was greatly discomfited at seeing so fine an opportunity escape him. Having failed to attain by dint of stratagem and subterfuge his object, which was that the Directorate should invest him with a dictatorship of European affairs, he could no longer refrain from giving vent to his vexation. He addressed us in such an imperious fashion that the Directorate could imagine it was listening to a master dictating his will. We were not the men to tolerate such insolence; a lively and heated discussion ensued, in the midst of which Bonaparte dared to threaten us with the resignation of his command both in Africa and Europe. Thereupon Rewbell, taking up a pen, and handing it to him without the slightest sign of emotion, repeated what he had said to him on a former occasion: "Sign then, citizen general." Bonaparte, abashed, did not sign, and withdrew in silent humiliation.

All these imperfectly known particulars have given rise to the statement that the expedition to Egypt had been an honorable banishment of the conqueror of Italy. Avoiding any explanation in regard to the matter, Bonaparte seems to have manœuvred so as to let the whole weight of the accusation fall upon the Directorate. The fact is that the original conception of this expedition was his, and that the Directorate, acquiescing perhaps with too much complaisance in the project, the distant object of which was to strike a blow at England, generously furnished Bonaparte with the means of realizing this great dream. Amid all the troubles surrounding us, I may truly say that we accomplished wonders. A magnificent fleet was equipped at Toulon. An immense number of transports and ships of war of all kinds were gathered together, equipped and provided with everything, in the neighboring ports. The most flourishing and settled State could with difficulty have produced so imposing an apparatus of strength and power.

After having called for all these resources diverted from the other services, which they had exhausted, after having seen them placed with such liberality at his disposal, Bonaparte would now no longer proceed to his post, and stirred up, both at home and abroad, innumerable intrigues against the Directorate, in order to impede its course. Still refusing to admit himself defeated, in the face of the clearly expressed refusal of the Directorate to allow him to assume the chief management of peace and war in Europe, he incessantly begged us to allow him to return to Rastadt, with the object of controlling the negotiations and once more becoming the arbiter of the destinies of the Republic. His importunities having filled up the measure, my colleagues nevertheless saw fit to treat him with one more mark of consideration, and commissioned me to call on Bonaparte in a friendly way, and notify him that the time had come for him to embark.

Great was my surprise, on the evening I called upon him in the Rue Chantereine, to hear him dwell with persistency on his trip to Rastadt, and the line of conduct he would follow on his return; thereupon I told him in a low voice, so as to protect at once his self-love and the secret of the expedition, that there was a more direct road for him to take, and that he had no time to lose; that such was the purpose of the Directorate, a purpose full of goodwill to him, since it was I who was charged with

communicating it, but none the less decided. Bonaparte hardly knew what to reply; presently he said, "If I have spoken of Rastadt, it was to throw inquisitive people off their guard." "I am satisfied with the explanation," I replied, "but you must justify it by starting without further delay."

On the following day Bonaparte appeared before the Directorate, which listened to him attentively and coldly, and began with the statement that he had made up his mind to proceed to Toulon. We informed him that there was danger that "the English might forestall him in the Mediterranean;" he replied that "he had come to take leave of us." He remained in Paris another four days, and finally left, accompanied by the faithful or unfaithful Bourrienne and Mme. Bonaparte, who goes as far as Toulon only, when she will proceed to Plombières to take the waters.

15th Floréal, Year VI.—The consideration of Talleyrand's proposition to declare war against the King of Naples had been postponed until the presentation of the report on the reasons in support of such declaration. Pursuant to those now laid before us by Talleyrand, Naples is to be notified that France will consider herself at war with the King of the Two Sicilies, if the slightest act of hostility is committed against Rome.

Conferences have been held between members of the Directorate and deputies in the *corps législatif*, for the purpose of discussing the means of excluding from that body several members recently elected who, as we are informed, are anarchist leaders. I move we should deal with the Royalist faction, and that the message of the Directorate does not omit the conspirators of that party, which I consider the most dangerous, since it has its roots in royalty. Regnier, of the Ancients, Chénier, Hardy, Bailleul, and Crassous meet every night at the residence of the President of the Directorate, in order to determine upon what they call a purge. Are they worthy of the lofty mission intrusted to them by the people, these deputies who thus sacrifice their Republican colleagues to the will of the Directorate and to their own, which represents nothing more than the fraction of a fraction? It is sought to exclude Lamarque, whereupon I question his friend Chénier on the subject; he replies to me in a circumlocutory fashion which reveals both fear and deference. Lamarque has suffered much in the cause of liberty; no misdeed can be laid at his door; he was absent and in an Austrian jail in the unhappy days of the Terror; he is rejected, while Bally and so many others are retained. Regnier and Merlin display a persistent animosity towards the deputies of the *corps législatif*, whom they do not like, and whom they would wish to expel. What unrestrained authority will not such a measure give to the dominant party in the bosom of the *corps législatif?* This is truly what is even now styled "a see-saw government." The plan submitted by Bailleul meets with marked opposition in the Five Hundred, especially on the part of General Jourdan. Merlin is very uneasy, and fears that the proposition will be rejected. Finally, by compromise, the sentence is modified by the suppression of the word "conspiracy." François de Neufchâteau asks that the assembly of the Oratoire be mentioned by name. The discussion is renewed, with the result that his proposition is rejected. I maintain that the majority of the elections are good, and that we have no right to interfere in them any further; that it behooves the Government to ward off all political shocks, and to confine itself strictly within constitutional limits, because a contrary course would authorize the *corps législatif* to go beyond them; that we should guard against making arbitrary arrests, and restore to liberty all prisoners who are not charged with serious offences supported by documentary evidence. Carried.

In the short interval preceding these fresh troubles, and during which the administration of public affairs has been able to resume its course, the Directorate has devoted infinite care to it. We have devoted ourselves to rectifying many things in the matter of financial legislation, and making changes rendered indispensable by the various phases through which the Revolution has passed. We have been assisted in this by the laborious and well-informed members of the Councils, and there were good grounds for hoping that order would be restored in all branches hitherto neglected. Among the deputies who may be mentioned as having most powerfully contributed to the reform of the financial laws was the unfortunate Hugues Destrem, of the Council of Five Hundred, whose energetic protest against the usurpation of the 18th Brumaire caused him to be transported to Cayenne, where he died. He was for a long time president of the Finance Committee, and actively participated in the framing of the Customs laws and those connected with the sinking fund and direct taxation.

The Directorate is informed by the Minister of

Police that Commodore Sidney Smith and his secretary, for the past two years prisoners in the Temple, have just been removed by a detachment of troops bearing an order from the Directorate. Beyond doubt this order is a forgery; this is plainly revealed on its production by the Minister of Police. If any one is responsible in this matter, it is the employés of the Minister and the Minister himself. We are one and all dumfounded. A look of intelligence passes between the Minister and Merlin. The latter thereupon looks at me, as if designating me to my colleagues; I cannot help seeing that it is sought to saddle me with the matter. Merlin remembers that when he was Minister of Justice and wished to hang as a spy Sidney Smith, taken prisoner at Havre, I raised my voice against so barbarous an act. I had demonstrated that Sidney Smith, an English officer taken sword in hand, was a prisoner of war, and nothing more. My opinion had indeed prevailed; but because I had spared the Directorate a crime, did it follow that either at that time or subsequently I and the jailers should connive at Sidney Smith's escape? Here again are prejudices and conclusions inspired by hatred. "Sidney Smith was attending to his business in escaping," is my remark; "you were not attending to yours in allowing him to escape."

Bonaparte has at last left Paris. He has reached Toulon, he informs me, and is about to sail. Henceforth Bonaparte assumes the title of Member of the Institut among his other titles; he even places it before that of general-in-chief in his proclamations and letters. The philosopher's cloak was in vogue in Bonaparte's day, just as the sectarian's was in

Cromwell's. That is why the latter talked Bible and theology, while the former talked mathematical sciences, and assumed as his principal title that of Member of the Institut. The hypocrisy of philosophy and that of religion are one and the same hypocrisy; the mantle of Tartufe varies according to the fashion, but what it hides—*i.e.*, the character—is the same.

I have once more been elected to the *corps législatif*. This circumstance seems to astonish and nettle the members of the Directorate. I tell them in the first place that I will decline the honor. Next day I hint that I will accept; that at all events I am resolved to withdraw from the Directorate.

From the 18*th to the* 30*th Floréal, Year VI.*—On the day of the debate of the elections, the 18th Floréal, Bailleul appeared in the tribune as *rapporteur* of the committee appointed as a result of Merlin's message. He had been *rapporteur* on the 18th Fructidor, and the vague passion which had left its imprint on his work had furnished Carnot with material for a terrible rejoinder, wherein the proscribed man had shown that irritation and anger, even when overshooting the mark, are still sources of talent and eloquence. An impression was abroad that, in view of the similarity of the measures about to be called for, a point of support for them was found in the remembrance of the 18th Fructidor. That day having witnessed a victory won over the enemies of the Republic, the speaker who had then held the floor considered himself doubly interested to take it again at this new juncture. It seemed to him that the popularity attached to the former triumph would repeat itself more boldly to-day, even in the support of an entirely different thesis, but one which he would not fail to present as bound up with the former; for such is our weakness, that we are always most inconsistent when we seek to appear as most consistent and unchanging. In the Fructidor affair, just as to-day, Bailleul was doubtless animated by the purest sentiment of liberty; but impressed with the idea that certain political selections constituted a danger, he considered only the present time and not future consequences. He began by laying down that it was necessary that "the abstract principles, a strict observance of which leaves the Government without support against audacious conspirators," should be made to yield to the force of events. The committee, admitting as a positive fact the existence of a "double conspiracy"—that of the Royalists, which is permanent, and that of the anarchists, which is intermittent—claimed that this admitted fact should serve as a basis for the conduct of the Council; hence the Council should reject both the Royalist and the anarchist elected, and "everywhere separate the tares from the wheat." Should any one plead principles in opposition to the foregoing, the committee's answer is that the first of all principles is the welfare of the people. Moreover, the facts are there to speak for themselves, and require no comment. (Carnot, in his reply to Bailleul in the matter of the 18th Fructidor, had strongly reproached him with having, in default of proofs, asserted as the greatest of all proofs that "one does not prove daylight." Was the argument any different to-day?) Bailleul goes on to say: "You have to select one of three courses: to admit all elections, to annul all elections, or to choose from among the elections. To admit all elections would be excessively dangerous; to annul all elections would be most impolitic; all that remains, therefore, is to choose from among the elections. The committee accordingly proposes to you the following project," etc.; and this project consisted purely and simply in the annulment of the operations of a large number of electoral assemblies, whose selections did not please for individual as much as for political reasons; then, by virtue of such annulment, to make a choice among the deputies elected.

On hearing this proposition, several deputies exclaimed that "the assembly was being taken for an auction market of animals offered for sale;" and indeed, whatever might be at that moment the opinion entertained as to the real or exaggerated dangers of the Fatherland, it was difficult not to be uneasy about the consequences of the new *coup d'état* which was being prepared. This was one more cause for regretting that the Constitution of the Year III. had not invested the Directorate with the power of dissolving the Chambers, or that, after having so unfortunately felt this gap at the time of the 18th Fructidor, the breach made in the Constitution on that day should not have been repaired at once, and that a fundamental and provident law should not have afforded protection against the recurrence of *coups d'état* which their very authors must fain look upon as catastrophes and the ultimate cause of the downfall of empires.

The astonished silence which at first pervaded the hall after Bailleul's speech was quickly followed by a most violent explosion. All wanted to speak, whether from one point of view or the other, but as all spoke at once, not a word could be heard. Threats quickly followed murmurings, and blows were about to come on the heels of threats, when, by one of those sudden transitions not unusual in large assemblies, a reflection thrown at haphazard quieted all minds. "The Royalists have their eyes on you; they will take advantage of our dissensions." This was a paraphrase of what Bernadotte had said to his division at the crossing of the Tagliamento: "Soldiers of the Army of Sambre-et-Meuse, the Army of Italy is watching you!" These words, spoken on the bank of a mighty river at the review of the troops about to cross it, had decided and gloriously terminated the second Italian campaign; this utterance, I say, was more felicitous in its original improvisation, which belongs to Bernadotte, than is its repetition, which now comes to preside over the defeat of principles. Nevertheless, the magic effect produced by these words hurled into the assembly, which seemed to impress it like the head of Medusa, prove that those who heard them were for the greater part Republicans at heart, and sincerely desired the establishment of liberty in their country; but, while agreed as to the common aim, they were unfortunately not so as to the means. When at last there came a chance for speakers to be heard, General Jourdan, Talot, Quirot, and Gay Vernon attacked Bailleul's project. No one combated it more sincerely and openly than did Rouchon, who said: "The principal and perhaps sole effect of such a measure will be to stir up against us the indignation of France and the contempt of Europe. I will not suffer our grave to be dug in such a fashion. The committee has not lacked light, but the wish to see.

It has closed its eyes to the real attack while a false one was being made. You were threatened with anarchy, when despotism was behind it! Beware, citizens, lest you resemble the timid birds, who, in order to avoid the bird of prey, fly into the clutch of man. Remember that the horse, having lent its assistance to man, as soon as it sought to get rid of its auxiliary found that it was bound. The fatal day of the 18th Fructidor would have produced other results had its register been closed on the 19th. I have no love for the anarchists, but with the project it is now sought to impose on you the next session will be only the *Parlement de Paris*. Moreover, have not these terrorists, with whom it has to-day been sought to terrify you to such an extent, been the favorites, the *protégés* of the Government ever since the 18th Fructidor? How is it that their presence has attracted attention for the past two days only? To sum up: the elections are neither entirely good nor entirely bad; but I assert that not one of them has been held with full freedom, and I ask that they all be annulled."

The man who had just spoken thus was reputed to be a Royalist, and hence the Republicans had at first considered it unnecessary to pay any great attention to his speech; they had noticed in it and remembered of it only that which affected them personally, as is usually the case with every one in his own cause. Quirot, while maintaining that the project of Bailleul was odious and inadmissible, sought less to combat it than to take up the aggressive portion of Rouchon's speech against the 18th Fructidor. "Rouchon," he exclaimed, "intimated that the 18th Fructidor was a fatal day." "I did not intimate it," coldly answered Rouchon; "I stated so most positively." Jourdan swore in military fashion that "the plan of Bailleul was equally absurd and destructive of liberty; but should the law be passed, he would be the first to submit to it." On hearing this declaration Chénier rushes into the tribune, kisses Jourdan, and, turning towards the assembly, says: "The project is the salvation of the Republic, the rampart of liberty. With it I no longer dread either Royalists or anarchists. I feel secure as to my fate and that of the people. We have sworn hatred to royalty and to anarchy; this project represents the fulfilment of our oath." Audouin and Jean de Bry express like sentiments. "Let us submit," soon becomes the general cry. "Before we submit," says Lamarque, "permit me, colleagues, to shed tears on the grave of liberty. You know my sentiments. I call heaven and earth to witness that no one in this assembly loves his country more than I do. I would wish to save it; but some power I know not of is dragging us towards slavery. This project seals our fate." "If you do not adopt it," exclaims Crassous, "scaffolds will be erected before a week has passed, and your bleeding heads will roll off them. I have spoken." The speaker, seeing that this rhetorical figure made a somewhat powerful impression on the assembly, thought it good policy to continue, and so he exclaimed in still louder tones: "I ask you, in the name of your wives, of your children, of your lives about to be attempted by the knife of the executioner, do you wish to be guillotined? Answer me!" "No, no!" replied all the deputies, ingenuously, putting their hands mechanically to their necks, as if better to secure their tottering heads; "no, no, we would not wish to be guillotined." The sentiment of terror had been communicated to all as if by electricity, and no more was needed. Their imagination had been worked upon; all gave in, and the project was adopted. Merlin has triumphed.

CHAPTER VIII

Calumnies spread against Rewbell—His proposition in regard to the drawing of lots—Projects of assassinations in Italy—The King of Sardinia urged to grant an amnesty—Jean de Bry desirous of entering the diplomatic service—He is sent to Rastadt—Treilhard a Director—François de Neufchâteau leaves the Directorate—A dinner at Merlin's—He flatters Treilhard—Bonaparte sails—The English land at Ostend—Discussion with Treilhard in regard to the presidency—The challenge of two lawyers—Who is to be president?—A few hours' interregnum—Rewbell wins the day—Mutual apologies—Rewbell's antipathy to Talleyrand—An anonymous screed—Circular letter from Talleyrand to the Directorate—Malta refuses to receive Bonaparte—The taking of Malta—Admiral Nelson in the Mediterranean—Capitulation of Malta—A disgraceful clause—Vaubois governor of Malta—A purchase and a resale—Bonaparte's barren marriage—With whom does the blame rest?—A trip to Plombières—Its twofold object—Beurnonville at the waters—Mme. Bonaparte meets with an accident—Rapinat in Switzerland—A scathing epigram and its author—Rapinat recalled, then left at his post—The Emperor of Austria refuses all satisfaction for the insult offered Bernadotte—Vigor shown by the Directorate—Revolution in Holland—*Coups d'état* copied from our own—Sieyès's funny story—Departure for Malta—Translation of the Pope—Suspension of relations with North America—Taking of *La Sensible*—General Baraguay-d'Hilliers—Diplomatic changes—Disturbances in Ireland—French troops in possession of the citadel of Turin—Affairs in Sardinia—England's agents—Fresh translation of the Pope—Kosciuszko in Paris—Veteran soldiers charged with anarchism—Two centenarians—Affairs in Switzerland—The conference of Seltz broken off—Propositions made to the Directorate in regard to military preparations—Fresh troubles in La Vendée—Letourneur's place taken by François de Neufchâteau—Our position in regard to the Empire—Our ultimatum at Rastadt—Fresh expedition to Ireland—General Hardy—Affairs in Italy—General

CHAP. VIII A FALSE REPORT SPREAD

Saint-Cyr recalled — Treilhard persecutes Bernadotte — The woman Desjardins and the Chouan Rochecotte — Rewbell's illness — A word in praise of him — Measures taken against England — Armies of the Rhine and of Italy — Law in regard to the military conscription — Bad faith of the Rastadt plenipotentiaries — Our envoys Trouvé and Brune — Incapacity of Treilhard and Merlin — Méchin commissioner at Malta — General Desfourneaux — The Minister Saavedra — Special press laws — Home and foreign affairs — Condition of Italy — Infamous pillage — General report made to the Directorate — Reorganization of our armies — Brune sent to Italy — General affairs — Talleyrand's plan in regard to Italy — The expedition to Ireland sets sail — Uneasiness of my colleagues in regard to the press — Uproar in the Five Hundred — Lucien Bonaparte, deputy — His violent propositions — The deputy Marquezi and *Le Journal des Francs* — His calumnies against me — He makes his appearance in my drawing-room — I feel inclined to drive him out — His apologies — Austria's great preparations — Rewbell takes the waters — Chabert and Porte — Fresh seeds of disturbances — Intrigues against me — Fresh rascalities — Prussia's neutrality — Conscription — Rewbell returns from taking the waters — The *Journal des Francs* suppressed — My dissatisfaction in the matter — I am in favor of trial by jury — Talleyrand and Truguet — Diplomacy — Talleyrand's infamous act — His intrigues against Truguet — Truguet as the lover of the Queen of Spain — What to think of it — Source of Talleyrand's hatred for Truguet — A few more denouncers — Séguy, Perrochel, and Carency — Truguet's noble behavior — Talleyrand's fresh calumnies — He seeks to implicate me — I defend Truguet — Atrocious proposition made by Merlin adopted — Truguet in Holland — The doctor-ambassador — Guillemardet's silly conduct — Bonaparte in Egypt — Blunder committed by Brueys — Disastrous naval engagement on the Nile.

EVIL-DISPOSED persons, actively engaged in calumniating the Directorate as a whole and individually, have spread the rumor that, when the time comes for proclaiming at the Luxembourg the outgoing of the member of the Directorate designated by lot, Rewbell will be the one excluded, because he has been guilty of fraudulent practices in regard to contracts for supplies. Rewbell is of opinion that the best refutation of such a calumny would be to draw the lots publicly, since no one could question the truthfulness of chance guaranteed by publicity. The majority of the Directorate oppose this proposition. Thereupon Rewbell has it recorded in the minutes. The drawing of lots is to take place to-morrow, the 20th, at eight o'clock in the morning, in presence of the Ministers.

Fresh assassinations are being planned. In Italy attempts are made to sow dissensions among the French, and to hold them responsible in the eyes of all Powers in whose dominions disturbances have taken place.

The Directorate enacts that the King of Sardinia shall be called upon to grant a general amnesty for political offences; that the general of the Army of Italy shall supply amnestied persons with the means of returning to their homes, whence the intrigues of England had caused them to be banished.

The Revolution seems to lose daily in its progress something of the moral ideal which constituted its first movements. A taste for offices has developed itself, without its being in all cases justified by a need of them; men are beginning to confound honors with honor, and sigh for offices, seek offices, which are called honorary provided they be also lucrative. A representative of the people, whose few speeches impregnated with a pure and austere morality delivered from the tribune might justify his being looked upon as a sincere friend of practical honesty and simplicity, Jean de Bry, on seeing Sieyès and several of his former colleagues appointed to ambassadorial posts, in his turn wishes to tread the paths of diplomacy; he is sent to Rastadt to take the place of Treilhard, appointed a Director. There still remain many matters to be settled with Germany and Austria at that congress; as to the difficulties naturally following upon the crisis resulting in the sudden departure of Bernadotte, we are agreed that they shall be dealt with separately by negotiators of the two Powers. These are to proceed respectively to Seltz, a little town situated on the banks of the Rhine. François de Neufchâteau, whom the drawing by lot has deprived of his seat in the Directorate, is to proceed thither on behalf of the Republic; Cobentzel on behalf of Austria. We learn that the latter has already reached his destination. Austria does not seem anxious to commit herself again with France.

There is nothing so distasteful to a government as the selection of a bad Minister whose inefficiency it recognizes, while unable to get rid of him from the fear of having or of seeming to have the weakness shown by instability. The citizen Dondeau, Merlin's *protégé*, after having exhausted the list of improprieties and follies, is succeeded as Minister of Police by the ex-deputy Le Carlier, a former member of the Constituent Assembly, and at present a commissioner of the Directorate in Switzerland, where he has given proofs of capacity and integrity.

From the 1st to the 10th Prairial, Year VI.—Treilhard, our plenipotentiary at Rastadt, has just been appointed a Director; he has lost no time in finding his way to the Luxembourg. We immediately proceed with his reception. After his installation a dinner is given at the President's. Merlin, who is the host, flatters Treilhard with an assiduity noticed by everybody; he suffers no one to approach the new colleague. The latter seems divided between the desire to respond to all the special attentions of President Merlin and that of conciliating all his other colleagues.

Bonaparte has at last embarked, and sailed from Toulon for Egypt on the 20th. But before leaving French soil the Parthian has fired his parting shot. He can rightfully rejoice at having bequeathed to us the beginnings of a civil war in the dissensions which have arisen out of the elections.

The English have landed at Ostend. Some two thousand of them have been made prisoners by only three hundred French, commanded, it is true, by General Championnet, one of the brave sons of the Army of Sambre-et-Meuse, accustomed to conquer irrespective of the numbers of the enemy.

Treilhard, who has been so impatient to take his seat in the Directorate, is no less eager to enjoy all the prerogatives it confers. He begins by telling me in confidence that he believes the presidency is his due; he speaks to Merlin also in the same strain. Treilhard is to preside, provided Rewbell surrenders his turn in his favor. In the evening Rewbell calls on Merlin; from what he has been told, he considers that the presidency belongs to him; he would protest were the Directorate to deny it to him. On the morning of the 7th Treilhard calls on me; he persists in the idea that the presidency is his, as successor to a Director whose turn he takes. The Directorate is to meet at ten o'clock to consider this great business.

The sitting opens. Rewbell takes the floor, and informs us of the calumnies with which he has been overwhelmed; he avails himself of them to show that his enemies might draw ill-natured conclusions from his condescension, were he to give up the presidency which is his by right; were he to surrender it, he would find himself deprived for sixteen months of this prerogative, whereas his colleagues would be deprived of it only for a twelvemonth. Rewbell is not prepared to endure such a disgrace; he flies into a rage. Treilhard replies to him that had he felt inclined to refuse the presidency, Rewbell's speech would have imposed on him the duty of keeping it. Words, even threats, are exchanged. The two champions "do not fear anybody; they are ready," they assert, "to fight a duel after the deliberation." The challenge of the two lawyers excites no little hilarity. Rewbell might have said all he had to say on the previous day, before the presidency was given to Treilhard. Larevellière, Merlin, and I consider that it must have fallen to the lot of François de Neufchâteau, Treilhard's predecessor. Rewbell maintains the contrary; his eyes glare; he turns pale and thunders by turns, and finally confesses that he may have lost his head owing to all the attacks of which he is the target. Thereupon Treilhard gives up the presidency. I at once point out that a presidential interregnum exists, and that there must be an end to this deliberation, which Rewbell might have avoided yesterday; while admitting that I am right, he persists in looking upon his exclusion as a disgrace. The majority decides that Rewbell is to preside, to be succeeded by Treilhard. It is proposed to convert this decision into an enactment; I oppose the motion: an oral agreement sufficiently covers such a matter. Rewbell, on seeing himself in possession of the presidency, ceases to be angry, and becomes as mollified as a child allowed to have its own way; throwing aside all rancor, he shows himself affectionate, and confesses that he was in the wrong in regard to Treilhard; the latter admits that he was in the wrong in regard to Rewbell; both request their colleagues to accept their apologies and regrets: granted. They embrace.

Talleyrand is more and more uneasy about his position, *i.e.*, the retention of his portfolio, since he now lacks the support of Bonaparte, who has sailed. Aware of the contempt in which he is held by Rewbell, he is continually trying to conciliate him by every means he thinks "will meet his views." But Rewbell insisted that even that which might "meet his views" should be presented above-board, for he detested stratagem and falsehood even in diplomacy. He was in the habit of saying: "He is the cleverest who shows it not." Talleyrand was therefore greatly surprised at seeing Rewbell anything but satisfied with the following letter he had written to me concerning our relations with the United States of America. "Everything," remarked Rewbell, "should be openly avowed and signed, and especially between republics, where still greater frankness and sincerity should be displayed."

CITIZEN DIRECTOR,
I have the honor of submitting to you several reflections, which I have had printed, in regard to the absurd communication made to the American Congress by the President of the United States. They seem to me to be within the bounds of the moderation we should display; they are not too offensive to Mr. Gerry, of whom we are desirous of making use, but severe against his colleagues; they are very nettling to Mr. Adams, whose liberticide policy they unmask; as a whole, encouraging for our friends in America. I believe that all this was required.

Moreover, the refutation is complete. I have not signed these reflections, as I believed that they should not be entirely official, while at the same time appearing to come from authority.

Greeting and respect.

CH. M. TALLEYRAND.

21st Prairial, Year VI.—Bonaparte, on arriving off Malta, has been refused leave to enter the port for the purpose of taking in a supply of water; on the refusal of the Grand Master, Admiral Brueys is commanded by Bonaparte to make preparations for a landing; everything is got in readiness to capture this important island; the star of Bonaparte, hitherto continually in the ascendant, decides the success of this incredible undertaking. The town of Malta capitulates on the 24th Prairial. The Knights of St. John of Jerusalem resign their sovereign rights in favor of the French Republic. Two ships of the line, two frigates, four galleys, and 1200 cannon are surrendered. On the same day Admiral Nelson enters the Mediterranean with sixteen ships of the line.

In regard to this inconceivable surrender of impregnable Malta, it is true that its knights have no longer anything in common with the brave men who rendered themselves illustrious at Rhodes. As a result of the capitulation, the French knights at present in Malta are free to return to France, where they are to receive a pension of 700 to 1000 francs. This clause is not inserted in the message sent to the *corps législatif.* It would be impossible openly to avow that the island of Malta had been sold by its Grand Master and his officers, and that pensions had been stipulated for each member of the Order. Bonaparte had been determined on victory at any price; little did it matter to him if he saddled the Republic with a burden. Vaubois was appointed governor of Malta. Vaubois was aware that Malta had been heavily paid for by Bonaparte; it is doubtless for this reason that he in turn considered it his right to sell it to the English.

At the time of Bonaparte's departure for Egypt his wife had accompanied him as far as Toulon. Two years of married life, which she coquettishly called "two years of love," had not resulted in making her a mother. Already a debate had arisen between the two upon the question with whom the fault lay. In the course of a talk at which I had been present, Mme. Bonaparte maintained that it was not hers, since she could display the fruits of her first union. She thought thus to evade the question of age, which in her case might entitle her to rest. Bonaparte made her realize it by saying to her that Creole women, earlier marriageable than those of less hot climates, ceased being productive at an earlier date for this very reason. As for himself, he believed he was fully as able to procreate children as to win battles. In order to put an end to the painful side of such a conversation, and rescue Mme. Bonaparte from the actual consequences of her age, I remarked that these suspensions or delays in conception were generally got rid of by a course of waters. Dufour, my physician, confirmed in his opinion by M. Portal, said that it was absolutely necessary that Mme. Bonaparte should take a course of waters at Plombières, and that the result would prove all that could be wished. This presented a double advantage to Mme. Bonaparte, viz., that of escaping the journey to Egypt, and of indulging in meetings, which were easier at Plombières than in Paris, because of the watchfulness exercised over her by the brothers of Bonaparte, interested in defaming her. So Mme. Bonaparte went to Plombières; while there, she doubtless had for courtiers all those in whose eyes she was reputed to be on intimate terms with myself, not to speak of the reflex lustre shed upon the wife of a general-in-chief by the importance of his functions. It has but to be stated that General Beurnonville was at the time at Plombières, for people to be convinced that this *chevalier d'industrie* was bound to be the chief cavalier of Mme. Bonaparte.

Her husband having, as was his wont, commended his wife to my care, it was a matter of course that she should write to me. She met with some accident or other, whereupon General Beurnonville became particularly attentive to her, and freely used both post and telegraph to better display all the luxury of his attention and devotion.

The doctor at the waters of Plombières, taking all the devotion of General Beurnonville seriously, thought it incumbent upon him, in order to be on a level with it, to send me daily bulletins more circumstantial almost than in the case of a queen. An extract from this correspondence is worthy of a place in the archives of *M. Purgon*. This is how M. Martines, the doctor at the waters of Plombières, expressed himself in his bulletins:

"The patient has no fever; she is beginning to walk; she sleeps well. Her pains have become endurable; the contusions are nearing resolution. The patient is to be purged to-morrow, because her tongue is covered with saburra and her stomach is often full of *flatuosités*. I fully hope that, following upon this purge, matters will mend and the patient will soon be able to once more take her baths and douches.

"It is doubtless unnecessary, citizen Director, for me to beg you to forward this good news to General Bonaparte, as well as to all persons particularly dear to the *citoyenne* Bonaparte.

"This day, 6th Messidor, the *citoyenne* Bonaparte took a light purge: three ounces of manna in a light decoction of tamarinds. This purge cleared away a large amount of bile, and the patient feels relieved. I do not consider that there are any further consequences to be feared from the fall of the *citoyenne* Bonaparte; in three days she will be able to take her baths once more."

From the 1st to the 14th Messidor, Year VI.—Rapinat, a brother-in-law of Rewbell's, and our commissioner in Switzerland, has serious charges brought against him. Numerous complaints are coming in on all sides; he is charged with betrayal of trust, and even thefts. It would seem as if the very name of this commissioner furnishes food for an epigram. And so it is that a most biting one sees the light of day; its pith lies almost wholly in the name of the man whom it scourges:

> La pauvre Suisse qu'on ruine,
>   Voudrait bien que l'on décidât
> Si Rapinat vient de Rapine
> Ou Rapine de Rapinat.

As the author of this epigram did not reveal himself, an individual, whose particular species of wit justified his being credited with this wretched effusion, attributed it to his own pen; although not its author, he perhaps ended in believing that he was, by dint of incessantly saying so. The plagiarist was Thurot, later Secretary-General of Police, etc. The actual author was a young friend of mine, who had accompanied General Chérin, Chief of the Staff, to Holland, and who had returned from that country fully impressed with the idea that Rapinat richly deserved the joke indulged in at his expense. It is moved and unanimously carried that the citizen Rapinat be recalled. I am unwell for a few days, and my absence is taken advantage of to repeal the enactment recalling Rapinat. This man Rapinat is not only an impudent extortioner, but a brazen-faced maker of *coups d'état;* he has dared to expel worthy citizens from the Helvetic Directorate, substituting for them most unworthy people, that is, people of his own kind. On our receiving the despatch giving us the particulars of Rapinat's doings, there is some talk of appointing as his successor Champigny-Aubin, a former *conventionnel*, an able, honest, simple, and modest man. Lengthy debates extending over several sittings ensue. Rapinat's enactment is repealed, but he is allowed to remain as our commissioner in Switzerland: a few members of the Directorate are delicate enough to wish to avoid wounding the feelings of Rewbell in the person of his brother-in-law; I do not see why being related to a Director should constitute a mantle of impunity for extortioners.

As a result of all Bonaparte's intrigues with our enemies, and of the authority they think they can find in his calumnies against Bernadotte, the Emperor of Austria refuses to make reparation for the insult offered our ambassador. Even if Bernadotte has been somewhat ingenuous and thoughtless in his expression of a genuine patriotism, nevertheless such charges, more or less unjust even when best founded, do not constitute a reason for assassinating an ambassador in the exercise of his ministry.

The Directorate declares that it wishes for peace, for the execution of the Treaty of Campo Formio, but that it will not forego the satisfaction it is entitled to demand. The Republic will not send a representative to Vienna until the reparation due Bernadotte is made.

A revolution, considered necessary, has just been carried out in Holland. The Executive Directorate is overthrown; a few representatives are expelled; this measure saves the country. It was concerted with the agents of the French Government. The Directorate recommends the newly-constituted authorities to govern wisely, and especially to guard against any reaction. The Dutch are under the impression that they have had their 18th Fructidor, not to say their 22d Floréal. There is nothing like the example of things the least imitable to attract imitators in politics as well as in less grave matters. In regard to this singular imitative disposition of the human species, I must here narrate a serious story which I have often heard told by a most grave man, who, from the very reason of the demeanor he ever preserved with imperturbable *sang-froid*, enjoyed the faculty of making his hearers explode with laughter whenever he so willed.

Sieyès was wont to tell that, while still a schoolboy in the lowest forms, he had been struck by a scene of childishness, which he had since seen repeatedly renewed, with a more extended application, in the great domain of politics. "One of my most mischievous school-fellows," he said, "one day conceived the idea of playing a singular trick on the rest of us: as he was passing by a mass of filth, he dipped his finger into it, and with what adhered made himself a disgusting mustache. All the others looked at him with horrified disgust. 'Now, then,' exclaimed the young scamp, 'we shall soon see which one of you has any pluck;' and once more putting his finger into the filth, he ran among us exhibiting it and saying boastfully: 'Let those who have any pluck follow my example.' Immediately thereupon those who had shown the most disgust rush forward, put their fingers in the same mass of filth, make for themselves similar mustaches, and, with fingers uplifted in triumphant fashion, chase each other, so loudly proclaiming to be cowards those who do not imitate them that the latter, intimidated, finally make up their minds, and in a very short while all have mustaches. Well, citizens," Sieyès would say, proud and happy over his anecdote, "such is the sheeplike nature of the human species! Let us therefore derive all the benefit we can from it."

18*th Messidor, Year VI.*—The French fleet and its convoy have sailed from Malta for Alexandria. The Pope is moved to the Chartreuse, near Florence.

The Congress of the United States of America suspends all commercial intercourse between France and America.

Nelson captures off the coast of Sicily the French frigate *La Sensible*, bearing despatches from Bonaparte and having on board General Baraguay-d'Hilliers.

The taste for offices and ambassadorial posts grows apace. Our former colleagues of the National Convention, more numerous than ever, were wont to say: "Why should we abandon to the aristocrats every social advantage, and all the prerogatives we have for so long modestly rejected?" I must confess that I am altogether of the opinion of the grumbling *conventionnels*. I believe that a republic cannot be founded without republicans, and that to maintain so new a social organization as ours in the midst of old Europe we have but one means—that of placing everywhere, abroad as well as at home, those men who are most deeply attached to liberty, and who have given pledges to it.

Lamarque is appointed ambassador to Sweden. Lacombe Saint-Michel succeeds Garat at Naples; the latter has been elected to the Council of Ancients.

Ireland is in a state of ferment; several districts have risen in arms against English tyranny. Engagements take place daily; the Cabinet of St. James gives way, and seems to abandon for a while its system of persecution and cruelty. The French Republic is not in a position to give open support to the Irish patriots. The Minister of Marine is instructed to ship arms and ammunition to them, and to take all means at his disposal to supplement these with a few troops. We are informed that the English, warned of our attempts in regard to Ireland, have resolved to carry the scene of the discussion into our midst, and that they have among us agents whose mission and hope is to sow dissension.

It is of importance that we should put our hand on these agents. The *corps législatif*, alive to the danger, authorizes the Directorate to make domiciliary visits during the space of one month, for the purpose of discovering and arresting the agents of England.

French troops have taken possession of the citadel of Turin, pursuant to a convention entered into with the King of Sardinia. General Brune has been ordered to take the city of Turin itself, if its government refuses an amnesty and does not withdraw its troops. A similar order is given in regard to Liguria.

The English squadron scours the Mediterranean in search of the one conveying Bonaparte. An engagement takes place between the French brig *Lodi* and the English brig *Eagle* off Porto Longo.

The Pope is transferred from the Chartreuse to Cagliari in the island of Sardinia.

The celebrated Pole Kosciuszko has arrived in Paris. The hospitable soil of liberty should be proud of welcoming the new Washington. Less fortunate than he, Kosciuszko has been unable to save his country by defending it; and left for dead on the field of battle, he reopened his eyes to see his Fatherland in the power of the Russians. What a lesson and what an example to France, if wisdom does not enlighten our courage, and if we allow the magnificent opportunity of establishing our independence to escape!

From the 20th Messidor to the 1st Thermidor, Year VI.—It continues to be the custom to denounce the anarchists; even our venerable veteran soldiers are embodied in this category, and their declining days are disturbed by persecutions and dismissals. These are so many false measures. Discontent has made itself manifest among the veterans, and their complaints are bitter. I propose that pecuniary help be given to these brave and maimed men, whom the law has excluded from the places they formerly occupied. The matter is to be seriously talked over with the Minister of War. Two of these worthy old men are almost centenarians. It has often been a real enjoyment to me, whenever I saw them, to compensate them in a small way for their misfortunes by my attentions. I have often sent to the Hôtel des Invalides for these aged representatives of French glory; they were conveyed to my residence in my carriage, and I would seat them at my table together with some other old soldiers who still bore within their battle-scarred bodies generous and resolute souls; so I was the first to set the example of the respect due to these noble ancient monuments, to these surviving remnants of our armies.

Rapinat continues to spread anarchy throughout Switzerland. He now seeks to get rid of Colonel La Harpe, whom he himself had recommended to us at the time of the organization of the Helvetic Directorate. Difficulties have arisen in regard to the offensive and defensive treaty. The French troops are not to evacuate Switzerland until after the conclusion of this treaty.

Conferences which had been begun at Seltz have been broken off without any result having been reached. If we wish to preserve peace, let us not forget that war and victory procured it for us. We should give all our attention to military matters; 120,000 men should be massed on the Rhine, and

80,000 in Italy. It behooves us to command the Minister of War to get ready the necessary supplies, compel all deserters to join their corps, recall all men on furlough, and at once lay before us a report on the results of the recruiting system. These are urgent measures enjoined upon us by the silence of Prussia, by English and Russian intrigues at that Court, by the armaments being prepared in Austria, and by the imperious tone of the Imperial delegation at Rastadt. The Directorate recognizes the urgent need for adopting all these propositions.

From the 1st to 25th Thermidor, Year VI.

La Vendée is once more being stirred up by the agents of the foreigner. Unfortunately, there still exists in the bosom of the *corps législatif* a party which gives its support to these enemies of all liberty.

The relaxation of Republican morality continues to invade all classes. Deputies of the Council of Five Hundred have once more begun to solicit several pecuniary advantages already refused to them on moral as well as on economic grounds. These deputies are, it is true, military men who have so far remained within the bounds of decency. If at one time they seemed to accept the austere morals of the Republic, the terror inspired by 1793 may have had not a little to do with their resignation. Nowadays death is no longer there to restrain them. But a truce to harsh comments. It is merely in this instance a matter of a few forage rations; although aware that the demand preferred constitutes an abuse, that military men not on active service are not entitled to these rations, the Directorate grants them to the military deputies.

Pursuant to our new agreement that an outgoing member of the Directorate is to receive a portfolio, the ex-Director François de Neufchâteau becomes Minister of the Interior in lieu of the stupid Letourneur.

The position we have taken up in regard to the Emperor is such that we remain in a state of war. We are consuming all our means of subsistence; disorganization ensues as a result of our inaction; both the home and the foreign enemy foment this state of disorganization. I ask that the Rastadt Congress be notified that our ultimatum is that the middle of the Rhine is to be considered the frontier, and that war is to be declared if this is refused.

We have seen that Bonaparte, after having made all his arrangements at Malta, has continued his journey to Alexandria; the English squadron is giving him chase.

The Directorate has finally resolved upon attempting a fresh expedition to Ireland; it is intrusted to General Hardy.

Discussions, slight at first sight, but most important in their results, arise in Italy between the civil and military authorities. We summon to us General Brune, in order that he shall enlighten us as to what is taking place in Italy.

General Saint-Cyr is recalled from Rome, whither we had sent him in consequence of the mutiny of the Masséna division. He was the wisest soldier and the one most firmly attached to discipline that we ever sent into that country, and it was an actual blunder to recall him.

Treilhard has already given us several specimens of a character ill-tempered and inclined to personal resentment; he seems to have a grudge against Bernadotte. Not that Bernadotte, like all weak mortals, has not committed political blunders at the outset of his career; it is because he has ceased committing them, because he has proclaimed himself in a striking fashion in favor of Liberty's cause, that he is to-day persecuted and that it is sought to cover him with disgrace.

A certain woman, Desjardins, comes to Paris from Le Mans, and hastens to call on the Directorate for the purpose of denouncing one Rochecotte, a leader of Chouans, who has recently arrived in Paris. Events have gone to show that this denunciation is not a calumniatory one; this Rochecotte is the same who since the Restoration has thought it incumbent upon himself to demonstrate, in memoirs which he has published, that he was always an avowed enemy of the Republic, and that for long years all his doings were influenced by this enmity, in order better to contribute to the extermination of liberty in France. General Verdière is ordered to arrest this Chouan, who has no right to be in Paris; the order is duly carried out.

Rewbell was a sick man even previous to the 18th Fructidor. His illness makes a progress painful to all the friends of this true statesman; his health has been undermined by the shock of all that has happened. I am afraid that I notice a considerable weakening in him; on nearing me he has shed tears. This Director possesses great administrative knowledge, and is well versed in jurisprudence and in international law. His is undoubtedly, as I have already stated, and as I willingly repeat, the most level head in the Directorate. He was my compass. Surrounded as we were by a labyrinth of laws, the intricacies of which were hard to master, I was able perhaps to bring a certain amount of natural common-sense to the understanding of them, but I was more familiar with the execution than with the scientific side of them; my inexperience oftentimes leaned on the luminous discussions of Rewbell, who enlightened my opinion and determined my vote. His departure from the Directorate would be a calamity which I should feel deeply.

I move that the twelve Spanish ships of war anchored off Carthagena should be united with the squadron of Admiral Brueys, for the purpose of attacking Admiral Nelson with some chance of success. It would be well for us to treat with Spain so as to obtain assurance from her that all the war-ships she is able to arm should proceed to Brest. This amalgamation of naval forces will furnish us the means of undertaking the great expedition to Ireland, which is necessary if we would wish to secure peace and tranquillity. England, who possesses the commerce of the world, also undertakes to be mistress of everything that sails the seas. The loss of Ireland will overthrow that government, deprive it of a number of its sailors, and bring it back to pacific and well-intentioned sentiments. The most active measures must be taken to make the sailors called upon by requisition join their ships; thereupon the Ministers of War and Marine are instructed to report.

The Army of the Rhine will very shortly number 120,000 men, that of Italy 80,000.

The Directorate devotes its sittings to framing a law relative to military conscription; such a law is urgently required; this is the true way to influence Austria.

The foreign delegates to the Congress of Rastadt daily prefer the most insidious demands; no end is being attained; each succeeding day sees the previous day's work taken up again. It is like Penelope's web. On the other hand, our negotiators are not meeting with any wonderful success. Bonnier, who goes to work with old and obsolete ideas and a peremptory manner, does much harm; as for Jean de Bry, he is little versed in diplomatic negotiations.

The disturbances taking place in Italy claim our attention more than ever. The Directorate, which has summoned to Paris Brune, Commander-in-chief of the Army of Italy, has had several conferences with him. All the disorders in the Cisalpine Republic seem to proceed from the presence in that country of the ambassador Trouvé, a young man as weak as he is presumptuous, who assumes an exaggerated authority based on the favor he enjoys at the hands of our colleague Larevellière. In order to bring about a peaceful state of affairs in Italy, it is necessary first to remove Trouvé. Larevellière would like to bring about a *rapprochement* between his *protégé* Trouvé and General Brune. The latter returns to Italy provided with fresh instructions.

The recent appointment of a Director, in succession to François de Neufchâteau, has nowise added to the elements of union and fraternity which we so need in order to strengthen our hands. Treilhard is a vindictive and haughty man, far inferior to his reputation on the occasion of serious debates in the Directorate. Merlin is a scribbler well versed in jurisprudence, but so circumscribed by his very knowledge of that branch, that he is unable to grasp what goes on in other spheres; he is a man who will belong to every succeeding government, and will register with admirable promptness the minutes of all their changes.

In conformity with my habitual desire, I may say with my religion—which I have always professed and practised as much as it lay in my power—to place patriots in public offices, I had for some time past extended a kindly welcome, having so far not succeeded in doing more than this, to a man who enjoyed in those days a great reputation for patriotism (a patriotism which he has perhaps since sought to perpetuate by an ardent imperialism), the citizen Méchin. He had served us in the course of the events subsequent to Thermidor, and had since been employed by Fréron in the South, but had not thereby acquired means enabling him to live comfortably. My colleagues were greatly prejudiced against him. Finally I obtained, but not without difficulty, their consent that Méchin should be sent as commissioner to Malta.

Another individual, who on all occasions came forward in quest of the most lucrative offices, on the grounds of his having been formerly employed in the colonies, General Desfourneaux, again makes his appearance; he is one of those mediocrities of the Beurnonville stamp, although on a lower plane, who by dint of worrying governments always extort something from them, owing to an importunity equalled only by their insignificance.

We are waiting for Prussia to come to a decision. The new Spanish Minister, Saavedra, appears disposed to work harmoniously with us.

The law placing journalists under the immediate control of the Directorate is about to lapse. Measures are adopted to prepare the public mind for its prolongation. I consider it proper to point out to my colleagues that a penal law and good courts allow the Government to deprive itself of a too dangerous power over the press. Governments in general, even free governments, dislike relinquishing attributes granted to them for a while. Equally mistaken are those who think to derive some additional force from laws of exception; the security of administrators as well as that of those governed is in the exercise and inviolability of the common law.

Just at this time (Prairial, Year VI.—May 1798), *i.e.*, the third year since the installation of the Directorate, I looked with some degree of pride at the past, with some trepidation at the present, and at the future with the greatest uneasiness. It was impossible for one who saw things in all the nakedness of truth not to perceive that the Directorate was daily losing a portion of the consideration acquired by the military triumphs of the last few years, by their results, and by the creation of several republics; now all that the Directorate might lose did not constitute a private, but truly a universal misfortune. Should it succeed in preserving the vigorous and dignified attitude proper to it since its installation, the mere fact of the good organization of the new constitutional States would constitute a useful example which could not fail to increase, without provoking any shock, the number of Republican governments, and place the representative at the very least on a level with the hereditary system. But the Directors who had joined since the 18th Fructidor did not possess the lofty conceptions and views enabling them to look this great object in the face. Merlin and Treilhard, with less ability than Carnot, or even Barthélemy, suffered themselves to be swayed by the same passions. They did not vote with Rewbell and myself; they worked upon the imagination of Larevellière, whom they often succeeded in winning over to their side; ill-considered proclamations against the anarchists [for which read Republicans] lowered the Directorate in the public mind, whether it was believed that it acted from error or from fear. One hypothesis being as good as any other for the purpose of accusing the Directorate, its enemies took up the course pursued by it at the time of the elections in Floréal, when a most legally elected majority had been sacrificed to a minority founded on force. The 18th Fructidor had pitilessly expelled the deputies opposed to the Republican party, but had not put others in their places. The 22d Floréal, more illegal and more cynical, had admitted to the ranks of the national representation, without titles and without mandates, individuals hitherto looked upon as honorable men in their private lives, but who were far from showing any sense of honor in the means employed by them to enter political life, and who were most properly styled "intruders." Since public opinion had in no wise consented to the law of the 22d Floréal, it caused uneasiness to the individuals who had become somebody by that law alone. Thus was established, outside as well as in the bosom of the national representation, an opposition from which the most fatal consequences might be feared.

Simultaneously the formation of the new States, the result of the victories of the armies of the Republic, gave us much trouble. We had undertaken to maintain and support that act, and this was a daily and even an hourly responsibility. Great discontent had followed upon enormous abuses in civil and military administration, the violent spoliations perpetrated in Italy by military commissioners, and by civil commissioners, another newly created body of hungry patriots. Among the generals, Masséna, chief among plunderers as foremost by his talents, had distinguished himself equally in both respects. Alarmed at this state of things, truly symptomatic of a state of decline, I had called for a few changes in the *personnel;* little had been gained thereby. The new-comers were as violent as their predecessors. Justly alarmed at this progressive retrogression, I considered it my duty to communicate my thoughts on the subject to my colleagues, and to direct their special attention to Italy. Here are some of my reflections:

"The districts of Italy wherein our victories have established new organizations are divided into three republics, the Cisalpine, the Roman, and the Ligurian. The city of Rome alone, the most recent conquest of French arms in Italy, contained enormous riches. What has become of them? They have been divided among a small number of military chiefs, and especially of the civil leaders.

"These riches, united with the annual contributions of the Cisalpine Republic, should have amply furnished France not only with the means of keeping up the army on a respectable footing during the whole of the campaign, but of paying several millions into the public coffers to meet the home expenditure; yet so far from this being the case, the Army of Italy is greatly in arrears; the soldiers are badly fed, badly clóthed, and badly paid; its present position is to be compared only to the distress it was in when vegetating on the Genoese coast, lacking clothing, bread, and boots. It is hard to say who has greater cause for discontent, the despoiled inhabitant or the victorious soldier. Is it to be wondered at that in such a state of things indignation should have given rise to breaches of discipline? Meanwhile peace is not being signed at Rastadt, and the Emperor is quietly despatching troops into the Tyrol and the Grisons. He is making formidable preparations for a new campaign. He occupies Venice and the mainland by virtue of the treaties concluded; he can by entering the district of Ferrara, which is insufficiently guarded, prevent the junction of the Army of Rome with that occupying the Cisalpine Republic. It is feasible for him to regain possession of Lombardy. The discontent of the populations, the destitution of the army, and especially the dissemination of the troops over a vast extent of territory, leave the road open to him—especially if he opens the attack, for he will be fully prepared, while it appears that we are not even ready to act on the defensive. A first victory for Austria will be ominous for the rest of the campaign if you do not adopt stringent measures for the repression of the disorder existing in our Italian affairs, and especially of the conflict of powers, the primary cause of the abuses existing in Italy.

"To compare this state of affairs with that established by our first conquests up to Frimaire, in the Year V., in the matter of finances: the army in Lombardy had been clothed, fed, and paid; a considerable amount of arrears had been paid off, and a few millions had been paid to the French Government. Lombardy alone had furnished these resources, with the exception of five millions paid by the Pope on account of the contributions levied on him at the time of the armistice.

"Let us now look at the political aspect of affairs. Up to the time Saliceti left the army to go to Corsica, he had successfully maintained an equilibrium between civil and military power. Since that time an unpleasant discord has found its way into the armies; generals have enriched themselves shamelessly and beyond measure. I of course except from among them those generals who, true to honor, have contented themselves with acquiring a disinterested glory; hence it is that they enjoy the confidence and esteem of the army. What would have become of it had it not been for new resources, albeit in part diverted from their proper use? Mantua, Trieste, and Venice were wealthy in riches and provisions of all kinds: Trieste, as well as the former depots, was given up to pillage; Venice was despoiled, as well as a portion of the fifteen millions paid by the Duke of Modena, who had sought a refuge there: this amount alone would have assured the maintenance and provisioning of the army during a year's campaigning. The army sustained itself, but would soon have suffered from extreme destitution in the midst of this abundance of resources if, at the height of this unparalleled disorder, the general and the higher administrators had not placed in safety a few remains for the needs of the military service. There were soon as many receivers and commissioners in the army as officers, and a large portion of the contributions levied found its way into their pockets. Then came the capture of the Capitol; the Directorate and the general-in-chief had taken measures which, instead of putting a stop to depredations, added new depredators through the despatch of new commissioners and *savants*, who came upon the scene with empty pockets. The general-in-chief was little versed in matters of administration. I have already stated that the military and civil authorities had quarrelled over the rich spoils of the Papal Government, and that this had excited the indignation of the army; that Masséna and even Berthier had been compelled to fly. Monuments of art were carried away, and in part sold abroad. Some of the most precious were sent to the Museum. Many others still adorn to-day the rich residences of the thieves. Thus vanished the treasures accumulated by seventeen centuries of fanaticism and superstition within the walls of the ancient capital of the world. It is painful to see that no punishment is inflicted upon a consul who enters into onerous bargains in the ports of Corfu, Malta, and Corsica, which he pays with national domains, unknown to the Minister of Finance. Each and every accountant administers as he sees fit, and in furtherance of his own interests. The Directorate should take measures to prevent the pillaging of Naples and Tuscany when we occupy them. Such corruption is not to be tolerated, for it would ruin our influence in Italy, and result in the hatred of the Italians for our great nation. What means will be at our disposal if war is renewed with a totally unprovided army? The Directorate should therefore repress the depredators and, if possible, make them disgorge, and not listen to any appeal based on personal affection when appointing its agents. All dishonest accountants are to be reckoned as enemies of their country. The authorities in whom is vested the law, and who are responsible for its execution, must not show indulgence to these plunderers. I call the attention of my colleagues to the foregoing observations, put together perhaps in shapeless fashion, but none the less the result of long and deep meditation."

Although in the habit of never speaking in the Directorate except on the spur of my emotion, under the inspiration of events and without any preparation whatsoever, and although I hardly ever put anything down in writing beforehand, I had deemed it best in this instance, in order to be sure of my ideas, to jot them down. They won me the individual and collective thanks of my colleagues. Results did not go to show that gratitude is akin to attention; still it is decided, in a general way, that the affairs of the Cisalpine Republic are to be looked into, and that it is to be organized in such a manner as to diminish the expenses it can no longer support.

The Directorate hurries forward the organization of the Armies of the Rhine and of Italy, so as to be able to reap success should the enemy attack us. Orders are issued to send the levies called out by requisition to join these armies. The granting of furloughs is suspended. The Army of Mayence, commanded by Joubert, is to be reinforced with troops and competent generals; the Army of Italy likewise.

After having conferred with the Directorate, Brune returns to Italy. He is commissioned with the execution of reforms, and with the putting into effect of the changes ordered in the Cisalpine *corps législatif* and Directorate. It has needed nothing less than the storm threatening us to induce the Directorate to intrust these measures to a general whose transcendent capacity is perhaps not on a par with his patriotism. Naples no longer conceals her hatred or her warlike preparations. Vienna is also making hers. Still the coalition does not dare so far to pronounce itself openly; it would like to compel us to declare war, in order to be able to charge the French Directorate with violating existing treaties. Prussia, seeking to use tact in dealing with the matter, still hesitates; she cannot expect the friendship either of the French or of the members of the coalition. Nevertheless, Sieyès writes that he hopes to win her over to a French alliance.

Treacherous intrigues continue to be carried on in Turin. This is the first enemy to whom we must mete out justice. It is impossible not to expel the king; he shall receive an asylum in France, should he ask it, and the Piedmontese Army shall be united with that of the Republic. A few picked troops only are to be left in the interior of Italy, for the purpose of supporting the organization and establishment of a representative government. Tuscany will also receive a republican organization. The General-in-chief of the Army of Italy is, by way of negotiation, to advise the King of Sardinia and the Grand Duke of Tuscany to take their departure. Talleyrand guarantees that he will succeed in demonstrating to the two sovereigns, through the cleverness of his agents, that "their departure is their own salvation." He undertakes to inspire them with such a desire, and with the necessity of promptly carrying it out, by putting them in fear for their lives if they do not immediately submit to their deposition. In the case of Messieurs of Sardinia and Tuscany turning a deaf ear to the musical voice of Talleyrand, and persisting in deceiving us, the General-in-chief of the Army of Italy is to speak to them in most peremptory fashion, and, as the slang phrase goes, "show his teeth," and order them to make haste and pack off. All these measures are commanded by the certainty we have acquired of a new and flagrant coalition. We are not premeditating an aggressive propaganda, but we are under the necessity of defending a new State, whose existence the older States cannot really wish to preserve. Hence we are compelled to invade the dominions of the King of Naples, for which purpose 25,000 men will be more than amply sufficient; the Army of the Rhine is to give battle, and, if victorious, to push on to Constance; its right wing will then be able to unite with the left wing of the Army of Italy, and the two armies will act in concert to overwhelm the enemy. If, as we demand, the King of Prussia should pronounce himself on the side of the Republic, the Army of the North, held in reserve for the purpose of watching him, will be free to join the Army of the Rhine.

The little expedition to Ireland is on the seas, in the hands of sailors who so far have not had much experience.

The expiration of the law on the newspaper press creates a strange uneasiness among my colleagues;

all manner of efforts are made to obtain its prolongation; as for myself, I dread the silence of the press far more than its excesses; a clear conscience can always brave these; the croakings of scribblers may sometimes give useful advice. The press constitutes a danger, say my colleagues. I answer them that there is nothing good in this world which has not its alloy, but that the annihilation of the press leaves liberty without any protection against despotism.

From the 1st to the 10th Fructidor, Year VI.—The Council of Five Hundred is a prey to great agitation. Violent motions are made against certain Ministers in regard to contracts, the granting of furloughs, and waste of the public funds. The Directorate is not specifically denounced in these attacks; but the Directorate is aimed at, in order to divert attention from the issue, and to engender the belief that the power which is compelled to defend itself is that which seeks to attack. Lucien Bonaparte, who has recently taken his seat in the *corps législatif*, has set to work to open the breach. A national representative owing to a fraudulent and illegal election, he must fain strengthen his position by fomenting intrigue and discord. The keeper of stores of Saint-Maximin—which he had, as we have seen, rechristened *Marathon*—at last sees himself in possession of a stage whereon he will be able to put to good use the resources of machination, the genius for which belongs to his family. The brothers Joseph and Lucien are to keep close guard during the absence of the great general who has been compelled to join the army. Lucien Bonaparte, brought forward by several of his colleagues, as well as by his own wickedness, enjoys the support of

General Lahoz, an envoy of the Cisalpine Government. Here is Lucien accusing the Directorate of wishing to change the constitution of France, as it has done in the Cisalpine Republic by way of experiment and to give an example. The Council nevertheless passes to the order of the day.

Following upon his skirmish, Lucien calls on me; I receive him coolly, and have a lively explanation with him. He replies: "I have done a foolish thing; I allowed myself to be influenced by the counsels of several of my colleagues." He confidentially denounces some twenty of them to me; he recognizes, he says, that the enemies of liberty "would like to attach themselves to him, and applaud all signs of agitation in the bosom of the *corps législatif.*"

As it so happens that sincere enthusiasm oftentimes interferes in intrigue with the result of becoming its dupe, I commission several of my friends, of whose wise and enlightened patriotism I feel sure, to confer with these exaggerated patriots, in order to win them back to the side of the Government, already spoken and worked against in a scandalous fashion. I learn from various sources that among those it is not allowable to class as dupes the deputy Marquezi, who has lent his name to the *Journal des Francs*, inveighs against me much more in secret than he does in public. I condone his accusation made publicly: that is his right; but I do not intend to submit to oblique and sly calumny. I know, moreover, that his calumnies and diatribes are coupled with intrigues which will not stand favorable explanation. For what reason does Marquezi inquire of General Guidal, the commandant of the

École militaire, what is at present the number of troops in Paris, and the spirit animating both soldiers and chiefs? Were I the man to believe every report made to me, I might seriously call Marquezi to account in connection with everything I hear about him. As to what concerns me personally, no need for me to have recourse to the public authority for the purpose of silencing calumny. Does Marquezi, in his ignorance that I am aware of all he has said against me, still wish to set me at defiance? In the evening he makes his appearance in my drawing-room. I blurt out that, already indignant at his cowardice, I am no less so at his presence under my roof, after all the infamous things he has spoken about me. I beg him to leave, not wishing otherwise to fail in respect to the character of deputy with which he is invested. Marquezi tenders me apologies, which I accept. I do not pretend that on this occasion, as well as on others, I was not wrong to let my violent temper get the better of me. In my youth I should have considered myself temperate had I contented myself with acting as I had just done.

We are informed in all directions that Austria continues her great preparations. It is time that the Minister of War should submit to us a plan of campaign co-ordinated with those of the generals-in-chief. The force of circumstances is leading us back to a state of war. The issue of it may not be favorable to us. The Republicans must not suffer themselves to fall a prey to sleep or lassitude. It behooves us to recall our pristine energy. Republics surrounded by monarchies can be established only by dint of constancy and courage. The French Republic must either triumph or be devoured.

Rewbell, who is ailing, has left for the waters; calumny has taken advantage of his absence to renew its charges against this Director. I am told that it will be my turn next. The factious and troublous spirit existing previous to the 18th Fructidor manifests itself boldly under divers forms. I am more than once truly justified in exclaiming: "You see now the fruits of the 22d Floréal!"

The seeds of dissension are being sown in every direction.

We are threatened with great difficulties.

From the 10*th Fructidor to the* 2*d Complementary Day, Year VI.* — On this occasion royalism and anarchism are truly hand in glove together; they join forces with the party in the *corps législatif*, which no longer makes any pretence to moderation. The committee appointed to inquire into the waste of public money opens an investigation in regard to Schérer, and seeks to include Rewbell in it. Meetings influenced by the deputies Chabert and Porte frequently take place; at a loss how to attack me, my enemies seek to blame me in my official capacity for my treatment of Marquezi, as if this affair were aught but a personal one, and as if I were not free to prove that I did not fear my assailants, whatever the pretext or the reality of their opinion. The intriguers who have fomented this wickedness carefully remain in the background, while behaving openly in a way contrary to their secret actions. The deputies Chabert and Porte, who are at the head of the intrigue, together with others who take a no less active part in it, and the brothers Bonaparte, who have a hand in everything that bids fair to cause trouble, call upon me. They seek to make me believe that they do not share the opinions of the enemies of the Directorate, especially of mine, and that they would come forward as my devoted friends were an attack made on us. I am not deceived by these double-faced men; still, I should like to be able to believe in their regrets and return to the fold. We so need peace among ourselves! I accept their protestations and invite them to dinner. Apparently there has been a reconciliation.

Prussia continues to let us know in a friendly way that she still preserves neutrality. We continue to believe in it so long as we shall continue to be victorious. The Directorate prescribes the following ultimatum to our plenipotentiaries at Rastadt: "The abandonment and demolition of Kehl, Cassel, and the citadel of Ehrenbreitstein; the middle of the Rhine to constitute the frontier line."

Simultaneously we are secretly engaged in filling up the skeleton organizations of the army; the conscription will add some 200,000 men—a sufficient number for the taking possession of Naples, Tuscany, and Piedmont.

Rewbell, back from the waters of Plombières, has again taken his seat in the Directorate. His absence was a kind of a widowhood to us. His presence is invaluable in connection with decisions to be taken in troublous times.

The *Journal des Francs*, formerly the *Journal des Hommes Libres*, is suppressed. Owing to the fact that I was the one who had most cause to complain of the deputy Marquezi, who lent his name to that sheet, I was pained at seeing this measure adopted. I would like to have been able to prevent it. When will the day come when the

Administration shall no longer enjoy such a prerogative, and the periodical and every other kind of press shall be amenable to the courts alone, and when the courts themselves shall be constituted with a jury, both in civil and in criminal cases, and no longer be aught but the organs of public opinion?

Governments, which have their weaknesses as well as individuals, possess in a special fashion that of refusing to confess when they have done wrong. For the very reason that Admiral Truguet had been deprived of the portfolio of Minister of Marine on the 18th Fructidor, which had given Talleyrand a place in the Cabinet, he had not been allowed to return to the Navy Department, in which he had displayed the soundest and broadest ideas; and, as he had been relegated to an embassy, it was still further resolved not to let him enjoy it undisturbed.

To be frank, the disposition of the Directorate towards Truguet was a kind of ill-feeling displayed against him before his departure, and since kept up. This ill-feeling, revealed by more than one member of the Directorate, afforded to any one who wished to avail himself of it a ready means of doing injury to Truguet. This was too plainly manifest for Talleyrand not to put it to use; it furnished him an opportunity to glide into our passions and chime in with them: a twofold triumph for him—that of furthering his own interests and of working to the detriment of another. It will be seen how he went to work, and how he attained his aim. Talleyrand, who sought to conceal his insignificance by every possible means, thought the principal one was to attribute great importance to his department, "in order to place," he said, "the diplomacy of the Republic on a level with that of the kings "—as if the first did not consist in the power of the cannon and the bravery of armies, as if the French Republic had ever had any other diplomacy than its victories, of which Talleyrand's diplomacy was assuredly innocent.

Simultaneously with his pretensions to elevate diplomacy, he was seeking to corrupt it in its principle, by adding still further auxiliaries of corruption to an institution already not highly moral in its practice, since it calls above all else for the privilege of hypocrisy, which constitutes its very essence. Hence he proposed to us, as if it were a discovery born of genius, the idea of establishing in connection with his foreign relations that to which the kings of France had long since had recourse—a double diplomacy composed of secret agents who should exercise supervision over the public agents, and supply us with police reports; in other words, interested information about ambassadors who were supposed to enjoy the confidence of the Government. When witnessing with what an air of solemn morality he was making this proposition to us, and what a luxury of perfidy he was displaying in our presence "to place the diplomacy of the Republic on a level with that of the kings," my mind reverted to what Mme. de Staël had so naïvely told me, when seeking to demonstrate to me that Talleyrand deserved the post of Minister of Foreign Affairs—that " he possessed all the vices of the new and the ancient *régime.*" He had, in the past, done his best to prevent us from again taking Truguet into the Ministry, and to have him sent to Spain as ambassador. Now that Truguet was transplanted to a foreign land, Talleyrand sought every possible means of doing him harm, sometimes by sarcasms in regard to what he styled his gallantries, and sometimes by more serious denunciations of what he called his Jacobinism, as if previous to the 18th Fructidor Talleyrand had not been more of a Jacobin than Truguet. Like all the rest, the affairs of gallantry were an invention of Talleyrand's. It is probable that, with a probity which did not exclude a certain shrewdness, Truguet may have thought that in order to penetrate the mysteries of the Court of Spain, it would be well to make himself agreeable to the Queen, since she it was who was really ruler. It is a fact that, owing to this intermediary, Truguet had undoubtedly obtained great results. On the one hand, he had secured justice for many of his French fellow-citizens whose interests had suffered detriment; on the other, he had succeeded in bringing about the dismissal of the Prime Minister and Generalissimo, the Prince of the Peace. Talleyrand drew from this the conclusion that Truguet had become the lover of the Queen, and paraded himself as such; that thus he was wanting in the gravity pertaining to his position, and was harmful to the interests of the Republic. I must fain confess that on this occasion I again listened too readily to the insinuations of Talleyrand. I likewise confess to having listened with too great a complaisance to the reports of several of his secret agents—notably those of one Séguy, whom he had placed at our disposal, of Perrochel, a secretary of embassy, and of the Prince de Carency, to whom I had granted, without sufficient thought, a certain amount of confidence, considering the slender pledges offered us by a man who had served us in so strange a fashion before and on the 18th Fructidor. Now it was acting on all the foregoing suggestions, which supported those of Talleyrand, that we decided upon recalling Truguet.

Truguet, although with gentle ways and with manners perhaps of the ancient *régime*, was one of the men who had taken the Republic most seriously. Truguet had merely called upon Spain to execute the laws of the Republic—a course justified by relations apparently sincere—to the extent that all *émigrés*, all refractory priests, and all others known as enemies of France should be expelled from Court. Talleyrand had been not only the defender but the instigator of all the greatest severities exercised in this connection.

But on this geographical point of Europe, in Spain as in France, Talleyrand sought to make money. He was bound, in all places and under all circumstances, to keep the oath he had taken with so much effusion at the time of his appointment to the Ministry, when, addressing Castellane and Benjamin Constant, he had said: "We must make an immense fortune, an immense one!" The overtures he had made in this respect to Truguet had not met with success, since instead of conniving at giving contracts for supplies to the creatures he had sent to Spain for that purpose, Truguet had been on the point of causing the arrest of Talleyrand's agents; at any rate, he had had them expelled.

So it came about that, thwarted by the crude honesty of Truguet, Talleyrand could not rest until he had secured his recall. Truguet, who had obtained so many favorable results for France, and who had tightened the bonds of the alliance of the Republic with a monarchy governed by the Bourbons, could not imagine that he deserved to be thus recalled, especially when his conduct was so perfectly in accord with the political sentiments of the Directorate and our common interests. It is said that Truguet, when angrily referring to the matter, indicated Talleyrand as the author of this strange perturbation. Truguet's unpardonable fault lay in having discovered the real cause of Talleyrand's intrigue.

Strong in his conscience, and universally respected at Madrid, the admiral-ambassador considered himself at liberty to make his preparations for departure at his leisure, and to remain some little time in a country where honest men bestowed on him an esteem based on the gratitude to which he was entitled for the improvements of which he was the author, and which the Spanish people were beginning to enjoy. This sojourn of the ambassador, prolonged a little while beyond the time of his recall, was construed by Talleyrand into a daring disobedience of the orders of the Directorate. At the very outside there was nothing more in it than a little satisfaction felt by Truguet in reaping the marks of esteem of a foreign nation, which sentiments were for him a pleasant offset to the injustice of his own government. It is possible that Truguet also entertained the hope of seeing his government, enlightened by the explanations he had made to it, reconsider the severe course it had adopted towards him. I was among the foremost to share this hope, when Talleyrand, continuing to take advantage of the hostile frame of mind of the Directorate, still further irritated it by making a fresh recital to us of the speeches which he styled the utterances of Truguet in Madrid against members of the Directorate, whom Truguet believed to be the protectors of Séguy, Perrochel, and de Carency.

On my seeming to doubt the violent language attributed to Truguet—a most perfectly bred gentleman, and one whom I did not believe capable of forgetting the proprieties of life, as Talleyrand was seeking to make out—the latter, taking me aside, said, in the most kindly and insinuating way, that "he owed it to his attachment to me not to suffer me to remain ignorant of the fact that I had been one of the chief objects of Truguet's diatribes." "That," I replied to him, "does not seem a reason why I should feel more severely inclined towards Truguet. You should even, had you any esteem for me, deduce that I should draw from that the contrary conclusion. Truguet," I went on to say, "has done excellent work while at his post: he has abolished the Inquisition; he has caused to be restored to liberty many who were in prison for their political opinions; he has protected French commerce; he has saved from ruin several of our most respected merchants; he has on all occasions shone by his integrity. Following upon the heels of an ambassador who had availed himself of the privileges of his position to indulge in smuggling, he has pursued an entirely different course; he has refused to avail himself of the most legitimate advantages of his position, and has truly re-established the opinion held of French honor by a conduct so different from that of his predecessor. Following upon such a public life, which constitutes an answer to everything, what do we care for a few particulars of his private life and all the reports of secret agents, who are nothing else than interested mischief-makers? Such are," I said to Talleyrand, "the early fruits of what you call your secret diplomacy. It is nothing else than trouble organized in the bosom of the Administration."

Talleyrand replied to me that "the nobility of my sentiments did not surprise him; that I was always and in all things a superior being, and the most generous man of all the lands in which he had travelled; but that although he would gladly imitate me on this occasion in so far as he was personally concerned, he did not consider he could do so when the honor of the Government was involved. A man had the right perhaps to remain silent in a personal matter, but it was otherwise when the question was a general one. Now what he was told about Truguet constituted an attack on the Directorate as a whole." Thereupon Talleyrand, who had so far carried on a kind of aside with me, suddenly raised his voice with an air of innocent emotion—the intention of which was, however, to make himself heard by my colleagues—and named them all, so that each one should become fully aware that he was being individually referred to. This was a bit of play-acting on his part, the object of which was that he should be asked for an explanation, which would enable him to read each one a lecture. His trick was rewarded with success. One and all of us in the Directorate presented to a phlegmatic and calculating man just so many vulnerable subjects, because we were all of us more or less irascible. The annoyances one meets with in the turmoil of public affairs may aggravate the dispositions already pertaining to stubborn characters; and when these annoyances come to us from subordinate agents who, dependent on us for their position, should apparently be bound to us by ties of gratitude, we think we are entitled to consider ourselves doubly wounded in our feelings, we see in those who undermine us so many ingrates, nay, traitors; nothing but a great loftiness of soul and reason can make us rise superior to personal resentment. Now Talleyrand had taken good aim, and succeeded in inspiring us with such a resentment against Truguet.

Of all the members of the Directorate, Merlin was assuredly not the one who would have been thought the most capable of rising to such superiority. He was the most narrow-minded of men in his conceptions, and the most easily irritated we had ever had in the Luxembourg. But always skilful, or at least daring, in screening his personal passions with the veil of the law, Merlin, who continued to deserve the praise given him by Bonaparte two years before of "never having lacked a law to make a crime appear innocent, or even to justify it"— Merlin says, in a cold and implacable tone: "My dear colleagues, no one is better able than I to define the insults of one of our diplomatic agents, or of any one else. You have given Admiral Truguet one of the finest embassies, in spite of his not having been one of us, and although he had not given any pledges to the Revolution. To speak plainly: he has not been a member of the National Convention. Consequently he has not voted for the death of the king, and has not, like us, burned his ships. What return has he made to our Government for the great favor it did him in appointing him to one of our principal embassies? Our treatment of him has been met with ingratitude; he has allowed himself to make remarks about our political conduct, and, according to what we are told by citizen Talleyrand, Truguet has even dared to speak in Madrid of our private morals, of our wives, of Mme. Merlin, and of ladies of my social circle. And yet since these ladies are received under my roof they can be only persons enjoying the highest reputation, who at the very least deserve that whoever will not speak of them respectfully should abstain from speaking of them at all. Still I am willing, as far as I am concerned, to forget the ingratitude and perverseness displayed in the conduct of the citizen Truguet. I think that if on this occasion we can, acting on the impulse of a mistaken generosity, withdraw our personality from the question, we cannot push this generosity to the point of suffering to go unpunished the agent we have recalled; and, since he has not yet returned to France, he must be considered as in open rebellion. I am aware of the objection that can be raised, one which doubtless constitutes his defence — to wit, that being no longer an agent of the Government, and having become once more a plain citizen, he enjoys the right of living where he sees fit. This would constitute a serious mistake in the case of several classes of citizens, especially those who may have been in the service of the Directorate, and who have accounts to render to it. Moreover, the passports duly received by Truguet were delivered to him only in his capacity as an ambassador; he is no longer one, hence he no longer enjoys the right of being out of French territory; and, knowing as we do what he has said of us, it must be admitted that he is truly in rebellion; ours would be the right to treat him as such, and to have him punished by law. I do not wish to urge you to adopt so severe a course, and I would be the first to incline to clemency. I therefore propose that you should content yourselves with looking upon Truguet as an *émigré*, and placing him on the list of *émigrés*, to be tried according to the laws of the *émigration*, if he ventures later on, and in spite of your prohibitions, to seek to re-enter France—in other words, to break his ban."

Larevellière and Rewbell considered the measure very severe; Treilhard merely looked upon it as unwonted; nevertheless, each individual member of the Directorate, whose weak spot Talleyrand had cleverly succeeded in touching, was thirsting for revenge. Taking advantage of this frame of mind, Merlin informed us that what he proposed was after all only comminatory; that it was merely a way of reaching a rebellious individual, by preventing him from returning to France for the purpose of defaming us; that his intention was to frighten rather than to harm him; that, as Truguet was not returning, he would not receive a scratch.

As a result of these honeyed words of Merlin's, one of our most honorable compatriots, one who had rendered the greatest services to our country, was to consider himself treated with indulgence when deprived of his citizenship and placed as a criminal on the list of our enemies. This was the subtle invention of which a man was capable whom France and Europe looked upon as the first of modern jurisconsults! Do, then, a knowledge of the laws, a profound acquaintance with jurisprudence, represent nothing else in the hands of certain beings than an additional means wherewith to deceive one's mind, lie to one's conscience, clothe wickedness with forms, and, in a word, legalize it? Without being very well versed in the history of the individuals who presided over the science of law, I am well aware that one Tribonius, perhaps one Ulpianus, were the deliberate slaves of the Roman emperors, and placed their talents at the feet of tyranny; but even under the odious emperors there existed men learned in the law who possessed consciences, while in modern times men like Donnat, d'Aguesseau, and Pothier have demonstrated that integrity was not incompatible with the genius of jurisprudence; and the picture of these men of so lofty a virtue consoles one for the existence of those who have shown themselves so totally different. But a truce for a while to the personality of Merlin, this veritable father of cunning, whom Bonaparte, General of the Army of the Interior after the 13th Vendémiaire, so thoroughly characterized, and who was subsequently to give further proofs of his vicious pliancy, when the new Tribonius should be free to become with impunity the interpreter of an emperor, and the tortuous applier of his so-called laws. Although almost all of us entertained of Merlin the opinion I am here recording—viz., that of a cold, treacherous, narrow, and perfidious mind—we were nevertheless captured by the *naïveté* of his speech. So Truguet was placed on the list of *émigrés*, a first triumph of what Talleyrand styled secret diplomacy.

Truguet, justly indignant at this treatment, may perhaps have said a few more sharp things about the virtue of Merlin and his female friends, as well as about Talleyrand and *his* female friends. But he took his sentence resignedly, and quietly retired to one of those countries where liberty had in days gone by ever found an asylum. Holland was then in the power of France; hence perhaps it was not at the time I recall a land quite as free as formerly. Still, the intrigues of Talleyrand and the wickedness of Merlin failed to trouble the existence of the honorable exile in that country.

The main object of the dismissal of the ambassador Truguet had been to give his place to a personal creature; Merlin, who had alleged that one of the weak points of Truguet was that he had been neither a *conventionnel* nor a regicide, had made arrangements to substitute for him a man after his own heart, one combining these qualifications. As such a one did he introduce to us Guillemardet, who had indeed been a *conventionnel* and a regicide, but at the same time was one of the least capable men who had sat in the Convention. He was one of those doctors of the Revolution; he was at one time a doctor, but a most mediocre one at that. The Revolution had, as in the case of so many others of his cloth, brought him into public affairs, but had not succeeded in lifting him out of his pretentious sphere; his small brain, void of ideas, had never allowed him to soar above the ways and views of *M. Purgon.*

Such is the specimen of the dignity of the French Republic which Merlin had succeeded in getting appointed to the Court of Madrid, by transforming into an *émigré* one of our best citizens, and one most hostile to the *émigration.*

As the new ambassador must needs justify his appointment, if only by his devotion, Guillemardet thinks he cannot better follow the instructions of Talleyrand than by sending us the silliest reports about the Queen and other important personages of the Court of Madrid; he is on the lookout, and alleges that he is on the track of the deepest intrigues, of which he believes he holds all the threads. On one occasion he lets us know that he has been informed by the Duke of Ossuna that a large amount of money has been paid to a secret agent, whose name he does not know. This anonymous agent is alleged to have undertaken, with this money, to prevent Larevellière, Treilhard, and Barras from revolutionizing Spain. The Duke of Ossuna denies having said so, and would make Truguet responsible for this statement.

Bonaparte has disembarked at Alexandria, which he has taken after a glorious engagement, the hero of which is Kléber. Several others have followed, and Cairo is his. He has left his fleet at Aboukir; there has been a difference of opinion between him and the Admiral. The latter states that he has not received any orders, while the former replies that he had advised him to enter the port of Alexandria provided there was sufficient water; in the contrary case, to find an anchorage in the Bay of Aboukir, and if this anchorage were unsafe, to proceed to Malta or to Corfu. Admiral Brueys, a courageous man, but of little nautical experience, has anchored in the Bay of Aboukir without taking all the necessary precautions, when he was liable to be attacked at any moment by the enemy. The English squadron has borne down on him; in lieu of sailing out to fight it, he has awaited it at anchor. Admiral Nelson, taking advantage of the space imprudently left open between land and the anchorage, has cut off the French squadron; an engagement *à outrance* has ensued, as a result of which we have lost nearly all our ships. This naval engagement, which lasted three days, is one of the most bloody ever fought at sea. The line of the French ships, which were moored with their broadsides to the enemy, was doubled by the English, and so found itself between two fires. The fight became terrible; an English ship mounting fifty guns was daring enough to cut through the line and to cannonade the flagship. In the heat of the action fire broke out on the *Orient* (120 guns), which blew up with a loud report. In spite of prodigies of valor, nine of our ships and two of our frigates have fallen into the enemy's hands. The *Timoléon* was set on fire, in preference to surrendering it. The *Guillaume Tell* and the *Généreux* made good their escape, together with a couple of frigates. Admiral Brueys has been killed.

The news of the disaster, which took place a month ago, has just reached us. The Directorate, while not the author of this appalling catastrophe, cannot shirk the moral responsibility of it. It behooves us to display a great amount of firmness; in this we shall not fail. The more acutely we feel this loss, the more courage must we show in enduring and repairing it. We will be avenged on the Continent for our defeat on the seas. But until the time comes for this revenge the disaster so justly deplored by France forms a fresh subject of reproach and accusation, which our enemies turn to their advantage against the Directorate. They have so long been on the lookout! Are our foreign enemies about to join hands with them and support their liberticide desires and attempts?

CHAPTER IX

France's first industrial exhibition—Fouché's distress—His police reports—His conversation with Bonaparte—Exploits of General Humbert in Ireland—The English general Cornwallis—Bonaparte's lack of foresight the cause of the disaster at Aboukir—Spain's tergiversations—An extraordinary levy of troops—Exportation of cereals—Belz and Bourin—Neapolitan affairs—Paul I. declared Grand Master of Malta by the Russian Knights—Treaty between France and Switzerland—Budget of the Year VII.—Consequences of the expedition to Ireland—European affairs in general—Brune and Trouvé—Brune and Macdonald—Lucien Bonaparte in the tribune of the Five Hundred—Successes in Egypt—Mosneron agent in the Île de France—Posters placarded against Marquezi and Guesdon—Treilhard their author—The influence of temperament on politics—Danton and Robespierre—Fresh seeds of dissension—Disadvantages under which our navy labors—Le Carlier replaced by Duval—Bread becomes dear—Hédouville at San Domingo—Toussaint L'Ouverture—Disturbances in Belgium—General Collaud—Uneasiness of the public mind—Electoral fever—Rouchon and Fabre de l'Aude—Merlin still anxious to proscribe people—His project combated by Rouchon—The latter's speech—His noble words do not find an echo—Shameful proof given to the Directorate by Fabre de l'Aude—Different destiny of these two men—Political assemblies—Joubert General-in-chief of the Army of Italy—He is ordered to take Piedmont—My secretary Botot—War against Naples and Sardinia—General measures taken—The Duke of Aosta—His assassinations included in the amnesty—Adoption of the *conclusum* of the French Ministers at Rastadt—English and Egyptian affairs—Uneasiness felt at home—Dismissals—The state of Europe—Joubert tenders his resignation—It is not accepted—Prince Henry of Prussia friendly to France—He is beset by Fouché and Vincent Lombard—Fouché chief agent for Italy—He denounces and is denounced—He clings to Joubert—Noble character of this general—His iron will—Moreau inspector-general in Italy—Triumphs won over Naples—Flight of Mack and of the King—Anarchy in the Army of Italy—Report on gambling-houses—Piedmont occupied—The commissioner Ancelot—Joubert threatened—His resignation accepted—La Tourette—Jourdan with the Army of the Danube—Distress of the Army of Helvetia—Formidable opposition to the Government—Measures taken against the transported deputies—Alarming march of the Russians—The Republican authorities enter Rome—Electoral manœuvres—The *Cercle Constitutionnel* and Talleyrand—Bonaparte's brothers denounce a Corsican parish priest—Overtures made to Russia—Alliance between Russia and England—Declaration of the Rastadt plenipotentiaries in the matter—Armistice concluded by Championnet—Treilhard calls for his dismissal—Everything satisfactorily explained—Treilhard's fury—Capitulation of Ehrenbreitstein—General Dallemagne—Agitation in the departments—Progress made by Royalism—Weakness of the Government.

From the 2d Complementary Day, Year VI., to the 10th Vendémiaire, Year VII.—The new Minister of the Interior, François de Neufchâteau, who has profound and extensive ideas in regard to agriculture, trade, and manufactures, has just established in the Champ de Mars a fair, wherein are exhibited for the first time French industrial products. He delivers a speech full of ideas and encouragement on the subject of arts and manufacturing industries, demonstrating to us their influence on the prosperity of a great nation.

Fouché, since his return from his post of military agent in the southern departments—a post to which I had had him appointed after the 13th Vendémiaire—is vegetating in Paris in the direst distress. He is perpetually pestering me to give him any kind of a place, or, as he would say, facetiously, a "placelet," which would supply the most urgent needs of himself and his wife, an ex-nun as poor as himself. Twenty times have I asked for the most humble place for Fouché, but in vain; the whole of the Directorate distrusts him. Pending the time when I shall be more fortunate in my petition on behalf of Fouché, I cause some little pecuniary help to be given to him, as to a revolutionist in distress. In order to make a show of earning his money he does police work for me—out of devotion, so he says. In a report anterior to Bonaparte's departure he has related to me a conversation held by him with that general, who had complained bitterly of the Directorate. Fouché alleges that the drift of this talk was that true patriots should lose no time in "blowing up the Directorate sky-high." Fouché pretends that he combated this strange idea of Bonaparte's, saying: "But is not Barras in it? He is your old friend, and he can surely not have ceased being so now that you have reaped glory." Bonaparte is alleged to have replied: "I can no longer reckon on Barras; on the one hand, he supports the Directorate; on the other, his is a revolutionary mind and a Jacobinical heart." These words of discontent, which begin to reveal Bonaparte's ingratitude towards me, are the sequel to the discussion I had with him on the day when, fathoming his ambition, vexed at his intrigues towards entering the Directorate, and no longer able to conceal my opposition to his aspirations, I said frankly to him: "You are seeking to overthrow the Constitution; you will not succeed; you will only accomplish your own ruin if you persist in your idea. Sieyès may have urged you on by his perfidious counsels, but he did not give you his confidence, nor did you give him yours, and both of you will end badly."

General Humbert has alone done his duty in the

expedition to Ireland; he has boldly landed at Bantry. A glorious success has crowned his prodigies of valor; he would have conquered and brought the island under subjection had he had more than 1200 men under him; attacked by Lord Cornwallis with superior forces, he has been compelled to surrender. Had General Hardy rallied to Humbert in Ireland with his 5000 or 6000 men, there is no doubt that the operation would have succeeded, as the inhabitants fully believed in it.

Letters from Naples unfortunately confirm the news of the naval engagement at Aboukir. This disaster is due, not only to the intrepid manœuvre of Nelson, but principally to Bonaparte's lack of foresight, and his contradictory and vague orders to Admiral Brueys.

The Cabinet of Madrid, in spite of all its friendly and fraternal protestations, is none the less united with our enemies; it is a member of the secret conspiracy of hereditary royalty against the new Republic. It is resolved to write to the Spanish Government, to demand that it should declare itself and make common cause with its ally the Republic.

A levy of 200,000 men is to be raised "in order to give the new coalition, which is secretly organizing, a public specimen of France's defensive resources." As a consequence, and pursuant to the report drawn up by General Jourdan, the first class of the conscription is to be called upon in its entirety, and the second also, should the first not produce the 200,000 men required. An excessive number of permits have been granted throughout Belgium for the exportation of cereals. Great abuses, calling for severe repression, have been committed. The

Directorate orders that a statement of exports shall be submitted to it by the Minister of the Interior. Merlin had asked for a permit for 600,000 cwt. on behalf of some jobbers, Belz and Bourin by name. The permit has been granted, and sold in the Paris market. These cereals were destined for Malta.

The Neapolitan Government is arming, and no longer conceals its hostile intentions; English ships are admitted into its ports. It is decreed that seven demi-brigades and 3000 horses shall be despatched to Italy, and that an army shall be formed in Rome, with orders to march on Naples. The Helvetic Directorate is to withdraw the 4000 Swiss now in the service of Piedmont; they may be of use to our Army of Italy.

The *baillis-commandeurs, grands-croix*, commanders, and Knights of Malta, constituting the Grand Priory of Russia, confer upon Paul I. the title of Grand Master of the Order of Malta. An uprising has taken place in Malta, but has fortunately been stifled at its birth. The massacre of all the French had been plotted; the leaders of the plot are arrested and sentenced to death.

Ratification of an offensive and defensive treaty between France and Switzerland.

The taxation for the Year VII. has been fixed —to wit, the land-tax at two hundred millions, and the taxes on movable property at thirty millions.

Letters received announce that three Russian columns are marching on Warsaw. Prussia continues to conceal the part she has taken in the coalition; it is painful to have to deal with so double-faced an ally. Sweden refuses to receive our ambassador. The final peace negotiated at Rastadt, such as presented by the protocol, gives to the Empire a centralization which would prove too advantageous to the coalition. Turin is up in arms, and war appears inevitable. Great measures are called for. I had in other days opposed the disbanding of the Army of Mayence and the sale of its artillery equipages. We are to-day compelled to replace them at great cost; it is to be doubted whether our present resources are sufficient to enable us to assume an imposing attitude. Austria is already moving troops; Russia likewise. Joubert is appointed General-in-chief of the Army of Italy. Championnet, recommended by the dying Hoche, is sent to the Army of Rome. Jourdan, who is still to retain chief command of this army, is to call upon it for any assistance he may consider urgent. Brune is to command the Army of Holland. Just at a time when there is a likelihood of impending attacks he has been deprived of the command of the Army of Italy for two reasons. The one reason is, that we do not find in him the talent necessary to cope with great operations of war; the other, that intrigues, born of rivalries between the civil and military powers, have been stirred up against him by the ambassador Trouvé. Brune has assuredly not been in the wrong in his discussions with Trouvé; he has even shown much moderation in his political behavior towards the Cisalpine Republic. But M. Trouvé is essentially the *protégé* of Larevellière. The latter, who has raised this presumptuous young man to a position higher than he deserved, continues to defend him in all things and against all comers. I have been unable to prevent Brune's change of command. For the past three years Brune had studied Italy, had administered and fought there with success, and was fully competent to respond to the expectations of his Fatherland. When I recall to my mind so many generals, who, so to speak, have passed in review before my eyes from the early days of our wars, I can perceive and I am entitled to assert that Brune is one of the ablest I have seen on the stage of the Revolution. His operations, always successful, constitute the first proofs of my assertion. These proofs are confirmed by all the plans and letters received by us from him while on active service, and which are deposited amid the archives of the Directorate or at the War Department. They contain sufficient evidence to refute the statements of those who have sought to blacken his fame. It was believed in those days that Macdonald was among his defamers; there is, indeed, some foundation for this charge in the jealous mediocrity of that general, for Brune was vastly his superior in military and political ability. Macdonald, in his turn, possibly enjoyed a different sort of superiority—that of the kind of dissimulation styled circumspection. It constitutes a kind of talent readily suited to phlegmatic beings, who, since they are not exposed to any *élan* of the imagination, can dwell tranquilly in the silence of their nonentity, the silence known as the wit of fools—one which has frequently so well helped Talleyrand in convincing people that he was a man of wit; this calculated and impotent silence, habitual to Macdonald, seconded by wary but ever relentless intrigue, may therefore have, in connection with Brune, won him some temporary advantage over the latter. Moreover, Brune, having been an ardent partisan of the Revolution from the very outset, together with Danton and Camille Desmoulins, or a follower in their steps, had derived from that a far greater reputation than he actually deserved, and this afforded his enemies a happy pretext for attacking him and denying him every other kind of merit. Now that of having been a sincere patriot has rarely been of any great service to those who have possessed the reputation of it. The Revolution constituting a perpetual engagement, its enemies, every time they have suffered defeat, may perhaps have been reduced to silence; but they have never been able to make up their minds to renounce their pretensions, still less their feelings of resentment. Thus the men of the Revolution properly so called, its first intrepid authors, of necessity incurred a hatred which did not end with their life, but followed them beyond the grave. There is nothing but to be resigned to one's fate and not to attempt to shirk one's responsibility when one has placed one's self at the head of so great an undertaking as that whose aim is to transform France, and perhaps the world.

Lucien daily makes more and more violent motions from the tribune in the Five Hundred; he is privately prompted by his brother Joseph, who disowns him publicly. These are the usual tactics of the Bonaparte family.

Bonaparte is master of Cairo; Lower Egypt has surrendered, and the beys are in flight.

> The colony of Île de France is being stirred up by agitators, who seek to detach it from the Republic. The worthy citizen Mosneron is despatched thither as agent; his reputation and conciliatory character will, I hope, be productive of good fruit.
>
> A placard aimed at Marquezi and Guesdon, editors of the

Journal des Francs, is posted throughout Paris; owing to my having had with Marquezi the altercation I have related, I have all the more frankly blamed such a proceeding, and have asked that the Minister of Police should be charged with bringing its authors before a tribunal. My motion is rejected for a reason I was far from suspecting: it is Treilhard who has indited these posters. Treilhard is an individual both hard-hearted and curt in every-day life. This defect has strangely increased since he has become a Director; he is beside himself, and in his insufferable haughtiness will hardly allow himself to be spoken to. He is the *Tuffières* of the Directorate. How much has not the more or less bilious temperament of private individuals fatally influenced the irritability of their characters when they have become public men? It is in this respect that Carnot has often seemed to me more deserving of pity than hatred. A physiologist of the Revolution has said, with some show of reason perhaps, that the whole history of Danton and Robespierre could be summed up in two decisive traits of the causes and consequences of their different destinies. Robespierre was bilious—in other words, malignant and distrustful; Danton was of a sanguine temperament—*i.e.*, generous and trusting. The temperament of trustfulness was bound to succumb to that of envy.

End of Vendémiaire, Year VII.—On every side I see mistakes and passions which co-operate with England's intrigues for the purpose of sowing discord in France, by introducing it in the first place between the *corps législatif* and the Directorate. It is hard to say where the misfortunes of the Republic will stop should such a rupture occur once more.

From the 1st to the 8th Brumaire, Year VII.—The little squadron conveying General Hardy to Ireland has been attacked by the English. Several of our ships have been captured. The Bordeaux division ought not to have sailed until after the landing of General Hardy in Ireland; now it has incurred a great risk; I had opposed its departure, but the impatience of the majority overruled me. I fear that the events happening on the seas will continue to justify the opinion of the little reliance that is to be placed on our navy until it shall have been reorganized.

Le Carlier, the Minister of Police, is replaced by a doubtless most worthy citizen, but one perhaps even weaker than Le Carlier—Duval, of the Seine-Inférieure.

It will be recollected that at its advent the Directorate found the system of provisioning in a most disorganized state. Ever since order has been infused into this essential branch of the public service, by the restoration of freedom to trade, we have felt at ease in this direction. We are told that murmurings, which threaten to develop into disturbances, are making themselves heard in regard to the dearness of bread. I move that the Ministers of the Interior and of Police be ordered to report on the proportion existing between the price of bread and that of wheat. My motion at first encounters opposition. Is it not the primary duty of all governments, with still more reason popular governments, to give their attention to the existence of the poor, and diminish, if possible, the price of the victuals indispensable to their daily consumption? The Ministers are ordered to report; in other words, the matter is postponed.

General Hédouville, in spite of all his cautiousness and diplomatic shrewdness, has not adopted the proper course in dealing with the colony of San Domingo. He has allowed himself to be shipped home with great politeness by Toussaint L'Ouverture, in whose hands he has left the military and civil government. This negro displays great superiority in filling both.

Hoche had, in the letter which he wrote to us on his deathbed, specially urged upon us to keep an eye on Belgium. Events justify his warning; Belgium is being stirred up by the enemies of the Republic. The harsh behavior of the authorities in levying the conscription enhances the ill-feeling; several *arrondissements* have risen in insurrection. General Collaud is sent with the necessary powers to re-establish order; several regiments of cavalry are placed at his disposal.

The new Minister of Police informs us that a secret uneasiness is becoming manifest among the population. Attempts are being made to foment disturbances; Royalism is conspiring; the malcontents are agitating; the leaders of both parties are in quest of a point of support, and will end in joining forces if the Directorate opens a breach to them by any intestine quarrel.

Letters from Belgium inform us that peace has been completely restored.

The annual electoral fever is already making itself felt, although the elections are only due in another two months. The Directorate devotes its attention to them. Some wish for moderate men only; how is it that these alleged moderates are the enemies of liberty, and that they always assume the mask of honesty?

I have already quoted the speech of the deputy Rouchon on the occasion of the debate on the law of the 22d Floréal. It is not necessary that a man should be of my opinion for me to render justice to an honorable character. It seems to me that he who gives noble proofs in this respect should be claimed by men of all parties who are possessed of conscience. For can there be different parties in questions of humanity and honor? I therefore believe that in my Memoirs, which I call historical, if I may be forgiven this pretension, I cannot omit a most important debate: one in which the deputy Rouchon is concerned, and also another deputy, who, on his own testimony, will appear in a totally different light—one who in those days was acting a strange part against the Directorate, a part which indeed procured him some few favors at the time, but which will in the future bring him many others, under the governmental *régime* succeeding the Directorate. This deputy is M. Fabre of the Aude. I must first state the conduct of the deputy Rouchon, in order that the difference between it and that of his opponent be better felt. This is what it was about.

Our colleague Merlin, who was not happy when not proscribing, and who ever had something new to offer us in this line, had conceived the idea of a law assimilating with the *émigrés* individuals who should have escaped transportation, or should have left the place of residence assigned to them. I had strenuously opposed this idea, as well as many others of Merlin's, finding in them a pettiness and a persistent and relentless cruelty which had always revolted me. It is conceivable and admits of explanation by all natural sentiments and the instinct of self-preservation that one should, on the field of battle, deal all the blows likely to secure victory, and that these blows should be more or less measured in the heat of the engagement, wherein it is a matter of saving one's own life and the political life of one's country at one and the same time; but, victory once secured, I was unable to conceive that the enemy should be hunted down in all the asylums wherein he sought a refuge, and whence he could no longer do any harm; that, when blows could no longer be dealt to him, it should be demanded that he come and surrender himself in person, under penalty of a severer punishment. Such was my opinion, publicly expressed after Fructidor, hence several men sentenced to transportation as a consequence of that day, notably Siméon, my compatriot of Provence, had trusted themselves to appeal to me, begging that I would try and mitigate the severity of their position. I had engaged to do so in my heart, as well as in the words I had spoken to the relations and friends who had interceded with me; it was on my part an engagement prompted by conscience, honor, and humanity, which I wished to carry out trebly on this new occasion. As the matter was to be discussed in the *corps législatif*, I was curious to know what would be said and with what result. One of my friends, who was in the habit of keeping me informed about everything, Bergoeing of the Gironde, brought me at once the speech delivered on the subject by the deputy Rouchon; it was in all respects similar to what I felt myself, and to what I had laid before the Directorate. It pleases me to transcribe this speech from the identical copy handed to me by Bergoeing; it was delivered on the 18th Brumaire (5th November). Rouchon began by saying that he formally declared himself opposed to the proposition of confiscating the property of the proscribed of Fructidor who had escaped transportation. He spoke the first sentences with so much animation that the adverse party, considering itself personally challenged, shouted: "Order! To the Abbaye with the counter-revolutionist, the Royalist!" But these vociferations, repeated with a sort of fury in all parts of the chamber, could not silence him. "The hackneyed reproach of Royalist," he exclaimed with energy, "does not impose on me; it will not prevent my opposing an act of tyranny which has no precedent, and a law which adds penalty upon penalty. Would it not be an atrocious thing to say to a man sentenced to the guillotine: 'If you do not come of your own accord to the foot of the scaffold, you shall be broken on the wheel or quartered?' Are we to be like those Indian monarchs who order their subjects to proceed to the frontier, there to have them hunted by wild beasts? I am well aware that the Sultan sends a cord to those of his viziers or bashaws whose death he desires, but I have not heard that he compels them to come and fetch it, under penalty of a severer punishment in case they refuse to submit to the one imposed on them. Read history, and you will see that men like Nero and Heliogabalus never adopted such cruel measures as those which are proposed to you. It is outrageous to use, as indeed it has been done, the words 'justice' and 'humanity' in connection with measures of confiscation and proscription against men who have not been tried; it is the ironical laughter of a man as he stabs his victim." At these words there was a fresh outbreak of shouts and insults against the speaker. Deputies sitting near him were seen to move farther away from him as from a plague-stricken man, which did not prevent him from continuing: "You must listen to me; the unfortunate beings I am defending have no rich commissariats, no sumptuous embassies to give me; . . . proscription is their lot."

The sitting at which M. Rouchon thus pleaded for wretched proscribed men will doubtless be taken note of by history. It is indeed remarkable that in an assembly of deputies, who all sought to prevent Rouchon from speaking, not a solitary one came forward in his support, thus emphasizing the fact that there was amid them but one man imbued with a feeling of justice, or at least who dared to fulfil the duties it imposes. As it is, Rouchon remained unsupported.

Great was my astonishment on receiving next morning from a deputy the statement which follows, this deputy being no other than the one who became subsequently an accomplice of the 18th Brumaire for the purpose of betraying the *corps législatif*, an act quite in accord with his antecedents—a deputy who since became president of the Tribunate only to betray the Tribunate, then a senator, a count of the Empire, then a supporter of the Restoration, and lastly a *pair de France*. It has been sought to explain this extraordinary conduct by the suggestion that his crying needs may have been its cause; that M. Fabre of the Aude was the father of ten or twelve children, whom he had to feed and bring out in the world. What kind of a paternity is it, then, that could justify a man indulging in such infamous deeds? Let us not attribute the baseness of M. Fabre of the Aude to his position as father of a numerous family; he merely followed the dictates of his character, which would have remained the same—*i.e.*, the type of all that is ignoble, even had he been a celibate. The following is his autographic statement:

"*Memorandum in regard to what occurred at the sittings of the 14th and 16th Brumaire, to serve as a reply to the calumnies of two deputies whom the Director Treilhard has, in spite of my entreaties, persistently refused to name.*

"No sooner had Rouchon entered upon his speech, and we clearly saw what he was driving at, than it became impossible for us to restrain our indignation. Personally I repeatedly, and with all my might and main, shouted: 'Close the discussion! Put the project to the vote!' Nevertheless, Rouchon was listened to till the end. He repeatedly interrupted the speakers who sought to refute him, and was determined to speak. Twice did I proceed to the tribune to beg that the President would grant me the right of speech for the purpose of closing the discussion; and, as the President did not vouchsafe any reply to me, I told the two secretaries sitting on his left that they should themselves point out to him that Rouchon was merely seeking to create trouble and even some scandalous scene, and that he ought at once to put to the vote of the Chamber the closure of the discussion. The secretaries repeated my words to the President. Hardly had I resumed my seat, a moment later, when the discussion was closed, and the project adopted, clause by clause. I sat on the first bench, to the right of the President, and my colleagues, among whom the only one personally known to me is Cochon, can state whether or not I rose in my seat for or against the project. I likewise invoke the testimony of the representatives Bergasse-Laziroule, Lehardi, and in particular Duviquet, who has reminded me that I was by his side on the steps of the tribune, together with others who were in a position to see and notice the way in which I acted. I must also point out that while in the tribune I suggested to the *rapporteur* a change in the text of one of the articles of the project, which article was liable to an interpretation adverse to the interests of the Republic, and that the *rapporteur* adopted this modification. When, at the sitting two days later, Poullain-Grandprey once more read the project, I do not know what I am alleged to have said; the fact of the matter is that I did not reach the Chamber until towards the close of the debate. I had left the Chamber with my colleague Robert of the Tarn, to speak with him about matters of interest to us both; on returning I sat down beside my colleague Izoré, of whom I inquired what had taken place. He answered me that that 'madman Rouchon' had again speechified at great length. I replied: 'The discussion ought to have been closed.' The several clauses of the project were put to the vote, and I rose with my colleagues to adopt it. Such are the facts, whence it is plain that the citizen Treilhard has been imposed upon when informed that I had voted for Rouchon. I did not hear of this calumny until the 22d of this month. On the evening of that day I called on the Director and informed him, as did also my colleague Villers, that, taking into consideration my principles and my past conduct, he ought not to have credited what had been told him. I do not know whether he still remains unfavorably impressed with me; at any rate, such an impression can be easily dispelled if he will take the trouble of verifying the facts herein submitted.

"FABRE DE L'AUDE.

"PARIS, the 24th Brumaire, Year VII. of the French Republic, one and indivisible."

If, in order to do justice to each one, I have considered it my duty to devote some little attention to M. Fabre of the Aude, and relate how fortune had crowned his conduct, I feel the need of saying a word about the fate of the only man who displayed courage and a sense of honor on this occasion. Rouchon had in store the fate reserved in all times and in all lands for men of character. A short while after he left the *corps législatif*, not to return to it. He did not, it appears, exercise any function until 1816, when he again became a deputy, and shortly afterwards attorney-general to the Lyons tribunal. May he, for the sake of those under his jurisdiction, have brought to his functions the vigorous equity he twice in one session exhibited in the *corps législatif!* I have dwelt with satisfaction on this last striking act of courage displayed in the Council of Five Hundred, just as one regretfully watches the last flicker of a light which is dying out. The quality most necessary in public assemblies is unfortunately the one which henceforth will be the most lacking in all the succeeding assemblies.

From the 1st to the 24th Frimaire, Year VII.— General Joubert, appointed to the command of the Army of Italy in the place of Brune, is ordered to seize upon Piedmont. Botot, my secretary, is sent to Milan with instructions for the general-in-chief.

We had for some time past been warned of the treachery of the Neapolitan Government; it now stands revealed. After having summoned our outposts to evacuate Roman territory, the Neapolitans have attacked us without further ceremony. As a matter of course they have been beaten by the Republicans. A declaration of war against Naples and Sardinia is submitted to the *corps législatif*, which decrees it. Joubert conducts this expedition with great precision, taking possession of the fortified towns in Piedmont and of the city of Turin. The King has capitulated, and been allowed to withdraw to an island which gives its name to the whole of his kingdom—Sardinia. Large depots of stores have fallen into our hands, and will be of value to us in future operations. Joubert, together with the Sardinian and Swiss troops, who have donned the tricolor cockade, is once more to take up his position on the Adige, and to reinforce with a few demi-brigades the French army occupying Rome. This operation assures the security of our rear-guard. Although Austria wages war against us, she has so far not succeeded in alienating the peoples from us.

The King of Piedmont, now merely King of Sardinia, might perhaps have been brought to Paris, but the Directorate neither needs nor desires such a spectacle. There is some talk of arraigning before a tribunal as an assassin the Duke of Aosta, who is accused of having caused to be committed, and of having actually committed, numerous murders on the persons of French citizens. The Directorate is not desirous of indulging in any such revenge, which might truly be called justice; it abandons to their remorse those who have been led astray by their ferocious passions, whatever their rank. The Directorate decides that the Duke of Aosta is included in the amnesty, which it considers a measure worthy of its generosity, and one good to adopt towards enemies, in order to be able to claim reciprocity in the matter of our friends. It is time reciprocally to have recourse to indulgent methods, and to show a mutual respect, wherein humanity reckons for something and distinguishes civilized peoples from barbarians. Clemency, like all other things, is learned in the course of revolutions. This word "revolution," which by its very etymology explains all the nobility of human destinies, sufficiently warns those who direct revolutions to beware lest the conqueror of to-day be the defeated of to-morrow.

The *conclusum* of the French plenipotentiaries at Rastadt is adopted. It has been delivered to the Imperial Minister for the purpose of obtaining his sanction.

The Republic is threatened at home and abroad. She has until now been able to look upon herself as invincible by reason of all her successive triumphs, due to the valor of her troops and the improvement of her generals on the field of battle. But we are far from possessing a like strength on the sea, which remains the patrimony of England, and her latest successes do but confirm her mastery over it. I propose the reunion of those of our ships at Brest with those in the Mediterranean, in order to be able to attack the English with superior forces, and then to communicate with Egypt. It would thus be possible to rescue the remainder of the French army and bring it back to Europe, unless our victory should be sufficiently decisive and consolidated for us to feel no alarm about the future in Egypt, in case my idea should be adopted. Admiral Bruix seems to me the only sailor capable of conducting this daring enterprise. The Directorate postpones the consideration of this plan until the receipt of despatches from Egypt.

The Government is not pursuing a course likely to reassure the citizens; frequent arrests are taking place and alarming them. Dismissals made on the sole ground of caprice unsettle functionaries in their positions, the rights and duties of which they can no longer know. This capriciousness increases the number of our enemies, and leaves us without friends. Political matters can be managed only by men: it is therefore necessary to select carefully those who are intrusted with the noble duty of governing their fellow-citizens; but when selections are made with discernment, some latitude must be allowed functionaries when once appointed. They should not be abandoned to the enmity of those whose primary duty is oftentimes to combat and condemn unjust pretensions. Lastly, it is not meet that the supreme government should interfere to too great an extent with the minutiæ of administration, nor with those pertaining to elections. When once one has competent officials, it is for them to see to the execution of the laws, without respect of persons. Justice must triumph, and the various parties be thwarted in the departments as well as in Paris, without any interference on the part of the Government. But in order to attain such a result the Government must have a system, and follow it without swerving.

The English are fitting out an expedition to Mahon. Spain displays a revolting apathy. Prussia is watching the course of events. The hazards of war will decide the side to be taken by these Powers. We are informed that a Russian column is marching towards Galicia.

General Joubert gives vent to his displeasure at the changes made in the Cisalpine Republic. He tenders his resignation, which is declined. I have given Joubert proofs of my personal affection for him. The Directorate, cognizant of our intimacy, begs me to write privately to Joubert, to induce him to retain his command.

Letters received from Prussia convince us that Prince Henry is still friendly to the French.

From the 25th Frimaire to the 20th Nivôse, Year VII.—The greatest discord reigns in Italy between the military authorities and civil agents. At a time when it behooves us not to send into that country agents who have not had a hand in previous agitations, I again call the attention of the Directorate to Fouché, who has been persistently rejected by my colleagues ever since his return from the military agency I had caused to be given him after the 13th Vendémiaire. Fouché was in the habit of daily standing in my ante-chamber, looking as doleful—I am not exaggerating—as a beggar. He was constantly getting M. Vincent Lombard to plead with me on his behalf. This Provençal, my compatriot, has spoken to me repeatedly of the devotion of Fouché to the Republic and to my person; he has positively demonstrated to me that the cleverness of his *protégé* in police matters was a pledge of his diplomatic ability, since there was no difference between these two sciences, which are supposed to be so important to governments. "If you are satisfied," Vincent Lombard would constantly say to me, "with the reports and views of Fouché in public matters, you can judge what he will do in a less difficult sphere. Moreover, Fouché is in the direst misery; he has a wife and children, but no bread. You have given employment to many men in the course of the Revolution, and he is a man if ever there was one. You have employed Talleyrand, who has many an antecedent which is no better than those of Fouché. I guarantee you," Lombard would repeatedly say, "that you will come to congratulate yourself upon your choice. Besides, Fouché's only salvation lies with you."

I had witnessed Fouché in the National Convention gravely compromising himself by revolutionary deeds of the most ardent type committed in the course of the most fearful missions. He was truly a man without a refuge, and outside the pale of the Revolution. Previous to the 9th Thermidor he had been the object of the hatred and fury of Robespierre, against whom he had conspired together with ourselves—indeed, in a most underhand way— pursuant to the priestly character derived by him from his Congregation of the Oratory; but, after all, he was one of the men who, if they did not make the 9th Thermidor, at any rate most frankly desired it. Vincent Lombard would say to me, with the warmth and adroitness of friendship, that "Fouché was entirely dependent on me; that I could not, after having protected and placed Talleyrand as a man of the Revolution, refuse my support to Fouché, who had more genuine and more sincere claims. It behooves you, citizen Director, ever to utilize the talents of patriots to the advantage of the Republic."

Italy had been plunged into anarchy; she needed a man of firm character and strong will to bring her up to the pitch of the Revolution when in presence of the army about to attack her; it was necessary to silence the dissentient parties and concentrate all minds on one idea—Italy's defence against the foreigner and her independence. For the foregoing reasons, perhaps also listening to the weak side of my heart, and once more conquered by his daily obsessions, I again suggested the appointment of Fouché. I believed that his daring and supple character might amalgamate with that of Joubert, the general-in-chief. So it was that I obtained that Fouché should be appointed our chief agent in Italy.

Fouché did not altogether belie by his conduct what I had expected of him in the matter of energetic action; but as he felt an inordinate desire to make money, and, as he said naïvely, "to make up for lost time," in lieu of seeking to restore order he would have prepared to perpetuate—at least, for some little while—anarchy, which offers the best opportunity for enriching one's self. Fouché was soon denounced to us on all sides, especially by the agents whom he had come to control, and who had become alive to the fact that he had superseded them. They could, moreover, be justly accused of all the troubles from which the Cisalpine Republic was now suffering. They ought to have warded them off, but perhaps they had incited them. Hence reciprocal denunciations, and thus difficulties, instead of being swept away, increased daily. Fouché was adroit enough to ally himself with and fasten himself on

Joubert, who supported him faithfully and in the most disinterested manner. Joubert, with a pronounced character of patriotism and the purest of intentions, had the disadvantages of these qualities. His was an iron will which nothing could bend when he had announced it; hence he always took the part of Fouché in all matters and against all comers. Joubert was an honest Republican, well educated and able, but for lack of affability in his character he could win only esteem and not love. Something more is needed to rally men and unite in a solid phalanx the friends of liberty; and it is only too frequent in the nature of rugged characters not to be insensible to the pliancy of subordinates, which is the most subtle of flattery. Hence Fouché had pounced upon this weak point in Joubert's armor to captivate him.

On assuming command of the Army of Italy, Joubert finds there General Moreau, whom, since the 18th Fructidor, the Directorate had considered it could not employ as a general-in-chief. In order not to leave him altogether without a position, we have appointed him inspector-general of the Army of Italy. It is in this modest capacity that Moreau has reported himself to Joubert, who, out of a feeling very much akin to chivalry, has sought to raise him from his humiliating condition. Not only has he held out a helping hand to Moreau by availing himself of his services, but he has admitted him to his intimacy; and if he can receive from this some good military opinions, we do not believe Moreau disposed to receive from it good counsel. Moreau is not a good confidant in this respect; he is unfortunately viewed as a mark and rallying-point for the counter-revolutionists, who look upon him as with them, by reason of his equivocal, or at the least uncertain, conduct during the days preceding the 18th Fructidor.

Meanwhile affairs in Italy are getting more and more complicated in every direction. The Neapolitans have attacked Rome; this position has in the first instance been evacuated, but immediately recaptured by the French army, and the Neapolitan army completely routed. A number of prisoners, cannon, and stores are all ours. The charlatan Mack, not only forsaken but pursued by his own army, is at the mercy of General Championnet, who is marching on Naples in all haste. The King only awaits him to fly; he is already in Sicily. Joubert advances on Leghorn, proclaiming that his sole object is to drive the English and Neapolitans out of it. I was of opinion that this step might have been deferred; it will probably draw upon us a sudden attack on the part of the Austrians, massed in large numbers on the Adige, in the Tyrol, and in the Danube. We require another two months to be prepared successfully to cope with the enemy.

Independently of all the worries that Joubert is exposed to from all the agents with whom he has to come into contact, he is greatly annoyed at the ceaseless attacks of newspapers which denounce and bring into disrepute all the authorities, showing no mercy to generals-in-chief. Chafing under all these annoyances, Joubert cannot moreover work harmoniously with our ambassador. The latter issues ordinances annulling the orders of the general-in-chief; by way of revenge, Joubert forbids the commander of the Milan garrison to pay heed to any requisition made by the ambassador. Anarchy and tumult are at their height. The Directorate decides that the

Minister of War and myself shall seek to reconcile the contending parties, and more especially warn General Joubert against the irritation stirred up in him by the impostures of journalists in the pay of the foreigner. All these firebrands are kindled in Paris; Paris is ever the hot-bed of all intrigues. I turn for a moment from our foreign affairs, in order to cast a look on one of the establishments existing in the bosom of the great city, an establishment which has always been a rock on which morality has split—I mean the gambling-houses.

The gambling-houses of Paris have ever been the object of ardent covetousness on the part of the corrupt men of the capital. The riches they dispense have in succession gone to the various Ministers, especially during the Empire. Mme. Bonaparte always received a considerable portion of them from Fouché; it is even said that, following upon the Restoration, the highest personages did not consider they were lowering themselves when taking their share. The information about individuals received by the Directorate may be of some interest nowadays, especially for several of those who are still living, and who have not ceased to follow the chances of fortune in this direction.

PARIS, 24th Nivôse, Seventh Republican Year.

POLITICAL REPORT[1]

ON THE GAMBLING-HOUSES, ON THE INDIVIDUALS KEEPING THEM, AND ON THE IMMINENT DANGER WITH WHICH THESE ESTABLISHMENTS, IN THEIR PRESENT CONDITION, THREATEN THE GOVERNMENT.

I had up to the present time looked upon gambling-houses merely in the light of immoral establishments, which the Govern-

---

[1] *Note.*—A copy of this memorandum has been sent to the Minister of Police.

ment should proscribe. I was therefore little inclined to create an establishment of this kind at the time the Minister of Police proposed the matter to me and offered to advance the necessary money. As I was utterly strange to such kind of speculations, I imagined that a sum of *three thousand francs* would be sufficient for the purpose of procuring a place, and meeting other preliminary expenses. I did indeed organize what is called a *partie de société* (private gambling-club) in the vicinity of the Palais-Egalité; now if my object had been to make money, I should have been greatly deceived in my calculations, for up to the present time the establishment has not yielded enough to pay the employees, and I am myself considerably out of pocket.

My entire attention has been devoted to carrying out the views of the Government; and in order to do this I did not consider it sufficient to acquire notes and information about the players, but thought it far more interesting to throw some light on the keepers of gambling-houses. My relations with the establishment I have created have connected me with persons thoroughly acquainted with everything connected with gambling-houses, and I am thus enabled to present a full and complete statement in regard to this branch of business. It gives all the personages interested in these kinds of speculations, both those who openly appear on the stage, and those who remain behind the curtain; and we presume that, after a perusal of this report, the Government, fully informed in regard to all the manœuvres practised in gambling-houses, which might be called genuine counter-revolutionist workshops, will feel the necessity of closing these houses; or at least, if administrative or financial considerations militate against the adoption of such a measure, of placing in charge of them men who have given pledges to the Revolution, and of whose loyalty there cannot be the slightest doubt.

With the object of introducing order into the following *exposé*, based on the various notes we have collected from the least suspicious sources, and while making sacrifices proportionate to their importance, we will first class numerically the houses under the control of the Excise, and next those independent of it, and which exist only owing to toleration or by the favor of the Government.

GAMBLING-HOUSES LICENSED BY THE RÉGIE.

1. *Rue Ceruty*, corner of the boulevard. — This house is kept by the *ci-devant* Vicomte de Castelanne, the Chevalier la

Mansellerie - Morainville, Baron de la Calprenede, and Diesbeck.[1]

Castelanne, in 1790, kept the *Club polonais*, in the Jardin-Egalité, with La Calprenède, Morainville, and the woman Villars. The foreigner it was who supplied the funds of this house, wherein a Russian prince, a bastard of the late Empress, lost 20,000 *louis*. The matter was taken up by the Mayor of Paris in person. The ex-Marquis de Lamberty came forward as proprietor of the establishment, and was fined 1000 *écus*, besides the costs of publicly posting his sentence.

After this check Castelanne and his partners set up the Club de Valois, in the Palais-Egalité. It was there, in '93, that the proposition was made to place the Dauphin on the throne. Thereupon Castelanne, Dillon, and the Prince d'Hénin were arrested. The first-named managed to escape from the Luxembourg prison; Dillon, less fortunate, was guillotined; while the Prince d'Hénin managed to cross the frontier.

After his escape Castelanne remained in concealment until after the 9th Thermidor, when he reappeared, and opened the Maison des Princes, at the corner of the Italiens. Again it was the foreigner who supplied the funds for this establishment.

On the 13th Vendémiaire Castelanne was at the head of the Lepelletier "section," together with Richer-Serisy, the Comte de Lanjac, and Lafond, a soldier of the Artois regiment. All were outlawed, but Lafond was the only one arrested and punished.

The storm over, Castelanne reappeared, and resumed his trade, which he has plied ever since. His partner Morainville, whom everybody calls a swindler and a thief, gives himself airs of importance with the players by speaking continually of his relations with the Directorate, and placing at their disposal his influence with the Directors.

Diesbeck, another partner of Castelanne, is a former soldier of the Artois regiment, and has all the qualities necessary to belong to such a set.

In regard to La Calprenède, he is a *ci-devant* Gascon noble, known as a swindler under the old *régime*, and he has probably not mended his ways under the present one. He does nothing but speak of the games he played formerly with "Monseigneur, Comte d'Artois." Previous to the 18th Fructidor he gave a

---

[1] Pencilled note in the margin of the MS.: *Lillebeck.*—G. D.

dinner to the deputies *fructidorisés*, with whom he was on most intimate terms, in particular little André of the Lozère.

Castelanne has also as a partner the ex-Marquis de Livry. Persons who claim to be well informed have told me that more than 20,000 *louis* had been made by the establishment in little games got up after the *trente-et-un* of the Excise had been played.

2. *Maison Egalité, No.* 113.—This house is kept by the ex-Countess d'Albain, who alleges that she enjoys the protection of the Directorate. The partner is one *ci-devant* Comte de Dourain, who occupies in the said house a private room where are held conventicles attended by the friends of the Pretender—*i.e.*, the purest and most pronounced Royalists.

3. *Maison Egalité, No.* 154.—This house is kept by Richard, of Lyons, and La Vitonière, of the Artois regiment. Richard kept the Hôtel Massiac in '91, '92, and '93. England supplied the funds for this establishment.

In '93 the said Richard went to Lyons to rejoin the famous Précy. At the beginning of '95 he disappeared, but returned at the end of the same year to establish the gambling-house he now keeps.

On the 13th Vendémiaire he participated in the doings of Lafond, Richer-Serisy, Castelanne, and other counter-revolutionists who came to the surface in those days.

4. *Gambling-house à la Chancellerie d'Orléans.*—This house is kept by Grandger and Maury, formerly attached to Pache's police. They are considered patriots.

5. *Club des Arcades du Palais-Egalité.*—This house is kept by Changrand, Nolet, Andrieux, Moulinet, and Garel. The first-named is a Knight of St. Louis, and one of the principal agents of the *ci-devant* Duc d'Orléans; the second, valet to the Duc de Villeroi; the third, ex-banker of the royal police; the fourth, valet of the ex-Minister Sartine, with whose friends he corresponds; the fifth, former valet of the Comte de Jumilhac.

It seems that this house has relations with Spain, whence, it is presumed, it derives funds.

6. *Maison Egalité,* 129.—This house is kept by one Descarières, a former officer in the king's military household, from which he was expelled. At the beginning of the Revolution he came out of the Temple, whither he had sought a refuge from his creditors, and opened a gambling-house. The foreigner has at all times

supplied the funds of this bank. Descarières was in partnership with the Spaniard Gusman, guillotined as a spy.

It was in this house that Rovère, Saladin, Aubry, Henri Larivière, and other deputies conspired previous to the 18th Fructidor. Here was kept the treasury of the Clichiens, whence they drew funds to pay their police, and make all the disbursements necessary for the counter-revolution they were meditating.

Descarières, previous to the 18th Fructidor, gave a daily dinner of forty to fifty covers; he still gives one of twenty-five, to which foreigners of all shades are most specially welcome.

At the time of the anniversary of the King's death it was necessary to be in mourning to be admitted into Descarières' establishment. General Colin, having gone thither in uniform, was not allowed to enter. This Descarières has a mistress who parades the most scandalous luxury. Her indecency has won her the name of "Beautiful Bacchante" of the Palais-Egalité, under which appellation she is known and designated.

7. *Maison Egalité, No.* 167.—The house is kept by one Mons, a German baron, formerly attached to Niquille, a peace officer, who gave him six francs a day; he is now very rich, and works for the interests of the House of Artois.

8. *Rue de la Loi, No.* 120—This house is kept by Ligny, a former valet of the *ci-devant* Duc d'Orléans, and by Serrière, the son of an inspector of police under the old *régime*. Both were surprised on the 10th of August while members of a bogus patrol, but were fortunate enough to escape.

Maison Egalité, No. 50.—This house is kept by one Asvedo, who has succeeded Monier. He has an apartment at a yearly rental of 18,000 francs, which he occupied for a year and a half without having any gambling in it; but this did not prevent him from giving four dinners per decade during the whole of that time. He had attracted to his house all the generals returning from Italy or Germany, and the most elegant and skilful strumpets "to work them."

This Asvedo, of Jewish origin, is a very intriguing personage, and found the means of meeting an excessive expenditure by supplying memoranda on the position of our armies to those who were willing to pay a good price for the information. He has taken a gambling-house only in order to better conceal his mission, or perhaps as a means of better fulfilling it.

HOUSES INDEPENDENT OF THE RÉGIE

1. *Rue Honoré, Petit Hôtel de Noailles.*—This house is kept by the widow Bentabole, who claims that she enjoys the protection of the Directorate. Her partner is one Cayeux, a former eating-house-keeper, who supplies the funds. This Cayeux has made his fortune with *étouffoirs*. *Trente-et-un* is played in this establishment.

2. *Rue Honoré, No.* 58, near the Place Vendôme.—This house is kept by the woman Raynal, who claims that she enjoys the protection of François de Neufchâteau and the police. She has several deputies as boarders. Gambling serves only as a pretext for the gatherings held on the second floor in the rooms of the notorious Sainte-Foix, former treasurer of Monseigneur, Comte d'Artois. Azon de Saint-Firmin and Simon, of Brussels, supply the funds for this establishment, which first flourished under the protection of the inspector d'Ossonville, transported in Fructidor. Bourdon, of the Oise, was one of the boarders of the woman Raynal, who supplies the deputies with strumpets. It is there that decrees have been and are still drafted. In the morning the talk is all *émigration* and supplies; in the evening it is gambling; those who do not play proceed to the second floor to "talk politics." We know what that means.

3. *Rue Honoré, Maison Vénua.*—This house is kept by the woman La Boucharderie, the mistress of the representative of the people Chénier. *La bouillotte* is the game played here. The frequenters of the house are military men and members of the diplomatic corps. Baronne de Stal contributes in part towards the expenses of the establishment by means of her gifts to one Vivian, who has at one time exercised control over the gambling-houses. This Vivian is an immoral man, suspected of having coined base *louis* and forged *mandats*. He lives at No. 26, Rue Marc. He is on very intimate terms with the La Boucharderie woman. Duperret, cashier of the police in the days of Sotin, has made a great deal of money out of this Vivian. The police have several times raided the house, but without discovering anything, owing to his having always been warned. His mistress is named Cauchois; she lives in the Rue de la Loi, near the Café des Colonnes.

The citizen Chénier seems to be ignorant of all that takes place in the La Boucharderie house, and to take no part in it.

4. *Rue de la Loi, Aux Trois Pigeons.*—This house is kept by the woman Vienay, an Orleanist. She is also on intimate terms with Vivian. *La bouillotte* is played here, and those frequenting the house are composed of the same elements as the frequenters of La Boucharderie's house. Raffet, a former military man, Rue Anne, Dollet, Maison Vivian, Rue Marc, and Demailly, Cour des Fontaines, frequent these two houses alternately. The aim of all these people is to rob the unfortunate, and, if possible, to bring about a counter-revolution.

5. *Rue de Cléry, No.* 66, near that of the Gros Chenet.—This house is kept by one Saint-Brice, a former lady's-maid, once attached to the service of the Dauphin. It is said that she has free access to the Directorate. She is a friend of Mme. Tallien and of Mme. Château-Renaud. The Pretender, whose cause she serves, has money remitted to her for her household expenses, and for the purpose of bringing together under her roof all the agitators of the party. She is an adventuress whose father kept a private lodging-house in the Faubourg Germain. She is married to a journeyman baker who received the cross of Saint-Louis during the last days of the monarchy.

6. *Rue Basse-du-Rempart, No.* 337, Chaussée d'Antin.—This house is kept by Mme. La Fare, a niece of Marshal de Biron; a year ago she was in great poverty. She became intimate with La Boucharderie, and obtained from the representative of the people Chénier that he should allow the latter to keep a gambling-house. She introduced her to many well-bred women as the protectress of the former nobles; it was due to her entreaties that Chénier, after having in the first instance spoken in support of the committee which called for the transportation of the ex-nobles, ended in recanting and laboring in an entirely opposite direction. Since that time La Boucharderie has received under her roof the former nobility, clergy, diplomacy, and general officers. All vie in paying court to her. The Minister Schérer is one of the habitués of the house. Gambling is indulged in three times every ten days. It is a place of gathering for the Pretender's friends.

7. *Place des Victoires, No.* 16.—This house, known as the *Club des banquiers*, is kept by the woman Fremont. Financial matters are here discussed; it is believed that it was here that the idea of wrecking the *Caisse des Comptes Courants* was conceived.

Houses of Assembly

1. *Rue Ville-l'Evêque, No. 987.*—This house is kept by one Bonnecarère, who has on his own account a gambling-hell where the Orleanists hold their conventicles.

2. *Rue Honoré, No. 90*, near the Place Vendôme.—The woman Laurine here keeps a furnished house wherein gambling takes place. The deputies who frequent this establishment may truly be called "the tail of Clichy." Not one of them but would vote that the present Directors be transported to Cayenne.

We might also mention the actress Raucourt, who is travelling just at present, as well as an Englishwoman named Eliot, first the mistress of the *ci-devant* Duc d'Orléans, and then of Prince d'Aremberg.

But there is a woman who deserves special attention: it is the woman Demailly, alias Charpentier, the former mistress of Barère, who, so the story goes, was in the habit of intrusting to her the secrets of the Committee of Public Safety; the said Demailly was in the habit of selling them to England. She owns a printing establishment at No. 470, Rue de la Perle, and a country-house at Meudon. Persons who claim to be well-informed say that were this Meudon residence searched, precious things would be found in it. This Demailly has been paid by England since the beginning of the Revolution, in exchange for Government secrets. She gives dinners at her house in the Rue de la Perle, but it is at Meudon that have been and are held counter-revolutionary committees.

During the whole of the time that Lord Malmesbury was in Paris the three women above mentioned saw him continually, while the Demailly woman even went to Lille to confer with him. It is the banker Pargot who supplied them with funds. As he has the care of the English prisoners in France, he was, as a matter of course, intrusted with paying the salaries of these women. It is asserted that he has in former days received, both from Switzerland and from England, eight million *écus* to bull the *mandats* and then to bear them.

We must not forget a Mme. Thiolon, nor one d'Aoust, her partner, living at No. 126, Rue Bonne Nouvelle. They were at one time the agents of d'Orléans, and are now the agents of England. The woman Thiolon goes on frequent journeys; she glides into all the ministerial offices to find out what is going on, and attracts all the heads of departments to her house by inviting them to dinner. She has asked for the "radiation" of Count de Senef, the friend of Gusman and of the Prussian Clootz. In the days of the Minister Sotin she obtained the administration of the gambling-houses, and ceded the undertaking to Vivian and Perrin for 1500 *louis* down, 21 *louis* a day, and ten per cent., without loss, on the profits. Sotin, by enriching this woman, has put her in a position to serve with more daring all the enemies of the Government.

The Present Régie (Administration)

One Delzen is at the head of the new *régie*. He is a former gambling banker of the former Princesse de Lamballe. Although an ex-hairdresser, he has, in days gone by, had the "honor" of dealing the cards at the Queen's. He had retired to Vernon at the beginning of the Revolution, and has on all occasions shown himself devoted to the House of Orleans.

An ex-Knight of Saint-Louis named Varnière, formerly a banker at Spa, and the Marquis de Gaville, a former cavalry captain and an elector of the 13th Vendémiaire, are Delzen's partners. Their bankers, croupiers, dealers, etc., are nearly to a man counter-revolutionists, possessing neither *cartes de sûreté* (tickets of safety giving name, address, and occupation) nor other papers to identify them—adventurers, in short, numbering in all over three hundred, scattered through the various houses of the *régie*.

It is with the enormous sums derived from these gambling-hells that the ex-Marquis de Gaville subsidizes the famished horde of the Pretender's friends, pending the time when happier circumstances shall enable them to make what they style a *coup*, and replace things on the old footing.

We shall refer more particularly in other reports to some of these personages, when speaking of the clandestine gambling-houses known as *étouffoirs*, which have so strangely multiplied ever since the licensing of gambling-houses; we shall give the list of all those haunts frequented by individuals known as belonging to what is styled the *Bande noire* (Black Gang), about which the commissaries of police and other agents hold their peace, because they have the best of reasons for so doing.

Such, citizen Minister, is the actual condition of the gambling-houses and of the persons interested in them. You will perceive that there is not a single one of the latter who cannot rightly be suspected of being an enemy of the Government. The gambling-houses are, we make bold to say, the hot-bed of all the counter-revolutionist intrigues. In them is to be found the treasury of all the factions. If the Government is desirous of winning a bloodless yet signal victory over all its enemies, it has but to close these their asylums. What is the use of closing our ports to English merchandise if Mr. Pitt is free to have in Paris gambling-house bankers who levy on their dupes the expenses of all these counter-revolutionist manœuvres?

Two reasons, it is averred, have influenced the Government in its decision first to tolerate and next to license these establishments. The sum derived from them monthly has seemed precious, considering the exhausted state of our finances. But, whatever the needs of the Public Treasury, it is assuredly money too dearly paid for if it supplies the foreigner with means for maintaining dissension in our midst, and developing germs of corruption. It is also argued that gambling-houses are necessary to facilitate the supervision by the police of counter-revolutionists and rogues; that they constitute a kind of trap into which these dangerous individuals fall. This may be true, but to obtain such a result they should not be at the head of these establishments, for if it is they who farm them, manage them, and lease them, it is in vain that the police send detectives into them; supposing even that they are not bribed, they will see only what it is wished to have them see; and, as the Government will rest on their vigilance, and their reports will be insignificant, the counter-revolutionists of every shade will be able, under cover of gambling, to carry on their intrigues, weave the threads of their plots, and put every kind of spring in motion, without the police receiving the slightest warning in the matter.

It is therefore absolutely necessary that there should be among those principally interested, such as the farmers, managers, and keepers of these houses, men absolutely devoted to the Government who are not merely sleeping partners; and in no other position perhaps is it more important to place safe men. Existing circumstances make this a paramount duty. Otherwise the gambling-houses, far from affording the Government the means of knowing and surprising its enemies, will simply be a veil thrown over their machinations—a place where they will be able to conspire with impunity, and to indulge in the ever-renewed hope of seeing their guilty manœuvres some day crowned with success.

From the 20th Nivôse to the 1st Pluviôse, Year VII.—To return to higher politics, which will no longer tolerate any digression breaking in upon them. We are entirely masters of Piedmont; the King of Sardinia is free to retire to the island that gives its name to his kingdom, and has sought a refuge in the dominions of the Duke of Parma, pending the time when he will cross over to Sardinia. Joubert has carried out to perfection the taking of Piedmont. The financial commissary of the Directorate, Ancelot, writes to us against the military authority, which he styles aristocracy, naming Joubert personally in his denunciation. The latter may perhaps not be altogether undeserving of blame, but it is alleged that he acts with far too much rigor. Nothing less is called for than the dismissal and bringing to trial of the general-in-chief who holds in his hands our military destinies on so important a point. It is Ancelot's friend Treilhard who speaks with less indulgence. The victorious Joubert, to whom we owe our first successes, which he alone can keep up, becomes angry and sends in his resignation. I vote that it be accepted, in order to ward off the measures with which he is threatened. Nevertheless it seems to be incontestable that the agent Ancelot, who allows his personal passions to govern him, is moreover stimulated by those of the corrupt men and enemies of the Revolution surrounding him— among others, one La Tourette, whom the Directorate has expelled from the army. Here is Italy in such a position that, were she attacked by Austria, she might perhaps be conquered in one campaign.

Haller, who has been employed by Bonaparte in a manner so profitable to both, reappears, eager once more to play a part; he seems to be a partisan of peace on terms hardly honorable. He requests that he be sent to Milan. He is not the man for this important post. Haller and Berthier have not left a good reputation behind them in Italy, especially in Rome; in connection with their last mission they have been charged with waste of public moneys, and even with stealing several precious objects from the Vatican. We have received official reports seriously incriminating them.

Championnet is under the walls of Capua. He has committed the imprudence of attacking the enemy's camp before having all his troops in hand; he awaits them with impatience, in order to seize upon the capital. It seems to me that there is too great a distance between him and the Army of Italy; it is to be feared that Austria will take advantage of Joubert's withdrawal to attack us; he enjoys the confidence of the soldiers. His is not a superior genius possessing transcendental conceptions of war, but he understands war in the sphere wherein his command has placed him.

We are possibly going to have our hands as full in Germany as in Italy. The Directorate, mindful of its triumphs on the Rhine, believes it best to fire the mind of the army by giving it a more distant destination, so the new army created to operate in that direction is called the Army of the Danube. Jourdan is appointed General-in-chief of the Army of the Danube. An enterprising activity is not the dominant quality of this general, who is, however, most commendable in many other respects. His first letters announce to us that he does not think he is in a position to act; they even reveal an alarming feeling of uneasiness on his part.

The Army of Helvetia is in urgent need of food supplies. Its general-in-chief, Masséna, writes to us in the strongest terms in this regard. This unfortunate position is the work of dishonest agents. As soon as Masséna has bread for his troops he will act vigorously against the enemy.

Public opinion seems to be getting more and more stirred up against the Government. Anarchy on the one hand and Royalism on the other seem to work harmoniously together, and threaten the public peace. It is necessary to reunite all citizens; Justice alone has the right to rally all, but she does not possess the means, as passions are at work. The Government should not adopt severe measures except when they are indispensable; its chief aim must be to reassure the mass of citizens in regard to their liberties and security.

Although the troubles raised against us are perhaps not foreign to the men and things which necessitated the 18th Fructidor, I do not consider I should cease to display the interest I have taken in the cause agitated in so lively a fashion and so eloquently pleaded by Rouchon, and in favor of which I have so sincerely pronounced myself, in response to confidence reposed in me by Siméon, and others among his unfortunate colleagues sentenced to transportation. As Siméon has most justly remarked to me in his letter, although the Directorate is free to assign the place of transportation, it is not bound to give the preference to that which, like Guiana, may be fatal to men's lives. Instead of rigorously pursuing measures adopted in the first hour of danger, we should diminish their severity, at least to the extent the law permits; let us therefore allow those who have been fortunate enough not to have crossed the seas to remain in Europe. I succeed in proving that this simple act of humanity is just and proper, and in conquering the exacting demands of the inexorable Merlin. As a result, it is enacted that the Île d'Oléron shall be the provisional place of detention of the individuals sentenced to transportation by the laws passed on the 19th and 22d Fructidor, Year V.

Events corroborate the information which had not more than half proved to us the designs of the new coalition. It is truly against France that the Russians are marching, having left their country in large numbers, and advancing by forced marches by way of Germany and Italy. We have addressed a note to Austria in regard to this extraordinary and decidedly hostile march. We have not received any satisfactory reply. The Directorate extends the time for a reply, but it behooves it to redouble its precautions, so as to be ready to face events.

The constituted authorities of the Roman Republic had been compelled, owing to the presence of the Neapolitan army, to withdraw to Perugia; they have now returned to Rome once more free, owing to the triumph of the Republican army which is now marching on Naples.

All parties are plotting together to get control of the impending elections.

Attention has been called to the founding of the

Cercle Constitutionnel, Rue de l'Université, in the Year V. So long as the thing in question was the making Talleyrand a Minister, the club lacked nothing of what was necessary to keep it in existence. It would seem that now that Talleyrand has a portfolio, the object of the club's foundation has been attained, for Talleyrand, himself both founder and member, has decided, ever since the road to fortune has been opened to him, to refuse paying the *Club Constitutionnel* the slightest assessment. I never was a member of this club, but since it is I who made Talleyrand a Minister, the honor is done me of believing that I must have been his colleague in the *Club Constitutionnel*. I am in consequence favored with a circular calling for the payment of expenses incurred in the establishment of this popular society. This missive ought naturally to have been sent to Talleyrand. I think it proper to forward it to this Minister, who is even now disposed to have so little memory for essential things, especially for those which may have been connected with his advancement.

It would be difficult for Lucien and Joseph Bonaparte to remain quiet amid the seemingly ever-increasing troubles. I receive from the two Bonaparte brothers (for now they always hunt in couples) a report on and a statement against a Corsican parish priest, who remained in the island at the time of its occupation by the English. This document, accompanied by personal statements of Joseph Bonaparte against the Pope, his authority, and his policy, seems rather strange to me in view of its appearance in such troublous times; but if one takes into account that Joseph Bonaparte has never pursued any course whatsoever not commanded, or at the very least permitted, by a sign from his brother Napoleon, one may catch a glimpse of the amount of treachery, bad faith, and both religious and political perfidy promised by this family, with which it has been an hereditary pastime to treat with derision all that is most sacred in heaven and on earth.

PARIS, 14th *Nivôse, Year VII.*

The Representatives of the People elected by the Department of the Liamone to the Council of Five Hundred to the Citizen Minister of the Interior.

CITIZEN MINISTER,

We beg you will lay the following facts before the Directorate :

The citizen Franchi, appointed central commissary in the place of the citizen Costa, is the parish priest of the village of La Soccia; he did not discontinue his religious functions during the English domination.

We beg you will add to our attestation of these facts that of the Corsican deputies, who have already been consulted as to the morality of the citizen de Franchi, but not as to his quality of parish priest and subject of King George.

It is not a question of ascertaining whether citizen de Franchi is an honest man, but whether he is a parish priest, and whether he was actively engaged in his functions as such during the English domination.

As there is no one to deny these two facts, we beg you will bring them under the notice of the Directorate. The Director Barras has authorized us to prefer this request. We have to point out to you—

1. That a parish priest who has exercised his functions during the English domination has, as a matter of course, taken the oath of allegiance exacted by the King of England from all the inhabitants of the island, especially public officials and ecclesiastics.

2. That during the English invasion, the Parlement of Corsica having sent deputies to Rome for the purpose of disowning everything that had been done in matters ecclesiastical under the

domination of the Republic, and with the object of again entering into the pale of the Catholic, Apostolic, and Roman Church, and the Court of Rome having sent to Corsica vicars-apostolic, and notably former counter-revolutionary bishops, all priests having preserved their parishes under the Roman *régime* have as a matter of course retracted the oath given by them to the civil constitution of the clergy of France.

3. That each and every act of these ministers of religion exercised under the supervision of the vicars-apostolic and of the returned episcopal *émigrés*, is an act equivalent to a formal retractation.

4. That this retractation takes place in the church, at the close of the mass, on the part of constitutional priests desirous of retaining their parishes after the return to the island of the vicars-apostolic and bishops who came from Rome.

As a matter of course the English agents have not furnished us with official reports; but this is to be expected from the nature of things (see Exhibit A).

The citizen de Franchi did, on the 3d of June, 1794, take part in a meeting in his parish church at La Soccia. This meeting, held pursuant to a letter from Paoli, then an outlaw, elected as a deputy to the General Assembly of Corsica—which pronounced the island's separation from France, and gave the crown of Corsica to the King of England—*Anton Dominico de Franchi*, brother of de Franchi, the parish priest.

It results from the foregoing, for all men of good faith, that it is a refractory priest who has been substituted for the citizen Costa, who has made every sacrifice for the Republic, and fought in Italy and Corsica against the enemies of France.

Citizen Minister, we count not only on your justice but on your zeal in bringing these facts to the notice of the Directorate. We ask for the reinstatement of the citizen Costa, or that some irreproachable citizen be substituted for him. While we are serving the Republic in positions which retain us near the centre of government, other brothers of ours are sailing the seas and braving every danger for the Republic; and that men who have lived as subjects of the King of England, that a refractory priest should enjoy the confidence of the Directorate, and be able to carry desolation into our department, and perhaps compel Republicans and the rest of our family to leave their country once more and seek refuge on the continent of France—

you must realize, citizen Minister, that no Frenchman of good faith exists who can do otherwise than smile at such a state of affairs.

For them, as for us, the time of persecution must be only that of the triumph of the enemies of the Republic. We have already suffered ours without complaining. We hope that, enlightened by the foregoing information, the Directorate will proceed with a new appointment which will restore peace in the department, and put an end to the cry of alarm so complacently propagated throughout it by the enemies of the Republic: "Woe to the friends of General Bonaparte!" The Government knows that the Republic and itself have no truer, no better tried, and no more ardent friends than all those bearing that name.

Greeting and fraternity,

A certified copy. (Signed) J. BONAPARTE
(Signed) BONAPARTE. and L. BONAPARTE.

EXHIBIT A

I am able, in this connection, to insert a fact which I know of my own knowledge; it will serve more fully to convince the citizen François de Neufchâteau. At a time when I was ambassador to Rome, Cardinal Zerdil, President of the Ecclesiastical Congregation, told me one day that, seeing the efforts of a few members of the Legislative Council of France to establish the Catholic form of worship in that part of the Christian world (this was previous to the 18th Fructidor), he considered the matter easy of accomplishment; that the Court of Rome would doubtless lend its aid to the scheme. He unfolded to me his plan, which consisted in applying to France the arrangements made in the matter of Corsica. The good man considered it quite natural that the episcopal *émigrés* should return, and that the intruders should be expelled, unless they took an oath of absolute obedience to the chief of the Roman and Apostolic Church, and abjured the errors of 1791. But what proves two other truths—viz., the hypocrisy and simoniacal greed of the Court of Rome—is the proposition made to me some days later by the Holy Father himself, to countenance an arrangement in regard to France's ecclesiastical affairs, provided the French would restore Ancona and even Romagna to him, so greatly did Rome reckon on our weakness and the religious fanaticism then being stirred up in France by the public authorities.

A certified copy.
(Signed) BONAPARTE.

From the 1st to the 15th Pluviôse, Year VII.—We now know as a positive fact of a treaty of alliance between Russia and England, pursuant to which the former supplies 45,000 men, now on the march. Our plenipotentiaries at Rastadt have declared that all negotiations would be broken off should the Empire allow the Russians to pass through its territory. It might perhaps be possible to divide this new coalition, whose interests are truly heterogeneous. I propose that overtures of peace be made to Russia. The Directorate adopts my proposition.

Having arrived under the walls of Capua, as the result of a series of triumphs won over the Neapolitans, Championnet has thought it good military tactics and sound policy to conclude an armistice previous to entering the town. Naples cannot escape the conqueror; she is in a state of ferment, the excesses of which are to be dreaded. The armistice has been signed with the Viceroy of Naples, Pignatelli. On learning that Championnet has given his consent to it, Treilhard there and then moves that he be deprived of his command. I ask that official news be waited for, and that Championnet be written to for explanations, before dealing so severely with a general worthy of esteem, and whose courage and integrity justify our suspending our rigors. And indeed we receive the next day despatches which justify and do honor to Championnet's action; hence the letter drafted by Treilhard to dismiss him remains null and void. The first letter written to Championnet by the Directorate stands, wherein he was ordered to take Naples, and to have Mack conveyed to Briançon, where he is to be carefully guarded. Treilhard flies into an awful passion: not only would he dismiss generals, but he would have everybody shot; the only honest men in his eyes are the agents Faypoult and Ancelot. I remark that both civilians and soldiers should be punished in an exemplary fashion for the excesses of every kind committed in Italy.

Ehrenbreitstein has capitulated; the garrison of 1300 men surrenders it only after a memorable defence, owing to lack of food; the German general Faber hands it over to the Republican general Dallemagne.

As the time for the elections approaches, agitation increases in all the departments; Republicans are alarmed at the assassinations; Royalism is making progress, and more blood flows. There is good cause for charging the Government with weakness, but it is going too far to charge some of its members with conniving at these excesses; yet such is the movement of passions in political fights that they say continually: "What is not with us is against us: you are opposed to the party supported by the Republicans, therefore you belong to the Royalist party." In the meantime public works are nearly everywhere suspended; if war is sufficient to occupy abroad a portion of the active population, public works are still needed to occupy those at home. Although, as a principle of political economy, the needs of society primarily regulate and create public labor, still, owing to the inequality dividing the classes, one class is always made to dominate the others; this is characteristic of what is called civilization; the rulers, who are the masters and dispensers of so many resources, have an important duty to perform towards the indigent class. Established as they are for the preservation as well as the protection of the greater number, they should be attentive to the needs revealed to them by suffering; nor should they lose sight of the claims of the body politic; lastly, they are chiefly responsible for good or bad social hygiene, for the revolutions which occur are, after all, nothing but an expression of the general uneasiness and despair at not having been heard.

CHAPTER X

Excesses committed by the lazzaroni—Horrible carnage—Embarkation of the King of Naples—Mack surrenders—Schérer succeeded by Milet-Mureau—Schérer general-in-chief of the Army of Italy—Young and old generals—The command of the Army of Italy offered to Bernadotte—His questions—History of the Army of Italy—Bernadotte's curious report—How he is received by the Directorate—Schérer appointed—Translation of the Pope—Position of the armies—Merlin's anger against Schérer—Mme. de Villars—Merlin is of everybody's opinion—Departure of the deputies for the Île d'Oléron—The tax on salt rejected—The theory of taxation—Charges brought against Championnet—Macdonald takes his place—Affairs in Germany—Death of the Elector of the Palatinate—Guillemardet at Madrid—His awkwardness—Contrasted with other ambassadors—Treilhard's violence—Critical situation of the Directorate—War voted by the Councils—Merlin's worrying conduct—His intrigues against me—He seeks to win over Guidal—His visit to the latter's wife—
—My aide-de-camp Avy—A screen—Merlin does the amiable—An indiscreet noise—Merlin's fright—His teeth a source of fear to ladies—Merlin and certain contractors—Progress made by Jourdan—Dissension between him and Masséna—Jourdan defeated—His retreat—Bernadotte's successes—He sends in his resignation—The Army of Observation suppressed—Bernadotte in the country—Burning of the Odéon—Prognostics—Calumnies—Painful letter of Jourdan's—D'Hautpoul and Decaen—Jourdan granted a furlough—Masséna provisional general-in-chief—His orders—Bernadotte's rivalry—Macdonald sees all his wishes gratified—Championnet court-martialled—The secretary Bassal—General affairs of the war—Admiral de Winter—General Daendels—Agitation at home—Great operation intrusted to Admiral Bruix—Jourdan's timidity—Schérer's position—Spirit displayed in the elections—My remarks to the Directorate—Cruel execution of the conscription law—A poor hunchback—Assurances of neutrality given by Prussia—The Directorate

wishes to arrest the Grand Duke of Tuscany and his family—Situation of the army of Masséna—Prince Charles does not know how to take advantage of his victory—Jourdan's double mistake—General Ernouf—Instructions sent to Masséna—Schérer's blunder—The ardor of the generals slackens—Schérer assumes the defensive—The Directorate blamed for his appointment—Marshal Souvaroff—Kray and Melas—Plan in regard to Italy—Larevellière's charges against Joubert—What was the cause of the disorganization of the Army of Italy?—Schérer returns—Moreau succeeds him—Dissension in the bosom of the Directorate—Jourdan's vigorous deed—An attempt to bring Vandamme and d'Hautpoul to trial—D'Hautpoul and Decaen court-martialled—Departure of Bruix—Fears of our envoys at Rastadt—The *émigrés* Digeon and Albigez—Confusion in the Army of Italy—The first military executioner of modern times—Schérer inspector-general—The brothers Frégeville—Orders to evacuate Italy—Treilhard charges the agents with depredations—Plans of war in Italy—Assassination of the Rastadt plenipotentiaries—Declaration presented to the foreign ambassadors by the Directorate—Who were the authors of this crime?—Manifesto addressed to all nations—The Clichy Club reappears—Plans of accusation—Moreau with the Army of Italy—Opinion of certain deputies in regard to the duties of the Directorate—It is proposed to change the laws affecting *émigrés*—The civil commissaries in Switzerland and their depredations—Fresh accusations against Schérer—Merlin follows in Carnot's steps—Pius VI. at Briançon, then at Valence—Discouragement in Italy—Bernadotte begs an extension of his furlough—He is asked to come to Paris—Gouvion Saint-Cyr, Sainte-Suzanne, and Delmas—General affairs of the war—Sequel to Prince Charles's mistake—How he receives the news of the Rastadt assassination—His letter to Masséna—Military tactics of the Russians—Prejudices against François de Neufchâteau and Talleyrand—Ministerial changes—Gourlade—Anonymous letter inserted in *L'Ami des Lois*—Who was its author?—I complain loudly about it.

From the 20th Pluviôse to the 5th Ventôse, Year VII.—As foreseen by Championnet, the lazzaroni indulge in all kinds of excesses, and make a furious onslaught on the French troops entering Naples. Championnet's soldiers, nevertheless, advance into the heart of the city on the 23d Pluviôse, fighting their way through the streets, which become a scene of frightful butchery; however, victory remains with us. The King of Naples has embarked for Sicily on board an English ship. Mack has fled from the fury of his army and the Neapolitans, and has put himself into the hands of Championnet, who, respecting his misfortune, has contented himself with requiring him to withdraw in the rear of the army. Mack is, it is reported, in Rome. The Directorate orders that he be arrested and conveyed to Toulouse, where he is to remain a prisoner on parole.

Joubert has left the Army of Italy; Schérer is to take his place; the Army of Naples is to be under his orders. Schérer's place at the Ministry of War is filled by the general of brigade Milet-Mureau.

We have been censured for appointing Schérer to the command of the Army of Italy, and I do not in the least deny that this selection was perhaps reprehensible and unsatisfactory. The wars of the Revolution had so far been carried on by young men. We had justly criticised the intrusting of military commands to old men by foreign Powers, and we were now committing the very fault into which they had fallen. But it must be said in defence of the Directorate that the nursery of young generals created on the field of battle had been greatly thinned out. Hoche, best of them all, not excepting Bonaparte, was dead. The expedition to Egypt had deprived us of Kléber and many others. It has been seen how the rest of the men who had distinguished themselves in the wars had been utilized, or could not be utilized as a result of civil discords. Towering above the best we had retained was Bernadotte.

After the retreat of Joubert, when it had seemed decided that should war be renewed a heavy blow was to be struck in Italy, I thought of designating Bernadotte for that purpose, as he had already distinguished himself on that stage, and had been recalled and sent to Vienna only owing to the obsession of Bonaparte supported by the intrigue of Talleyrand. The Directorate, still imbued with the prejudices bequeathed to it by Bonaparte on his departure—prejudices which had been carefully nourished by Talleyrand—rejected my proposition in the first instance; but as the need of military talents—which governments would like to ignore, but with which they cannot dispense when they have to carry on a war—soon compelled them to come to terms, my colleagues agreed to allow me to offer the command-in-chief of the Army of Italy to Bernadotte.

Bernadotte inquired of me in the first place what would be the forces placed at his disposal. It was impossible for me to mention a greater number than actually existed, or an amount greater than the one we could really supply. Bernadotte said to me: "This will not suffice, for Italy is destined to experience the first shock. The Russians, who are reported to be on the march, will, should they reach their goal, begin operations in this quarter; Helvetia and the Rhine will not see war until subsequently." Bernadotte thereupon gave me the complete history of the Italian campaign from its very beginning. He demonstrated to me that it was a veritable mistake to imagine that Bonaparte had, during his two years of command, accomplished such great things with small means; that he had had enormous means at his disposal; that Kellermann, who had been looked upon as having done nothing, as being merely an ornamental general, had with his Army of the Alps constituted the bountiful rear-guard which had constantly provided the Army of Italy; that during these two years Kellermann had done nothing but review and send troops to the Minotaur, which had devoured the greater part of them, and was destined to devour many more hereafter, if but allowed to do so. "Bonaparte," he said, "has never ceased calling for more troops, and you, citizen Directors, have never ceased granting them to him. They amounted to something, did my 20,000 men of the Army of Sambre-et-Meuse, which I brought to him, and which he enjoyed causing to be called *messieurs* by the citizen soldiers of the Masséna and Augereau divisions. And yet I imagine that my boys of the Sambre-et-Meuse were as good citizens as those of either Masséna or Augereau. I think that they proved at the Tagliamento and Gradisca that they did not go in quest of the *citizens* to do their work. Our troops are excellent; they are the best in Europe; they possess every possible quality; with them it is possible to go to heaven or to hell. But there is a certain numerical force which cannot altogether be dispensed with in war, in view of the immense developments occurring nowadays, when a large extent of territory has to be guarded, fortified towns to be garrisoned, and a steady advance to battle maintained. You may rest assured, citizen Directors, that Bonaparte did not accomplish something with nothing; and although a man may not be, like him, an executioner of men, a certain quantity of troops is necessary and indispensable when he is face to face with bellicose nations incessantly renovated and constituting an actual deluge of population."

There was much picturesqueness, in accordance with his ordinary form of speech, in what Bernadotte was telling me, but at the same time a substratum of truth, of facts, and sound reasoning which could not be ignored. I asked him to put his remarks in writing, in order that I might lay them before the Directorate, so as to present his very ideas.

On the following day, just before the opening of the sitting, Bernadotte brought me in writing the observations he had promised me the day before. The document embodied the whole of his conversation, with the exception of what he had told me in regard to Bonaparte; it contained a series of facts, of deductions skilfully concatenated, a perfect exposition of all the requirements of the Army of Italy, an explanation of all the sites, an enumeration of all the fortified towns, a plan showing all the roads, a designation of the rivers and mountains, the physical and moral reason of everything that had been done on this vast stage, what could be done on it at this juncture, and the means necessary to insure success. It was one of the most logical, eloquent, and convincing documents I have ever perused in critical moments.

Full of the emotion I felt, I presented this remarkable work of Bernadotte's to my colleagues, who shared my feelings. The Minister of War was present, and had listened silently, as if assenting. "Well, citizen Minister, what have you to say to it?" we asked him. Schérer replied that something remained to be said; that there were many truths in Bernadotte's *exposé*, but also much that was theoretical, and which would have to stand the test of experience; that he considered he knew enough of the wars of the Revolution to know that they could still be carried on with the means remaining to us; moreover, that notwithstanding France's fecundity, nurseries of men could not be manufactured by merely stamping on the ground; that it was impossible to detach troops from the other armies; that the Army of Italy had all that the Government could and should give to it; and that, properly led by a good general, it could still win signal victories. "You would undertake its command on such terms?" inquired Merlin. "Yes, citizen Director," was Schérer's reply; "I would not refuse a burden I am seeking to place on other shoulders." "Well, then, why should you not yourself assume the command of the Army of Italy?" "Citizen Directors, I know but to obey." Thereupon two of us exclaim: "General Schérer is appointed commander of the Army of Italy." Thus it was that Schérer, on the impulse of the moment, was appointed commander of the Army of Italy upon the refusal of Bernadotte, who had declared that he could accept the command only on the conditions given, written, and signed by him. Rewbell and I did, it is true, make some remark as to Schérer's present condition. We considered him even more aged than he really was, by reason of the infirmities which would detract largely from his activity in a campaign.

In the midst of these difficult times both at home and abroad, the person of the Pope is a source of continual embarrassment to the Directorate. It is a phantom which may have some importance in the hands of those of our enemies who least believe in the holiness of the very Holy Father.

The Directorate demands that the Pope be handed over to us, for the purpose of being conveyed to Spain. It is alleged that he cannot endure the fatigue of travelling by carriage.

The Austrians are moving on a large scale. Jourdan, appointed general-in-chief of the three armies of the Danube, of Helvetia, and of Observation, is to occupy the centre; he is to command in person the Army of the Danube, Masséna that of Helvetia, and Bernadotte that of Observation. Jourdan is ordered to march forward and head off the Austrians. The Emperor has remained silent in regard to the advance of the Russians. Masséna is empowered to allow himself to be called by the Grisons, and to cause the Austrian commander to be notified that he must evacuate them; otherwise he will not enter that canton.

Merlin is furious against Schérer. The reason alleged for this is that the Minister of War has not given Mme. Villars, Merlin's mistress, certain presents she has asked for. And yet it was Talleyrand who had been commissioned by Merlin to commend Mme. Villars to Schérer; but it would seem that, pursuant to his custom, Talleyrand began by commending himself in this affair, and did not give the things expected by Mme. Villars the time to reach their destination. Merlin cannot submit to this disappointment, which has resulted in his being temporarily excluded from the good graces of Mme. Villars, and compelled to make all kinds of personal disbursements in order to make his peace with her; he indulges in personalities against Schérer, which Rewbell easily refutes. Proofs of his prevarication are necessary before accusing a Minister; we should gratefully accept them. "The proper time to have laid them before us," says Rewbell, "was when Schérer was there to reply, and not after he had left for the army." Rewbell adds that a love of peace alone prevents him from divulging circumstances too painful for the Directorate to listen to, and which would probably compel it to take sides against the accuser of our colleague. As usual, Merlin ends by chiming in with us all. He would in the first place have liked to have seen the command of the Army of Italy taken away from Schérer and given to Muller, a creature of Mme. Villars. The new Pompadour or Du Barry has a poor mouthpiece for support. Unable to prevent the appointment of Milet-Mureau to the Ministry of War, Merlin has, as usual, ended in voting for him. Merlin goes about saying that Rewbell and I have caused Schérer to be appointed to the command of the Army of Italy, whereas it has been seen that Rewbell and I opposed this appointment owing to our misgivings in regard to the age and health of General Schérer.

Merlin believes he is avenged of his failures by securing the appointment of civil commissary at Turin for one Senover, a creature of his.

Discord makes fresh progress in the bosom of the Directorate. Rewbell is with me in seeking to preserve the harmony so necessary among the members of the chief authority of the Republic towards which all eyes are turned; but our efforts are singularly thwarted by Merlin, who, like Carnot, Barthélemy, and Letourneur, is in his turn stricken with a fit of panic in connection with his message of the 18th Floréal. At each sitting he presents enactments calling for dismissals. As the preponderating opinion is always his, and he believes that nowadays the Royalist opinion shows strength, he acts accordingly. Thus it is a mistaken idea to call him either a Royalist or a terrorist, for Merlin is nothing; he is merely timorous and weak, and it is because he is weak that he is often wicked. Ever since the law of the suspects of the 17th of September, 1793, to the present time (end of Pluviôse, Year VII.), he has been, and most probably at a later period he will be, no less wicked should other *régimes* call his malignant genius to their aid.

Several individuals sentenced to transportation, among others the deputies Gau, Dumolard, Lomont, Boissy-d'Anglas, Villaret, Siméon, Paradis, Muraire, Mailhe, Doumerc, and the ex-Minister of Police Cochon, take advantage of the favor shown them by the enactment of the Directorate of the 28th Nivôse, and proceed to the Île d'Oléron, to avoid having their names placed on the list of *émigrés*. Shortly afterwards the deputies Pastoret, Duplantin, and Noailles likewise go thither.

From the 5th to the 10th Ventôse, Year VII.— At the very time that an almost universal war demands fresh resources wherewith to meet the most urgent needs, the Government sees itself deprived of the ordinary resources on which it is entitled to depend principally; the salt-tax is rejected by the Council of Ancients. Its deputies at their last meeting, held at the residence of Larevellière-Lépeaux, had foreshadowed this in their conversation. It was, indeed, possible to agree with them up to a certain point, but not absolutely, for if the most productive taxes are those which are portioned out among the generality of the citizens, great attention should be paid to those that have that effect; they must not be suffered to become onerous and unbearable; on the contrary, from the very reason that they fall on all classes, efforts should be made to render them lighter, in order not to sacrifice the classes which would be crushed by them, while the same taxes would not be felt by the other classes.

Now that Championnet has by his skilful manœuvring and intrepidity so gloriously terminated his Neapolitan campaign with 8000 against more than 80,000 men, it is alleged that he lacks both character and deportment for so important a mission. It is true that the victorious general has offended the cupidity and vanity of the civil commissioners. The latter allege that they have claimed nothing but the rights of the civil power in view of the encroachments and ramifications of the military power. The Directorate, taking this point of view, lays the blame on Championnet, and has ordered his recall, his arrest, and his trial. The upright, generous, and too frank conqueror is succeeded by one of his lieutenants, who before and since the opening of the campaign has not ceased intriguing against his general-in-chief. This sycophant, by dint of underhand manœuvres, has succeeded in casting doubts on the ability of Championnet and building his own reputation on the ruins of his chief's. And yet Macdonald, accustomed to believe himself or to make others believe him to be an able man, is at best but a Talleyrand, to whom it would be easy to compare him morally and physically in more than one respect: the same pallid complexion, a stiff neck, the face in the air like the nose; the same vague, haughty, insignificant, and incomprehensible expression; a silent, mysterious, and phlegmatic demeanor; the most composed stiffness, akin to immobility itself. Macdonald, like Talleyrand, would be more suitably dressed in ecclesiastical garb than in military uniform.

Jourdan has crossed the Rhine, and taken up his position beyond the Black Mountains. We impatiently await news from Masséna. He must have occupied the Grisons in the case of the Austrians having refused to evacuate that canton. Fresh Russian columns are, like the first, marching towards the French frontier, and great movements of troops are taking place in Germany.

Charles Théodore, Elector of the Palatinate and of Bavaria, has just died at the age of seventy-five years. The Duke of Zweibrücken, Maximilian Joseph, aged forty-three, succeeds him. The death of the Bavarian causes uneasiness to several Powers, some of whom assert that the successor is a friend of the French. Prussia and Austria seek to estrange him from us; but his first acts, explained to us by his envoy, lead us to hope that he will pronounce himself in favor of France. Will his position leave him free to do as he pleases? Prussia still affects neutrality, and adopts no definite course; she singularly dreads an alliance between the Emperor and France. The Emperor of Russia develops symptoms of insanity.

Our position in regard to Spain is as badly represented as it is little understood by our ambassador. Guillemardet, as bad a diplomat as he is an ignorant doctor, has succeeded Truguet at Madrid, and commits acts of awkwardness at a post which calls simply for a little deportment.

Guillemardet, who has never seen such good times, has imagined that he was going to find everywhere the familiarity of our ways in the Convention. He is ignorant of the fact that gravity and dignity are most compatible with Republican manners. Franklin, while at the Court of Louis XVI., set the example to be followed in this respect. He was the shrewdest and most dignified of the diplomats of his day. His was the task of winning over a monarchy to a newly born Republic—one whose steps were undoubtedly very uncertain in its early days. He attained his object without having betrayed his simplicity or modified the frankness of his character. Besides character and frankness, wit is also required in order to use these natural means in an authoritative way. Now this is just what our former colleague Guillemardet lacked above all things. It has been seen that his selection was one more of those we owe Merlin. Guillemardet has committed all the improprieties which do harm to intercourse between ambassador and government. Having learned that Truguet was far advanced in intimacy with the Queen of Spain, Guillemardet has thought it proper that he should in his turn take a part in the affairs of the inner Cabinet by being gallant to the old Queen and boorish to the old King. This was just the way to set everybody against himself. By everything that Guillemardet has so far done wrong as regards his mission he has more than deserved to be dismissed. Merlin succeeds in getting him retained at his post. Sieyès at Berlin, Reinhard and Belleville in Italy, are the only diplomatic agents showing themselves able, worthy of their functions, and suitably representing the Republic.

The *corps législatif* is divided in an unfortunate fashion. The impending elections are disturbing men's minds. The repeated dismissals of Republican officials cool the ardor of the patriots, thus favoring Royalist hopes. Discontent becomes general. Treilhard displays his ill-temper more and more; he is, alone, more violent than all the past and present members of the Directorate. We are nearing a terrible reaction. There is not a good citizen who is not charged with being an anarchist. What deputies will the elections bring forth? Friends of the Republic? Where are they to be found, if indeed any still exist? What support are they receiving? Fresh troubles are brewing. They encourage the belief, which our enemies are seeking to spread, that it is impossible to establish a representative government. The Directorate might ward off the catastrophes with which we are threatened by turning a deaf ear to the voice of passion, by welcoming and utilizing all talents, by governing without allowing itself to be disturbed by events, and pursuing the even tenor of its course without turning round to see or listen to attacks in no way to be feared, were the authorities to remain united among themselves.

From the 10th to the 24th Ventôse, Year VII.

Hostilities have begun with marked success in Helvetia; they are about to begin on the Rhine and in Italy. The Directorate has too long delayed proposing war, which was inevitable; it is declared with acclamation by the two Councils.

Rewbell and I are subjected to the calumnies of a party which seeks, so it says, "to oust us." It would seem that Merlin is no stranger to these instigations; we have beyond doubt entered upon a struggle with him; he is forever scribbling and writing out dismissals, and persists in bringing them to us for our signatures. We tell him that such measures, by introducing disorganization, lead to anarchy.

In addition to this, Merlin worries us with his annoying interference in matters of administration. I am told that he is undermining me personally in all kinds of ways unworthy of any man having any respect for himself. He knows that I have caused General Guidal to be appointed commandant of the *École militaire*, and that this officer, who comes from my part of the country, is particularly dear to me. He has him brought into his presence, together with Mme. Guidal, by the deputy Mathieu de l'Oise, who is doubtless unaware of the use he is being put to. He asks them if I have concerned myself about their fortune, adding that it would be a very easy matter for me to do so, considering the wealth I possess; he speaks to them of my splendid dinners, of my expenses at Grosbois, and of my large retinue, which is that of a lord. "Since Barras does not concern himself about them, he will do so himself; he is fond of military men; he is their protector, and always defends them much more than does Barras, whose Provençal whims and sallies he little heeds." To convince Mme. Guidal of the interest he takes in her, Merlin is gallant enough to say he would like to pay her a visit at her residence—in the evening of course, needless to say, in the absence of her husband. On learning that Merlin is to call on her the next day, I send my aide-de-camp Avy to her house; she places him behind a screen. "I am going," says Merlin, "to give you a proof, *citoyenne*, of the interest I bear you. The Minister of Police is at my beck and call, and consequently I can dispose of the gambling-houses, which are under his control. I abandon the Royalist Milet-Mureau to the Triumvirate; as to Schérer, he is the accomplice of Rewbell."

Merlin had sat down with rapture by the side of

Mme. Guidal, edging closer towards her as he spoke, when all of a sudden he hears a loud noise. It was the sword of my aide-de-camp Avy, which had fallen to the floor. Merlin is frightened out of his wits, and tremblingly inquires, "What is happening? Where am I then?" "Fear nothing," says Mme. Guidal, "something has fallen down which an orderly left behind him." Merlin's fears are not quieted; it grieves him to take such sudden leave of Mme. Guidal, and he begs her to accompany him to his carriage, which he has left at the gate of the *École militaire.* Had I heard of all this from the lips of Mme. Guidal only, I might have thought she was embellishing a tale; but the words and particulars related to me by my aide-de-camp harmonized in every respect with Mme. Guidal's version. She told in a laughing voice that the large, protruding teeth of Merlin had, just as he was seeking to become amiable, frightened her as much as the falling of Avy's sword had frightened Merlin. General Guidal was likewise sought out by my colleague, and had several talks with him, afterwards warning me to beware of an enemy all the more dangerous because he was hidden. About the same time I was given a document in the handwriting of Merlin, which might have implicated him in a hardly honorable transaction in regard to a contract for army supplies. I did not make any use of it, but I owe it to truth not to make such an assertion without producing the document.[1]

From the 24th Ventôse to the 11th Germinal, Year VII.—Jourdan has crossed the Rhine, and is to

[1] I have been unable to find this document in the papers of M. de Saint-Albin.—G. D.

advance against the Prince Charles, but he is merely groping about, while imagining himself full of a resolution which does not form part of his character; he is beyond doubt sincerely devoted to the Republic, but he lives in dread of compromising himself, and does not know how to take quick advantage of circumstances. Masséna feels nettled at being placed under the orders of Jourdan; still, the latter is his senior, and up to the present time his superior, from the importance of the military achievements with which his name is coupled. The Directorate commissions me to write to the two generals, to restore harmony between them.

Masséna has entered the Grisons, where he has made seven or eight thousand Austrians prisoners, together with their general. Jourdan has attacked the Austrian posts, without at first encountering any resistance. I confess that I greatly fear that this is merely a ruse to make our army advance without sufficient precaution. And indeed our vanguard is soon afterwards attacked; General Lefebvre, after prodigies of valor, as is his wont, is wounded; several demi-brigades and regiments cover themselves with glory, but are overwhelmed by numbers. A heavy fog clears away, and Jourdan, seeing the immense line of the enemy, gives orders for a retreat, which, if indispensable, he might have facilitated by supporting his vanguard. Had Jourdan immediately brought all his forces to bear on the Austrian left, he could yet have turned and defeated them; such rapid movements are proper to the French, and have ever stood them in good stead. Assuming even that he had not beaten the Austrians, Jourdan could still have easily joined our

Army of Helvetia, which was under his supreme command. Such a reunion would have enabled him to resume the offensive in a very short while, especially if the Prince Charles penetrated into the mountains and sought the bank of the Rhine. Instead of manœuvring thus, Jourdan has entered the passes of the Black Mountains, and the *début* of the campaign of the Year VII. is a retreat. Unfortunate beginning! Sinister presage!

Meanwhile Bernadotte has acted promptly and skilfully with the corps of observation he commands on the Bas-Rhin. He has taken Mannheim, and occupies excellent positions. He has issued proclamations full of vigor to his army, which he has thus fired; but his troops are far from numbering the thirty thousand we had promised him; his staffs are not filled, while nothing but untrained recruits are sent to him. It requires all Bernadotte's talent to make something of them. And yet, with this phantom of an army, Bernadotte succeeds in temporarily commanding the respect of his troops. But, after having struggled successfully for some months with his army, which existed on paper only, Bernadotte, seeing that the brunt of the battle is to be in Helvetia, refuses to remain at a post where he cannot reap the highest glory, and sends us his resignation. The Directorate suppresses the Army of Observation, which, barring its commander—who has done something and given it the semblance of an existence—is really nothing else but a surfeit of staff. Bernadotte retires to the country-house of one of his aides-de-camp (since Marshal Maison) on the banks of the Simmeren.

From the 11th Germinal to the 2d Floréal, Year

VII.—The Théâtre-Français, recently renamed the Odéon, has been destroyed by fire. Those who are fond of detecting an ill omen in everything that happens, hold that the burning of a building in such close proximity to the Luxembourg forebodes no good. Others say boldly that the Directorate, in order to better isolate itself and not be exposed to the wrath of a large popular gathering, has itself caused the Odéon to be fired, so as to clear the avenues to the palace. This way of viewing the simplest things shows the disposition of the people towards the Government, and especially that which the enemies of the Directorate were kindling against us.

The General-in-Chief of the Army of the Danube, Jourdan, writes to the Directorate that several officers, among them d'Hautpoul, Decaen, and others, have not seconded him in his efforts. "The former," he says, "did not charge the enemy's cavalry when it debouched into the open. The latter has dared to censure my conduct and impugn my authority." Jourdan's letter is saddening, as it indicates that he has lost the confidence of his army; he asks to be allowed to appear before the Directorate in order to enlighten it as to what is going on in the army. The Directorate authorizes Jourdan's proceeding to Paris. His command is temporarily given to Masséna. The latter is instructed to gather together all his forces for an attack upon the Austrians. The Army of Observation had been previously suppressed, in order to reinforce Jourdan with the few demi-brigades composing it. Bernadotte had not made any difficulty about serving under his former chief of the Sambre-et-Meuse; it would seem that he is not as well disposed to be under the orders of Masséna, whose rival he has been at all times; and it is known that military rivalry oftentimes constitutes well-defined hatred.

At last Macdonald, who for a long time has yearned for a chief command, is at the height of his ambition; he has taken the place of Championnet. The latter, who has left Naples to proceed to Milan, pursuant to an order of the Directorate, has been arrested in that town by the ex-Minister Schérer, now in command of the Army of Italy. He is court-martialled for having suspended the action and authority of the civil commissioner of the Directorate attached to his army. The arrest and bringing to trial of Bassal, the former secretary of the Roman Consulate and of Championnet, is likewise decided upon. Bassal is, moreover, charged with pilfering at the time of the retreat of the French army.

Insurrections have broken out in various parts of the kingdom of Naples. Discontent reigns in the Roman State, as it is completely ruined; the Army of Naples may be cut off, should Schérer meet with reverses compelling him to retreat. On the other hand, the Prince Charles, on seeing Jourdan's retreat and the discouragement of his army at this false measure, finds himself free to direct considerable forces towards Italy, or penetrate into Helvetia, leaving behind a portion of his army to keep the French in check in the Black Mountains. As is customary with him, the King of Prussia awaits the issue of the opening of the campaign, so as to make doubly sure to which side victory will fly. The Elector of the Palatinate, who was to receive the support of Prussia, sees his dominions invaded by Austria, who occupies them. We learn from letters that England is meditating a descent into Holland, where she has many partisans. Admiral de Winter and General Daendels proclaim themselves to be sincere friends of the Republic.

At home the foreigner is fomenting agitation, while the Government increases the number of malcontents by fresh dismissals. Changes should be made after due reflection and with moderation; the Republican Government should deal severely only with convicted intriguers. The impending election of a member of the Directorate adds fuel to the prevailing agitation. Some wish to see Sieyès elected, others Abrial, Le Carlier, etc. It is not the best-equipped man, or the one who offers the best pledges in the matter of ability and probity, whom it is sought to call to the Government; it is the one who is believed to harmonize best with the passions of the party selecting him.

A great operation is about to be carried out: Admiral Bruix, the most distinguished of surviving naval officers, has gone to Brest to take the twenty-four ships and sail for the Mediterranean; he has orders to avoid an engagement, to give assistance to Malta and Corfu, and to land a few troops and provisions in Egypt. Having accomplished this, he is to give battle to English, Portuguese, Russian, and Turkish squadrons in the Mediterranean; this done, he is to retire to Toulon. The Directorate has commissioned me to lay before him the plan of this expedition, which, it will be remembered, I was the first to conceive. If Bruix is seconded, his mission will be productive of great advantages; his forces are superior to those opposed to him.

It has been seen that Jourdan had, immediately upon his first reverses, intrenched himself in the Black Mountains. This general, who is capable of military conceptions, and brave beyond doubt, like every Frenchman, lacks great daring, and is ever fearful of being beaten, so he is necessarily bound to be frequently defeated. Had he rejoined Masséna, it is more than probable that he would have triumphed over the enemy.

Schérer has been partly successful on the Adige, but no striking advantages are to be expected from his command, although he is perhaps the best equipped and one of the ablest men of our period: on the one hand, his age and the infirmities besetting him do not leave him the necessary activity to put his plans into execution; while, on the other, many prejudices are at work against him. A general despised by public opinion cannot exercise any ascendency over his army.

The successive and various mutilations to which the *corps législatif* has been subjected seem to have deprived electoral movements of all life. The elections display a sad state of apathy. Few citizens have taken part in the primary assemblies. The public spirit is dead, and the Government has declared itself too strongly against alleged anarchy not to give the Royalist party the idea of making common cause with it, and determining the selection of those whom they consider most proper to foment the dissensions they are meditating. A strange abuse is made of the word "anarchist" when applying it indiscriminately to all patriots. The new-born Republic can maintain itself only by the union of the Directorate with the immense number of Frenchmen who love it. Such is the state of discouragement and the lack of confidence nowadays that people say: "It matters little to me: the Government and the Councils favor our enemies; they are delivering us up to their slaughterers in various parts of France." In our debates at the Directorate I am continually compelled to repeat to Merlin what I was wont to repeat to Carnot previous to the 18th

Fructidor—that the small number of men dubbed anarchists could be easily won back to moderate opinions, and that the erroneous course pursued by the Directorate increases the number of our enemies. I again and again tell my colleagues that we have to defend ourselves against royalty and nearly the whole of Europe, and that in order to withstand such an attack we need all the courage of our united fellow-citizens; that so formidable a coalition is to be repulsed only by dint of sheer strength, which is to be found in the people alone—in short, that you cannot establish a republic if you mean to dispense with Republicans.

It is with pain that I see that the system which should be pursued to ally all against the common enemy is no more observed by the military than by the civilian class. The harshest and most inexorable methods are employed in calling out the conscripts, who nevertheless, of the purest French blood, compose the flower of the population. The Minister of War informs us that an unfortunate hunchback, belonging to one of the Belgian departments, has several times been arrested, dragged from prison to prison as a conscript, when his patent infirmity had secured his exemption in due form from military service. Merlin finds additional reasons why the wretched hunchback should be made to enter the ranks. It seems to me that I can hear the Swiss who, ordered to bury the dead after a battle, and considering he should treat the wounded similarly, said with naïve abruptness: "To listen to them, not one of them ought to be buried." I vainly oppose the rigors of Merlin; I call to my aid the spirit of the law in its execution; we must avoid being compared to the Committee of Public Safety, which ended in becoming tyrannical by progressive acts of the most extreme rigor. Our unjust deeds, already guilty in themselves, will also serve admirably the party opposed to us in the Councils. If we deviate from the constitutional line, we set an example which is bound to react against us. The Directorate lends an attentive ear to my remarks; I see that my colleagues are becoming seriously uneasy as to our situation; still nothing is done to ameliorate it, to reassure the *corps législatif*, which it is sought to imbitter by impressing it with the belief that the Directorate is meditating fresh *coups d'état*. 'If the Government wishes to be strong and respected, it should, I go on to say, be Republican and just; passions should be silenced; the Republic's friends should be protected; all prejudices and denunciations should cease. Will it be believed that these simple remarks draw forth the following reply from Merlin: "You are forever giving support to the wearers of Phrygian caps who seek to kill the Directorate"?

The King of Prussia once more assures us that he will remain neutral: I have stated that personally I placed little faith in that wheedler, who will keep his word if we win signal triumphs; in the contrary case he will make common cause with our enemies.

Tuscany is occupied by our troops. It is proposed to despatch a messenger to Schérer with orders to arrest the grand-duke and his family, and convey them as hostages to Briançon. The measure is adopted after a debate extending over several sittings; our orders will reach their destination too late, and we shall thus be spared a fresh embarrassment. I prefer, in every way and in anticipation of all possible events, that such hostages should be held far away from us, rather than be close at hand and dependent on all the fluctuations of politics.

Italy is in a deplorable condition. Cruel exactions have

stirred up the people to rebellion. Our army is in the midst of all these elements. Masséna is to assume temporarily the chief command of the Army of the Danube; he has not yet developed his talents on so large a scale as Jourdan, but he has more daring.

Prince Charles, who has just beaten Jourdan, has no more taken advantage of his victory than he has deserved it. He has allowed the French army to retreat towards the Rhine, when he could disperse it by cutting it in twain, attacking it in the rear, and capturing all its artillery. Jourdan has committed the twofold blunder of having abandoned his army too soon, and especially of having had himself replaced, even temporarily, by Ernouf, his chief of staff—a personage whom he always keeps at his side by reason of his servility, but who certainly possesses no other merits than his baseness and corruption.

The Directorate orders that all fortified towns on the Rhine be placed in a state of defence; Masséna, after having strongly garrisoned them, is to despatch to Switzerland all available troops; he is to threaten the Austrians from the Tyrol to Bâle, while waiting for the reinforcements which we are going to send him to enable him to resume the offensive.

The instructions sent to the General-in-chief of the Army of Italy are to feign attacks on the enemy's front, threaten it at all points, and assail it at a single one. Instead of carrying out this plan and turning his adversary with considerable forces, Schérer has attacked the enemy between Verona and Legnago, an operation which, even if successful, could not give great results; it is, moreover, easily seen from these first engagements that the ardor of the military chiefs is beginning to slacken; they have acquired wealth, and Bonaparte, by loading them with riches, has made so many laggards of them. Schérer takes up defensive positions; this is the only method of waging war suitable to his age and infirmities. The Directorate is once more censured for having given him the command of so important an army. Merlin and Treilhard believe that everything can be remedied by dismissals, both military and civil; that, in order to fill the ranks, the conscription of 200,000 men must be carried out with greater severity. Just so many pretexts for the enemies of the Government to attack us in all directions, especially when our armies are beaten; for the military glory acquired by us in our earlier years has established as a principle that the French Government can maintain itself only by victories.

2d Floréal, Year VII. — Marshal Suvaroff has received from Paul I. the command of 80,000 Russians, who are to act with the Austrians against us. The Russian has reached Verona, where Generals Kray and Melas tender him the general command of the army.

Considering the condition of Italy, would it not be advisable to evacuate Naples and Rome, after having placed in authority the men who have shown the greatest patriotic ardor and the deepest hatred of their former masters, and to send thither officers who are on the retired list, with orders to organize bodies of troops capable of imposing respect and revolutionizing the country? The inhabitants should be assured of the return of the Republican army, which should indeed come back immediately after having defeated the Austrians. The uniting of 30,000 men withdrawn from Naples and Rome with the Army of Italy would undoubtedly compel the enemy once more to cross the Mincio and the Adige. The usefulness and urgency of these measures are not understood by my colleagues, before whom I persistently lay them. Yet the General-in-chief of the Army of Italy is authorized, in case of absolute necessity, to end matters by an evacuation.

Larevellière inveighs strongly against Joubert, charging him with having disorganized the Army of Italy. Larevellière is mistaken: the disorganization is due not to Joubert, an able soldier and a man of noble character, who has done his best, but to the intrigues and rivalries of the civil commissaries, who, beginning with M. Trouvé, an intimate and creature of Larevellière's, have incessantly sowed discord; they have compelled the interference of the Directorate, which, at so great a distance and amid so many covert denunciations, has perhaps been deceived as to the really guilty, and has, in the first place, punished the innocent. Larevellière cannot listen quietly to these remarks, and flies into a rage, which is appeased only because we laugh over it.

Schérer asks to be allowed to return; he designates Moreau as his successor. The Directorate confirms his choice; Moreau is perhaps not altogether a stranger to the intrigues which have paralyzed Schérer.

Larevellière is entirely devoted to Merlin, who cajoles and dazzles him by the promptitude and the quantity of his work. Now that I see serious dissensions established in the Directorate, I do not intend to inveigh against Merlin as he has inveighed against Rewbell. It is quite enough to have made one 18th Fructidor, and I have not the slightest desire to begin another. If possible, I shall work harmoniously with Merlin, in order to thwart the common enemies of the Republic.

Jourdan, wishing to prove to us that he can act with firmness in difficult moments, has dismissed

Generals d'Hautpoul and Vandamme, who did not obey with sufficient promptitude on the day of the battle of Stockach; he attributes to them the check he has received. It is proposed to bring d'Hautpoul and Vandamme to trial. Roberjot denounces them, and the German newspapers are unanimous in censuring their conduct. The retreat of Jourdan is laid at their door. Treilhard and Merlin clamor for their trial. As for myself, I am of opinion that, considering present circumstances, we should be less precipitate in adopting such a course towards soldiers who have rendered distinguished services to the Fatherland, and who may still do yeoman's work in defence of the Republic. I therefore cause the motion to be postponed until such time as the Minister of Foreign Affairs shall have laid before us the letters accusing them. Nevertheless, Decaen and d'Hautpoul are court-martialled for insubordination. Treilhard and Merlin insist that the Directorate shall proceed with rigor; they are blind to the fact that the persecution of the most experienced officers leads to the disorganization of armies, and that we are in the presence of the enemy.

From the 5th to 8th Floréal, Year VII.

The Minister of Marine, Bruix, left yesterday to take command of the great fleet. A despatch-boat is sent after him, to instruct him to fight if the enemy persists in following him; otherwise he would risk being placed between two fires on reaching the Strait of Gibraltar.

Our plenipotentiaries at Rastadt express fears as to their safety; they ask to be recalled. The Directorate orders them to remain at their post.

Merlin in vain demands the erasure from the list of *émigrés* of Digeon and Albigez, priests in the department of Aude.

From the 12th to the 27th Floréal, Year VII.—Schérer reaps the consequences of his ill-calculated attack; he retreats in disorder, abandoning his artillery and stores. The French army has taken up an unfortunate position behind the Ticino, and will doubtless shortly abandon it in order to cross the Po again; it is to be feared that, in the state of confusion in which the army finds itself, we shall not be able to keep open our communications with Italy, and shall lose the passage of the Apennines.

It has been seen that the greatest military butcher of modern times, Suvaroff, has taken command of the enemy's troops. This great sacrificer of men will soon be seen at work.

The Directorate appoints Schérer inspector-general of the troops in Holland; he is one of those who best understand this branch of the service. General Frégeville, who is far from being as capable as Schérer, but who is upright and brave, is appointed inspector of the cavalry of the Army of England. The Frégeville whereof I speak is the elder of two brothers, both cavalry officers. The other is known by his connections of pleasure and interest with the brothers Bonaparte. I am not aware that he is distinguished in any other way.

The order to evacuate Italy is despatched, but very late. The patriots who wish to follow the French army are to be protected and to receive assistance; a like measure is adopted in regard to the Cisalpines.

Treilhard is beginning to admit that Ancelot and other agents have committed malversations while with the Army of Italy; he moves that they be brought to trial; he is informed that it would be necessary to bring to trial the whole of the administrative staffs of our armies. At last, on my motion, the Directorate decides that 15,000 men shall be detached from the Army of Helvetia to join that of Italy, and that troops shall likewise be despatched to the latter from home.

Previous to this arrangement, the idea had been entertained of ordering Masséna to attack—a dangerous measure, which, had he been beaten, would have thrown open to the enemy our Swiss frontier. In conformity with my advice, the plan of an immediate attack has been abandoned. Masséna will, for the time being, content himself with defensive operations.

We receive by despatch the appalling news of

an event for which no precedent is to be found in the annals of any civilized community. The Republic's envoys to Rastadt, the deputies Bonnier, Roberjot, and Jean de Bry, have been assassinated by a detachment of Austrian troops, the Szecklers Hussars, almost under the very walls of Rastadt. Bonnier and Roberjot are dead; Jean de Bry, covered with wounds, has miraculously survived. Will such a crime, by exciting a universal sentiment of horror and indignation, at least stir up the energy which should punish its authors? After imparting the news of the crime to the *corps législatif*, the Directorate presents to the foreign ambassadors in Paris a declaration compelling them to pronounce their horror of the deed. Azara has signed it. Sandos-Rollin takes it, promising to sign it. Staël has demanded his passports for Sweden.

Historians, when subsequently relating the various circumstances connected with this unheard-of crime, seeking its cause and attempting to discover its authors, have been divided upon the question, variously attributing the crime to the English Cabinet, the soul of the new coalition, to Queen Caroline of Naples and her favorite Minister Acton (at the time with her a fugitive in Vienna), and to the Austrian Ministry. If, after the usual presumption, the crime is to be laid at the door of him who derives advantage from it, the probability is to be found in the motives of the three culprits I have just named. It was in the interests of the English Cabinet, in order to maintain the new coalition it had cemented, to render impossible all *rapprochement* between France and the members of the coalition, England's stipendiaries. The Queen of Naples, driven out of her kingdom, and ever the implacable enemy of the Republic, of which her sister Marie-Antoinette had been the queen, brought to bear in this connection a fury inflamed by her desperate position. The Austrian Government, which the policy of the Directorate had rather skilfully detached from the interests of the empire, was eager to become acquainted with all the means by which the French negotiators had hitherto deprived Austria of many of her supports. Such are the presumptions which history may admit as proofs, by adding to them the many auxiliary circumstances mixed up with modern war, and which make it a distinct kind of war, by reason of the passions that inspire it, and of the question which these have put to the belligerents on either side—the "To be or not to be" of Hamlet. Historians who claim to have reached the final limits of discovery, and who have been credited with great sagacity, have asserted that the Szecklers Hussars, who are known to have been the assassins, were in no wise the soldiers of that corps so highly esteemed in war, but French *émigrés* who had disguised themselves with its uniform. One thing is certain—that, after all that has been said and written on the subject, the humane utterances of the Archduke Charles did not result in securing the detection of the crime, that Austria never gave any lucid explanation, and that the papers of the legation, carried away by the assassins, and turned over by them to the Vienna Cabinet, have never been returned to France.

The Directorate issues a manifesto to all nations and all governments. The ferocity of the Austrian Government warns Republicans of the fate in store for them at the hands of monarchs should these be triumphant.

The Clichy Club, looked upon as dead since the 18th Fructidor, has again begun its manœuvres, influencing everything; nowadays it assumes popular colors. This is the club which foments discord between the *corps législatif* and the Directorate, as well as among the patriots, and it has become formidable owing to our state of weakness and disunion. We are informed that as a forlorn hope a deputy in the tribune is to call for the impeachment of Merlin, Schérer, and Rewbell, to be followed by that of Barras; libels have been prepared, money scattered, and again there is talk of proclaiming the Constitution of '93. Gibbets are once more to be erected, and the members of the Government are to be the first to try them.

General Moreau is appointed to the command of the Army of Italy in the place of Schérer. If Moreau succeeds, all the honor will be his; should he meet with reverses, all the blame will fall on the Directorate, which has designated him as a partisan of Pichegru's. It was but yesterday that Pichegru, Joubert, Brune, and Bernadotte were called scoundrels and anarchists by Treilhard. I confer with many members of the *corps législatif* who come to me apparently in good faith; they seem to me convinced of the necessity of union in order to save the Republic. I convey to my colleagues the expression of all sentiments likely to reassure and quiet them; I entreat them to remember the high regard in which the Directorate was held at the time of its installation, when it showed itself united. Division had weakened it, and driven off the Republicans, without whom triumph over its enemies was impossible. I entreat my colleagues to ponder and to adopt the indispensable measures which the Constitution offers us, in order once more to place the Republic and its essential institutions on the pedestal of glory attained at the cost of so many sacrifices. Fear kills governments as well as men; in the present instance it caused the Directorate to turn a deaf ear to my words.

18th Floréal, Year VII.—A new proposition is made to the Directorate—that of ridding itself of the erasure of the *émigrés*, and of closing the list. I would eagerly adopt such a measure, had the list of *émigrés* and the legislation in this connection been drawn up with more discernment both as regards men and things; but during the National Convention, and towards its close, a number of southern patriots were inscribed on that list; some have been killed, the survivors ruined; it is time to break what is a terrible weapon in the hands of the factions. In lieu of finishing or consecrating their legislation, we should, on the contrary, reform it. It would be tantamount to restoring life to so many affairs now checked; it is time to organize liberty and frame less severe laws in regard to citizens who go abroad. Postponed.

Two civil commissaries are in Switzerland, and are harassing that unfortunate country; it is moved to recall them; Rewbell secures the postponement of the matter.

Denunciations continue pouring in against Schérer, at whose door are laid all our reverses in Italy. I advise the ex-Minister to retire to the country. Although the sincerity of his intentions may be a most legitimate defence in this matter, still it behooves him to pay some heed to public opinion in regard to a great calamity, and at least not to defy it.

Merlin, Carnot's successor, but lacking the latter's talent, comes every day, as did his predecessor, and brings us little bulletins against the Republicans, whom he calls anarchists.

From the 20th to the 27th Floréal, Year VII.—Pope Pius VI. is conveyed to Briançon by order of the Directorate. He is accompanied by a few archbishops and bishops. He is quartered at the General Hospital, where a suitable apartment has been prepared for him; in a little while he is removed to Valence.

General Moreau is occupying positions from Turin to Genoa; he is impatiently awaiting his junction with the Army of Naples. If Macdonald arrives, and the two generals come to an understanding, they will be in a position to cope with the enemy. Turin, Mantua, and Coni are, it is said, provisioned. The dissensions among the leaders of the troops, the disrepute into which Schérer has fallen, have in less than a fortnight destroyed the fruits of so much glorious labor.

Steps are taken to render secure and fortify the towns and defiles in the Alps. In accordance with my motion, it is determined to establish a camp at a short distance from Lyons and one at Antwerp.

A portion of the Cisalpine Directorate and *corps législatif* has gone over to the enemy; the deplorable condition of Italy is due to Trouvé's administration. This man, of churlish character and narrow views, has so worried and tired the people that he has driven them to the point of despair. The civil agents have fled and returned to France with their plunder, and the people of Italy, whose independence we created, are abandoned to their executioners. The Directorate would have warded off all these misfortunes if, frankly taking up the new question of the organization of a great Italian republic, it had declared its policy. A policy which would have united all would have been in itself sufficient to defend itself against the whole coalition.

In Helvetia Masséna is maintaining his reputation for defensive warfare, with which he is thoroughly acquainted. Bernadotte is still in retirement at Simmern, whence he writes to us for a furlough: Achilles sulking in his tent. In the first instance the Directorate writes to Bernadotte denying his request; but, the Army of Observation having been suppressed, I am of opinion that we can no longer keep him there, nailed to a post which has ceased to exist. Moreover, circumstances are becoming every instant more difficult, and it is not a matter of indifference to have one's friends at one's side. Bernadotte writes and causes to be told to me that he is "the best among my friends; that his bowels yearn for me; that he presses me to his heart." Moreover, when in command of the Army of Observation he displayed a patriotism more decided than ever, and revealed talents deserving a larger field. I rather like Bernadotte; I enjoy loving this Gascon who says he loves me, this Gascon who is not very strict about keeping his promises, but who promises so gracefully. In spite of Merlin and Treilhard, I succeed in having it decided that Bernadotte may return to Paris. My beloved colleagues greatly dread his presence.

General Gouvion Saint-Cyr has, at my request, just been employed in Italy. Sainte-Suzanne has left the army, as also Delmas, wounded. Discord is making rapid strides among our best generals; our apathy and our reverses are emboldening the coalition. Information is laid against deputies who are in communication with the foreigner; in order to avoid the danger attendant upon letter-writing, when feathering their own nests, they prefer making their own journeys. The enemies of the Republic no longer conceal their hope of avenging the 18th Fructidor. Everything is done to discourage the conscripts, while the Treasury again has recourse to its system of throwing obstacles in our way, just as it did previous to the 18th Fructidor. Hence money, arms, and provisions are all lacking everywhere at once. In the midst of all this our Minister of War informs us with charming candor that he is busy seeing to his daughter's wedding. Prussia is trying to pick a quarrel with us about the boundary. The Courts of Vienna and St. Petersburg are seeking to have our ambassador dismissed from Berlin, as they have succeeded in doing in the case of our ambassador to Spain. We must put our Prussian frontier in a state of defence. Fortunately, the Berlin Cabinet has not inherited the character and resolution of the great Frederick.

Prince Charles has let slip the occasion to attack us; he is apparently slumbering in Suabia. He has given us time to cover ourselves in Italy, and even in Helvetia.

On being informed of the Rastadt assassination— which it seems hard to hear of without experiencing a sentiment of horror — Prince Charles does not seem to have been deeply moved. He writes a cold and insignificant letter to Masséna on what he calls the "Rastadt affair." Such coldness might be almost akin to complicity, did not the archduke enjoy a reputation for loyalty, which does not suffer him to be suspected of such criminality.

> The Russians are fighting without order, but they rarely retreat; they are experts at burning, assassinating, and stealing.
>
> François de Neufchâteau and Talleyrand, especially the latter, are in bad odor with a portion of the *corps législatif*. The former has incurred censure for influencing the elections. The latter has for enemy Rewbell, who has not yet been able to comprehend him, who sees him in everything that happens, and who foresees what he will do in the future. Gourlade is once more mentioned in connection with the Ministry of Marine; he is a trumpery fellow, altogether unsuited to the post; he is rejected.

Poullain-Grandprey, one of the active leaders of the *corps législatif*, sends me the letter of a *conventionnel* to a legislator, printed as a supplement to *l'Ami des Lois.* It is a diatribe against the Republicans, who are, as usual, designated under the names of Jacobins and anarchists. Poullain-Grandprey informs me that the letter is producing a bad effect, in view of the apparent threat with which it concludes. I ask that the Minister of Police be summoned, in order that he may be asked who has ordered this officious publication that it is sought to make appear official. My colleagues display hesitancy in replying, and look at one another. I call for an explanation. Merlin replies: "It is the Directorate that has caused it to be printed." "In that case there should be some record of such a decision having been reached after a deliberation." I protest against any insertion being made without its having been discussed. Larevellière and Merlin declare that they will, if necessary, sign the document in question. I call upon them to do it, adding that even should they do it at this late hour I still openly condemn all these anonymous writings as unworthy of a Republican Government; they merely tend to increase disunion between the two great powers. Thereupon follows another furious outburst against the anarchists. I reply, as I did previous to the 18th Fructidor: "Well, I also am then an anarchist, since you thus dub Republicans. The faction of which you are the dupes sounded me before sounding you, under pretence of the country being in danger. Let us not stray from Republican institutions; let us remain in harmony with those who profess to love them; no reaction; our enemies are powerless if not supported by a *corps législatif* which has been skilful in entrapping members of the Directorate. You would to-day shackle the liberty of the press; it amounts to depriving the Government of the only light which can save it. Liberty, and the people, who are capable of defending it, can alone save the Republic."

CHAPTER XI

Rewbell retires from the Directorate—My regrets at his departure—Sieyès's hatred of Rewbell—His sarcasms—Old women who govern Sieyès—The sway exercised by old women over certain men—Sieyès hated in his turn by Merlin and Treilhard—Sieyès a Director—Treilhard's sudden change of feeling towards him—Meeting of deputies at the Bibliothèque with the object of restoring union—Garreau's speech—The deputy Destrem—Violent expression of his sentiments—Vigorous apostrophe of Larevellière to one of the speakers—Rewbell's probity avenged—The Helvetic Revolution—Italy's deplorable condition—Treilhard's fears—Rudeness of three passers-by—Attacks on Schérer—Jourdan at the *corps législatif*—His plans—His remarkable letter to me—My reply—A conversation over the letter—A dinner in my apartments—Dufresse desirous of printing a diatribe against Championnet—I oppose it—Sieyès received into the Directorate—Kind attentions showered upon him by Merlin and Treilhard—Sieyès, "the Desired"—Merlin's terrors—Means of restoring quiet—Sieyès's opinion—Despair of a few patriots—Happy negligence of the enemy—Masséna in Switzerland—Bruix fails in his mission—The English talk peace—The Spanish fleet dispersed by the winds—Treilhard's haughtiness wounds his former colleagues—The Five Hundred call for a report on the state of the Republic—They declare that they will hold permanent sittings until the report is delivered to them—Bergasse-Laziroule—Project of law directed against Treilhard—It is adopted—Night sitting of the Directorate—Treilhard retires—Merlin and Larevellière accused—Boulay de la Meurthe and Digneffe de l'Ourthe make a violent attack on Merlin—A firm man needed with the 17th military division—Bernadotte discontented with some of the Directors—Joubert's twenty grenadiers—" A corporal's guard!"—I tender Bernadotte the command of the 17th military division—He wishes to cede it to Joubert—His aides-de-camp oppose his desire—Joubert accepts—Gohier succeeds Treilhard—The

Councils seek to impeach Merlin and Larevellière—I try to obtain their resignation—They refuse it—A violent scene in the Directorate—I address Merlin directly—He withdraws—A deputation of the *corps législatif* calls on me—Régnier—Marbot—Merlin and Larevellière resign—The 100,000 francs are denied the outgoing Directors—Bailleul's pamphlet—Sieyès's New Year's gifts—In praise of Gohier—Roger-Ducos and Moulins Directors—Joubert the butt of the factions—Semonville and Mlle. de Montholon—Schérer indicted—Consequences of the seesaw system—Assassinations—Bourguignon Minister of Police—Quinette Minister of the Interior—Progressive humanity of the Revolution—Joubert sent to Italy—Last bond of union between Gohier and Sieyès—Mannheim demolished—Project of Français de Nantes—Duchesne gives his support to it—Lucien Bonaparte opposes it—Joseph intrigues—Message from the Directorate—A secret committee called for—Lucien opposed to it—The motion rejected—Jourdan's proposition—Lucien's discontent—Defeat on the Trebbia—Macdonald's blunders—Weakness of the new Directorate—The English fleet on the seas.

FATE has decided that Rewbell is to be the next outgoing member of the Directorate. In my innermost conscience I wish I could leave instead of him and change places; I even go so far as to talk to Rewbell about making an attempt to bring this about. He proves to me that it is not feasible, and that, moreover, his personal safety does not suffer his remaining in the Directorate even a few hours longer; he would have resigned before this, had he not feared to appear as yielding to the unjust attacks directed against him. Moreover, he is in great need of rest; hence there is nothing to prevent his entering the Council of Ancients, to which he has just been elected. Rewbell embraces me in a friendly way, and urges me to remain at my post, pointing out that it is my duty to do so, in order to protect the outgoing Directors. "Without you," he says, "we should run the risk of having our throats cut." In speaking thus Rewbell was treating me kindly, but he was giving me credit for more power than I possessed. It was Rewbell who was the soul of the Directorate. It was he who from the very first day had made it adopt the vigorous course which had obtained for us so many results at home and abroad—results which had won us the respect of Europe. I confess that on no longer having Rewbell by my side I felt myself deprived of a powerful support, and I conceived alarms far more serious than those I had felt hitherto: formerly the only danger apparent to me was that of life; nowadays it was liberty itself and its institutions which were threatened; it was no longer a question of individuals, but of the very essence of things.

It will be remembered that, appointed a member of the Directorate after the 13th Vendémiaire, Year IV., Sieyès had refused the Directorship. The ostensible reason assigned by him for his refusal had been the state of his health; the true reason was his antipathy to Rewbell. This antipathy had been conceived at the time of a mission they had fulfilled together in Holland, when that country was occupied by a French army under Pichegru. I know not in regard to what trifle these two representatives of the people, intrusted with such important interests, had fallen out, for they were thoroughly agreed as to the vital question of the establishment of liberty. Rewbell, by nature violent, but kind-hearted and incapable of rancor, had sincerely believed in the reciprocal oblivion of the incident promised by both at the time. But Sieyès, if it cannot be called spite, had at any rate one of those priestly memories which are said to be most tenacious. Never had he spoken well of Rewbell; he had often spoken very ill of him, indulging in sarcasms which bordered on calumny. To quote an example, he pretended that Rewbell, while a member of the same Government committee as himself, had occasionally carried away wax-candles in his pocket; he was in the habit of telling this story and others, which he did not improve by embellishing them with very poor jokes, which were repeated by ancient dames, the friends constituting his private circle. I have more than once noticed this weakness of certain most distinguished men for intercourse with old women, and the sway they exercise over these men, who are, moreover, considered self-willed and of inflexible character. Does it perhaps arise from the fact that, for a long time exercised in the knowledge of our weak points, which they have been enabled to detect under circumstances of intimacy, these ladies have on mortals moved by a passion or some idea or other the advantage possessed by cold and invulnerable beings? Does it arise from the fact that the poor Samsons who abandoned themselves to these old Delilahs are already minus the locks which would prove their defence? Since an old woman exercised sway over Louis XIV., old women—no comparison between him and the King intended—could full well exercise sway over Sieyès. To drop the subject I will quote, as a specimen of his sorry jests received by the aforesaid ladies, the following, which did nothing less than impugn Rewbell's probity: "This Monsieur Rewbell," he would say, "must needs take something daily for the benefit of his health."

Be it as it may in regard to the wicked sarcasms, Rewbell is now out of the Directorate, to the great joy of the enemies of the Republic. I do not think that these latter otherwise possessed any great affection for or confidence in Sieyès; but he bears a reputation for colossal ability, which circumstances alone have prevented him from developing hitherto. The Directorate is as weak in talents as in character, and needs strengthening. It is the sense of this actual need of a man who may assist and sustain me, a sense sincerely felt by a large number of patriots who have faith in Sieyès, which causes all eyes to be set on him. Sieyès is, in his turn, far more hated by Merlin and Treilhard than ever he hated Rewbell. They do all they can to prevent his appointment, which circumstances have brought about, and they are compelled to resign themselves to it. Sieyès is appointed a Director in succession to Rewbell. I view with sincere pleasure this appointment, which may be of great help if Sieyès, less a slave to theory and abstract ideas, will work with the Government and amalgamate himself with his colleagues.

After having labored to prevent the appointment of Sieyès, Treilhard thinks better of it — like an adroit courtier who appears to have committed a mistake, but who has quickly been weaned from it; just as much as he had been opposed to Sieyès, just so much, he said, after mature reflection, he now declared himself to be his partisan; so henceforth Treilhard will be on the best of terms with Sieyès. May this sentiment only last.

Twelve deputies have been commissioned by a number of others who have met at the Bibliothèque to wait upon the members of the Directorate, and come to an understanding with them, in order to allay all fears and to re-establish the union which is so necessary between the two powers. Garreau, one of the delegates, made a speech, and seemed to me to be under the impression that he was displaying energy because he declared himself exclusive in the matter of Republicanism. The deputy Destrem, a most estimable and still more energetic man, perhaps no less vague than Garreau, declaims with virulence against the rich. It is not the sentiment of the agrarian law which inspires Destrem, for he is personally reputed to have a large fortune; he calls for popular societies (clubs) everywhere; he would like to see the nobles crushed—those enemies of the human race ever since Adam. Other deputies complain of dismissals, of public moneys pilfered; Larevellière vigorously apostrophizes one of them who is for the nonce the mouthpiece of the brothers Bonaparte, who are actively intriguing. Larevellière casts the blame of this pilfering of the public funds on the men attached to Bonaparte's command while in Italy, and on others even more closely connected with his person. Larevellière is on the point of naming the contractor Fesch (afterwards cardinal), the keeper of stores of Saint-Maximin, Lucien Bonaparte (afterwards Prince Lucien), the war commissary Joseph (subsequently Joseph, King of Spain)—all these names are on his lips, which I close with my hand, and put an end to the sitting.

I have told how, in the first days of the Directorate, we five had entered upon an agreement pursuant to which each one of us was to pay 10,000 francs to be given to the outgoing member. The sum was no more than what would afford the strict means of existence to him, who would have been altogether without means. The reason actuating us in the matter led us to take a somewhat less pinching measure in favor of the one whom fate should henceforth withdraw from our midst; hence we agreed to allot a sum of 100,000 francs to each outgoing Director. This sum was to be taken by the Minister of Finance from the general funds not set apart for any special purpose. We likewise decided that each Director might take with him his carriage and horses. Since the *corps législatif* allotted us yearly our expenses for the equipment of our household, such an expenditure was legitimate from the fact of its being sanctioned. Rewbell enjoyed all these privileges, in spite of all the calumnies of which he had been the butt; he was in need of them; nowadays it is recognized that his probity was equal to his ability.

From the 1st to the 10th Prairial, Year VII.— The revolution in Helvetia has perhaps increased the number of our enemies, owing as much to the resentment felt at our military severities as at the pilferings of our civil agents sent into that country. At heart the Swiss never were our friends; by depriving us of their neutrality, which was the best they could give us, they have compelled us to guard a more extended line of frontier, and we have lost the means of employing at stated points the large masses which determine victory; but the members of the Directorate are so obstinately in favor of the Swiss Revolution that the Minister Milet-Mureau is reprimanded in a lively fashion for having but feebly approved of it; and yet our position in Switzerland is such that on our experiencing a check we should be hunted down by the inhabitants themselves.

Everything is going from bad to worse in Italy. Moreau has lost his position about Alessandria; his army is broken up: a portion of it has proceeded to Genoa, and another towards Saluzzo, in order to keep open communications with Mont-Cenis. The 15,000 men drawn from Switzerland and brought into Italy were intended to prevent this disastrous dispersion of our forces.

Treilhard has actually entered upon a struggle with a number of combatants who have no existence, but who, so he imagines, are continually at his heels. He comes panting to one of our sittings, and complains of having met in the galleries of the palace three men who did not doff their hats to him. The Directorate refuses to take notice of such a matter. Just at present it is a prey to the greatest anxieties· Assassinations are multiplying; complaints are growing louder; men's minds are getting inflamed; the irresolution of the Directorate is emboldening its enemies. Schérer is the scapegoat upon whom all denunciations are showered, but it is really the Directorate which it is sought to injure, and at which blows are being aimed in the person of Schérer.

Jourdan, back from the Army of the Danube, where he had met with so little success, and thinking he could justify his defeat at Stockach by casting the blame of it on the Ministers, the generals, and the contractors, had resumed his seat in the *corps législatif;* he was seeking to win back some of the consideration which a defeated general always loses, even when he can furnish the best of reasons for his defeat. A noisy display of patriotism has oftentimes constituted a resource for public men placed in an awkward position. Hence it came about that Jourdan posed as the vanguard of patriotism. I believe that this sentiment of patriotism truly dwelt in his heart, but the gorgeous setting he gave it was perhaps as much a reaction against his surroundings as his actual impulse. He believed that his military exploits, his honorable rank in the *corps législatif*, conferred upon him the mission of assuming the right to speak first and treating with me on a footing of equality, as if I alone constituted the Directorate. Although Jourdan had repeatedly called on me, he had told me hardly anything since his return. On seeing me he would always seem as if he had something to communicate; then he would go away, expressing regret at the silence he always preserved. At last, on the 13th Prairial, I received from him the subjoined letter, enclosed in an envelope bearing the following superscription:

The Director Barras is requested to break the seal of this letter himself, and not to communicate it to any one until after having read it.

The Representative of the People,
JOURDAN.

PARIS, the 13th Prairial, Year VII. of the Republic.

The Representative of the People JOURDAN, *of the Haute-Vienne, to the Director* BARRAS.

CITIZEN DIRECTOR,

When the Fatherland is in danger, it behooves courageous citizens to save it or perish with it; it is in accordance with this principle, my knowledge of the danger threatening the Fatherland, and my conviction that you are a courageous Republican, that I address you on so important a subject. I am going to unbosom myself freely to you, and, if I have been mistaken as to your character and patriotism, I shall certainly be the victim of my zeal and confidence. If, on the contrary, you are the man I believe you to be—*i.e.*, a Republican and a friend of the people—you will reap the honor of having saved the Fatherland, and I shall be, as far as I am concerned, satisfied with having co-operated in bringing into action your courage and patriotism. Nobody knows of this letter. Never shall anybody know of it except with your consent. I am consequently placing myself entirely at your mercy, and I assume the danger of so delicate an overture. To come to the subject.

The Army of Italy is destroyed; that of the Danube is too weak to allow of the hope that, even in spite of the courage of the soldiers composing it and the experience of its commander, it will not be compelled to evacuate Switzerland. The maladministration of the agents of the Directorate abroad has everywhere caused the French name to be looked upon with horror. The brigandage of the Chouans is assuming a fearful persistency at home. The assassinations of patriots are multiplying and spreading with alarming rapidity. The public officials are, generally speaking, weakened, and do not shine by their Republicanism. The laws are not executed, or, if so, in a listless way. The Republicans are despised, the people are succumbing under the load of taxes, and are loudly voicing their discontent at the existing state of affairs. The conscripts are not leaving, or make good their escape before reaching their destination; Republican institutions do not exist; there is no public spirit; all Frenchmen are groaning under the burden of oppression; they feel the need of shaking off the yoke oppressing them, and the majority of them are, do not doubt it, more inclined to revert to the previous form of government than to endure any longer the one now in practice. . . . Such, citizen Director, is the analysis of the situation of the Republic. You assuredly see the necessity of promptly remedying all the evils afflicting the Fatherland, and preserving it from all those threatening it. You surely see that if the action of the Government continues to be uncertain or ill-directed, the result will be that our foreign enemies, acting in harmony with the Royalists at home, will take advantage of our unfortunate situation to make us destroy one another, and then re-establish in France the ancient form of government. I might, citizen Director, point out the causes which have brought about all the evils afflicting us; but it is not part of my plan to address reproaches to the Directorate. Quite the contrary, I feel with all Republicans the necessity of casting a veil over the past, as well as of arresting the progress of these evils by prevailing upon the Directorate to bring about a change in the state of affairs. All parties feel the necessity of making a change in the present order of things. The party which we will call Directorial—pardon me the expression—is composed, generally speaking, of men who, lacking both character and loftiness of soul, would willingly bow their heads under a despotic power, provided such power gave them offices in its turn, and suffered them to exercise their despotism over their subordinates. To these people are joined all Royalists, who feel full well that in the existing Government the power most opposed to the return of royalty is the *corps législatif*, and who, doubt it not, will in the first place strain every nerve to dissolve the national representation; inasmuch as the government of five approaches nearest that of one, it will then be easy for them to attain their end. This party, citizen Director, has as its main object the conferring of dictatorial power on the Directorate. Assuredly, did I think this measure capable of saving the Fatherland, I should support it with all my strength; but it will be easy for me to prove to you the dangers and impotency attendant upon it. The dangers consist in the substitution of a despotic and arbitrary for a regular and representative government. You are aware that governments have a natural tendency to extend their powers and prerogatives, and that the suspension of the exercise of the rights of the people has always resulted in despotism. I would enlarge upon this far more did the limits of a letter permit; but what I have said will suffice if I content myself with proving the impotency of the means. I find the proof of this impotency in the experience of the past. Previous to the Revolution the Government was concentrated in the hands of a small number of persons covered with the cloak of royalty; the people were oppressed, and possessed the liberty neither of writing nor of speaking. The Government concerned itself about nothing except to extort money from them and to grind them down, and still the Government was unable to maintain itself by its own efforts; it was compelled to summon the representatives of the nation, whereupon the magic of royal authority vanished; the needs of the State were made known; the nation recovered its rights, found the means of saving the State, and drove far from our frontiers the numerous enemies already settled on a portion of them. The Revolution was made by the people, by whom it can alone be maintained. No sooner have the people been kept aloof than the Government has once more been beset by all the dangers of the ancient *régime*, and fallen a prey to its impotency. The means of action have diminished in proportion to the keeping of the people aloof from public affairs. The more authority has been limited to a few the more has the public spirit been weakened, the more have means of action decreased; and these means would become absolutely null were the French people again brought under a despotic government. I leave it to you to reflect, citizen Director, whether such a thing be possible at the present time; and, assuming such a possibility, I leave it to you to say whether you wish to become one of the instruments of tyranny.

The other party, which I shall call the Republican party, seeks to restore the *corps législatif* to its proper status and revive the public spirit; it seeks to kindle in the people an enthusiasm whereby it will make great sacrifices to repair past mistakes; its aim is to stir up Frenchmen with the principle of the preservation of their liberty and its benefits. It would like to see the Republic one of men and not of words; it seeks to put a stop to the Machiavelian system which, by dividing Frenchmen into factions, is leading them all under the despotism of a small number of individuals—a system which, while tiring the people, makes them detest the authority governing them, and causes them to yearn for a change. I shall not stop to demonstrate to you the absurdity of this denomination of anarchical faction, a denomination which serves as a pretext for all the vexations inflicted upon the true friends of the Republic; this faction exists only in the minds of a few individuals who are not very dangerous, and in the minds of those who, under pretence of preserving the people from an imaginary danger, would rivet on them the chains of slavery.

Such are the two parties which actually exist, citizen Director. It is for you to choose. These two parties are on the point of locking horns unless a few courageous men turn the scale in favor of the second, and quickly make it impossible for the first to act. This honor is reserved for you, citizen Barras; declare yourself, then, strongly and loudly against the party I have just designated under the denomination of Directorial, and soon all

Republicans will rally to you in a compact body, and the triumph of liberty will be assured. Your colleagues—whom I accuse of all the evils afflicting us, and who nevertheless are, I believe, less guilty in intent than in fact—will follow the impetus given to them by you, when they see that you are determined to resist them; and they will soon recognize the necessity of a change of system in order to avoid greater misfortunes. Then will the Republic be saved without any shock; confidence will succeed the uneasiness and distrust agitating the *corps législatif* and the Directorate. Together we shall revive the public spirit, and create means as prompt as the danger is imminent; we shall be seconded by all patriots. Royalism, frightened by this reconciliation, will conceal itself and cease to agitate our unhappy Fatherland. The courage of the defenders of the Fatherland will assume fresh consistency. Frenchmen will have a Fatherland because they will be free, and as soon as they shall have a Fatherland they will know how to defend it, to preserve it from the dangers threatening it, and to make it triumph. Your colleagues will find the arms of the patriots ready to receive and protect them. At least I can assure you on my honor that I, who have the courage of writing this letter to you, will become their defender. If, on the contrary, you leave the patriots in a state of uncertainty much longer; if, as a consequence of this uncertainty, your colleagues, instead of devoting themselves to the search of means to save the State, continue to oppose the patriots, traduce the national representation in the public prints which have sold themselves to them, threaten the *corps législatif*, consider the Republic from their standpoint only, and its prosperity only in their self-preservation—then, I frankly declare to you, the energetic Republicans will perish or save the Fatherland; and, if compelled, they will attack the Directorate constitutionally. The latter may, in an unconstitutional fashion, disperse the *corps législatif*, and even put to death several of its members; but, as honor is dearer to them than life, this consideration cannot stop them; besides, they are aware that the violation of the Constitution in their persons would prove the precursor of the ruin of the Directorate, and that the people, weary of their painful position, would shake off the yoke that oppresses them. Save, therefore, the Fatherland, citizen Barras, save the *corps législatif*, save the Directorate! It is in your power to do so if you will only pronounce yourself strongly against the existing system, and arrest with your firmness its disastrous course. When you shall have fully determined to carry out this resolution, let the patriots know of it; they will then do everything that is necessary to second your efforts; you may then play a grand part in your country; such a part is worthy of your courage and character.

Greeting and fraternity.

JOURDAN.

Should you have any communication to make to me, you might let me hear from you the day after to-morrow. I am going into the country to-morrow, not to return until the evening of the following day.

On receiving this letter from General Jourdan, I was in no wise surprised at the sentiments of patriotism embodied in it; I was and am pleased, I repeat, to believe that they filled his heart; but the repetition of the most sonorous words made use of in the crises of our revolution did not seem to me a happy choice, nor to show a right appreciation of the period in which we lived. In the first place, the military idea that "the Army of the Danube was too weak to allow of the hope that, in spite of the soldiers composing it and the experience of its commander, it would not be compelled to evacuate Switzerland," seemed to me the expression of a despair not at all suited to a French general who had seen and done difficult things in war, and who, having just returned from the Army of the Danube, should not have despaired of it in such a fashion, to the prejudice and dishonor of the general who had taken his place; the world knows how gloriously Masséna has since given the lie to Jourdan's melancholy forebodings. Throughout the remainder of Jourdan's long letter I find a lack of precision in the ideas and a vague declamation, of which my readers may judge. As far as I was personally concerned, I found, concealed under Republican forms, an appeal to my courage and character almost akin to a fashion of tendering me the dictatorship—a thing not at all to my taste. As to the *ensemble* of things and the situation of the Republic, it was not at all putting it correctly to say that the tendency of the Directorate was the reestablishment of the ancient *régime*, and that its mistakes originated with this system, or to accuse of such a combination those members of the Directorate who, from our point of view, were as deserving of reproach since the 18th Fructidor as before. In spite of all the accidents encountered amid the struggle of the factions, it was not right to say that a despotic government was being substituted for a representative one. The Directorate was doubtless being continually attacked, collectively as well as individually; every private group and every public print daily said and published unmercifully everything our enemies could imagine against us. We were even done the honor of being called tyrants. Now, rulers whom you can call tyrants to their very faces are not very formidable ones.

For the rest, rendering justice to the sentiment of patriotism animating the author of the letter, although finding too much prodigality and vagueness in his demonstrations, I sent for General Jourdan and thanked him sincerely for the mark of confidence he had shown me. I made to him, with all the consideration which esteem commands, all the remarks I have recorded, and many more. He agreed with the correctness of my reasoning when I told him that "our position was far from being as desperate as he claimed; that we had weathered far greater crises; that we should emerge from this one by dint of courage and will, but with a will enlightened; that the Revolution was no longer in its infancy; that it triumphed by organization; that nowadays it was merely needful to perfect this organization in all its branches; that the framework was there, both civil and military; that the French nation was robust and inured to war."

General Jourdan seemed to drink in these words with genuine joy, and to regain courage on hearing me say that matters were not in the least desperate. He advanced towards me, and confidently yet respectfully waited for me to take his hand. I did so with emotion; I even embraced him. On taking leave of me he said, in a voice as if broken with tears, "Ah, citizen Director, it is again for you to save the Fatherland; you only half saved it on the 18th Fructidor; you must perfect your work; it is you who must save the Fatherland, citizen Director!" "My dear general," I replied, "all of us will together save the Fatherland by clasping hands with the nation, and showing it that the high authorities are united by mutual esteem." I invited General Jourdan to dine with me on the following day; he did not fail to come. Our conversation was again very much the same, and on his once more saying to me, "Citizen Director, it is for you to save the Fatherland," I replied to him, in a determined tone, "My dear general, you are too kind; not I alone, but all of us, will save it, and will save ourselves. . . ."

A desire was shown yesterday to insert in the newspapers a diatribe of General Dufresse's against Championnet; I opposed it, Milet-Mureau being present. I considered it sufficient to bring Championnet to trial, together with Decaen, Vandamme, and others. As the trial of these generals is being called for daily by public opinion, some of the members of the Directorate declaim against the freedom of the press, which is the organ of publicity. "Without this freedom," I say to my colleagues, "there would be neither Republic nor Directorate."

From the 10th to the 25th Prairial, Year VII.—Perrin des Vosges and Poullain-Grandprey have in a marked manner contributed to the appointment of Sieyès. Treilhard, unable to resign himself to the idea in the first instance, had gone so far as to say to Talleyrand: "Well, then, you have at last succeeded in getting your Sieyès." He can no longer show the same ill-temper over this appointment. The question now wears a different aspect. Sieyès, most legally appointed, and, moreover, enjoying the public favor, comes to the Luxembourg from Berlin; he has to be received with the honors due his rank, and the show of respect merited by a colleague who is to work with us on terms of friendliness and mutual regard. Merlin, who had no less than Treilhard opposed the election of Sieyès, thinks it incumbent upon him to use every effort to ally himself with Sieyès. He goes so far as to say to him that "he has been as much desired as awaited for a long time past in the seat he is about to occupy." Sieyès, "the Desired," returns thanks with a protecting smile for this compliment, to which he considers himself fully entitled.

There are no means of reassuring the frightened imagination of Merlin in regard to his personal safety; especially does he attach great importance to anonymous letters which he pretends he receives daily: he does nothing but whisper about them with the Minister of Police. Every day I realize more and more the loss which the Directorate has experienced in Rewbell. My colleagues rave against the *corps législatif*, and talk of nothing less than of "decimating it." While looking on such utterances as merely explosions of anger, Sieyès and I are far from approving them. A suitable means to restore calm and revive the public spirit would be, according to my opinion, to reinstate the Republicans who have been dismissed, and restore confidence to the armies by giving them Republican leaders, for whom they are clamoring. I charge four agents principally with acts of treason, which have delivered Italy over to the enemy. I propose to send back there, without further delay, General Joubert. Moreau will be better placed on the Rhine, which is familiar ground to him. Masséna is not equal to a large command; his is not the brain to conceive a vast combination; but as regards bravery, all things can be expected of him. And yet this quality, so eminent in him, is perhaps tempered with some degree of caution, since Masséna, having acquired fortune, dreams continually of acquiring a larger one— a thing liable to diminish the confidence of the troops in him.

On seeing how all our reverses realize our melancholy predictions, I raise my voice against the system of vexations and persecutions which has deprived us of our chief supports abroad as well as at home. In the recent changes made in Cisalpine officials were not men placed in power who were notorious for their Austrian leanings? Merlin replies that it is degrading the Directorate to suppose it is an accomplice in this matter. I point out that the Directorate weakens itself when tolerating such selections, and degrades itself in ignoring the services rendered to it, and which it still has the right to expect. Sieyès comes to my rescue, and says in a grave and firm tone: " In monarchies the friends of the kings are called to public functions; in a republic the friends of the republic should be called." A certain number of patriots who are filled with alarm meet together and propose organizing a Republican Vendée; this is altogether despair; we must not entertain the idea that we have come to that as yet. The nation has delegated its powers to us; we hold our magistracy from the law; it is our duty to enforce respect for it.

Fortunately the enemy seems to have let slip the opportunity of destroying Moreau, who has sought refuge under the walls of Coni and in Genoa; nor has the enemy acted promptly against Macdonald. It will now be less easy for it to prevent the reunion of the two armies, whereupon we shall again be in a position to defend our frontiers, and soon, with 50,000 men, to resume the offensive against an enemy which is widely scattered. Moreau has, it is thought, committed a mistake in dividing his forces.

In Switzerland, Masséna, with 60,000 men between Geneva and Bâle, wishes to retain command of the whole of this territory; he is scattering his forces and daily fighting engagements, the only result of which on either side is an exchange of blows. Prince Charles has hardly more than 30,000 men. Were he to concentrate them on a single point he would win advantages over a few weak points of all our positions, which extend over too long a line. A war of invasion and of masses is the one suited to the French. The warrior who is capable of bold conceptions does not limit his efforts to attacks on an intrenchment; he pushes his masses onward, gives battle, wins, and rushes forward to gain other victories.

Admiral Bruix has been unable to carry out his mission in the Mediterranean, where the English have become his superiors in force. There is talk of peace in London, provided we make the sacrifice of Egypt and Belgium. The Spaniards who have not been beaten by the English have been dispersed by the winds, and have sought shelter in Carthagena.

Treilhard has been appointed to the Directorate before the expiration of a full year after his service as deputy. From the time of his attaining power his brutal outbursts have offended and disgusted many deputies, who have come into contact with him in regard to general and private interests. They have said to him bluntly, "You boor, you shall pay dearly for all this!" These deputies now believe that the time for revenge has come.

Some days ago the Council of Five Hundred asked the Directorate for a statement regarding the position of the Republic at home and abroad. In view of the crisis through which the Republic is passing the answer was too long delayed. After several days of patient waiting Poullain-Grandprey ascended the tribune, and, in the name of several united committees, secured the adoption of a message ending with the declaration that "the Council will hold permanent sittings until such time as it shall have secured the information it insists upon receiving." The Directorate replied that it had adopted the same measure, and that at eleven o'clock at night of the next day it would satisfy the demands of the Council. Bergasse-Laziroule, chairman of the committees in whose name Poullain-Grandprey had spoken, announced that a large number of members had zealously striven to assist these committees with whatever information they possessed in the matter; that he came to bring the result of their conferences; and that he was about to propose the proper means whereby the Republic was to be lifted out of its state of uneasiness. All that had to be done was to repair a manifest violation of Article 86 of the Constitution, an article reading as follows: "Reckoning from the Year V., no one shall be eligible for the Directorate during the exercise of his legislative functions, nor during the year following his occupation of a seat in the Legislature." Treilhard had been appointed a Director on the 26th Floréal, Year VI., and, as a matter of fact, his functions had not ceased until the 30th Floréal, Year VII. As a necessary consequence there had not been the interval of a year, as laid down by the Constitution. The objection was an excellent one, but it would never have been raised had Treilhard not been coarse and insolent towards his former colleagues. The *rapporteur* dwelt on the fact that "it was the same session which had appointed the citizens Barthélemy and Treilhard." Hence he moved the following draft of a resolution: "The appointment of the citizen Treilhard to a seat in the Directorate is declared unconstitutional; he shall therefore divest himself of his functions at once, and his place shall be filled according to the provisions of the Constitution." This draft was at once adopted and sent to the Council of Ancients, which had likewise declared itself *en permanence*. A committee was at once appointed, and at one o'clock in the morning it moved the adoption of the resolution, which was carried without a debate.

The *corps législatif* having annulled the appointment of Treilhard, the members of the Directorate are immediately called together in the apartments of the President, and in the dead of night. Larevellière opens the proceedings by saying that he foresees with sorrow great misfortunes if the *corps législatif* is permitted to pursue the line it has adopted. Larevellière would like to summon the commander of the troops and the Minister of Police, in order to take steps to reject the law removing Treilhard. The latter, not possessed of sufficient modesty to remember that he is advocating his own cause, declares that the execution of such a law becomes extremely dangerous for the remaining members. A deep silence ensues; I break it with the remark that the Directorate has neither the means nor the right to prevent the execution of a constitutional act. Sieyès adds that he does not see any danger inherent in the execution of a constitutional act. Larevellière and Merlin grow angry. The law is officially delivered to us, and Treilhard, rising, says to me, "What do you think of all this?" My answer to him is that he must conform to the law. Treilhard, downcast and with tears in his eyes, bows deeply to the Directorate, and makes the announcement that he "withdraws." Thereupon all retire for the night.

The dismissal of Treilhard is not a sufficient sop

to the spleen of the Councils and the universal discontent arising from all the military and political events attributed to the Directorate. Unwilling to attack the Directorate as a whole, and perhaps not believing that they are doing so, the deputies now denounce Merlin and Larevellière as administrators incapable of performing their high duties. Boulay de la Meurthe charges Merlin with being a man of narrow views, of petty decisions, and of great revenges, profoundly Machiavellian, if indeed capable of anything profound, fit to be the Keeper of the Seals of Louis XI., but in these times fit to be only a bailiff or an attorney's clerk. He charges Larevellière with rabid fanaticism, and with giving his mind far less to government than to establishing his new religion. The deputy Digneffe de l'Ourthe says that the modern Cæsars and Marii have plotted the overthrow of the Republic and the restoration of Belgium to Austria. According to him, Merlin has been nothing less than a Duke of Alva towards his country. These comparisons were perhaps somewhat stretched by the imagination of this Belgian, when he bedecked Merlin with a resemblance to Marius, Cæsar, and the Duke of Alva; Boulay was more equitable when making a bailiff of him.

The speeches delivered in the Councils were finding an echo in society and causing a fermentation to whose term and consequences it was not possible to set any limit. At such a juncture it became necessary to have a man with brains and heart in command of the 17th division. I had at first thought of appointing Bernadotte to it. Released from his Army of Observation by its suppression, and authorized by the Directorate to proceed to Paris, Bernadotte had promptly done so. He was at present in the city with General Joubert and other generals not on the active list. He was daily conversing with them of the political changes which their personal positions, and doubtless also the public interest, caused them ardently to desire. Bernadotte was personally dissatisfied with the Directors who had delivered him over to Bonaparte, when the latter had sought to take him out of his military career and bury him in diplomacy. These same Directors had, in a certain measure, refused him justice in the Vienna affair, when listening to what Bonaparte had said previous to his departure for Egypt, on the occasion of his appearance before the Directorate with Talleyrand, when both had with so much bitterness cast the blame of the whole affair upon the ambassador by representing him as quarrelsome. Bernadotte was likewise justified in feeling discontent at the lack of appreciation displayed at his noble refusal of the command of the Army of Italy. In lieu of gratitude being shown him for his excellent counsels, he had been sent to the weakest of the armies on the Rhine—that of Observation, which, without the activity and talent of its leader, would have been merely illusory.

Filled with all these recollections, which seemed akin to resentments, Bernadotte was in the habit of calling on me daily, again and again offering me his services and assuring me of his devotion even to death. He would return to the patriots in the Councils, receiving a warm welcome at their hands. During the time of uncertainty attendant upon the overthrow of Treilhard, military men and deputies were speaking of lending assistance to the party determined upon the expulsion of Merlin and Larevellière. General Joubert, who had carried out Holland's 18th Fructidor, dethroned the King of Sardinia, and whose deeds were always suited to his words, would say: "A lot of time is being wasted in talk; I shall put an end to it all, whenever it is wished, with twenty grenadiers." Bernadotte, in whose hearing this energetic utterance had been made, seeing that he had been outflanked, and in order to recover his ground, remarked: "Twenty grenadiers! That is too many; a corporal's guard is enough to clear out the lawyers."

This utterance of Bernadotte's was reported to me; he himself, on leaving the antechamber of the hall of the Council of Five Hundred, wherein he had thus spoken, repeated it to me. "Well, then, general," I remarked, "we shall give you the command of the 17th division; you shall have no violent operation to perform: all that is required is to preserve order and prevent all excesses on the part of the Republicans against the recalcitrants." It was permissible for me to believe that such was indeed Bernadotte's desire, since I had heard the proposition from his own lips.

But just as I was under the impression that I was doing nothing but accepting his offer, Bernadotte appeared to me seized, I will not say with great fright, but at the very least with an embarrassment hard to describe. He was as if choking at being taken at his word; it was not, I repeat, cowardice: it was the despair of an irresolute man who saw his words caught on the wing, and who did not know how to extricate himself. Bernadotte, after a few moments' silence, which was not customary with him, said to me: "Citizen Director, General Joubert came to Paris before me; he has taken in this connection an initiative such that I might perhaps be showing but little delicacy in disputing. I beg you will permit me to go to him myself, and lay your offer before him, as behooves a comrade."

Bernadotte left me, promising to return the same evening. I learned that, while pacing up and down the hall of the Palais-Bourbon adjacent to that wherein sat the Council of Five Hundred, he imparted to several friends the offer I had made him of the command of the 17th division. His aides-de-camp, all men of genuine character—character since proven by their deeds—the citizens Maison and Maurin, at that time only lieutenant-colonels, and who "thou'd" and "thee'd" their general, according to the custom of the day, said to him: "Accept the honor which seeks thee. Do not go after Joubert just to give him precedence over thyself. Thou sayest and believest thou art without ambition; thou wouldst prove it all the better by doing on the day that is approaching what should be done for the common weal, and by doing nothing in thine own interest." The irresolute man was unable to triumph over his nature. Hence Bernadotte went to Joubert. The latter, unmindful of the sharp practice by which he was put forward, resolutely accepted the temporary command of the 17th division, declaring himself no less resolved to give it up the day after he had fulfilled his mission.

The patriots are enraged against Larevellière and Merlin. The *corps législatif* no longer sits *en permanence*. Gohier succeeds Treilhard. On the morning of the 30th great excitement reigns. Deputations from the *corps législatif* call on me in succession; they are uneasy in regard to the dispositions of the Directorate. I reassure the deputies, and pledge them my word that they have no cause to be alarmed, and that I personally guarantee their safety. At eleven o'clock yet another deputation, which wishes to see quiet restored, demands that Merlin and Larevellière resign; should they refuse, a decree of accusation and arrest will be issued against them within twenty-four hours. I have a talk with Larevellière, and counsel both him and Merlin to resign. Both decline. I offer to tender my resignation with them if they decide to do so at once. I point out to them the fearful intestine commotion contingent upon their resistance. The Councils are fully determined; hence there is nothing to do but to make this sacrifice to the common weal.

My colleagues persist in their refusal. "Well, then," I say to them, "I shall go and explain myself in the presence of the Ministers." And, indeed, upon entering the hall of the Council I ask the secretary to keep a strict record of everything that takes place. Thereupon I recall to those present everything I have done for a long time past to re-establish union between the *corps législatif* and the Directorate, everything I have proposed for the purpose of warding off the misfortunes now afflicting the Fatherland; it is because its enemies have remained unpunished that matters have reached so serious a point. I appeal to the Minister of War, who admits that I have done everything to send troops to the armies abroad. I appeal to the Minister of the Interior, who confesses that I have never proposed any dismissals to him. Although the commissary of my own canton is acting in a most shameful manner towards a certain family, which he does not cease molesting, I point out the fact that he has not even been dismissed, in spite of the request of the central commissary. Under such complicated circumstances, and when administrators as well as those under their jurisdiction have for so long been worried and harassed, at a time when the general uneasiness is imputed to the Directorate, does it not become necessary that those in power should withdraw and give way to new men? These, coming to power free from prejudices and passion, might save the Republic. Are we, considering the state of disrepute into which the Directorate has fallen, still able to accomplish this end? I announce that I too shall be the first to hand in my resignation.

Pained at the humiliating position in which I see my colleagues placed by this urgent demand for their resignations, I would assuredly not have abused their position to press matters; but their unjust recriminations, their insults, and their stubborn refusal authorize me not to renounce the advantage my personal behavior confers upon me. Have I not the right, and am I not under the necessity, to recall that I have for a much longer time past been opposed to calamitous propositions, which I have constantly combated? I appeal to the Ministers in regard to several essential facts. I charge Merlin with treason, cowardice, and hypocrisy. I reproach him with his inveterate ill-will towards everything Republican. I tell Larevellière that he was the cause of the loss of Italy, that his intentions are good, but that, abandoning himself to deceptive inspirations, he has committed many mistakes.

As I was thus roughly handling Merlin, Larevellière remarked: "I render justice to Barras; the Fatherland's danger inspires him with this patriotic anger." Merlin was quite out of countenance, and from time to time sought to mumble some silly remark. I reply to him: "If you wish to defend your honor by impugning mine, I accept your challenge. You have played here the *rôle* of Carnot without possessing either his talent or his qualities; the pair of you have done the Republic more harm than all its enemies together. Hasten to decamp; thou canst no longer sit with propriety in the Directorate." Thereupon Merlin adopts the course of there and then leaving the Directorate without uttering another word.

On my return home I found more deputations from the *corps législatif* awaiting the result of the sitting of the Directorate; at their head was Régnier. I inform them that what had taken place could in no wise be considered final. The Council of Ancients and the Council of Five Hundred are still *en permanence*. Marbot writes me, as do several other representatives, to inform me that security cannot be re-established until the two Directors Merlin and Larevellière are out of office. These deputies next call on Merlin and Larevellière and obtain their resignations from them. On my returning to our council-room I found Merlin, who handed me the two resignations. I told him the matter did not concern me, but the *corps législatif*. Merlin then assured me that he would so behave as to destroy the bad opinion I entertained of him. He begged me to forget everything, and embraced me with tears in his eyes, as did also Larevellière. The sitting was at an end.

Larevellière causes me to be asked by Valette, his friend, if the Directorate will not give him the sum fixed by our last agreement, that of 100,000 francs, as in the case of Rewbell. I reply that I shall prefer his request; the proposition is rejected on the ground that it is perhaps not strictly constitutional, and that it might draw upon the Directorate fresh reproaches from the bosom of the *corps législatif*.

The deputies have promised Larevellière that he will in no wise be molested upon his tendering his resignation. I have obtained their word of honor on this point. If the *corps législatif*, the majority of which is decidedly Republican, stands firm and within the limits of the Constitution, and if the Directorate works in harmony with it, the Republic can still be saved. If this last resource fails, then I see nothing but a return to revolutionary measures to preserve it.

Bailleul, who has been entangled in his swaddling-clothes ever since the 22d Floréal, does not know how to disencumber himself of them. He might perhaps do so by maintaining a certain silence never lacking in dignity; but, as he must forever speak, Bailleul thinks it incumbent upon himself not to hold his peace, and publishes a fresh pamphlet, in which he declares that he "fears more the Russians who are in the *corps législatif* than the Russians who threaten our frontiers." Bailleul perhaps entertained such a fear, but it was neither shared nor approved of by the nation. Bailleul would like to see attached to the Directorate a committee of deputies taken from both Councils, which committee's duty should be to investigate, in concert with the Ministers, all branches of the Administration. Bailleul confesses that he will "willingly be a member" of this commission; and he simultaneously confesses that this plan does not perhaps harmonize exactly with the preconceived ideas of the liberty and independence of the powers. It will be seen that if on the one hand Bailleul does not lack a certain amount of ambition, he displays a greater ingenuousness and modesty in his revelations.

Sieyès asks that he be reimbursed for the gratuities which he says he gave on his journey from Paris to Berlin and on his home trip. He asserts positively that these sums are over and above the expenses already paid by the Ministry of Foreign Affairs.

From the 28th Prairial to the 18th Messidor.—Treilhard is succeeded by the former Minister of Justice Gohier, an honorable veteran in the ranks of patriotism, enjoying a great popularity, and a man of decided and positive character.

The places of Merlin and Larevellière are taken by Roger-Ducos and Moulins, two men of very limited capacity. Moulins owes his elevation to his Republicanism. The utter nullity of Roger-Ducos is the very reason which has caused Sieyès to have him appointed, in order to have a slave at his beck and call.

I give a dinner to all the members of the Directorate. General Joubert is invited to it. This general, by reason of his good reputation and its ascendency in the councils of the Fatherland, is already the objective point of all the factions which would make use of him. There is a well-known theory of intrigue which, within his hitherto narrow sphere, Bonaparte has in the first instance practised on his personal account, previous to extending it over a larger field. This theory consists in worming one's self into power through matrimonial alliances. This means, no less than many others, is familiar to the citizen Semonville. He has broken in to this art, if I may so speak, his step-daughter, Mlle. de Montholon, who receives orders to make herself agreeable to General Joubert, captivate, and marry him.

Foreign and home intrigue is triumphant, and the Government falls into complete disrepute. Moulins, so some say, is a match for Barras: they would like to introduce duelling and pugilism into the Directorate. The *corps législatif* denounces Schérer; he is abandoned and handed over by the Directorate to the commissary attached to the criminal tribunal. We are no longer living in a time when Ministers are considered inviolable, and protected from the people by the executive power which has appointed them its agents.

The revolution of the 30th Prairial, since this name must needs be given to it, was really the counterpart of the 22d Floréal of the foregoing year. Thus Gohier, Roger-Ducos, and Moulins, the Directors succeeding Treilhard, Larevellière, and Merlin, were those who in the Year VI. had obtained the suffrages of the electoral assemblies in whose bosom the Directorate had engendered divisions by means of minorities which it had caused to predominate over actual majorities. Nowadays it is the excluded who succeed the excluding. I would fain believe that, carried away by the passion of fear, Merlin himself had not foreseen the consequences of his hare-brained policy. Alas! the consequences of the 22d Floréal are to prove still more unfortunate than is now imagined. This fatal day conceals in its bosom germs deleterious to the Republic.

Assassinations are still being committed in the departments, where Royalism is showing a bold front. The Directorate busies itself with changes in the civil and military authorities. Bourguignon is appointed Minister of Police on the recommendation of Gohier, and Quinette Minister of the Interior on that of Sieyès.

If, during the first moments of an agitation which was likely to become far more serious, we appointed General Joubert to the command of the 17th division, just as we had appointed Augereau on the 18th Fructidor, we had in no wise done so in order to consummate a *coup-d'état;* as far as I am concerned, I had neither dreamed of nor desired one. Nay, I would have opposed one in a most decided way. All we wished was to have done once and for all with the authors and chiefs of the dissension reigning in the bosom of the Directorate. The entire mission of the commander of the armed force of Paris was visibly accomplished in the mere fact that he had awed the disturbing elements, and that order was restored in one direction at least.

Just here those who observe revolutions afterwards and at their ease may, in regard to the occurrence of the 30th Prairial, which has been styled yet one more "day," notice a fact hopeful in itself—one which even now shows the progress of humanity displayed in the course of the Revolution. The early "days" of the Revolution are signalized, up to the 13th Vendémiaire, by the death of the vanquished. On the 18th Fructidor transportation only was resorted to. On this occasion dismissals were considered sufficient. This species of amendments to the early ferocity truly bears a resemblance to a progress of civilization. It is no longer permissible to kill one's enemies, nor even to transport them: all that is possible is to dismiss them and put others in their place. If what I here call a progress of humanity is styled by others the weakness of a government powerless to do more, my reply is: "Honor and courage to the peoples who once more regain such control over their affairs that weak governments meet their requirements! Political and individual liberty will equally be promoted."

Since Joubert's mission is now fulfilled, he is of opinion, and I agree with him, that he can better serve us with the army. I therefore renew my motion of reappointing him to the chief command of the Army of Italy. He enjoys the esteem and the confidence of the soldiers. Sieyès, who, it is believed, has already his eye on Joubert, in view of the execution of certain projects revolving in his brain, opposes my request in the first instance; but a few days later, driven to it by necessity, he joins Gohier in once more taking up my motion, and Joubert is sent to Italy. Gohier and Sieyès are here one, perhaps for the last time. These two Directors seldom agree, and in the future will do so still more rarely. "The man who has returned" from Prussia is haughty, seeks to play the protector, and couples bantering with a tone of superiority. Gohier is not the man to submit to this.

The Directorate has consulted Masséna as to whether it is just now of advantage to retain the position of Mannheim in so far as the town is connected with the operations on the Rhine. Masséna, without vouchsafing any explanation, orders its demolition. The Directorate learns that he has done so as the result of his having sold the town and the materials.

7th Messidor. — Français de Nantes announces that, considering existing circumstances, the Commission of Eleven has seen fit to embody in one measure all the fundamental principles, the application of which is capable of remedying the harm done by the liberticide system adopted by the old Directorate.

He states that the measure he is about to present will permeate all the fibres of the body social, not to irritate it, but, on the contrary, to appease or ward off all irritation. The following are the principal dispositions of the measure: "The wishes of each and every faction, when in a minority, are not to be considered; each and every agent of the Directorate or commissary who proclaims himself authorized to influence elections shall be declared guilty of an infringement of the sovereignty of the people; the law of the 19th Fructidor is hereby repealed, in so far as it empowers the Directorate to keep about Paris a larger number of troops than allowed by the Constitution; the Directorate is deprived of the power of delegating the faculty of issuing warrants for arrest. Under no circumstances shall it enjoy the power of dispensing with the interrogation of persons arrested within twenty-four hours. No military officer shall be dismissed without trial. Article 24 of the law of the 18th Fructidor shall be applicable only to priests who have not taken the oath, or, having taken it, have retracted it; no society devoted to political questions shall be formed unless by virtue of an ordinance of the municipal, indorsed by the central, administration. This ordinance shall be executed only provisionally, and up to the time of its final indorsement by the Directorate; no sale of military equipments, armament, or munitions of war shall be made unless under a law passed on the motion of the Directorate. The *corps législatif* denounces to the Directorate the conduct of agents who, whether at home or abroad, have stolen, infringed upon the sovereignty of peoples, and betrayed the Republic. The Directorate shall cause them to be brought to trial."

9*th Messidor.* — On the measure presented by Français de Nantes in the name of the Commission of Eleven coming up for debate, the deputy Duchesne took the floor in order to make a few remarks, the object of which was to modify it. He moved to refer back the whole of the measure to the committee. Such was also the opinion of a few right-minded men. The first and most formidable opponent of any modification whatsoever of the proposed measure was, as usual, Lucien Bonaparte, who exclaimed that " when the body social groans under the weight of tyranny, it frees itself by a spontaneous movement only; if it lets slip the opportunity, it does not find another for a long time. The Triumvirate has neglected nothing to oppress France. A salutary crisis has torn the Republic from the hands of the three despots. We have promised justice to the Republicans, and we must keep our word; but too often have they been deceived!... If a step backward is taken, the Fatherland is doomed, its friends condemned to silence; nay, more, I say, they remain at the mercy of the daggers of Royalism. Any declaration of principles is looked upon as useless. Is such a declaration of principles useless when it protects the officers of the army from arbitrary dismissal? Will it be useless when the Republicans reunite to revive the flames of patriotism? Will it be useless when its effect is to suspend any interference on the part of individuals rendered suspect by their constantly revolutionary behavior, to give the preference to soldiers who have served in the camps of the Republic, and whom Royalism alone has caused to be proscribed? Lastly, is it useless when its effect will be to give to public opinion a genuine energy? I tell you solemnly if you slacken the movement imparted to the political machine, if you delay re-establishing the equilibrium and restoring to the people their rights, Royalism will triumph, and the Republic will derive no benefit from the downfall of the Triumvirs." Thus spoke Lucien Bonaparte; thereupon, with ever-increasing violence, and railing at his humble colleague, he moved and carried the adoption of the order of the day against any modification. Joseph Bonaparte, who did not know how to speak, but only how to intrigue, supported his brother with all the underhand practices at his command. Such was at that time the behavior of the brothers Bonaparte! Here do we truly see the keeper of stores at Saint-Maximin with all his ardor, and the commissary of war Joseph with all his habitual low cunning!

In response to all the agitation and requests of the *corps législatif*, we address to the Councils an *exposé* of the facts setting forth our political position, and a *résumé* of all our sentiments. After having cast his eyes over this message, the Secretary of the Five Hundred assures the assembly that it is of the highest importance, and that, in his opinion, it might perhaps be fitting to consider it in secret committee. Thereupon Lucien Bonaparte exclaims: " This message either deals with diplomatic matters, or is a reply to the information you have asked for. In the first case, I indorse the motion for a secret committee; but in the second, I call for publicity. It is right that the French nation and its armies should know the actual situation of the Republic. I ask that the message be read in public." " Seconded!" exclaimed a large number of members. Portiez de l'Oise reminded the assembly that the Directorate, when promising a second message, had declared its intention of revealing matters entitled to the greatest secrecy, called for a committee of the whole, and received murmurs as sole answer. Grandmaison opposed it strongly. " The nation," he said, " has been oppressed, and led to the brink of the abyss; it must be frankly shown the greatness of the evil."

In consequence of which the Secretary read the message.

" Deep wounds have been inflicted on the body politic; they must be probed. The Directorate can no longer conceal the dangers with which the Republic is beset." (Interruptions.) General Jourdan sees fit to interrupt the reading of the message for the purpose of saying that the Commission of Eleven had engaged in a work it intended to submit after the reading of the message, and that it would make a demand for men and money. As a consequence, too great a publicity could not be given to the reasons which might determine the grant of what was asked for. The Secretary resumes: " It is true that a fatal system and unjust prejudices have kept away from public functions honest and able citizens, and put in their places weak or careless men. Nearly all the administrations require purging; the public spirit depends on the proper organization of the constituted authorities, and there is no public spirit when the authorities are tyrannical and persecuting. In a large number of departments the temple of justice has become the impious asylum of brigands covered with Republican blood. On the signal given by the assassins of Rastadt, the Royalists and fanatics are in motion. They already infest and desolate several western and southern departments. Purchasers of national domains, citizens known for their attachment to the Revolution, are despoiled and murdered in their own houses while in the arms of their wives and children. Civil war is on the point of breaking out anew. These innumerable evils are the fruit of a want of forethought which has suffered our armies to dissolve and our munitions to become the prey of pilferers. We flattered ourselves with vain hopes at Rastadt, while neglecting the means of preparing for war. Our frontiers are threatened; a coalition which would be formidable to everybody but a Frenchman is arming in every direction. Let us oppose to it the energy of the friends of liberty. Let us hurl back to the land of slavery these barbarians vomited by the North. Let us reassure the country by the organization of an imposing force. Let us instil fresh life into all the branches of the public service which the insufficiency and non-incoming of taxes have paralyzed. Citizen representatives, the Directorate feels it incumbent upon itself to tell you and the nation that the body politic is threatened with total dissolution. The dangers are doubtless imminent, but they arise solely from the bad use or the abuse of our means. The first and most powerful of these means is the energy of the people. Appeal to it, give it your support, and at your call, at that of the Directorate, Europe will see this energy display itself greater and more terrible than ever. The Directorate couples with this message the reports of some of the Ministers; you will find therein fuller particulars and the indication of a few means which you will weigh in your wisdom." Only twelve copies of this message were printed.

Jourdan thereupon spoke on behalf of the Commission of Eleven; he made the assembly see the necessity of stopping by means of prompt measures the almost general movement organized by the Royalists, and moved that it should be ordained—(1) that the conscripts of all classes shall be called upon to serve; (2) that they shall be organized into battalions or companies; (3) that free companies shall be formed for the departments of the West; (4) lastly, that one hundred millions shall be borrowed from the richest class.

All the foregoing was unanimously adopted, because there existed in the Councils a sincere desire to meet the actual needs of the Fatherland; but this was not sufficient for the disturbers. Hence it was that Lucien Bonaparte went about proclaiming that "all these measures were in no wise sufficient; that it was tantamount to sprinkling rose-water; that the people, who alone saved empires, should be called upon; that 100,000 sans-culottes of the faubourgs should be sent into the Chaussée d'Antin, and the palaces of the aristocrats be turned over to them; that this would infuse fresh life into the nation; that up to now only thieves had held both the lowest and the highest positions."

While we are combating these domestic troubles, I cannot forget that our first duty is to repair, at least in part, the individual acts of injustice committed by the Directorate previous to Prairial. To me this is a pleasure as well as a duty. Merlin no longer being there to maintain Truguet on the list of *émigrés*, I move the repeal of the measure adopted in this respect, with the result that Truguet, one of our best citizens, is no longer considered an *émigré*. Rejoicing at being allowed to return home, he writes me the following letter:

PARIS, 23d *Messidor, Year VII.*

My heartfelt thanks to you, my dear Barras, for the zeal you have displayed in obtaining from the Directorate the justice I had claimed. I have learned that you undertook to attend to this matter yourself, and that you eagerly seized the opportunity of giving me this fresh proof of your friendship. As soon as I feel somewhat reposed I shall call upon you, to express to you my gratitude in person. I embrace you.   TRUGUET.

Meanwhile the news we receive of our military affairs is bad. We learn that Macdonald has fought and lost the battle of the Trebbia. Nothing was more urgent than that he should join forces with Moreau. He has unfortunately lost much time in Tuscany, where, it was believed, he was detained by personal business, and did not debouch from the Apennines into the plains of Piacenza until very late (end of Prairial). Had he pushed forward sooner he would have found the enemy scattered, while Suvaroff was swaggering in Turin. While the Austrians and Russians combined were unable at this moment to oppose 30,000 men to him in any one direction, the French united under Moreau and Macdonald could put forward 50,000, and an assured victory would have ended the campaign. General Moreau had conceived this excellent plan, but had lacked the energy to execute it. He was content with seizing the chief command and exacting obedience from Macdonald. Experienced military men think that the latter, by delaying his union with Moreau and not working in harmony with him, has not only compromised the Army of Italy, but lost us Italy itself. Is he to be considered guilty of such an intention? No, undoubtedly; but such is the result, even if it be merely looked upon as caused by a misunderstanding, the outcome of rivalry. This is not the first time that Macdonald has revealed a selfish and jealous character. The consequences of such a moral disposition are most fatal when it rules men intrusted with important interests, and especially when they command in chief armies on which depends the fate of States.

Libels are freely circulated. Discord is on the increase. The new Directorate, which is styled regenerated, repairs nothing. If only the measures enacted were promptly executed, the Republic might still be maintained at home and abroad; but the inaction of the Government, the opposition of a portion of the Councils, render null and void useful measures wrenched with difficulty from a small minority; hence it is that acts which are said not to be the expression of the national wish fall powerless.

We learn that an English fleet has left English ports. This news seems to wake up the Directorate as if with a start. Orders are despatched to Holland and along our coast. The French squadron now at Carthagena is to return to the ocean, to be joined there by the Spanish.

CHAPTER XII

England's budget—The *Club du Manége*—Difficult position of the Government—Dispositions of the Emperor of Russia—Again besieged by Fouché—He is sent to Holland—Macdonald's behavior in Italy—News of Bonaparte's death in Egypt—His widow calls on me—A pathetic scene—A transformation—Doctor Dufour—Mme. Bonaparte's conjugal sentiments—Family affairs—She complains of hard times—The casket—A deposit—My aide-de-camp Avy and my fifty thousand francs—Mme. Bonaparte's gratitude towards fine young men— Financial legislation —A tendency towards order—End of the sittings *en permanence*—A general levy—A loan of one hundred millions—A Minister of War—What constitutes a good general?—I propose Bernadotte—Sieyès's opposition—Bernadotte Minister—His acceptance—He wishes to appear as having shown disinclination—Sieyès's opinion about the Ministry—He proposes Bourdon—"Léopard" Bourdon—Παντακάκα—A word as to Talleyrand's rapacity—Talleyrand's influence over Sieyès — A wish to transport the ex-Directors—Augereau, Porte, and Moreau de l'Yonne—Address from the department of the Gers—The Triumvirs—Calumnies against Rewbell—His reply—The necessity of a victory—The tour of Admiral Bruix—The *corps législatif's* attempt to conciliate public opinion—Lucien Bonaparte's motion—Prussia's conduct — The brothers Bonaparte anxious to make Ministers—Their intrigues to circumvent Bernadotte—The citizen Miot—A secretary-general—Bernadotte's grand behavior—Championnet reinstated—Bernadotte's touching letter—Letter to the generals of division—State of the Directorate—General Moncey—Everything forebodes a commotion — Law on the repression of assassinations — Affairs in Switzerland —Talleyrand charged with a host of misdeeds — Reflections on the Rastadt assassination—Plans in regard to Germany and a few other States of Europe—Arming in a hurry—Violent charges against Talleyrand—He seeks to explain his conduct—He calls on me while I am in bed—A bundle of pamphlets—Protestations of devotion—Caresses

CHAP. XII   MALCONTENTS PAID BY ENGLAND   441

and demonstrations of fondness — An extract from the apologetic pamphlet—Talleyrand resigns—He is succeeded by Reinhart—Robert Lindet Minister of Finance—Cambacérès succeeds Lambrecht — Fouché once more — He is appointed Minister of Police — Bernadotte's prediction about Bonaparte — Miot *aîné* and Miot *cadet* — Bernadotte's little cot — Birth of the future Prince-Royal of Sweden—Bernadotte's extraordinary activity—Constitutional conversations—Joseph betrays himself—Was he acting in concert with Sieyès ? — The latter's plans — Fouché's eagerness for the Ministry—The actions of office-seekers—Réal's position; his puns — A letter from him; what I think of it — Mme. V. de Châtenay—Her solicitations—The commissary Dupin—The Tort de la Sonde lawsuit—Mlle. de Châtenay's cleverness— My uneasiness — Réal a commissary — Political fortunes due to women—Mme. de Staël and Talleyrand—Lemaire—Réal's witty saying.

From the 19th to the 25th Messidor, Year VII.—It has been said over and over again that England's gold paid the malcontents. This assertion cannot be considered entirely void of foundation when Pitt is seen bringing the expenditure of England for the present year to £59,308,322, or, in *livres tournois*, 1,423,997,328.

A club having its headquarters in the *Manége* furnishes the opportunity for gatherings, and these gatherings give rise to all kinds of accusations. It is reported to us that cries of " Long live the King!" " Long live the sans-culottes!" are heard alternately. Authorities and citizens are watching each other. Each party frightens, and is in its turn frightened. Here is the Council of Five Hundred debating whether it is to indict the two ex-Directors. And yet I promised them, on the strength of the promise made by the deputies, that they should not be molested if they tendered their resignations. A hostile hand is urging on dangerous measures. Confidence no longer exists when a government has lost it. Can we hope, then, to recover it? Civil war is organizing at several points; our foreign enemies are acting in concert and approaching our coasts.

Holland is threatened with a landing by the English. We are informed that the Emperor of Russia, besides furnishing his contingent for Italy and Germany, is desirous of taking part in the naval attacks planned on several points, and that in regard to the operation meditated against England he has bound himself to supply 20,000 men. At this juncture Fouché, formerly proposed to me by Vincent Lombard, and whom I accepted as agent in Italy, again presents himself to me under the wings of his patron. He is of opinion that all Italy's misfortunes would have been avoided "had he been left" at the head of affairs in that country. A revolutionist could alone have coped with all the Austrian, Russian, and English counter-revolutionists. He could still save Italy were he sent thither with Joubert. He prefers this request in the name of his honor and of the common weal.

Although not so fully convinced as Fouché that he had deserved as much esteem as it pleased him to award himself in regard to affairs in Italy, I was of opinion that he had acted far more rightly than his adversary, the citizen Trouvé. Besides, I believed that the means of repulsing our enemies, once more advancing on us in coalition, lay in opposing to them the very Revolution which they were pursuing with fury, and in opposing it to them like a Medusa. I move that Fouché be sent to Italy.

My colleagues are of opinion that Fouché did not behave in Italy as well as he claims; that he devoted his special attention to money; that if he opposed the doings of a few commissaries, rivalry was his only motive, or, to speak in vulgar language, he spat in the dish to prevent others from touching it. If Fouché must absolutely be employed, the Directorate thinks it more advisable to send him to Holland, where he will give the support of his patriotic energy to General Brune, who has not much of the sacred fire within him, although a man of the Revolution. As to Joubert, who is a man of strong and determined character, he does not need strengthening with the support of the revolutionist Fouché, who has hardly any other but motives of interest for desiring to return to Italy, and who, with his customary suppleness, has acquired too great a hold over Joubert. For all these reasons Fouché is again sent to Holland. He is to concert with General Brune to protect the Republic against the announced invasion.

It has just been seen how Macdonald preferred to give battle rather than to unite with Moreau, when by joining hands they could together march on the enemy and overwhelm him. The worthy pupil of Beurnonville, no less ambitious, no less covetous, and no less mediocre than his master, Macdonald, has preferred compromising the welfare of Italy.

Just at this time I received, by way of Geneva, a letter informing me that Bonaparte had perished in Egypt as a consequence of a rising of the natives. The news of his death was not long in spreading, and, although I had not imparted it to Mme. Bonaparte, she soon heard of it through public rumor, whereupon she came in haste to the Luxembourg, whither she had been preceded by a few persons, with the object of knowing the truth of a piece of news that was circulating throughout Paris. Mme. Bonaparte enters all in tears, flings her arms about my neck, and, as if she had lost all power of utterance, can do no more than embrace me and cry. All of us present cannot believe anything else but that, better informed than ourselves, she has come to apprise us of the exact truth, when, after having released me from her embrace, she drops into an arm-chair, begs for ether so as to be able to breathe, and says to me, in an extraordinary transport: "Is it true? Is it an actual fact?" Even then I hardly know to what she refers, and I am as much astounded as are the rest. She continues: "Is Bonaparte truly dead? Is the news official?" "No, madame, the news is not official, and it lacks confirmation. Amid the hazards of war, in a hostile country, amid barbarians, who can tell? The life of Bonaparte is more astonishing than would be his death. Still, that which may be possible is, for all that, not certain." Mme. Bonaparte's hopes seem to revive. Once more does she open her eyes, which her swooning has for a moment closed. She turns her gaze upon us, then looks about her with a kind of uneasiness; she is going to speak, when, suddenly altering her mind, she feigns swooning once more, and begs my leave to enter my library with a trustworthy servant who has charge of the linen of the household. A moment later she sends word to me that she feels exceedingly ill. I dismiss the persons who have remained in the drawing-room, with the exception of Dufour, my physician, whom I take into the library with me. We find Mme. Bonaparte quite composed and almost smiling. Showing the same confidence and frankness towards my physician as towards myself, she exclaims: "Well, are all your visitors gone? Are you rid of them?" Once more she looks uneasily about the room. I send the servant out of it, when she asks: "Well, then, Barras, is it quite sure that Bonaparte has been assassinated?" "So I believe," is my reply. "The news comes from a correspondent who has no interest in lying." "Ah! ah!" Her features brighten up at last as she says, frankly: "Ah, I breathe freely. Ah, my friend, if it be a fact, I shall no longer be so wretched if your friendship towards me is continued. In times gone by it was thought that Bonaparte was in love with me, and that he married me because he loved me dearly. He is a man who has never loved any one except himself; he is the most ingrained and ferocious egotist that the earth has ever seen. He has never known anything but his interest, his ambition. You have no idea to what a degree he has forsaken me. Would you believe that I have an income of barely 100,000 francs. When I say income I should say annuity, for it is Joseph who has the control of the whole of the capital, and who pays me my allowance every month. If I venture to ask him—a thing most painful to me—to make me a quarter's advance, he refuses. He tells me I have no rent to pay, because I have my little house in the Rue Chantereine. Instead of considering this mediocrity, he makes it a reason for not paying me my monthly allowance in advance. I am desirous of having a country-house. I have mentioned the matter to you before, my good friend. It is a little place on the Saint-Germain Road. The environs are charming. The owner, M. Lecoulteux, would sell it to me at a low price; all that he asks is 80,000 francs down. Would you believe that Joseph has dared to refuse me this amount? I begged him to advance it to me out of my annuity. He replied to me that an annuity was not paid until it fell due; moreover, that mine was but a life annuity. What infamy! It would have been impossible for me to pay the first instalment if those good folks of the *Compagnie Bodin*—to whom, it is true, I rendered great service in Italy—had not given, lent me, 50,000 francs. I require a like sum to meet my engagements, and I do not know where to find it. Come, now," she goes on to say, "is he really dead?" "I believe so." "Ah! one wicked man the less! You cannot conceive, my good friend, of what this man is really made. He dreams of nothing but wicked deeds; he is perpetually inventing some trick to play upon this one or the other. He must needs worry everybody. How his brothers enjoy his confidence! Them only does he trust. How well they understand one another! I am sure that Joseph has a fortune of his own of thirty millions, and he plays the poor man! I have not more than three millions in precious stones and diamonds; besides, at one time he tells me that he gives them to me, at another that he lends them to me. It would not surprise me were the whole pack of them to dispute my right to them were I a widow to-day. Look here, my friend, you must render me an important service by allowing me to deposit with you the casket containing my jewels and diamonds. It will set my mind at ease, and if I no longer have Bonaparte, with my diamonds and my personal property, I shall at least have wherewith to live. Meanwhile, my dear friend, you must oblige me by lending me 50,000 francs, in order that I may pay an instalment on my country-house of Malmaison. You run no risk in losing them, since I am handing you securities for ten times the amount. Come, now, my friend, I shall at once go into retirement at Malmaison. This will be in accordance with the decorum suited to widowhood. It will enable me to receive you as often as it pleases you to visit me there. There shall be a bed for Mme. Tallien, one for you, and accommodation for your servants. Moreover, you may look upon the house as your own. It shall be the little branch cot of Grosbois. You shall rest there from your labors in the Directorate. I will do all I can to make your stay a pleasant one."

I thanked Mme. Bonaparte warmly, and told her that, being fortunate enough to possess a country-house, I should not leave to any one the care of receiving me and putting themselves to expense to give me pleasure; that, above all, I should still less consent to receive as a deposit diamonds and jewelry constituting for her a most precious and legitimate resource in case of misfortune; that as I chanced to be in a position to advance her some money, I should consider myself unworthy of the name of friend were I to accept security of such a nature; that I did not lend money on pledges; that as I was able to hand her the money she believed she stood in need of, I was personally grateful to her for the fresh opportunity she was giving me of being useful to her; that if, fearing the rapacity of the Bonaparte brothers, she really wished to place her diamonds and jewels in safe-keeping, I knew of no safer place than the house of her notary, Raguideau, and that she should make the deposit of them with him.

And indeed Mme. Bonaparte hastened home to put everything promptly in order. She carried her casket to Raguideau, then hurried back to me, to inform me that it had been done. A minute later she asked for the 50,000 francs, which she said she urgently needed. I sent them to her on the following day by my aide-de-camp Avy. He, together with my money, was received with the gratitude which Mme. Bonaparte as well as Mme. de Beauharnais could never help displaying towards fine young fellows.

Messidor, Year VII.—The *corps législatif* passes a law establishing, for the Year VII., the land-tax at one-quarter of the territorial income. Could the agitation reigning at home but cease for a while there is in that part of the government that has reference to administration a tendency towards order from which France would immediately feel the most happy effects. The *corps législatif* pronounces the cessation of its sittings *en permanence;* they had been decreed on the motion of Lucien Bonaparte, who would still like to preserve this violent state of affairs, which pleases him in view of all his ulterior designs.

But it is necessary to resist the foreign coalition, and, as the factions dare not show dissent on so important a point, the *corps législatif* passes a law ordering the general levy of all classes of the conscription, and the raising of a loan of one hundred millions.

As it is at the same time necessary to utilize the resources thus placed at our disposal, we bethink ourselves of appointing a Minister of War whose energy will make up for the mediocre talent, and especially the nullity of character, of the present one. Several military men are proposed. Sieyès thinks that a Minister of War need not be a soldier; it is sufficient that he should be an administrator. I reply to Sieyès that if he had seen military matters at as short range as I have he would know that it is impossible to be a good general without being a good administrator; for the first thing to do before setting an army in motion and directing it towards the point where it is to win a victory is to provide for its existence. To provide for its existence means to feed, clothe, and arm it. All this is within the province of the general as well as of the administrator; or, rather, if the general is not an administrator in this respect, he is nothing. I believe, contrary to the opinion of Sieyès, who fears to see at the head of the Ministry of War a general of ability, that we should choose a man who has won the confidence of the army—one whose resolute character will carry weight. Just at present all is in a state of dislocation: some of our generals have been deprived of their commands, and are on the point of being brought to trial; the soldiers are worn out with fatigue, and ask to return to their homes, to drag them from which nothing less than a powerful voice is needed; a man held in high estimation by his character and deeds is required. I ask my colleagues if they are not of my opinion. All share it, even Sieyès, who makes me a sign of adhesion most flattering for the principle, but implying also that one should beware of putting it into application. I propose Bernadotte for Minister of War.

Gohier and Moulins second my motion. Sieyès, who, I had imagined, was on my side just now, opposes it. He says that Bernadotte is a hot-headed man, a Gascon if ever there was one, a man who did not make up his mind to become a patriot until twenty-four hours ago; that this is no guarantee for his future conduct; that a republic needs the truth, that Bernadotte is in no wise inclined to submit to this law, that he belongs to the land of Henri IV., and is a liar like the good King. Sieyès was going to pursue his argument, with the indorsement of his colleague Roger-Ducos, who supports him through thick and thin, and would have supported him had he even said the exact contrary. At the close of his speech Sieyès proposed the intendant commissary of war Alexandre.

I resume speaking in order to say that Bernadotte is indispensably the man we need at the present time; just now we have not only to preserve the public spirit of France, but we have to give it an impulse, and to revive it in all branches of the war of the administration. I add that Bernadotte, brought up in the art of war, is acquainted with the whole of its hierarchy, from the lowest to the highest rank; that he has been an honest and enlightened administrator in his sphere; that he has the genius of organization; that he is capable of strong and extensive combinations; that, appointed by us five months ago Commander-in-chief of the Army of Italy, previous to the appointment of Schérer, he declined the post, giving admirable reasons for his refusal—reasons full of wisdom and enlightenment, which have been unfortunately and cruelly justified by all the disasters in Italy.

Gohier, Moulins, and I constitute the majority; the appointment is put to the vote, and Bernadotte is selected as Minister of War in succession to Milet-Mureau. Bernadotte, who had remained in Paris since the 30th Prairial, just as he did after the 18th Fructidor, in order to derive some benefits, or at the very least receive some compliments on his presence—Bernadotte passed his time in saying to those who spoke to him of the possibility of his becoming a Minister, that "never would he consent to take such a place; that he could do no good in occupying it; that he had never desired it; and that he would not take it even nowadays." As a result of all these assurances that he would not become a Minister, Bernadotte, on receiving his appointment, wrote to us at once eagerly accepting it. He wished just as much not to be a Minister, on this occasion, as he had wished after the 18th Fructidor not to be general-in-chief or ambassador, but merely a French citizen feeling honored with this title and trying to deserve it by taking repose in a thatched cottage with his retiring pension—

> . . . dans un endroit écarté
> Où d'être homme de bien il eût la liberté.

Bernadotte has since said, and allowed it to be printed (perhaps he himself caused it to be printed), that the offer of the Ministry of War having, in the first instance, been made to him by the brothers Bonaparte, who had been commissioned so to do by Sieyès, had been met with a refusal on his part; that the same offer had been renewed to him by General Joubert, on the part of the Directorate; that repeated entreaties from several quarters that he should accept the portfolio had encountered the most stubborn refusal on his part; that his personal friends had likewise failed; and that in the end his resistance had been conquered by his wife and his sister-in-law.

I do not, I must confess, see how this luxury of resistance was necessary to the honor of Bernadotte; why it should have been necessary that a new Volumnia and a new Veturia should have cast themselves at the feet of this immovable Roman in order to make him unbend and induce him to deign to accept a position as honorable as it was important. I am of opinion that Bernadotte was truly worthy of Ministerial honors; that he might know he had the requisite qualities; and that he was entitled to a desire to put them to use in a distinguished post that enabled its holder to display the means given to him by nature. But it is in Bernadotte's nature to indulge in forms even more uncertain than his will; he considered it good taste, and perhaps obligatory shrewdness, because of his birthplace, never to confess to the desire he might feel for anything whatsoever. Was this apparent modesty in regard to high governmental positions, as in regard to the national representation, inherent to the very infancy of constitutional manners, which, when grown older, will suffer a man openly to solicit both a portfolio and a seat among the deputies? Upon the whole, I repeat, Bernadotte, fully able to fill the position of Minister of War of our Republic, had no cause to decline it, and could have put his shrewdness to a better use than to a bootless refusal, and one which is seldom successful, since everybody knows that hardly any one refuses a Ministry, or is made a Minister in spite of himself.

Sieyès, though he has suffered defeat by the appointment of Bernadotte, makes a pretence of not having in any way renounced his principles as to what should and might be the capacity and incapacity of men destined to become Ministers. All Ministries, he argues, are merely organized machines; it is enough to have at their head men who are not totally illiterate, and who read what their head clerks bring to them for signature. This is the way affairs are conducted throughout Europe; the kings are not as good as their Ministers, while the latter are not and need not be as good as their clerks. They would simply lose themselves amid the mass of details; theirs it is to reserve to themselves the thinking out of matters, to fulfil their duty, especially towards their sovereign, whom they should not leave in ignorance of anything likely to interest him. As the sovereign is everything, those whom he appoints must watch over and for him. Personally, I should like each of our Ministers to have in his department an organized police, which should, within the sphere of its attributes, gather everything affecting us, and report the same to us individually; for, after all, we are the Government, and were some misfortune to happen to one of us, the State, which we represent, would truly be in danger. We may do ourselves this justice without any exaggeration of our merits. In view of everything that is taking place about us, the plots of the several factions now bestirring themselves, the chief quality we must look for in a Minister is that he should be sincerely attached to our persons; this constitutes the best guarantee of his Republican principles, since we are the representatives of the Republic.

After having so eloquently demonstrated how, in order to be a Minister, it was unnecessary to be acquainted with the particular branch intrusted to one, Sieyès sees fit to give an example in support of his system by offering us as Minister of Marine the citizen Bourdon, naval commissary at Antwerp. He is truly one of those individuals such as Sieyès desires. Bourdon professes to be deeply attached to the person of Sieyès, just as he has so often asserted that he was to mine; for all that, he amounts to less than nothing. I am not going to blame Bourdon for having had as a brother Léonard Bourdon, whom Fréron, in mockery of his persistent conduct in the system of terror after the 9th Thermidor, had jestingly dubbed "Léopard" Bourdon. No one in this world is responsible for his brother any more than for his father; but what I consider really reprehensible in the citizen Bourdon is, that he has allowed himself to be hoisted into the Ministry when unfit for it by intrigues not to be explained except by motives of interest scarcely honorable, originating with Talleyrand.

An exceedingly witty journalist of the period, who even at that early date had detected all that this name of Talleyrand embodied in the matter of sinister presages for the liberty and morality of the country, could find none but a Greek word to express the concentration in one man of what Mme. de Staël called "the vices of the ancient and new *régimes*." This word was παντακάκα, which, I believe, signifies all that is the very worst. As to Talleyrand's specialty in the matter of receiving bribes, I find among my papers the following memorandum in my own handwriting: "Talleyrand has received from M.

Sinking, Hamburg's envoy, 500,000 francs for the treaty; he has received a similar sum from Venice, and an enormous sum from Spain, for the purpose of influencing the elections and causing our fleet to be recalled."

Now this is the way Bourdon got on in the world through Talleyrand. The latter exercised a paramount influence over Sieyès. He went about proclaiming him to be the greatest man in France, which enabled him to fill the mind of Sieyès with whatever it pleased him to tell him in regard to men and things. Talleyrand, feeling his position insecure, sought to fill all approaches to the Government with his own creatures. This constituted, in case he was compelled to bend before the impending storm, a combination which might enable him to return afterwards; this was what Talleyrand called having a future before him. It was therefore sufficient that Talleyrand should have spoken to Sieyès of Bourdon as a man most deeply attached to his person for Sieyès to take him under his wing. We consented to appoint Bourdon Minister of Marine in order not to afflict Sieyès too much by appearing to oppose him in all things.

The idea of proceeding against the ex-Directors is not abandoned in the *corps législatif.* Augereau and Porte have come to me to propose that the ex-Directors Larevellière and Merlin should be transported, or at the very least banished from France. I was unable to restrain my indignation when they added: " It is in your power to do what we ask of the *corps législatif;* say but the word and it is done." I replied: " What, then, has become of your promises that they should not be molested on resigning?

Such conduct seems hardly honest to me; if need be I shall expose it; my own conduct shall be based on the frankness I profess. Your motion, if discussed in the *corps législatif*, will be scandalous, and I will share the fate of my two old colleagues. If I was compelled to join issue with them when their conduct was harmful to the Republic, I should unite myself to them in adversity."

Moreau de l'Yonne likewise calls on me in regard to this projected impeachment. I refuse to listen to him, telling him I am prepared to share the fate of my two former colleagues. Passing to a less exaggerated resolution, Moreau de l'Yonne tells me that he should be the first to defend me were I attacked. My final answer is: "I do not need any defender; my conscience is free from reproach."

On the 28th Messidor an address from the department of the Gers is read to the Council of Ancients, calling for the punishment of the Triumvirs. "May this epoch," says the address, "be that of the return of all powers to constitutional limits, in order that the French nation may no longer groan under the yoke of the individual caprices of absolutism."

This word "triumvirs" has for some time been repeated with a latitude justifying a fear that everybody—at least, all former Directors—may be included in it. Rewbell has in a special fashion been the object of innumerable direct and indirect calumnies, which have pursued him ever since he left the Directorate, and which have pained him singularly. With the firmness of a man who feels himself strong enough to meet every accusation, he takes the opportunity of replying to those directed against him in every address, just as if by agents who are put forward and who follow the impetus imparted to them. Says Rewbell: " No honest man will be persuaded that it is the public interest which calls for this mass of libels distributed gratuitously to hawkers on the sole condition that they shall cry them at the top of their voices in the streets and crossways. I do not believe, as has been pretended, that these libels are the work of representatives of the people; I see in them nothing more than the hand of an impious coalition seeking to profit by our divisions. Only scoundrels can say that I have invested ten millions abroad; they do not believe it themselves, and all their utterances against me do not prove anything, except that I do not belong to their gang. We are most guilty simply because we have not enlisted under their banners. I say *we*, because it is sought to send my two unfortunate colleagues to the scaffold, and me with them. And yet we have served the Fatherland with zeal, courage, and probity. If we have committed mistakes, they have been involuntary; if we have fallen into errors, it has been in spite of ourselves. How many times have I not bewailed the disorders which were magnified, and which harmony might have put an end to! Much has been said about peculation and waste, cases of which were daily being denounced to us; they constituted a source of anxiety to us, and not a day passed that we did not seek to reach and to repress them. I hated acts of rapine. This word is not immaterial, for the name of Rapinat has been played upon; but if Rapinat be a thief, if he has not denounced unfaithful purveyors, if, to put it briefly, he has not performed his duty, let him be punished, but let justice dictate what his punishment shall be; let us no longer give ear to vague declamations; let us cease to allow ourselves to be deceived by knaves who cry out 'Thieves!' [What furnished, according to French character, an opportunity of adding to the epigrams and wretched puns to which the name of *Rapinat* had given rise, was the fact that this man, whose name was already so expressive, had in Helvetia, so it was said, a secretary named *Forfait* (heinous crime) and a deputy named *Grugeon* (*gruger quelqu'un*—to live upon somebody); and it was pretended that all these people were related to Rewbell, although he was in no wise connected with any one of them.] We have been denounced as usurpers of power. I declare that, as I was expecting to leave the Directorate at any moment, I was willing that the Government should have enough strength to repel all oppression, but I was not willing that it should possess enough to oppress me. We are reproached with having exiled Bonaparte! Bonaparte allowing himself to be exiled! Is this not an insult to him? Posterity may pass a severe judgment on his expedition, which I had constantly condemned, even apart from the unfortunate affair of Aboukir; but our contemporaries should not be surprised at our having yielded to the genius of a man who had an answer to each and every objection, solved all difficulties, and overcame all obstacles. The reverses of the armies are laid to our doors; we intrusted all the resources of the Republic to men who had been fortunate so far, but whom fortune forsook, and to others whose glory, although temporarily dimmed, had not been effaced; but where is the government which can be suspected of desiring reverses that can but recoil on it? Are we traitors because victory did not answer our expectation? We have never despaired of the welfare of the Republic, either at the time we took the reins of government or in the course of the several crises it has undergone. And yet there are those who thirst for our blood; we are offered up as a sacrifice to our enemies; it is sought to make us the expiatory victims of the 18th Fructidor. What a day of triumph would that not be for royalty on which it should see our heads roll from our bodies into the dust! Let the revolutionary *régime* be recreated; let every idea of revolution, republic, and liberty be effaced! Drag to the scaffold the founders of French liberty; drag us thither one after the other! Such is the wish of the Cabinet of St. James. Begin with us; let us be devoted to infamy and to death; and, indeed, we do not wish to survive the Republic. But if it be not sought to re-establish the *régime* of terror which would kill the Republican Government, why are its forms assumed? Never did we stand in greater need of union; the emissaries of the foreigner are watching us; they are sowing dissension among the patriots of various shades. Let us be circumspect in the approval we grant to addresses. If blood is required, let it be shed with justice and not with fury."

From the 25th Messidor to the 4th Thermidor, Year VII.—One of the greatest misfortunes of a new government—and this misfortune is the consequence of a long war—is the necessity of winning victories every day. Our position is entirely dependent on the success of the armies.

Admiral Bruix has left Carthagena, followed by the Spanish squadron, and has gone to Cadiz.

They have anchored at Rota, in lieu of sailing towards the French coast, in order to come up with the English squadron blockading Rochefort. A large squadron is being equipped at Chatham, writes our correspondent; its destination is the French coast.

The *corps législatif* has attempted, but in vain, to conciliate public opinion. Lucien Bonaparte, by virtue of one knows not what intrigue, proposes to the Council of Five Hundred that it should pronounce an oath of fidelity to the Constitution.

We are informed that the Prussian Cabinet is actively engaged in seeking to discover the state of public opinion in France; it is constantly procuring information as to our projected measures and military resources; should it consider the latter insufficient, it will make up its mind to declare itself against us. Our troops on the Rhine are to remain stationed there. We have in this direction only 25,000 men, independently of the garrisons of fortified towns; a few battalions are ordered to join them; this will suffice for the present to check Prussia, which will not so soon break with neutrality. This Power will be emboldened to consider itself strong if we display weakness in our dealings with it.

Following the calculations of their covetousness and personal ambition, as well as the execution of the mission intrusted to them by the General-in-chief of the Army of Egypt, the brothers Bonaparte greatly desired to have at least Ministers of their own, since they did not possess enough of Directors. It had not been necessary for them to further Bernadotte's interests with us: Bernadotte's interests were ours, and we all liked him; but in ascribing to themselves the honor of his appointment they hoped to acquire a great ascendency over him. They were desirous that he should appoint as his secretary-general one of their creatures, their mere tool, the citizen Miot *aîné*, formerly Joseph's private secretary; but Bernadotte, seeing the trap, had the good sense to refuse Joseph's *protégé*, and to take, in conformity with the advice of his aide-de-camp Maison, a young man who was a friend of his—an excellent citizen, whose talent and political sentiments were known to him, and who had already made a name through a few historical essays, and was well thought of by the principal men of the Revolution and of the war, who had been his masters.[1]

No sooner had Bernadotte been appointed a Minister, and uttered his first vows of Republicanism, than he immediately became an object of terror to the Royalists; they nicknamed him "the man of Vienna with the little flag"; they remarked that he was "going to plant little flags everywhere"; but, rising superior to all these bawlings of the aristocracy, Bernadotte, really in his place at the Ministry of War, surrounded by a good staff and filled with the noble sentiment of the mission he had to fulfil, was not long in justifying the expectations the patriots felt the need of placing in him, as well as the reasons which had moved me to demand his appointment. In a first proclamation replete with sentiment he has declared that he "would not rest until he had obtained food, clothes, and arms for his

---

[1] It is M. Rousselin de Saint-Albin who is here referred to.—G. D.

old comrades"; he has reassured and electrified all; he has once more conciliated to us the military men alienated by the cavilling administration of Merlin, who sought to make war, politics, and revolution subject to all the chicanery of the law. Bernadotte has proposed to us the reinstatement of Championnet, whom Merlin relentlessly pursued, and whom he persisted in seeking to bring to trial by virtue of I know not what law having no reference whatever to the case and to the military circumstances; we have, on Bernadotte's proposition, appointed Championnet General of the Army of the Alps, under Joubert, Commander-in-chief of the Army of Italy. The two generals hold each other in high esteem, and sincerely love the Republic; they will necessarily work in harmony. Bernadotte, on sending Championnet to the Army of the Alps, has written to him a letter most touching in its eloquence. Such accents, recalling as they do the palmy days of liberty, kindle the hope that the Republic will live and endure.

It pleases me to quote this very remarkable letter of Bernadotte's to General Championnet, in order to do justice to the writer:

PARIS, 20*th Messidor, Year VII.*

Bernadotte, Minister of War, to General Championnet.

The Directorate, by its enactment of the 17th inst., appoints you Commander-in-chief of the Army of the Alps. Thirty thousand brave men await you, impatient to resume the offensive under your orders.

A fortnight ago you were in prison; the 30th Prairial has freed you. To-day public opinion accuses your oppressors; hence your cause has, so to speak, become a national one. Can you wish for a happier fate?

Others enough there are who find in the accidents of the

Revolution a pretext for calumniating the Republic; for men such as you, injustice is a reason for bearing your country a greater love. It has been sought to punish you for having upset thrones; you will avenge yourself on the thrones still threatening the form of our government.

Go, my friend, and cover with laurels the traces of your chains; efface, or rather preserve, the honorable mark they have left. It is not unprofitable to liberty to constantly place under our eyes the outrages of despotism.

I embrace you as warmly as I love you.

BERNADOTTE.

Bernadotte, Minister of War, to the Generals of Division.

The Directorate has just intrusted the War Department to me. If, when the Fatherland is in danger, it were permissible to consult one's tastes, you may believe, general, that I should have refused the Ministry, and that I should already have rejoined my comrades; but, seeing the dilapidated state of all branches of the Administration, I felt that there were several kinds of courage, and the very difficulty of the undertaking has constituted for me the obligation of accepting it. My efforts are wholly devoted to the relief of my brothers-in-arms; a no less imperative need for the armies is the union of those who lead them. Our enemies have calculated upon the rivalries of our generals, and hope to convert them into discords; let them know to their cost the meaning of emulation among free men.

Why have our enemies won successes? Let us say it frankly: it is because they have attempted to do what we did in the first place; and, when they followed our example, we seemed to unlearn victory; but despotism cannot long ape liberty, and we shall soon have seized once more the weapons which are ours alone.

The false and hypocritical moderation so long tolerated disappeared on the 30th Prairial.

Let burning activity succeed marasmus; let generous ardor, mother of all the miracles which have cast honor upon and caused the Republic to be respected, reappear with her latest triumph! Men who say that they never belonged to any party, except that of the Republic, will inveigh against our ardor. Let us begin by answering the Russians.

I have seen the glorious days when generals did their duty on the field of battle six times over, and the promotions given us then were the price of these extraordinary efforts. Liberty is to be regained by an equal development of virtues and energy.

To attain this result it is sufficient that you should be mindful of your past, resume your valor, and stir up all generous souls. At the sound of your voice the children of liberty, who are to be its saviors, will spring from the ranks; be on the lookout for them, and point them out to me immediately; they shall promptly receive promotion; those are the men who will vanquish Europe.

Above all, let the will of the generals-in-chief and its execution be one.

Friendship and trust. BERNADOTTE.

Bernadotte, when following the promptings of his heart, did not perceive that if there was now a new Directorate, a *regenerated* one as it was called, yet it could not dissociate itself from everything that had been done by the former one; in the first place, it would have shown bad taste on the part of the newcomers, and next, the consequences of such action would have been fatal, in so far as the several parties were concerned, if each time one government succeeded another it undertook to sit in judgment on its predecessors. As for myself, as will doubtless be expected, unable to abdicate my personality, I found myself in a most painful position when seeing acts in which I had shared denounced in so direct and merciless a fashion.

As a result of the 30th Prairial, all military men and civil functionaries who had been previously dismissed came forward to be reinstated. At their head was one whose principles had been looked upon as most equivocal, although he loudly protested his devotion to the Republic—viz., General Moncey. This general did not believe that his patriotic services were quite sufficient to obtain my interest, so he invoked the interference of two of my female relations who he knew saw me in my home circle. The day will perhaps come when General Moncey will be one of those who will least remember what I have done for them; this is what justifies my not losing the memory of it when coming across the letters wherein he presents his humble petition to me, dwelling on his deep and respectful gratitude, while of course, like all petitioners of the period, conclusively demonstrating to me that he is a very great friend of liberty. This was doubtless a means of reaching my heart, but it was at the same time a means of obtaining the favor of that power of which I was one of the dispensers, and of which military men, giving me a greater share than I desired, wished that I should be the dictator; since they generally called me their father, I am entitled to honor myself with the recollection that Moncey was once one of my children, just as he was one of the children of the Republic in Messidor, Year VII., when I did myself the pleasure of having him reinstated.

The exaggerated motions made in the *Club du Manége* afford fresh pretexts for attacking this society, which is composed in part of honest Republicans. Not only wisdom but courage and devotion are needed to maintain the Republic, in view of the existing state of affairs. It is necessary to act with vigor against those who are rending it; to welcome those who are prepared to defend it, and who are interested in so doing. The Directorate is uncertain as to whether it will at once send into Belgium the officers and sergeants on the retired list, with the object of placing them at the disposal of the general in command in that country; he could employ them in the parishes for the purpose of preserving order, and their presence would be of some use in maintaining the public spirit.

From the 5th to the 12th Thermidor, Year VII.— The *chouannerie* is taking up arms in the departments. The West is again stained with blood; English guineas are circulating, just as they are believed to be still circulating in Paris. As usual, the most audacious will be the conquerors.

A law is passed for the purpose of repressing brigandage and assassinations at home. It empowers the administrations to seize hostages among the relations of *émigrés* and *ci-devant* nobles.

We are still arguing as to the causes of our reverses in Switzerland, when it might be possible, by uniting our scattered forces, to attack the enemy with advantage. Our secret agents in Switzerland and on the right bank of the Rhine informed us that Prince Charles had withdrawn 25,000 picked troops which were face to face with Masséna, and that he was marching them towards the Lower Rhine; this relieved Masséna, and furnished him the means of attacking with advantage the troops so diminished in numbers which remained opposed to him, and warding off by a certain victory their junction with the Russians whose arrival was announced.

The movement of the 30th Prairial, which dealt a blow at the Directorate, is still considered incomplete and a failure, because the places of a portion of the Ministers of the old Directorate have not been supplied. Talleyrand, who has not only had a hand in all Directorial revolutions, but who has followed them actively and even gone beyond them with his exaggerated devotion, would like not to be subject to the common law, and so to remain constantly in office. As is his wont, he believes himself fully entitled to this. His principal claim to consideration is that he is "deeply attached to the persons of all the present Directors." He has used the same language towards all the Directors he has seen follow in succession, and whom he has assisted in having removed. Meanwhile a storm is gathering both in the Councils and abroad. Everything seems to unite for the purpose of charging Talleyrand with a host of misdeeds.

Men's minds are a prey to every kind of suspicion. The recent assassination at Rastadt is among the things which most inflame them. People say that this awful assassination, inexplicable in so many ways and so perfectly diplomatic, will probably have the same fate as the mystery of the Man with the Iron Mask, and that its secret will be buried in an eternal night. This unparalleled crime has been imputed alternately to England, to Queen Caroline, and to the Cabinet of Vienna, the imputation being doubtless based on the probable interest each one of the parties might have in the perpetration of the deed. It would seem that, independently of their willingness, which I do not contest, the primary instigators and movers in the affair were French *émigrés* disguised in the uniform of the Szecklers Hussars. Such is the version most supported by special details which were sent to us at the time from abroad by several of our Ministers, and confirmed in Paris by the correspondence of the foreign ambassadors. "After all," I remark to my colleagues, "had we not in so cowardly a fashion tolerated the outrage inflicted upon Bernadotte, we should not now have murders to avenge. Impunity ever emboldens crime. Let people compare this weak conduct of ours towards the Austrian power which abhors us with the extreme severity we have used in regard to the slightest peccadilloes of small States both Republican and friendly. Yet, in pursuing a weak course with them, we should not only have created fresh enemies, but have alienated all our friends. Such is but a part of what we have done to lose the fruit of seven years of victories. And yet we were not lacking in resources.

"What is not Talleyrand's share of responsibility in all our misfortunes? All of them are at present attributed to him by the justly exasperated Republicans. At the head of his accusers was the *Journal des Hommes Libres*, which published a recapitulation of facts of too serious an import for me to deny them a place in my Memoirs. Let us examine cursorily the different circumstances in connection with which the French policy is called to account. Beginning with Germany, said the accusers, would it not have been possible to enter Vienna some time ago? We might have 'Germanized' a portion of this vast district and 'Republicanized' the remainder by befriending the small States, and secured a 'long neutrality' on the part of the King of Prussia by rendering him some important service, such as, for instance, assisting him to have the Imperial crown pass alternately between the Houses of Brandenburg and Austria. Ought we not to have succored, or at least left free to act as they saw fit, the inhabitants of Suabia? But we preferred calling them anarchists; the Emperor does not call them differently.

"As to Switzerland. All we had to do was to encourage the good Republican spirit, but it was preferred to pillage and rule with a rod of iron; and yet it might have been remembered that the Swiss were naturally deeply attached to their independence and their money, and we might have foreseen the results of our missions à *la* Rapinat.

"As to Italy. She was all for us, and showed friendliness to us in every way. What have we not done to lose her? It was far more easy to retain her, but then fanaticism would have received its death-blow. A bishop could not permit so great an impiety.

"As to Holland. The opponents of the stadtholders were, willing or unwilling, necessarily devoted to us; their only salvation lay with us. Was anything left undone that could make them disaffected? Was it then imagined that the King of Prussia would love us in more Republican fashion than the Dutch?

"There are only four ways in which we can wage war against the King of England: (1) by attacking Hanover; (2) by an attack on Portugal; (3) by fitting out as many privateers as possible; and (4)—which would at the least be as good as all the rest—by freeing Ireland. What have we done in all this? (1) Against Hanover, which is infinitely dearer to George (German at heart) than the whole of Great Britain. Did we invade it? No; while on the contrary his friend, relation, and co-religionist, the King of Prussia, caused Hanover to be included in the neutral zone. Is this not evident? (2) As to Portugal. Did we invade that precious English colony called the Kingdom of Portugal? And yet its conquest would have been infinitely easy, while Lisbon is, as everybody knows or can know, the veritable London of the continent of Europe.

"Had we caused Portugal to disappear as a kingdom from the map of Europe, the King of Spain would not have loved us for it, we admit, because kings love 'with great difficulty' even their brother kings; while, as to democratic republics, these will always produce on them the same effect as water on a mad dog: all kings are *republicophobes*. But even if the King of Spain had not loved us, at any rate it is certain that by handing over to him Portugal, wherewith to aggrandize his dominions, even his own interests would have compelled him to serve us, and the forced services of kings are infinitely preferable to their friendship; we should thus have obtained Brazil as our share without any difficulty, and not only opened up fresh sources of commercial wealth far surpassing all our former ones, but, by a species of magic operation, our merchants might perhaps have once more become attached to the Revolution, as in '89. At that date they thirsted for honors; now the alluring bait of riches would once more have caused their generous souls to expand. Commerce must be spoken to in its own language: well, then, honors (always in the plural) and riches are the veritable mother-tongue of merchants of all countries. To succeed with them, no other idiom must ever be used.

"But, even admitting that we might have been unable to realize all that we have just pointed out, it is at any rate certain that the taking of Lisbon and Oporto would have been, next to the independence of Ireland, the most fatal blow that could have been dealt England. This is why we did nothing of the kind. We not only did nothing against Portugal, but we did a great deal for her. By speaking of an invasion it was not intended to make, and by coupling with it the redoubtable name of Augereau, we have put the English on their guard; hence you see with what powerful armaments they have ever since defended themselves. We should have acted, not spoken: then would Portugal, or rather Portuguese England, have been lost, and Talleyrand...[1] [The recurrence will be noticed in the nature of these reproaches of an idea which dominated a great portion of the Republicans of the period, one which is ever present to their minds—to wit, that Talleyrand, from the early days of the Revolution, during the time between his emigration and his return to France, and especially while in the Ministry, was never anything but the agent of England.]

"As to encouraging the fitting-out of privateers: it is incontestable that the enormous ephemeral power of England is principally fed by her commerce, which is formidable, both by the gold she piles up by robbing the whole world, and by the corruption she sows almost everywhere. By destroying England's commerce it is evident that we should be depriving its government of the means of subsidizing Russians, Turks, and Austrians, and corrupting, as it does at home, ——s, and ——s, and ——s (*sic*).

" The most efficacious means—the only one, perhaps, which we possess—of dealing a fatal blow at this fatal commerce is, plainly, privateering—a thing which the vast extent of our coasts and the large

---

[1] These dots are in the text.—G. D.

number of our ports on both seas enable us to do to so great an advantage. What could England's fifty vessels of the line, coursing up and down the ocean at great expense, do against two thousand corsairs which we might easily have equipped at fifty different points, while holding our large war-ships in reserve for a more opportune time? The fable of the lion and the gnat demonstrates most powerfully the excellence of this system. It shows what a single gnat can do against a lion. What, then, could a few large ships, necessarily scattered few and far between, do against a swarm of corsairs? It is clear that on this hypothesis we have all to win and nothing to lose; for England's commerce is everything, while ours is nothing.

"We should, it is true, have lost a few corsairs, but, to make amends, the capture of a few richly loaded ships would have helped to counterbalance the inconveniences resulting from the suspension of commerce. Well, then, what has been done? · In lieu of encouraging ship-owners by all possible means, we have never ceased to discourage them, and unceasingly to parade 'the respect' due to the property of neutrals; and God knows that the neutrals! etc., etc. (*sic*). As if in war it is not sought to do the enemy every possible injury; as if any scruples should be entertained about taking from the enemy what it possesses; as if war, which is in its nature nothing else than murder and theft legitimized, imposed on us the duty of respecting the property of brigands, whose only desire is the annihilation of the Republic!

"There remained a final means of dealing a deathblow at England: the liberation of Ireland, a country which unites with the most ardent desire of being free, or, rather, of being, for no one is who is not free—which unites, we say, with this precious disposition that equally precious, especially for France, of abhorring the English. What have we done to restore liberty to these unfortunate islanders—to give them that liberty which would have supplied us with an implacable enemy against England at her very gates, nay, almost in her bosom? What have we done to make them free?—or, rather, what have we not done to rivet their chains, to ... (*sic*). But here the pen drops from our fingers. It needs a bishop, an *émigré* in England of long standing, the creature of d'Artois, and even more than all that, to explain this horror. We close here the enumeration of the means which might have easily been employed to annihilate our enemies."

The accusers of the old Directorate, collecting in this fashion all the imputations especially concerning our foreign relations, demonstrated by this enumeration, and in the most convincing manner, that incapacity and worse had been displayed in every direction; that everywhere a hand one could not or would not see constantly served in our midst the monstrous coalition of emperors and kings who, in their atrocious fury, have sworn our ruin. Lastly, the accusers said that they had torn to shreds the veil hiding this hand, and revealed it in all its hideous nudity. They found still another connecting link in the fact that to serve Austria and England efficaciously, it was of importance to unite in the hands of one regulator the portfolios of Marine and of Foreign Affairs. "And indeed," they said, "the *émigré* bishop Talleyrand has triumphed over all obstacles; he holds both."

"Yes," they repeated, "the man who is the cause of our ruin is the eternal Bishop of Autun, who, as a *ci-devant* Grand Seigneur, and especially grand charlatan, formerly knew everything without having learned it, since to be an adept at intrigue is not to be learned, and a man can be a clever knave without being literary—this man, who, as a Court bishop, was never able to write except with the pen of his vicar-general (Desrenaudes); this man, who, as an *émigré*, can only desire a counter-revolution; who, as an Anglomaniac in all the parricidal strength of the term, has sworn France's ruin, beginning with her navy and ending with her Constitution. One must be even more stupid than this vile and debauched intriguer is perverse, not to see that the man has had himself made Minister with the sole object of accomplishing the ruin of the Republic. Let the country therefore make an end of this political excrescence, and stifle the counter-revolution at last; and in order that we may not be charged with pointing out evils in every direction without suggesting a remedy we shall," Talleyrand's accusers went on to say, "lay before the *corps législatif* a remedy most simple in itself, but one most decisive in operating good—a remedy in no wise harsh or revolutionary. It is the simple repeal of the law striking the name of the Bishop of Autun off the list of *émigrés;* then will the country be saved; everything will then resume its usual course, and the privileged traitor of the ancient *régime* will cease to be as monstrous a traitor under the present one." Such is pretty nearly a very succinct *résumé* of the indictment drawn up in those days against Talleyrand by the greater part of the Republican journals.

Vigorously pressed as he was, and this daily and more and more by the most determined Republicans, Talleyrand felt that he could not escape the necessity of presenting an explanation of his conduct. This method is, in his system, a most rare proceeding, and one which he has ever used very sparingly. For some days past I had been ill abed. Talleyrand writes to me to beg permission to call on me "in my bed."

> Not seeing you at the Directorate, I wished merely to have news of you. See me for a moment at your bedside.
> Eternal attachment.
> TALLEYRAND.

It was, too, his wont, in what was then the state of my health, to say to me on the preceding day whenever he wanted something: "Permit me to call on you to-morrow, when you are abed." Without my having granted the permission asked for, and although my physician was opposed to my receiving anybody, because of the high fever and fits of sweating that kept me abed, Talleyrand none the less calls on me with a packet or bundle of pamphlets, similar to the one formerly hawked about Toulon by Bonaparte, when he so respectfully and with so much ardor brought us his *Souper de Beaucaire.* Talleyrand, looking quite discomfited, informed me that his enemies, who were only those of the Republic, were strangely calumniating him; that they harried him to this extent for the sole reason that he was attached to liberty and to my person; that if it was sought to get rid of him by killing him morally in the first place, it was for the purpose of then killing him physically; that the object of all these attacks was, in the end, to reach me personally; that he was, with some show of reason, looked upon as a stumbling-block in the path of all the evil designs formed against me; that, all things said and done, nothing frightened him; and that under all circumstances, whether Minister or plain citizen, he would "make me a rampart of his own body."

I replied to Talleyrand that I was most grateful for the sentiments of devotion expressed by him, and for the "rampart" he offered me, but that I did not believe that this was the point at issue; that the first thing to be done was to look after him, since he was the object of the present burst of anger. Talleyrand assured me that all that was engaging his attention was the public weal, and that it was only with that in view that he had composed a pamphlet; that he had brought it to me, feeling confident of my approval, and of my communicating it to my friends.

I had spoken to Talleyrand with the twofold vivacity engendered by my sickness and his importunity. My physician, Dr. Dubourg, a witness of the conversation, thought that my health would suffer were it prolonged; he therefore requested Talleyrand to withdraw, telling him frankly that he had increased my fever. Talleyrand, affecting to be grieved at this to tears, moved closer to my bed, as if to embrace me, begging my forgiveness, and remarking that friendship had no dread of fever; that any friend would be glad to catch another's fever, if only he could cure him thereby. In his manner, of which his little notes, ever respectful, bear the trace, there was so much persistence, so many demonstrations of affectionate sentiments, that one might have been justified in believing that the cynicism of the ex-bishop would not have felt any repugnance at attempting the seductions of another sex, for the purpose of taking its advantages. As for myself, the disgust instilled into me by the kind of purring of the dry and flattering caresses of the "angora" made me preserve all the gravity natural to me, and did not permit his familiarities to reach me. I would not, even in my private Memoirs, stoop to such petty recollections did they not add a few additional characteristic traits to the physiognomy of the courtier.

It has been shown that the idlest of mortals could rise very early, and that the man most phlegmatic in so far as the interests of others were concerned could be most tender and ardent where his personal interests were involved. It will be pointed out to me that this way of feeling and acting is perhaps not altogether confined to Talleyrand, and that it is somewhat common to human nature; that egotism is part of men's natures; that all animal, vegetable, and even mineral organizations have their individuality, which separates them from other species, and even from individuals of their own. I admit, myself, the superiority of the invincible law which is the very nature of all beings, but I will add that in these very laws there is a measure, a natural limit, which is not overstepped by reasonable beings. People will be able to judge hereafter whether Talleyrand has ever considered himself bound by such measure and limits. Without, however, seeking to avenge myself otherwise of all the fatigue inflicted upon me on this occasion by the cynical courtier who was desirous of embracing me as I lay abed and of catching fever, I think I owe it to history, which requires to be informed about certain personages more or less worthy of its notice, to transcribe here a few passages from the pamphlet of Talleyrand—a pamphlet which is interesting by reason of the past, and still more so by reason of the future—in regard to which he was making such fine advances, and contracting such great engagements.

It is undoubtedly a source of encouragement for me to be able to recall, when entering upon this strange justification, with what eagerness, with what joy, I joined the ranks, in 1789, of the first and most sincere friends of liberty. This recollection fills me with a satisfaction of which even the present injustice cannot deprive me. It is true that I should be unworthy of having served so grand a cause were I to presume to consider as a sacrifice what I then did for its triumph. But I may at least be permitted to be surprised at the fact that, after having so justly earned the implacable hatred of the clergy and the *ci-devant* nobility, I should draw upon myself the same feelings of hatred on the part of those styling themselves the bitter enemies of the nobility and clergy, and who nevertheless, when venting their fury against me, seem to be desirous of avenging their destroyed privileges and their overthrown pretensions. Greater still is my astonishment when I discover that these who are so bitter in their hatred, these indefatigable fabricators of the calumnies which the journal entitled *Des Hommes Libres de Tous les Pays* delights in circulating, are nearly all themselves either ex-priests, ex-nobles, or even princes.

What, then, do they say—these men who are not French, or those among the French whose good faith they have succeeded in deceiving? That I have been a member of the Constituent Assembly? Ah! I knew full well that at heart they would never forgive those whose names shine among the founders of liberty. I knew full well that the men who did not experience those first enthusiastic impulses of the French people in 1789; that those who in those days shamefully joined in the cold raillery with which the sublime enthusiasm of the nation was insulted; that, lastly, those who in the Revolution came forward only when they indulged in the hopes that, having failed to ward it off, they might at least succeed in rendering it odious—nourished a secret indignation against the Assembly which first proclaimed the Declaration of the Rights of Man; that they especially showed greater favor to the anti-revolutionary party of this Assembly than to the party which was the cradle of the Revolution.

They say that I am only a *constitutionnel* of 1791, and pretend that I do not offer any pledge against the overthrow of the Republic.

Strange allegation! Even if one refused to see that the men pursued with the greatest fury by the counter-revolutionists of whatever stripe are undoubtedly those who first labored over a constitution in France, since that was the first stride, and an immense one, towards the Republic; even if one would not reflect that the greater number of those who hurl this strange insult at me could reproach themselves, in the event of a counter-revolution, with nothing more than a few utterances which would be most readily condoned; even if, lastly, it would be contrary to truth to say that a patriot of 1789 who did not hesitate to swear allegiance to the Republic, and who repeated his oath on most solemn and decisive occasions, has no mercy to expect from a French government which should not be Republican—it will be incontestable for whosoever shall not have closed his eyes to all light, that in the present state of effervescence of men's minds three suppositions only are possible: Either the Republic will establish itself on a firmer basis amid all these shocks, or we shall be annihilated amid the confusion and destruction of all Powers; or royalty will return to enslave us, with an increase of rage and tyranny. Any other supposition is in my eyes chimerical; and I have beyond doubt given sufficient pledges against the two last-named *régimes*. It is well known what fate the two have in reserve for me, and even the kind of preference they would grant me. It is therefore proven, and proven a thousand times over, that I cannot have any other wish than the consolidation of the glory of the Republic.

It cannot be repeated too often that the true and most certain pledges which can be offered to the Republic consist incontestably in a clearly pronounced love for the liberty which, since 1792, no Frenchman, unless in a state of madness, will seek outside of the Republic; in the open manifestation of this sentiment from the very origin of the Revolution; in the feelings of hatred constantly earned on the part of France's most irreconcilable enemies; in the union of all the kinds of interest and happiness which can attach a man to a *régime* under which he has exercised high functions, and to the glory of a country one has learned to cherish more and more during a three years' absence; in the profound conviction that the Republic which has cost us so much cannot perish except in torrents of blood, that he who would dare to lend his aid to this horrible event would probably be its first victim, and that his name, like that of every traitor, would reach posterity loaded with the weight of general execration; in all the human sentiments which cause one to look with horror upon a universal convulsion wherein would be ingulfed the lives of so many citizens, so many relatives, and so many friends; lastly, in the national honor which should be the life of a Frenchman, and which rouses the soul at the very idea that Russians and Austrians, after having ravaged our country, should insolently come and dictate laws to us. Such are assuredly the most reassuring pledges, and all these, I do not fear to say, I present.

The author of a libellous pamphlet has dared to say that, in the course of what he calls my emigration, I left England to go to America, where, so he alleges, I donned the white cockade. No, I did not leave England, but the English Government ordered me to leave it at twenty-four hours' notice, and in this its hatred conferred on me a most honorable distinction. I went to America, it is true, for I could not feel safe except in a free land; but it is as false as it is absurd to say that I donned the white cockade. So ridiculous an idea could not have even entered my mind. The same absurd story is repeated in regard to my sojourn in Hamburg, on my way back to France. I appeal, in regard to this mendacious allegation, to the testimony of the citizen Reinhart, at that time the envoy of the Republic to Hamburg, and to the citizen Lagau, our consul in that city. Let them say if I was not, like themselves, constantly bedecked with the national colors.

At all events such reproaches, however grave their object may be, are but trifles when compared with those the weight of which it is sought to make me bear. I hasten to say it: were a single one of them founded, I should be the most criminal functionary of the Republic.

The whole of this narration of patriotic deeds of Talleyrand's, all this expense of eloquence, was almost lost—at least, for the time being. Talleyrand's hour had come; he could no longer remain a Minister in view of all he had done and all that was imputed to him. Even if the Directorate wish to retain Talleyrand, it can no longer do so, for the public voice pursues him. Seeing that he must make up his mind to go, he resolves that since he must leave the Ministry he will at least put in his place one of his own creatures—a man whose nullity of character is coupled nevertheless with a certain amount of capacity, who will be considered a mere stop-gap, and who will keep the seat warm for his predecessor. Hence the Directorate, accepting the resignation of Talleyrand, tendered as it has just been seen, appoints in his place the citizen Reinhart, commissary in Switzerland.

Robert Lindet, a former member of the Committee of Public Safety, which intrusted him with the management of the finances and of the food supplies, when he displayed so much probity and capacity, is appointed Minister of Finance in the place of Ramel.

The place of Lambrecht, Minister of Finance, is filled by Cambacérès, an *ex-conventionnel* who, a member of the first Council of Five Hundred, has not joined it since; but, as he has been smitten by the law of the 22d Floréal passed against the assembly of the Oratoire which had elected him, the revolution of the 30th Prairial is bound to consider Cambacérès as one of the victims of the foregoing administration who are entitled to consolation and reinstatement. It is in virtue of this fact that he receives a portfolio.

Thus all the Ministries are regenerated just as the Directorate has been, since the Minister of Police, Bourguignon, has been appointed only since Gohier's entrance into the Directorate, and on that Director's motion. But Bourguignon's place has been greatly coveted, because large benefits are supposed to be attached to this Ministry—in particular, the farming-out of gambling-houses, and so many other good perquisites which morality cannot own, but for which covetousness is ever on the lookout.

Once more does the faithful friend of Fouché, M. Vincent Lombard, come to me one fine morning to lay before me the claims of his beloved candidate in the following strain: "The mission of Fouché in Holland had indeed for its object the compensation of him in a certain measure for the wrong done him by recalling him from Italy; it is doubtless an honorable position, and one suited to a free man like Fouché, sent to a free people; but when all is said and done, this embassy is in fact an exile, for if Fouché can be useful anywhere, it is surely in Paris, where everything converges from all parts of the world; and then, citizen Director, if there is any one truly attached to you, as patriot, as revolutionist, lastly, by an analogy of character and sentiments—any one, in fine, who loves you with his whole heart, is it not Fouché? Where can he better serve the Republic and yourself than in the Ministry of Police? You absolutely need at that post a man wholly yours, to inform you of and defend you against all revolutionary or counter-revolutionary attempts; you cannot have a more able Minister, one who has a better knowledge of men and things since 1789. Fouché has not only been a factor in the Revolution, he has climbed it and broken it upon the wheel, if I may so speak; he is its master; and no one in this world is more capable than he is of presenting all the cleverness and daring which can be desired of a Minister...."

I felt many personal objections to Fouché, and was sure to meet with others from my colleagues—in fact, many more than I entertained myself. For some days did I hesitate bringing up the matter, and I was not desirous that Lombard should again mention it to me. He returns to the charge just as we are discussing with some degree of uneasiness the gatherings of the *Manége* (Riding-School), which now take place in the Rue du Bac, and against which it is impossible not to proceed with vigor. He tells me that Fouché is alone capable of dealing the vigorous blow which will undoubtedly become necessary to save the Directorate from the wickedness of its bitter enemies, disguised under various forms. At each of the sittings of the Directorate fresh denunciations, fresh alarms pour in; there are daily complaints against the incapacity and even the helplessness of the present Minister of Police: he is not able to cope with the increasing disorder; he hardly sees it, can afford no explanation of it, much less repress it. It would seem that Fouché, in his interviews with the Minister Talleyrand on his return from Italy, had succeeded in interesting him in certain respects; he has especially done so by impressing him with the idea that he was on the best of terms with the patriot generals, such as Joubert, Brune, and Championnet. Talleyrand, who always sails with the wind, and believes that Fouché's military connections can very well harmonize with his revolutionary ones, becomes Fouché's protector in Paris, just as he has become that of Victor Hugues in the colonies. He speaks of Fouché to Sieyès, who is prejudiced in more ways than one against his former colleague in the National Convention; but Sieyès is greatly afraid: fear is his ruling passion. Talleyrand, cleverly appealing to this sentiment, says to Sieyès: "At a time when the Jacobins are showing themselves so audacious and so violent against you, none but a Jacobin can fight them vigorously hand to hand, and knock them down. There is no better man for that than Fouché." Sieyès, a fortnight earlier, would have shrunk with horror from such a selection, but now he will no longer be ill-disposed towards Fouché, since Talleyrand has told him that the famous terrorist can alone save him.

Fouché, who had for a long time exercised his faculty for police work (it has been seen how he had been in my service in this capacity), did not cease casting his nets as far as Paris from the Hague, where he had been only a few days; he had, when leaving our capital, borne away with him the hope of being recalled by circumstances. The Ministry of Police was in particular the avowed goal of his ambition. On Vincent Lombard again coming to me to advocate with increased persistence the claims of Fouché, I finally ventured to mention his name before the Directorate, on the day when its members, greatly discontented with the gentle methods which they called the incapacity of Bourguignon, seemed to be agreed that a change was necessary. Great was my astonishment at seeing Sieyès give me his warmest support, and hearing him say: "If we are decided upon selecting this energetic man, we should not adjourn until the matter has been settled. A special messenger must at once be despatched to the Hague to recall and bring back immediately the new Minister of Police." He was thus implying his appointment, which had hardly been mentioned; and, acting in a revolutionary way, *i.e.*, without observing any forms, he declared the appointment made. But his motion required to be supported. Gohier, the creator of Bourguignon, would not suffer that his creature should be touched. "You will never," he remarked, "have a more honest man." "This is not sufficient," came the answer; "your honest man must needs be active and sagacious." In spite of Gohier's opposition, Fouché is appointed Minister of the General Police; and in conformity with the motion made by Sieyès, a special messenger is despatched to the Hague, so that the new Minister may reach Paris without delay.

A few days after Bernadotte's entrance into the Ministry, Sieyès had, I no longer recollect in what connection, brought up the question whether Bonaparte should be recalled from Egypt. I owe it to Bernadotte to record that, without beating about the bush, he bluntly remarked to the man who had started the subject: "It is doubtless the *man* you wish to recall in order that he should fight by our side in Europe; as to General Bonaparte, you know his taste for the dictatorship; now, under the circumstances pressing us, would it not be tendering it to him were we to send ships to bring him back?"

It has been seen how Bonaparte, General-in-chief

of the Army of the Interior after the 13th Vendémiaire, had, in order to have a man devoted to him, sought to have Murat placed in command of the Guard of the Directorate, while from the Army of Italy, in the Year V., he had again made the attempt, which had once more been thwarted. It has been seen also how, immediately after the appointment of Bernadotte, the brothers Bonaparte, following in the steps of their brother the Egyptian, had sought to take possession of the Ministry under his name, by introducing into it a secretary-general of their own. I have named him: it was M. Miot *aîné*, since one of the most shameless servants and adulators of the imperial *régime*. (This M. Miot is not to be confounded with his brother, M. Miot *cadet*, attached to the Army of Egypt, who has written on this expedition a work wherein, especially in the second edition, Bonaparte is appreciated with some political justice.) Having failed in this method of taking possession of the Ministry, the brothers Bonaparte would not let go the prey they thought they had in General Bernadotte by way of their connection by marriage, Bernadotte having married the sister of Joseph's wife. In consequence of and under cover of this alliance, the brothers Bonaparte did not cease worrying Bernadotte, in the first place to obtain from him the placing and promotion of all their creatures, and very soon to make the power of the Minister serve their ulterior projects.

Bernadotte, who lived in the Rue Cisalpine, at the farther end of the Faubourg du Roule, had not given up his residence, which was nothing more than a little cot hardly worth 20,000 francs; but he was attached to it because he had purchased it with the fruits of his military savings. (The smallness of fortunes and moderate requirements are traits depicting the times.) An additional reason for Bernadotte to love his little cot was that his wife had just given birth in it to a child, the only one they ever had, and who is to-day the Prince-Royal of Sweden, heir-presumptive to that Northern Crown.

But while still residing in the Rue Cisalpine, Bernadotte, rising every day at three o'clock, was at the Ministry of War, in the Rue de Varennes, by four o'clock, together with his private secretary, who was at the same time secretary-general to the War Department; the latter lived in the Faubourg Saint-Honoré, and Bernadotte picked him up as he drove past in his carriage. Bernadotte's aides-de-camp who chanced to be in Paris were utilized in an administrative capacity. On entering upon his Ministerial duties, Bernadotte had issued an order that no matter of business should remain not disposed of or at least not examined and replied to beyond twenty-four hours; and he had given such an impulse that this order, which at first sight seems impossible of execution, was rigorously carried out, and everything was daily posted up. Just as he had stated in his proclamations, he had everything to reorganize, to create, as well as 100 battalions of 1000 men each and 40,000 cavalry to raise. After devoting to these operations and his daily reports on them to the Directorate some fifteen or sixteen hours' toil, he would return to the Rue Cisalpine towards seven o'clock, and dine there with his secretary and his aides-de-camp. The Minister could never come home, where his wife was lying-in, without finding there, under the pretext of the health of Mme. Bernadotte, the brothers Bonaparte, or at least Joseph and his wife; while Lucien, intent on another combination, was away in another direction, the greater portion of the time attending anarchist gatherings for the purpose of taking part in them, or at the Directorate, in order to spy upon us, and to give an account of our thoughts and actions to the Sanhedrim of Bonaparte.

Joseph, who during the first days of the installation of Bernadotte as Minister had approached him only in regard to individual interests, soon broached the matter of general interests, then spoke to him about the persons composing the Government, soon of the Government itself in its constitutional principle—at first in regard to the necessity of changing its members, then of " reforming," *i.e.*, "overthrowing the institution itself."

At first Bernadotte acted, perhaps, wrongly in listening too quietly to the insinuations of the Corsican delegate, and discussing the possibility of the various changes. There are sacred things, such as the fundamental law of a country, which you cannot touch without actual danger. But Bernadotte, recently admitted, owing to the course of events, to the most daring discussions justified by these very events, did not think that there were certain questions which might be excepted at least from the domain of private conversation; he seemed, on the contrary, to believe that each and every one might undo a constitution and make it over again: thus he believed that were the number of Directors reduced from five to three, one of whom should retire every five years, the Constitution might endure with this modification. He had an idea that from this combined renewal of magistrates would issue an order of patricians qualified to constitute the administration of the State. Bernadotte was under the impression that he derived this idea from the Roman Constitution, which he had probably looked at in a superficial way, and of the military part of which he was better able to judge than of the civil. He saw in the French Constitution of the Year III. a certain analogy with the consular rights and the rights of the Roman senators. According to Article 135 of the Constitution of the Year III., no one could henceforth aspire to become a Director without having previously been a member of one of the two Councils, or Minister, etc. Now, as Bernadotte already fulfilled one of these conditions, it was natural that he should, from motives of ambition, remain attached to a form of government which had already raised him to a point of elevation which placed him on a footing of equality with crowned heads tributary to or under the protection of the Republic.

The speculative ideas which I here record as enunciated at the time by Bernadotte are those at least to which he has since confessed. While granting that the Béarnais general had in him at that early date great germs of ambition, it would perhaps be crediting him with more than he then possessed to attach to his ideas, and especially to the expression of them, as far reaching a view as the one since developed by events. For I think I am entitled to say, in defence of the men who have since shown themselves most eager in this direction, that not one of them probably harbored the thought of an elevation overstepping the laws of the Republic. Moreover, apart from the principles which the laws and morals of the Republic may have inculcated into them, they had before them, in the matter of ambitious soarings, examples that afforded little encouragement, and attempts which had brought but little luck to those charged with them; nay, who is there among the generals mowed by the revolutionary scythe who can truly be charged with having really sought to break faith with the Revolution? From Lafayette, nowadays so well judged, and who so miraculously survives, down to Custine, Houchard, Biron, and so many others who perished, what is there to prove, I repeat, that any one of these generals was a traitor to the liberty of his country?

Bernadotte was in the habit of seeing me daily at the Directorate, when laying his work before it; he would besides come and talk with me, and confide to me a portion of the things I have just related, minus the ambitious ideas which his exuberant personality did not go so far as to lay bare. His Republicanism seemed to be impressed with the idea that its special mission was to combat the ambition of others. It was with this idea in his brain that he told me one day that Joseph, whom he was beginning strangely to mistrust, had, in a recent confidential talk, spoken to him of the possibility of the return of his brother the Egyptian. Bernadotte informed me that he had preserved sufficient presence of mind to conceal his indignation; but that Joseph, having detected the surprise he could not control, had been alarmed, and had sought to take back what had escaped his lips, and weaken its import by remarking (thus betraying his innermost thoughts) that what he had said was mere conjecture on his part—"a probability" which, he nevertheless confessed, with a certain amount of nonchalance, might some day become a reality; for, "Bonaparte having conquered Egypt," Joseph concluded that "his expedition was terminated, as nothing remained to be done in that direction." Bernadotte said he had replied to Joseph: "Egypt conquered! Say, at most, invaded. This conquest, moreover, if you will insist on so calling it, is far from being assured: it has kindled anew the coalition which was extinct; it has made the whole of Europe our enemy; and has compromised the very existence of the Republic. Besides, your brother has no right to leave the army; he is acquainted with the military laws, and I do not think he would care to incur the penalties laid down by them; such a desertion would be a serious matter; your brother must be aware of the consequences it would entail." Joseph left a few minutes afterwards, seemingly regretting a conversation in the course of which he had betrayed himself, although he had derived from it the advantage of ascertaining Bernadotte's sentiments in the matter; it likewise taught him that, in view of the Béarnais's character, it was not so easy to win him over to his side as he had expected. According to the explanation Bernadotte gave me of matters, he seemed to think that even at this early date Joseph Bonaparte was acting in connection with Sieyès, who, he believed, had commissioned him to feel the ground. Bernadotte said that on leaving him Joseph had gone to Sieyès to report, and that this Director, before whom all this had been laid with both simulation and dissimulation, had there and then conceived a dislike for Bernadotte; that his ill-humor, born of this beginning, had incidentally been increased by everything connected with it which presented Bernadotte as an absolute Republican, unwilling to listen to any agreement having for its object the modification of the persons and institutions established by the Constitution of the Year III. Bernadotte was impressed with the belief that he had discerned and recognized in several conversations held with Sieyès that the idea of a great innovation in, or at least a certain revision of, the Constitution of the Year III. was already then a combination, a hope, and a fixed determination in the mind of Sieyès.

Fouché has received Sieyès's messenger at the Hague, reinforced by one from Vincent Lombard; he does not come post-haste, but flies: he is with us on the fourth day dating from his appointment. He had at once set out on his journey, which goes to prove that he had some expectation of leaving for such a destination. He had slept neither day nor night, and came to "place his respectful devotion at the feet of the Directorate."

When one has for some length of time exercised a great power, notably the one which confers offices representing fortune itself, he acquires little by little an experience enabling him to become quickly acquainted with and to judge the ruses of the men who seek to attain a particular goal. The best known and yet the most common and most frequently used consists in resorting to actions altogether contrary to the thoughts that it is really meant to express. Thus the majority of men asking for places begin by speaking of retirement, modesty, and disinterestedness. I had seen so much of these methods that I generally expected them, and instead of causing me any great surprise, they merely provoked my amused contempt; but however much one may be on one's guard, by dint of expecting such things to occur, there nevertheless crop up unforeseen novelties. In support of this, I must here record an anecdote which is recalled to me by a letter, which I came across while writing these Memoirs, from a person who has since those days played a most active part. I had been acquainted with Réal of old in the revolutionary days: it was at the very time when he was public prosecutor to the extraordinary criminal tribunal instituted in Paris on the 10th of August; next he was deputy-attorney to the Commune, which took the place of the tribunal of the 10th of August. In spite of his deeds, anything but equivocal in a revolutionary sense, Réal had not been considered as pronounced as it was required to be in those days; having one fine day had the misfortune to run counter to Robespierre, he had been on the point of paying with his head for this act of opposition; cast into prison previous to the 9th Thermidor, he owed his life to that day of deliverance. He had, by means of witty and reasonably patriotic political writings, seconded the movement of the 9th Thermidor, without, however, advocating reaction—nay, having even sincerely done his best to prevent any excesses resulting therefrom. I had employed Réal when intrusted with the provisioning of Paris between the 9th Thermidor and the 13th Vendémiaire. He was without employment, and stood in great need of it. I had been satisfied with his services. He had displayed activity and intelligence on the 13th Vendémiaire. I had noticed him in the ranks of the "sacred battalion" of patriots, who have been styled "terrorists"; and he had shown all the courage that can be expected of a lawyer—that of having a well-oiled tongue which exhorted others while its owner kept out of the fight. Since then, having taken up his pen to tell the story of the battle, he had written an historical account of the 13th Vendémiaire and of what had led up to it—an account which I cannot praise without being suspected of some partiality, since Réal had to a great extent based his work on his conversations with me, which conversations he styled excellent notes. My readers may well believe that I did not furnish those wherein he is so prodigal of compliments towards me; it is true that while he was preparing his history I had become a member of the Directorate, and I admit that Réal probably addressed his amiable phrases rather to the Director than to the individual. At all events, treated better than any one else by the historian of the 13th Vendémiaire, I had tried more than once to make my colleagues sharers of my gratitude; but I had never been able to obtain for Réal anything more than an order for politico-literary work. He had given great satisfaction, and had been well paid, as things went in those days. I had since then attempted to procure him an administrative or judicial position; but on the one hand he was pursued by the personal enmity of Merlin, who reproached him with having defended a famous Belgian called Tort de la Sonde, against whom Merlin entertained a personal spite (and Merlin's hatreds were not of the kind which are ever smothered); on the other, my colleagues reproached Réal with not being sufficiently serious, and with unceasingly indulging in puns and buffoonery. Rew-

bell and Larevellière were in the habit of saying:
" It is impossible to place at the head of affairs and
put prominently before the public a punster and inveterate joker." Réal, whose lack of success did not
diminish what he called his gratitude towards me,
had not ceased coming to the Luxembourg, and he
was among those who generally paid me a visit in
the evening. Just as the fresh commotion breaks
out between the *corps législatif* and the Directorate,
I suddenly receive the following letter:

PARIS, 8*th Thermidor, Year VII.*
Réal, counsel appointed by Court, to the citizen Barras.

It is with a feeling of confidence that I recall myself to your recollection, and, I venture to say, your friendship.

I had, for some time past, become an entire stranger to public affairs, and returned to my old profession. I had devoted my time to pleadings, I had just returned from the country, when two of my friends spoke fo me of a fresh anarchist conspiracy, informing me that I was designated as one of the chiefs of this new conspiracy. My first impulse was one of contempt, and an involuntary smile rose to my lips; but this very morning a third friend has spoken to me of these same rumors, and assured me that I was truly one of the chiefs of the conspiracy which is to overthrow the Directorate, the Councils, etc.

It is difficult for me to believe in conspiracies, and I become incredulous when calumny makes me their chief or agent; but, instructed by experience, I cannot afford to neglect such rumors.

I declare that especially since the elections, nettled in an equal degree against the exclusive honest folk who have styled me a terrorist, and the exclusive patriots who have excommunicated me as a Chouan, I see neither the one nor the other. Surrounded by pleaders, I besiege the bar, and I try to make a living and sufficient money wherewith to pay my impatient creditors, lifting up my hands like Moses, and forming wishes like a hermit who has detached himself from a world which tires and bores him.

Such is the only conspiracy which absorbs every moment of my life.

In the name of the sacrifices I have made, in the name of the few totally disinterested services I have rendered, in the name even of the strange abnegation in which I live, have I not the right to hope for rest or oblivion?

Of you, citizen Director, of you who must know and esteem me, I beg tranquillity. These denunciations, the species of consistency given to them, are, I venture to say, a public calamity. Let my denouncer be arrested; let me be brought face to face with him; and if I do not at once prove that these underhand practices are the fruit of the most detestable intrigue, let me be condemned.

I would fain believe that these rumors have no consistency, and that you will laugh at my crazy fears; but, in view of what was said at the time of the elections, I have cause to dread the worst.

I am to-day what I was in those days, and you will do to-day what you did then: you will render me justice, and secure me the only thing I ask—tranquillity. Greeting and respect.

RÉAL.

This letter contained several peculiar statements at which I was entitled to be surprised. In the first place, there was nothing in the actual political movements likely to draw attention to Réal more particularly than to any one else. Besides, Réal was one of the men who were most assiduous and regular in paying me court; he never missed one of my Directorial *soirées*, and since his return from Vendôme, where he had defended the Babouvists, we had not heard of any special accusation against him. Why, then, did he come and defend himself against one which did not exist? Why speak with such ostentation of his determination to lead a retired life, and of the new projects of his modest labors? There is in this something which looks neither frank nor spontaneous, and which is necessarily connected with some particular desire. I considered that I did not owe any answer to Réal's letter, because I really did not think he was in danger; but had he been, I should certainly have answered his expectations by defending him with all my heart.

Now, while Réal's letter is still quite fresh, I receive a visit from a lady with whom we were both personally acquainted, Mlle. or Mme. V. de Châtenay—for, as a canoness, she was entitled to be "damed." Mme. V. de Châtenay was a woman of great wit, and still greater erudition—a regular reinforced Benedictine. She had made her mark in literature with several translations of English novels, notably with that of Goldsmith's *Deserted Village*—a little work of a few pages, very small in volume, but full of sentiment, and alone sufficient to make the reputation of a writer. Mme. V. de Châtenay was the author of *Le Génie des Peuples Anciens*, a work of her own no doubt, if we may so call a book which has been made from so many other books—a kind of review of the progress of the human mind, but which did not wipe out the recollection of the picture drawn by Condorcet.

Mme. de Châtenay was accustomed to speak with perfect frankness; she was so authorized by her position, by the family duties she had undertaken, and which she had fulfilled with much moderation and ability. She was so openly on an intimate footing with Réal as to enable her, without further consequences, to confess that she took a lively interest in him. So she came, following close upon Réal's letter of retirement, in the first place to confirm its contents and to laud the simple tastes of her friend. Then, without any transition, she told me that it would be better, for him and for the Republic, if Réal would consent to re-enter public life; and thereupon she informed me that she knew the Directorate's present commissary in the department of the Seine could not fail to be removed shortly, as many changes were about to be made in the administration of the department. Réal, she repeated, had no ambition; but since a certain course was about to be adopted in regard to the administrators of the department belonging to the old Directorate, could anything be better than to give the most important place, that which was to exercise supervision over the others, "to our friend Réal"? She said "our friend," and did not hesitate to say so on her own account, because Réal had shown her much kindness in troublous times, and then, over and above all, because he was personally attached to me, because he would lay down his life for me. Such are always the methods employed by those who seek positions towards those who give them. It will be seen hereafter how long these feelings of attachment endure. A consideration based on fact, which Mlle. de Châtenay further pointed out to me, was that Réal, who had so much wit, knowledge, and capacity of every kind, and who was entitled to the highest positions, had been constantly deprived of them by the hatred of one man; this man was Merlin de Douai, who had got his deserts on the 30th Prairial. The reason why Merlin had borne such ill-will towards Réal, said his lady patron, was that Réal, in a lawsuit in which he had defended one Tort de la Sonde, a Belgian, a few years previously, had almost caught Merlin red-handed in an act detrimental to his reputation for honesty. This is what Merlin had never forgiven Réal; but now that Merlin had been found out to be the wickedest of men, it was not right that his victims should suffer from his animosity; nor should a revolution which had meted out his deserts to so perverse an individual be suffered to perish: men should now be called to office whose interest it was to prevent the return of Merlins and maintain the revolution of the 30th Prairial.

Mme. de Châtenay, who had good grounds for so speaking, added with vehemence: "You, Barras, to whom France is indebted for the finest features of the Revolution, and who are the father of the most distinguished citizens and soldiers of whom our country is proud—for, indeed, is it not you who have made Bonaparte, Hoche, Talleyrand, Fouché, and so many others who owe you fortune, honors, rank, and fame? I do not pledge myself in regard to those whom I do not particularly know, but I do pledge myself in so far as Réal is concerned. I swear it to you on my faith, Barras; it is possible that, among those whose names I have just recalled, some outweigh Réal in brilliant military or diplomatic deeds; but none of them—I challenge all, even the first of them—surpass, nay, equal Réal in the matter of devotion, generosity of heart, and sublime patriotism."

Somewhat moved by this harangue, I was saying to myself with a certain feeling of pride, yet not devoid of perturbation: "It is true that it is I who have produced Bonaparte, Talleyrand, and so many others!" But while admitting a fact to the credit for which I was really entitled, I was not sure, when reflecting over many circumstances which sprang to my mind, whether I had acted so wisely after all. Unable as I was to deny the importance which the personages just referred to had assumed in public affairs, their own betrayal of their innermost character filled my soul with an ill-defined and unexplained uneasiness agitating it in a singular fashion. We sometimes have these secret presentiments, the results of many traits we have not taken the trouble to consider in their *ensemble*, and which would quickly dissuade us from the resolutions we take against our own instincts, and which we seize as if in spite of ourselves.

Independently of the kindly feeling with which Réal's eloquent patroness may have inspired me, I felt towards him an interest based on his presumed gratitude for the services I had rendered him at different times, and a sincere desire to console him for the persecutions he had suffered as the result of Merlin's hatred. I promise Mme. V. de Châtenay to propose Réal to the Directorate as commissary in the department of the Seine. I keep my word: Réal is appointed. Here is one more actor whom I have put on the stage; later on will be seen the part or parts he will play in the drama the performance of which is fast approaching. Without desiring to anticipate a judgment of the individuals who will in turns flit by in it, or of characterizing them otherwise than by their sayings and doings, I cannot refrain from here making an observation which drops from my pen, forcibly recalled by the primary causes which have connected the beginnings of several large fortunes with my protection. The principal personages, who but a short while ago appeared so very low, and who will be placed so high by the course of events—with the exception of General Hoche, who pushed his way by the sole strength

of his merit and the ascendency of his genius—all
ingratiated themselves with those in authority by
means of members of the fair sex. Thus, as a first
example, Bonaparte. We have seen his first intrigues as early as the Year II., when the vile courtier of the wife of the representative Ricord, in order
to maintain himself and secure promotion; we have
seen his manœuvres with Josephine and his marriage,
in order to obtain the chief command of the Army
of Italy. To pass to Talleyrand. It has been seen
how he was supported and his interests furthered
by Mme. de Staël. We now see Réal, in a secondary sphere, pushed forward by the same means. It
cannot be said that these gentlemen owed the devotion of the ladies to the fineness of their physique;
all, including Bonaparte himself, whose celebrity has
since created his physiognomy, and caused it to be
proclaimed magnificent and either Greek or Roman
—all these gentlemen, I say once more, with the exception of Hoche, the only one who did not have
recourse to such means, were certainly not the peers
of Antinous. I have here to record a still more
melancholy reflection in regard to their conduct: it
is that after having made use of women in the interests of their ambition, they rivalled one another in
ingratitude; having squeezed the lemon, they threw
away the peel. I do not refer to Réal, for posterity
will not busy itself with the results of his *liaison*
with Mme. V. de Châtenay. But it has been seen
how Bonaparte divorced the woman to whom he
had sworn eternal fidelity at the altar, and on the
very day of his coronation. In the case of Talleyrand—legally married to Mme. Grand when he
believed this union useful to his position, then sepa-

rated from her when he considered he no longer needed her—it was merely vulgar ingratitude, which goes hand in hand with all the worries and mortifications of his every-day life; but his ingratitude towards Mme. de Staël did not end with negligence and forgetfulness. From all that she told me herself when I saw her once more in 1814, she entertained no doubts that Talleyrand had been the moving spirit in the persecution she had endured. "I was unbearable to him," she said to me with a laugh, "as Agrippina was to Nero; and yet I was not quite his mother, at least in years," added this superior woman, who yet always let her sex appear, and wished it to appear. "I had literally given him bread, my dear Barras, previous to the time when you made a Minister of him on my recommendation. What did I not do for him? Just recall to your mind how I importuned you on his behalf. In spite of all this, had it been in his power to treat me as Nero did Agrippina, if he had been able to drown me by means of a boat with a trap like that of Anicetus, he would have done so, nay, he would do so still; and why? Because I gave him bread and made him a Minister."

There is no need, when seeing the shameful ingratitude towards women of these notable intriguers who made their fortunes through them, of being told that their relations in this connection partook more of calculation than of sentiment; indeed, can such calculating spirits ever have loved? They had judged beforehand all the devotion of which women who believe themselves loved are capable; they found therein a powerful resource wherewith to attain their object. I will add, as a supplement to their talents in the way of perfidy, that while women's delicacy of feeling delivers over this kind of speculation to beings vile enough to abuse it, perhaps the difficulties attendant upon their intercourse with men, the compulsory restraint of their sentiments, make it necessary to their position that they should have recourse to shrewdness and craftiness, the exercising of which for the benefit of their lovers still further develops in these latter the dispositions they already have from nature. Mme. de Staël was doubtless full of her subject, when in one of her works, entitled *De la Littérature Considérée dans ses Rapports avec les Institutions Sociales*, she says: " It is, so to speak, the negative vices, those composed of the absence of qualities, which need attacking. We must point out certain forms behind which so many men conceal themselves, in order to be personal in peace and perfidious with decency."

As for myself, who have as much as any other man been exposed to all the attractiveness belonging to intercourse with women, I confess I may have sought in it rather the pleasures of the senses than the immaterial joys of the ideal; but I feel sure that no spirit of calculation ever entered into any *liaison* I may have had. When believing that I loved women for their own sakes, it is possible that I may have loved them somewhat for my own; but I have not to reproach myself with having thought of making them the instruments of my ambition or of my interest; this never entered my mind, for it would have seemed to me a base action. In all political and private circumstances, I believed that the man who knows his own dignity must get on in the world by his own resources and his personal strength.

At the same time that we appointed Réal commissary to the department of the Seine, we gave the place of commissary to the *bureau central* (since the Prefecture of Police) to the citizen Lemaire, a former professor of the University of Paris, a man of wit and of business capacity, although he had been principally devoted to the cultivation of literature, while deeply attached to the principles of the Revolution; it was he who, after having weathered many acts of injustice and political intrigues, a well-equipped student of antiquity, brought out a magnificent edition of Latin classics, and became the Dean of the Faculty of Letters of Paris. Réal, as commissary to the department of the Seine, presented to us the commissary of the *bureau central*, and, introducing Lemaire to me, said: "Citizen Director, the Directorate has sometimes been charged with having appointed to public positions incapable men who paraded their profound devotion; I venture to assert that in the matter of devotion we can stand comparison with anybody; as regards capacity, permit me not to pass judgment on myself; but I can assure you that of the two individuals now in your presence, one at least is possessed of wit." I invited the two commissaries to dinner; both showed themselves most amiable and charming; I soon discovered that Réal's jest came from modesty, and that both commissaries were undoubtedly men of wit.

But the liveliness and intermixing of these recollections cause me to anticipate too quickly and too far ahead the sequel of my Memoirs. Enough of the Réal episode; events are on the gallop and do not suffer any further digression.

CHAPTER XIII

Affairs in Germany—Orders given to the Franco-Spanish squadron—Fresh demagogic clubs—The *Société du Manége*—Joseph and Lucien Bonaparte alter their tone—I send for Lucien; my reprimand; his pantomime; Joseph's attitude; his answer; was he a representative of the people?—Eyes turned towards Egypt—Visit of Joseph and Lucien to Mme. Bonaparte—Their sally against me—Demagogic exactions in regard to the Directorial habiliments—Fouché's universal science—Project of transportation—Astonishment of the Directorate—The seesaw—Projected measure against the Jacobins—The *Manége* closed—Tissot's harangue against the employés—Félix Lepelletier's projected address—Fouché's ideas—Fresh accusations against Merlin and Larevellière—Siméon; his obsequiousness—Siméon to be transported—I protect him—Siméon's revolutionary principles—An anti-Bourbon speech—Siméon under Bonaparte and under Louis XVIII.—The Portalis—Siméon's letter and memorandum on transportation—I lay them before the Directorate—His petition is rejected—Fouché and Sieyès—The transported priests at Rochefort—They appeal to me—Sieyès takes their request for an epigram—How it is received—Petition of the transported priests.

Thermidor, Year VII.—We are again informed that the King of Prussia is preparing to attack us, "should our reverses continue." The Army of Helvetia still remains in a state of inaction, thus enabling Prince Charles to pour troops on the Lower Rhine. It is to be feared that he may direct a portion of them on Mannheim, and thus, acting in concert with the English who are to land in Belgium, cross the Rhine. It is two months since I proposed to detach 15,000 men from the

Army of Helvetia; had this been done, Turin would have been ours. It is now necessary to send troops on the Rhine; I make a special motion to that effect. If Masséna still persists in his assertion that he cannot act in Helvetia, he will be sent on the Lower Rhine, where 35,000 men will at least be able to arrest the march of the enemy.

The Directorate had ordered the Franco-Spanish squadron to leave Cadiz and proceed to Brest; it has gone thither, without rallying the ships at Rochefort. Orders are given to Admiral Bruix to go and take them, and fight the enemy if it is still on station.

Demagogy, incited and fomented by the brothers Bonaparte, did not consider it possessed sufficient power in the Legislative Councils, and required reinforcements from the outside. Lucien and Joseph Bonaparte were the first to solicit such reinforcements from the faubourgs themselves. This portion of the population, so full of life in the early days of the Revolution, had met with such painful disappointments that it had for some time past inclined towards quiescence; and although it was not a fact, as has been stated since, that the people had given in their resignation (for never have those who do not possess anything on earth resigned in favor of those possessing everything), it is nevertheless true that, considering the actual condition of the lower classes of the nation, it was impossible to set them in motion without great efforts. The instigators had therefore thought they could not do better, as a compensation for the loss of the dispersed people, than to form new clubs; such had been the object of the formation of the *Société du Manége*.

The brothers Bonaparte, Joseph and Lucien, who

were inciting to all excesses in secret and even in public, seemed already to discover, amid existing circumstances, the right to assume an entirely different tone from the one hitherto assumed towards the Directorate. Formerly they had unceasingly worried and fatigued us collectively and individually with all sorts of requests for themselves, their relations, and their friends, and these requests were invariably for money; nowadays they considered themselves entitled to assume the tone of their new position, Bonaparte having left them with a considerable amount of funds to enable them to live in opulent style, and to receive all the intriguers who might co-operate in their designs. These Corsicans, who were a short while ago humble and beggarly petitioners, now set up for lords of high degree; and their lordships, as yet unable to soar on their own pinions, made use of the name of the *corps législatif*, claiming that their insolence duly represented its sentiments. They incessantly called —now in the name of committees of the Councils, again in the name of the Councils as a whole—both on the Ministers and on the Directorate; on one occasion a threat against us escaped them of their "brother, the General"!

As for myself, irritated by or rather indignant at this disturbing and vulgar conduct of Lucien, I considered that the many services I had rendered him and his family conferred on me the right to show him some severity on this occasion, so I summoned him and his brother Joseph into my presence. When specially commending both of them to me at the time of his departure for Egypt, Bonaparte had said to me in the most positive fashion that "it is necessary to keep a tight bit-rein on that worthless scamp Lucien, who since leaving Corsica has given us so much trouble." On his coming into my presence, I could not help telling him in strong terms how much his present conduct inspired me with discontent. I pointed out to him that it may have been necessary for him to be young and ardent like the Revolution in 1793, but that it was time to become staid and wise like her; that the *régime* of excesses was a thing of the past; that it was impossible to return to it; that I thought he, Lucien, had sowed all his revolutionary wild oats when entering the *corps législatif;* and that he might have done himself credit in that assembly. As for me, I thought that he would have seized the opportunity to cause to be forgotten the keeper of stores of Saint-Maximin, the spoliator of the goods of the Republic, the plundering commissary of war, the insensate speechifier in the clubs of the South; that his whole past might be excused and condoned by his good behavior; but were he to continue, I should have something to say to it, and should unmask him; that he would in vain invoke the authority of his brother; that the military services of this brother were one thing, and could never constitute for him the right to embezzle at home and disturb the Republic.

Joseph, a witness of all I said to his brother, gave me, in his pantomime, the measure of his character. Hat in hand, and in the most respectful attitude, he seemed to try and meet my gaze, in order to give to my words the humblest adhesion; he even muttered something to the effect that "it was indeed necessary to be wise," moderate, and not give way to one's passions. While speaking thus, I noticed that he nudged Lucien with an air of connivance; I saw him also step on his foot, in order to make himself better understood, and impose on him the silence of policy.

The tribune Lucien, that fecund speechifier, remained as if changed into stone by my words, which seemed to have a Medusa-like effect on him, and he withdrew with humbled and bowed head, saying: " Citizen Director, I am fully cognizant of the interest you have always shown towards me and my family; I shall endeavor not to be unworthy of your kindness, but I have my duties to perform as a legislator, as representative of the people. The people are there! . . ." He repeated the word " people " with an accent more sonorous than had ever been heard at the saturnalia of Saint-Maximin. " I respect the people as much as you do, and with more sincerity," I replied; " in my present position I consider myself equally a representative of the people, for it is the people who have delegated to me the supreme magistracy, and all functionaries, from the highest to the lowest, are the creatures of the people, and cannot lose sight of this source; but, citizen Lucien, a most important question might be to know in the first place whether you are a representative of the people. The official report of your election is said to contain several flaws, and even forgeries, with which you, Lucien, are accused. From an excess of consideration for your brother, and owing to the gravity of a matter so greatly compromising you, I took upon myself to prevent its being followed up; in so doing I doubtless did wrong, for it might have seemed a connivance on my part; beware of making it necessary for me to give an explanation of the affair, and think that the best thing for you to do is to remain quiet." Lucien sought to reply, and once more use the word "people," which he repeatedly bawled out. "Be silent," I said to him. "When one loves the people, one should render one's self worthy of loving them by not deceiving them, as you do; I will show you up to the people themselves if you persist in not understanding me."

Joseph, seeing that I was getting more and more excited, led his brother Lucien away, renewing his apologies and tendering "the homage of his respectful gratitude for all that I had done for his family and himself, who was proud to have received at my hands his first and his last position." He asked me with a great show of emotion "if we had news from Egypt." When witnessing the glory of his brother and his brilliant position, he could not overlook the fact that it was to me that he owed it; never would he forget it. "And you," I said to him, "do you not write to him? Have you no direct news from him?" Joseph and Lucien were one in asserting to me that "they had no news of the General except through the Directorate."

I learned that on leaving me the two brothers had, contrary to their habits, called on their sister-in-law, Mme. Bonaparte, whom they very seldom saw, and with whom they were always wrangling. They inquired of her "whether she had more recent news from Egypt than their own." She had none, and for a very simple reason—to wit, that, receiving her letters almost always under cover to them, they took good care not to deliver them to her, and suffered her to receive only what suited them. Thereupon they plied her with questions in regard to her former relations with me, as to what remained of them, and as to the manner in which she corresponded with her husband. Whenever she should wish to write to him, they were ready to see that her letters reached him; just at present they had several opportunities of forwarding correspondence." These opportunities consisted in little vessels which they secretly and frequently despatched to Egypt, and not a week passed without their supplying the General of the Army of Egypt with information as to what was taking place in Paris.

Mme. Bonaparte called on me next day, and informed me that the two brothers had begged her to remain silent as to their conversation, in the course of which they had indulged in diatribes against me. The sickly-sweet and wheedling Joseph had been as outspoken as the impetuous Lucien, and the two Corsican brothers had gone as far as to say that I "deserved to be *killed;* that it was absolutely necessary to get rid of me in one way or another; that this would be a good way of opening the doors of the Directorate; that it was I who had prevented the General from entering on account of his age; that it was absurd, abominable, etc.; that I should pay for it!"

Meanwhile the Bonapartist machinations were already bearing their first fruits. After having troubled themselves about individuals by bringing about their expulsion, the plotters soon turned their attention to things; in order to attack the institution, ere long they began to attack the very forms and habiliments of the Directorial magistracy. Thus the demagogues who thought themselves merely democrats made the discovery that the splendor of the Directorial costumes constituted not only a violation of equality, but a pernicious attempt to warp the ideas of the masses, more accustomed to be influenced by sentiment than by reason. Thus, they argued, "this extreme magnificence," as they styled it, had evidently been imagined merely to enable us to enter into intimate and special relations with our enemies by subjecting ourselves to the ways of foreign governments, whose custom was to prefer splendor to simplicity and wealth to virtue. We were accused of having feared to frighten them away with a too Republican simplicity. Happily, they went on to say, the Constitution does not prescribe anything in regard to the amount of gold braid to be used in the making of a Directorial mantle. This was a short and quick way of reaching the conclusion that one could first deprive the Directorate of its habiliments, and then overthrow it; for, without attaching to men's habiliments any greater importance than they deserve, it is nevertheless certain that the regard attached to functionaries is composed of an *ensemble* which cannot be meddled with, even partially, without the whole of it quickly being affected. Attack a private individual in his dress, dress him, undress him to dress him again, whichever way you do it, is it not equivalent to treating him as a child, as a puppet? Thus did demagogic exactions multiply, and, from all I learned from various quarters, there were no malevolent designs, no anarchistic projects of subversion, which could not be traced to the active instigation of the brothers Bonaparte.

The moment Fouché had taken hold of the Ministry of Police, all disorders were of course to cease immediately. So Talleyrand had assured Sieyès, with the result of having him precipitately appointed. The Directorate, Talleyrand had said, could not fail to be at once tranquillized and at ease. We are far from being so. Well, at least we are to see this famous police genius, on whom one has so greatly reckoned, at work.

The first sitting at which Fouché makes his appearance is spent in respectful salutations, and promises of boundless devotion to the Directorate. At the second sitting at which he appears, he has as yet hardly had the time to become acquainted with the affairs of his department. Sieyès calls upon him to make a report on the state of France, and in the first place of Paris, which is the hot-bed of all agitation, and where dreadful plots are being hatched at the present time. Far from being annoyed at so abrupt a question, Fouché replies that he "knows everything, and that he undertakes fully to deserve the confidence the Directorate has placed in him by guarding against everything; but there is a time for all things: the Directorate shall not have to wait longer than the next day, when he will lay before it the most satisfactory measures, fitted to put an end to everything."

On the following day, at the opening of the sitting, Fouché enters with a self-satisfied air, and says: "Citizen Directors, I am sure that I am not behindhand in carrying out your orders; I shall begin by asking you to make the following enactment: 'The under-mentioned citizens, who have not bowed to the decree of transportation pronounced against them on the 18th Fructidor, Year V., are assimilated with the *émigrés:* Bayard, Bornes, Cadroy, Couchery, Delahaye, Duplantier, Henri Larivière, Camille Jordan, Jourdan (André-Joseph), Imbert-Colomès, Lacarrière, Lemerer, Mersan, Madier, André de la Lozère, Marc-Curtain, Pavie, Pastoret, Polissard, Paire, Montaut, Quamère-Quincy, Saladin, Viennot-Vaublanc, Vauvilliers, Dumas-Ferrant, Vaillant, Portalis, Blin, Carnot, Miranda, Suard, and Morgand.'"

On hearing this rolling-off of names of *fructidorisés* we all looked at one another in astonishment, seeking to recall to our memory whether we had asked anything approaching this of Fouché; and, as not one of us could remember anything of the kind, Sieyès, more astonished than all the members of the Directorate put together, addressed Fouché in the following terms: "Citizen Fouché, this is not what the Directorate has asked of you. You come and take up our time with the *fructidorisés*, who are to all intents and purposes dead, and you do not tell us a word about the Jacobins, who are unfortunately very much alive, and far too alive for the public peace." Fouché replies in the most imposing tone: "Citizen Director, so sincere was my intention of realizing your views—and I thought I was surely doing so—that I have not seen fit to prefix to my proposed enactment any report or preamble. Since you call for an explanation, I shall have the honor of supplying it to you. You are desirous of repressing the Jacobins, the ultra-revolutionists who are now engaged in attacking us through their clubs, which are again springing up. I am just as convinced as anybody else of this necessity; but if we wished to assail the enemy in front, it is doubtful whether we should succeed; we must therefore turn the position; to put it plainly, we must maintain our popularity before engaging in a struggle with the Jacobins, and make a distinction between agitators and true patriots. In order to do this it is, above all things, necessary to first strike a blow at the Royalists. All Jacobins will agree with us on this point; then, on the following day, we can fall upon the Jacobins themselves."

25th Thermidor, Year VII.—Sieyès inquires what Fouché means by "the following day." Is it a week or a fortnight? Fouché replies that he intends it shall be "to-morrow itself, the 26th Thermidor," since to-day is the 25th. This is assuredly coming to the point as quickly as possible.

And, indeed, Fouché brings us on the following day the draft of an enactment ordaining the closing of the political society of the *Manége*, which has met in the church of the Jacobins, in the Rue du Bac, ever since, pursuant to an order of the committee of inspectors of the Council of Ancients, they had been compelled to leave the *Salle du Manége* (Riding-School). The proposed enactment is adopted. Fouché asks that it be immediately despatched to General Lagarde; he carries it away with him, and vows that the orders of the Directorate shall be carried out at once.

This somewhat tranquillizes Sieyès. On the following day Fouché, on appearing at the sitting of the Directorate, says to us: "Citizen Directors, your orders have been executed: the *Manége* of the Rue du Bac is closed, never to open again." He had proceeded with this closing just as Tissot was warmly perorating on the purging of employés, eloquently remarking that "as for himself, he was a citizen first and an employé afterwards!" At the same moment Félix Lepelletier was presenting the draft of an address, the principal propositions of which were to instil anew a democratic spirit into the Government, to assure the security and freedom of political societies, to make the rich bear the hazards of war, to create a general federation, etc. " Now," Fouché went on to say, " I beg your permission, in order to consolidate this operation, to do everything to cause it to be regarded as mild and conciliatory; it is necessary to console that portion of the patriots which may feel aggrieved, irritated even; it must be proclaimed that the Royalists would be strangely deluded were they to detect in it any advantage for themselves; that the Directorate is essentially Republican, that it goes hand in hand with the Republicans, and will never part company with them." " That's right," remarked Sieyès; "gild the pill for them, but make them swallow it, and let us no longer be exposed to plots the object of which is to alarm all good citizens. France has now been in a state of revolution for over ten years, and needs tranquillity. To deny it to her would be to mistake the state of things, and to expose ourselves to a violent reaction." Fouché withdraws with an air of self-confidence, not to say patronage. He seems to assume a higher tone in proportion as he thinks he can discern that the Government is disunited, falling into disrepute, and consequently growing weaker and weaker.

In spite of the positive refusal that I have returned to the deputies who have approached me on the subject of taking up the indictment against the ex-Directors Merlin and Larevellière, the idea is in no wise given up; there are men in the Council of Five Hundred to whom troubled waters are a necessity. Lucien Bonaparte is forever at their head. Fortunately the ballot disposes of this relentless motion, which is rejected by a large majority. Next day it is a fresh project: the Council of Five Hundred appoints a committee of its members which is to submit to it measures for the public safety. Ah! the first measure of public safety would be the sincere union of the authorities into whose hands the Republic believes it has committed the care of its defence!

I had seen a great deal of Siméon ever since the installation of the Directorate, when in the Year IV., almost up to the period of the 18th Fructidor, he was in the habit of coming to me to ask for places for some one or other of his friends. His letters and conversation had always agreed in telling me, adroitly and under the most agreeable forms, that it was most desirable that all functionaries should become united by a mutual interchange of services, as they undoubtedly were united as to principles, although they did not appear to proclaim it. When one has been born in a province, in which he has also spent a number of years, he is accessible to many recollections attached to his early existence. Those of my compatriots who knock at this door are not mistaken, believing that it will be opened to them, and that they can touch a chord which finds an echo in my heart. The Provençal Siméon had therefore successfully and repeatedly appealed to me in the matter of several personal requests. It had afforded me pleasure to grant them, and he had made a delicate use of this kind of compatriot's privilege. A native of Provence, he would approach me with the accent of our country, supplementing it with a few words of the familiar patois; this always had the desired effect. This is how we stood: sincerity on my part, and on that of Siméon an apparent cordiality, which at the same time he expressed in most respectful language.

I have mentioned Siméon as one of the deputies who, previous to the 18th Fructidor, had called on me, so they said, with intentions of peace and conciliation. I do not like to believe that a man is false enough to follow two different lines of conduct. I would therefore fain believe that M. Siméon really desired what he told me, to the effect that " the legal authority should remain with the Directorate"; but why did he not loudly proclaim from the national rostrum to which he had access, and from which he was listened to with deference by virtue of his talent, that which he came and whispered confidentially in my ear? That, therefore, happened to Siméon which occasionally happens to men who are trimmers: he fell between two stools. I did my best to rescue him from the transportation decreed as the result of the victory of the 18th Fructidor; but it is a great mistake on the part of those who are outside the pale of events to attribute these solely to those who seem to be their masters. Apparently they do control events, but for all that they are not masters of them. Nobody is master of the consequences resulting from a political movement when it is once launched on its course. Is even the commander-in-chief of a regular army himself master when the *mêlée* has begun, and the intoxication of courage has carried away men's brains and almost caused them to burst? Hence, as I have already said, I tried in vain to rescue Siméon; he has done me the justice to recognize that my efforts were sincere, and indeed repeatedly testified to the fact as long as I remained in power. In those days (in the Year VII.) Siméon several times did me the justice of believing he could appeal to me in all confidence and security. Independently of the need he might have of my protection in order to soften his fate, he seemed to me to feel the additional need of proving that he was deserving of my good opinion of him, in the matter of patriotism and pledges given to liberty and the Revolution. Thus, as a purchaser of national property as early as 1791, Siméon proved that he had frankly applied his whole fortune to this kind of investment; he had, in particular, devoted a considerable sum to the purchase of two estates—one in the territory of Puivert, in the *canton* of Cadenet, in the department of Vaucluse, which had cost him 42,600 francs; the other in the department of the Var, in the *canton* of Hyères, 220,000 francs, in partnership with a friend, like himself a purchaser of national domains. I recall these facts, the proof of which I find in my memoranda, not for the purpose of taking an unfair advantage of the fact that misfortune may dictate obsequiousness and a show of agreement on the part of a proscribed person towards the functionary to whom he appeals, because he stands in need of his influence, but for the purpose of cheerfully acknowledging that Siméon had not been an enemy of the Revolution, as may have been subsequently believed. Who, for instance, could have told me, and have told Siméon himself, that on emerging from so many vicissitudes he would return, as a consequence of the 18th Brumaire, to become the member of a tribunate; that in this tribunate, chiefly established for the defence of the institutions and principles of the Republic, he should declare in favor of the establishment of the Empire, not only against the Republic to defend which he had received a mandate, but also against the dynasty of the Bourbons, which assuredly ought to have been pursued with less violence, by reason of all its misfortunes, of its position which had become inoffensive, and of its existence almost obliterated from the memory of Frenchmen. This did not prevent Siméon from saying, with a lack of generosity (I here transcribe an extract from the officially reported speech of Siméon, such as I find it in a letter sent me by one of my friends, who wrote jestingly: " Well, this is the man whom you formerly transported as a Bourbonist!" I have no hesitation in admitting our revolutionary error: let us then listen to the tribune Siméon, as he speaks on the 10th Floréal, in the Year XII.):

" The catastrophes which strike kings are common to their families, just as were their power and their happiness. The incapacity which delivers over their persons to the thunderbolts of revolutions extends to their kinsmen, and does not suffer that the helm which has fallen from their feeble hands should again be intrusted to them. Great Britain was compelled to expel the children of Charles I., after having taken them back.

" The return of a dethroned dynasty, overthrown less by its misfortunes than by its faults, would not suit a self-respecting nation. There can be no compromise in regard to a question so violently settled.

" If we are tired of the Revolution, have we no other resources, when it has spent its force, than to place ourselves once more under a yoke broken twelve years ago? If, indeed, the Revolution has been stained with blood, are not those guilty who kindled among us the fury of demagogy and anarchy—who, congratulating themselves while seeing us rend one another, hoped to seize upon us as a prey weakened by self-inflicted wounds? Are not those guilty who, carrying from country to country their resentment and thirst for revenge, incited the coalition which cost groaning humanity so much blood? They sold to the Powers, whose clients they had become, a portion of the inheritance in which they begged those Powers to reinstate them. And are they not now redoubling their efforts with that government, their ancient enemy as it is ours, which, betraying their cause while at the same time combating us, would not, had it the power, again place them on the throne, unless as those powerless nabobs of India whom it has made its vassals?"

I have shown no hesitation in confessing to the revolutionary error which had made me take Siméon for a Bourbonist. I shall, nevertheless, once more return to my feeling of uncertainty in regard to this matter, when reflecting that he is the same man who, by reason of his hostility towards the Bourbons, fully demonstrated by his conduct as well as by his utterances and his writings, was constantly employed by Bonaparte, as Councillor of State, as Minister to his brothers, and who has since been employed by the Restoration, and been a Minister of Louis XVIII. Without invoking any other conjectures, the matter may be reduced to this: that men of flexible and useful talent, who couple with this talent a natural absence of character, or a strong determination never to have any, may entertain great hopes of ever being in active service under all governments. The habit of pleading for and against, whatever the nature of the case, often to the degree of not remembering it one's self (which is the essential characteristic of the legal profession, the one first exercised by Siméon)—this habit, I say, may likewise tend to facilitate and encourage the primary dispositions of mind of those who are not born with a decided taste for truth. This explanation of Siméon's life finds still further confirmation in that of his relatives the Portalis, who from father to son have displayed a flexibility which has enabled them to be capable of all things under all *régimes*. Have we not seen the last of the Portalis dynasty twice obtain portfolios in the reign of Charles X.?

To return from the digression into which I have been forced on once more seeing all these personages in my mind's eye, and to cease anticipating events, I come back to the position to which Siméon was then reduced. It is not the most brilliant of his life; it is certainly not the least honorable. He was in distress, and I may truly say that this constituted a claim to my consideration—to me who never knew any enemies except on the field of battle, and then not on the next day. I may, without complimenting myself, lay claim to the motto:

Il suffit qu'il soit homme et qu'il soit malheureux.

So it came about that Siméon, continuing to appeal to me with the fullest confidence, sent me, through one of his relatives, a memorandum in support of all the personal complaints he addressed to me from time to time, and which, under the simple appellation of *Remarks on Transportation and the Methods of Carrying it Out*, set forth a series of truly luminous arguments worthy of the celebrated lawyer of Aix. I cannot better do justice to Siméon than by transcribing this document, truly remarkable from its dialectics; it may somewhat compensate for the cold diatribe against the unfortunate Bourbons—a diatribe which I regret having been unable to let pass unnoticed, in order that history may render to each and every one the justice due to him.

CITIZEN DIRECTOR,[1]
When, on the 16th Fructidor, Year V., I had the opportunity of talking frankly with you on the state of affairs, you were enabled to judge from my visit to you and my utterances how far I was from being a conspirator. My confidence touched you, so I have been told, and even led you to show some interest on my behalf on the eve of the 18th. I was deeply moved at this. I have given you the only proof of my gratitude which misfortune has left at my disposal—that of addressing you on every occasion I thought it possible to solicit some mitigation of my fate. The time had not arrived; far from it, for here, after the lapse of a year, is a fresh measure of rigor.

We must bow to the laws, but we need not for all that despair of the humanity of those intrusted with their execution, and to whom they have left a necessary latitude in carrying out a measure of public safety affecting a whole body of men. They will doubtless avail themselves of the power left them of being humane; they will at least use it for the benefit of those who will seem least dangerous to it, for it has repeatedly been said on several occasions, in fact quite recently, that all were not equally guilty.

The power possessed by the Directorate of designating the place of transportation is set forth in the law of the 19th Fructi-

---

[1] The autograph of this letter is inserted in the manuscript of Barras.—G. D.

dor. It is confirmed by the law passed on the 19th Brumaire. It is therein enjoined upon us to present ourselves before the central administration of the department, there to be informed as to our ulterior destination. The Directorate shall give its orders in regard to this destination. It is free to assign to us, as it may see fit, various localities, either in the departments beyond the seas or in neutral countries, we being compelled to prove our arrival and residence there by means of certificates from the Directorate's envoys.

Guiana is not a country exclusively assigned by any law or general enactment as a place of transportation. Moreover, transportation has not been organized. It may be suffered in any other French department, in Corsica, in the Île de France, just as well as in Guiana or in neutral countries. Thus the Directorate has sent the Bourbons to Spain, by virtue of the same law which affects me—that of the 19th Fructidor.

It is well known, citizen Director, that Guiana and death are pretty nearly synonymous. It will perhaps seem to you, as well as to your colleagues, that circumstances no longer require that so dangerous a place of exile should be assigned to a man for whom, as it is said, most of those who have sentenced him feel some pity.

I shall shortly claim justice of the Directorate in this respect, but I shall first solicit your good-will and protection. I place in your hands the fate of a wife and two children, to whom I am still necessary. If I may no longer serve my country, to which I have devoted myself with assiduity and disinterestedness, suffer me to be still useful to my family, which nevertheless does not wish to buy my modest patrimony with my life.

I had already expressed to you, citizen Director, the desire that Holstein should be my place of exile; it is a neutral country sufficiently distant from the frontiers of the Republic, and is moreover foreign to all political movements. I persist in my desire, and beg you will favor it.

Failing this, I should prefer Holland. Failing this also, and if I must needs go to a land belonging to the Republic, Corsica.

Ever since the cruel guarantee exacted for our obedience, by threatening us with the shame and penalty of emigration, our transportation will surely not be preceded by a useless imprisonment, the only effect of which would be to weaken the strength required to endure a cruel exile, and to defer it.

The Directorate will doubtless also, by granting us a delay before we proceed to the place of transportation, provide, as allowed by the law of the 19th Fructidor, for our most urgent needs. As far as I am personally concerned, I should require one thousand *écus*, to be obtained from the tax-gatherers of the departments of Vaucluse and of the Var, out of the income of my sequestrated properties.

It may be, citizen Director, that my wishes, however just they may seem to me, will be granted in part only. Whatever may be in the nature of a refusal will be attributed by me merely to an insurmountable rigor, while it will be a pleasure for me to credit you with everything partaking of a favor. I already find some consolation in persuading myself that you have been kindly enough to listen to my prayer.

Greeting and respect.

SIMÉON.[*]

REMARKS ON TRANSPORTATION AND ITS MODE OF EXECUTION.

The law of the 19th Fructidor has laid down that various individuals therein named should be transported to a locality "to be determined by the Directorate."

It set forth also that the laws pronouncing the expulsion of the Bourbons should be executed, and the Directorate was likewise commissioned to "designate the place of their transportation."

Fifteen out of the sixty-five individuals named were arrested. The Directorate sent them to French Guiana.

It caused the Bourbons to be conveyed to Spain.

Several individuals transported to Guiana have left it; they have broken their ban, and the Directorate has placed their names on the list of *émigrés*.

Now the law of the 19th Brumaire compels those sentenced to transportation by the laws of the 19th and 22d Fructidor, Year V., to apply to the central administration of the department wherein they dwell, for the purpose of obtaining information as to their ulterior destination. Should they fail to comply, or, having complied, disappear without undergoing their transportation, they shall be assimilated with the *émigrés*.

The Directorate shall therefore give its orders to the central administrations, in order that they may be enabled to inform all applying to them of their ulterior destination. Many, if not all, will apply, feeling confident that the Directorate will cause rigorous laws to be executed without superfluous rigors, and with the humanity which should characterize the chosen men to whom a great and generous nation has delegated the exercise of its powers.

Believing this, permission is asked of the Directorate to submit to it a few observations.

1. A transportation pronounced, as the motives of urgency of the laws of the 19th Fructidor, Year V., and 19th Brumaire, Year VII., proclaim, by "extraordinary measures," and as "a means of public safety," should undoubtedly be executed with all the care demanded by the public welfare, but perhaps without the rigors proper to transportation inflicted by a judicial conviction. In accordance with this, persons transported for the public welfare should be expelled from the Republic, just as those transported pursuant to a court sentence; but their exile might be rendered less harsh, for, as remarked by the *rapporteur* of the law of the 19th Brumaire, "It is precautions that have been taken against them; it is not penalties that are inflicted on them."

2. The law of the 19th Fructidor left the Directorate entirely free to select the place of transportation, because it alone could judge of the limit to be given to the "precautions" taken; for the reason also that the law smiting promptly and *en masse*, it was proper to give the individuals involved in the generality and celerity of the measure the means of obtaining in its execution facilities which, without nullifying it, should render it less cruel.

3. In addition to this intention being worthy of the humanity of the *corps législatif*, it will moreover appear consistent with wisdom, if it be taken into consideration that our laws still remain silent as to the definition and the nature of transportation, that it could not do otherwise than leave in the hands of the Government the execution and choice of the one just decreed.

4. Transportation was substituted by our penal code for exile and banishment. Exile used to be pronounced in ancient republics, as more lately by modern monarchies, as a measure of security, and by an act of the government; banishment, on the contrary, was within the province of the tribunals; but exile, banishment, and transportation are but one and the same thing under three different names: the expulsion from a territory, and

consequently the deprivation of the rights enjoyed therein as a citizen.

No law of the Republic has organized transportation; no law has modified the general idea we have just given of it; none has pronounced as to its duration or perpetuity; none has stated whether it should be suffered at a greater or lesser distance, in continental departments or in departments beyond the seas, in the isles of the ocean or of the Mediterranean, in neutral countries or simply on French territory.

This silence of the laws leaves to the humanity of the Directorate all the latitude it can desire. For, whenever a penalty is not subject to exclusive means of execution, he who is charged with inflicting it is free to employ means more or less severe; he enjoys a discretionary power. It may even be that no exclusive locality of transportation was fixed in order to confer this power on him. The intention probably was that transportation should be, like confinement, more or less rigorous, according to the circumstances, of which the executive power is necessarily the best judge.

Hence it follows that transportation to Guiana is not made compulsory by any law.

5. Nor does transportation to a French department seem to be necessarily called for. The laws not having spoken, it is not known whether the transportation which they have fixed as capital punishment is merely expulsion from the territory or relegation to some locality of the territory.

It should be pointed out that relegation to some locality of a territory is not transportation properly speaking. With transportation is naturally coupled the idea of expulsion beyond the frontiers. In Guiana or in any other continental department, the transported person is still on the soil of the Republic, which is one and indivisible, and of which the colonies form an integrant part.

The English transport according to the nature of the crimes, now to Botany Bay, and again to their Western or Eastern colonies, or even to neutral countries. Quite recently they had fixed upon the United States of America as the place of transportation of several Irishmen. If these States refused to allow this, it is doubtless owing to an intrigue of the London Cabinet, which has sought further to persecute zealots for liberty; it is in consequence of the hatred and prejudices they seek to inspire against those who strive to shake off the yoke of kings, and restore to the peoples their rights.

Be this as it may, the English, when transporting to their colonies, expel from the State, because they have a metropolis of which the colonies are only a dependency; but France has no metropolis: its colonies form part of the Republic. Transportation to the French colonies is therefore in this respect in contradiction to the word "transportation" and its primitive idea. It is merely a relegation to a department of the Republic; and if this be French transportation, it will be carried out whatever may be the department designated. If the Directorate has seen fit, on certain occasions and in regard to certain individuals, to assign more distant and less healthy departments, it is free, on other less dangerous occasions, to designate for others departments nearer home and more salubrious.

6. It is equally free to designate neutral countries, since such designation, far from being prohibited, would more strictly constitute transportation or banishment from the Republic.

How, it is asked, can any supervision be exercised over individuals transported to neutral countries? The answer is: Through the agents and envoys of the Republic in those countries, by compelling the individuals transported to procure from them certificates of residence.

Can it be true that it has been argued that to transport to a neutral country would be tantamount to a permission to emigrate? What comparison can there be between emigration, which is a voluntary desertion of the Fatherland, and transportation, which is a banishment pronounced by the Fatherland itself? The *émigré* absconds and disobeys; the transported individual leaves and obeys: he is a disinherited and outcast child; it is not he who forsakes his mother. He is suffering a penalty. And where is the Frenchman to whom such a penalty is not sufficiently poignant? If it be asked whether the neutral Powers will tolerate the presence of transported individuals, the answer is: Do they not tolerate the *émigrés*, except in places from which the government has requested they shall be excluded? Is not asylum part of the law of nations? Has it not been observed in all times and by all nations, except in the case of great criminals whose extradition they reciprocally grant?

7. The facts confirm all that has just been said as to the

power vested in the Directorate to designate as places of transportation French departments or neutral countries.

The transportation decreed by the National Convention meant only banishment from the territory. The priests subject to transportation received passports enabling them to leave the territory; they went whither they chose, generally to the nearest country.

The National Convention decreed transportation to Guiana expressly only in the case of four of its members. This special aggravation of the penalty has never been converted into a general rule. Hence it comes that the law of the 19th Fructidor has left the selection of the locality to the Directorate; hence it is that the law of the 19th Brumaire did not enjoin upon those transported to proceed to the prisons of Rochefort, as laid down in the draft of the law. This would have been equivalent to assuming that there is no place of transportation other than across the ocean; and the law states that those transported would receive, each in his own locality, information of their ulterior destination, because it wished to vest in the Directorate the power of fixing it at will.

This law has also mitigated the project, in that it assumes that the transported individuals who shall inquire as to their destination will proceed thither freely, since it has foreseen the case of their disappearing after having learned it. The law has indeed taken such strong guarantees for the continuation of their obedience in the penalties of emigration and death that it can well spare them the sufferings of a transfer and the Government the expenses attendant thereon.

In short, the Directorate has done what we claim it can do. The law of the 19th Fructidor commissioned it, in the same terms, to designate the place of transportation of the sixty-five individuals named and of the Bourbons. To the latter it assigned Spain. It caused to be conveyed to Guiana those of the sixty-five who had been arrested. Every day sees *émigrés* sentenced to transportation conveyed to the frontier, so that they shall suffer their penalty in neutral lands. It follows, therefore, that transported individuals may be sent to various places, and even to neutral countries.

8. There remains to answer the objection: Why should those of the sixty-five who have still to be transported be treated any better than those arrested fifteen months ago?

The answer is, that circumstances do not perhaps call for the same severity; that those who remain to be transported are obeying the law of the land; that up to the present time their residence in France has not given the least cause for complaint; that it constitutes a proof of their confidence in the wisdom and humanity of the Government, and demonstrates that they are far from seeking to engage in anything likely to disturb it; lastly, that it is allowable to show some preference among people who are not equally guilty and deserving of suspicion.

Thus it is that prisoners are placed in this or in that prison, and kept in more or less close confinement. Transportation is susceptible of the same distinctions. It will none the less be executed whether all the transported persons be sent to Guiana, or scattered through other departments (such, for instance, as those of Corsica), or, like the Bourbons and the priests transported by the National Convention, conveyed to neutral lands.

It is more than permissible to show preference to certain persons: it is even necessary, especially after the statement made by the *rapporteur* (Boulay de la Meurthe) on the events of the 18th Fructidor, that innocent victims had been stricken by the rapidity of the measures of the 19th, and when it has again been repeated from the tribune of the Ancients, at the time of the passing of the last law, that all are not equally guilty.

The Directorate is therefore free to assign to the less guilty a transportation to neutral countries, and to all transportation to habitable places. That which is within the latitude of its powers is certainly in its sentiments of humanity, which are averse to rigors neither called for by the law nor necessary to its execution.

Résumé.

The mode of transportation and the place where the penalty is to be suffered are not positively specified.

Transportation to our colonies partakes more of a relegation to a department than of a transportation beyond the limits of a republic.

Relegation to neutral countries is more properly a transportation.

The general and special laws which now call for execution leave the Directorate free to select the place of transportation.

Transportation to foreign countries was more practised under the National Convention than transportation to our departments beyond the seas.

The Directorate has had recourse to both methods since the 19th Fructidor, Year V.

It can therefore do so once more; and by making use of its powers in this respect, it will affix to the 18th Fructidor a seal of humanity and moderation, which is within its power.

Lastly, whatever the place assigned to this or that one, it is free to assign a different one to others.

The law of the 19th Brumaire has secured a sufficient pledge for their obedience to allow them to go, of their own accord and within a specified time, to the place of their ulterior destination.

Impressed with the correctness of Siméon's course of reasoning, as well as with the justice of his request, I laid the matter before my colleagues, and succeeded, in spite of the impatience caused by what they styled "personal grievances," in getting them to listen to the reading of Siméon's statement. Each of them was individually of the opinion that Siméon had given expression to a well-grounded request, and that it should be granted, but the Directorate as a whole considered that it should be rejected. It will astonish only those who have had no acquaintance with political assemblies, or with simple associations comprising a still smaller membership, to see what a difference there is between individual men and the same taken collectively. The justice which the former are fully prepared to do is oftentimes refused by them when forming a body. It was Sieyès who formulated the following objection: "Because we closed the *Manége* yesterday, do the Royalists imagine that we are going to devote our attention to them to-day? They will soon find out their mistake. The best we can do for these people is to turn them over to the scrutiny of the Minister of Police, who will, if needs be, report to us thereon." Fouché returns on the following day, bearing Siméon's statement; he pretends that he has carefully examined it, and found in it only "nonsense," unworthy of engaging the attention of the Directorate, whose attention should be wholly reserved for the dangers actually threatening it. Sieyès replies with vivacity: "You are quite right; the present must engage our attention. The transported persons are transported persons, and must be so; let them cease worrying us!"

As I did not as yet consider myself beaten, I saw fit to produce a still more cogent argument in favor of Siméon, by reading an extract from his letter conceived as follows: "Ever since the cruel guarantee secured for our obedience by the threat of the shame and penalty of emigration—" I had hardly commenced this sentence, which gave proof of proud and generous sentiments against emigration—this but too real characteristic of the enemies of the Republic, with whom Siméon was so wretched at seeing himself associated—when I was most violently interrupted by Sieyès, who, supported by Fouché, called for "the order of the day in regard to persons sentenced to transportation, *émigrés*, in short, all aristocrats, and to take up the present question—that of the Jacobins."

A short time previous to these discussions I had received a complaint from the transported priests at Rochefort, setting forth their hardships and all their rights to the mitigation of these. For it is a circumstance which has oftentimes recurred in my life, that even in the midst of most troublous political times, when I seemed to be in the front rank and play the most formidable *rôle*, all that were defeated or in distress have ever appealed to me in full confidence, as if to a natural protector from whom the most was to be expected. These poor priests of Rochefort prefaced their memorandum by quoting Article 2 of the Rights of Man in the Constitution of the Year III.: "No person shall be condemned without having been heard or legally summoned before a judge." Generally speaking, the oppressed, to whatever party they belong, or have belonged, are the first to seek to avail themselves of the principles to which they used to pay the least attention, or towards which they even affected contempt. It is an altogether natural homage due to principles that, inasmuch as they are the salvation of all, each in turn must claim them. Moved as much as convinced by the complaint of these poor priests, I considered it my duty not to defer laying it before the Directorate, in the hope that the fit of anger that had vented itself on the Jacobins and the persons condemned to transportation might calm down, by way of compensation, in the case of the priests. Great was my astonishment on seeing Sieyès, seemingly believing that I sought to level a satirical remark at him, by my remembering that he "had formerly been a priest," or rather that he had never ceased to be one, since it is only a priestly hatred which can indulge in such violence, exclaim: "Why do you come and speak to us of your transported priests? They are either transported or not; if they are, they are dead, so there is no further need to trouble ourselves about them. This fact once established, it is unnecessary for me to pass to a second supposition. Your Rochefort priests no longer exist, and no longer constitute a debatable question, so let us pass to the order of the day; we can show the petitioners no other indulgence." Fouché, a witness of this sally, which he was in a better position to appreciate than anybody else by virtue of his personal antecedents, said to us, while looking at Sieyès with an approving smile: "Citizen Directors, I shall watch these moderate petitioners no less than the other enemies of the Republic. I can discern the full import of their conduct, even though they bow to you in the respectful attitude of supplicants. Moreover, pardon me the expression, we have other fish to fry just at present." Thereupon Sieyès, bestowing on Fouché a kindly and satisfied glance, remarked: "Citizen Fouché, you must devote your serious attention to the Jacobins. They are, over and above all, our enemies; still, this does not imply that you should lose sight of the *fructidorisés* and of the transported priests, but the attention bestowed on the latter must not be withdrawn from the former; you must keep your eyes open, and see everything at one and the same time." I consider the complaint of the transported priests an historical document, and so I reproduce it here in full.

Memorandum on Behalf of the Transported Priests at Rochefort.

"No person shall be condemned without having been heard or legally summoned before a judge" (Rights of Man, Article 2, Constitution of the Year III.)

One hundred priests, or thereabouts, are imprisoned at Rochefort in various jails; a further considerable number have been arrested, and are to join them there; the greater number remain in hiding. All have in prospect the melancholy fate of a mortal transportation; among them are many sexagenarians and infirm men, who for a long time past have claimed the benefit of the law exempting them from transportation. Not one of them but laments seeing himself thus proscribed without trial.

And yet everything combines to solicit for them from the Government of the French Republic the forms of judicial procedure—(1) their just interests; (2) the public satisfaction; (3) the honor of the Government.

When discussing a cause of such interest to humanity, we are far from losing sight of the respect due the authorities; we speak on behalf of faithful citizens, on behalf of ministers of charity, who would be the first to disown anything savoring of the bitterness of passion.

We will point out to you before entering upon our subject that this is not the first time such a measure has been adopted in the course of the Revolution, under the plea of the general security. No one has the right to censure the precautions taken by the Government; it is a matter of principle that the authorities are entitled to respect; but everybody has the right to claim justice, and in a republic especially the laws are open to the scrutiny of all citizens. . . .

If those who wield power have modified their opinion in regard to the excessive hardships involved in those measures in more difficult times, if the priests arrested in those days have been released, with what confidence may we not hope that a Government organized at last on more solid bases will not refuse to those actually imprisoned the means of defending themselves against the charges of which they are victims.

1. The just interests of the ministers of the Catholic religion demand that they should have a legal trial; in every civilized society it is the incontestable right of the accused to be heard in defence of the charges brought against him. The Government which protects the citizens is responsible to the mass of them for the manner in which it disposes of each one of them individually. It cannot smite a single one without accounting for it by an authentic declaration; this declaration' is its judgment. A judgment is the application of the law, made to one or more citizens, pursuant to certain consecrated forms; these salutary forms constitute the foundation of the common safety; they constitute for society the justification of the punishment inflicted on the guilty. The Constitution of the Year III. numbers this principle among the rights of man; and it may truly be said that

it was less established by human laws than engraved in all hearts by the Author of Nature.

Every person charged with crime enjoys this resource. Summoned and arrested in the name of the law, he is interrogated in regard to the misdeeds of which he is accused; he is confronted with the witnesses; he may even produce witnesses in his defence; the charges brought against him and his answers are discussed by two juries in succession; lastly, the court appoints counsel to assist him. If he succumbs after the agents of the law have exhausted every possible means to ascertain either his guilt or his innocence, conviction is the determining cause of his condemnation. He is never subjected to any penalties other than those the law has laid down for his crime; the justice of our code does not admit of retroactive effects in the laws.

Legislators, and you, depositaries of the supreme power, will you deny to ministers of religion what the law grants the greatest criminals? No, you may be deceived, but you cannot be unjust. Permit us to draw for you the picture of their treatment and sufferings. It is well occasionally to lay before the chief power particulars which distance hides from its view; and when these particulars are cruelties, one is sure of moving your sensitive souls, and of interesting your sense of equity.

After six years of an almost continuous persecution (the result of the revolutionary confusion of which you promised the nation to wipe out the slightest trace), after having been despoiled of their goods and chattels, prevented from exercising their ministrations, driven from their asylums, deprived of their pensions, ever harassed and threatened, oftentimes incarcerated, they were beginning to breathe freely under the ægis of the order which you substituted for anarchy; the people were giving themselves up to the feelings of joy with which a return to calm, the freedom of practising their religion, and the presence of their pastors inspire them—when these pastors are suddenly carried off by soldiers who cannot tell them even the cause of their arrest.

They are seized, dragged and carted away, exposed to the inclemency of the weather in the midst of winter, and nightly cast into cells, as if they were the vilest criminals, no distinction being made in favor of age or infirmity. Among the number are octogenarians, whose diet is bread and water, whose couch, straw; during their long journey they have owed their life to benevolent hearts. Confined to-day, some in prisons, others to the number of about 120 (including laymen) in one habitation, they have to choose between the severity of the cold and the contagion of mephitis; there, deprived of everything, they languish in misery, suffering from privations and from the anguish caused by their embarkation, which, in the case of the majority of them, will put an end to their painful existence.

These are the unfortunate beings who are entitled to a trial. Were they guilty, it might perhaps be considered that they have already been excessively punished, for the sufferings of a man are to be judged in proportion to his physical faculties, his infirmities, his age, and his habits; and yet we have here victims only; it is for the tribunals to show us criminals among them.

Directors, your humanity will throw open these prison doors; by making inquiries and resorting to legal procedure you will discover how you have been imposed upon, and how difficult it is for those in high places to guard against the influence of intriguers, the primary cause of all prejudices.

What will you find in these cells? Men all the more astonished at suffering in them that neither their conscience nor the public voice reproaches them in any degree with a lack of the fidelity they owe the Republican Government.

Some were arrested as infringers of the law of the 19th Fructidor before they had even time to become acquainted with it, since it had not yet been published in the places where they resided; others, although they had already taken steps to execute it. Some, condemned *in globo* on a mass of charges, not one of which had any actual justification; others, reputed guilty for having conformed to the requisition of the authorities, pursuant to the express orders of the generals. Others, banished in spite of the capitulations guaranteeing the security of their departments; all denounced, generally speaking, by some obscure enemy, in defiance of the testimony of their communes. All the Catholic priests in the French Republic might just as well have been proscribed.

Perversity has no other assurance than that which it finds in doing harm under cover of darkness; but would it show as great a firmness were it called upon publicly to proclaim its accusations, furnish proofs in support of them, and face the discussion of them? Let it not be said that the priests are disturbing elements, and that it was needful to smite them without employing the ordinary forms. These forms are sacred to everybody; they are indispensable to the condemnation of criminals, whoever these may be. Reasons of State justify the sudden carrying off of a person charged with a dangerous crime, but it must be done in order to place him in the grasp of his judges. No man is presumed guilty until he has been so judged.

It is sought to make out that Catholic priests are disturbers of the peace: their trial will prove that they have ever preached peace, and peace only; it is sought to make out that they are rebels, and no act of rebellion can be proved against them. Confining themselves to the duties prescribed to them by religion, their principle is that religion does not make politicians of its ministers, but submissive Christians; that it does not allow them to interfere in the revolutions of empires, nor to pass judgment on the rights of those governing them, but that it imposes on them the obligation of respecting even the most rigorous authority, and condemns every act of rebellion as a crime. "Obey and suffer" is their motto.

If the law of the 19th Fructidor has invested the Directorate with the power of transporting seditious priests, it has not exempted it from the formalities which are absolutely necessary to prove that they have fomented disorder. The law does not confer so strange a power, and there is no authority which would welcome it. Following upon an arrest which it considered to be rendered necessary by circumstances, the Directorate has not on that account renounced an exhaustive inquiry into the charges which may be brought against the prisoners.

They are men and citizens; they must be judged with humanity and equity. In that case inquiry will be made into the genuineness of the misdemeanor, its concomitant circumstances, the results of it, the intention, liberty, and morality of each of the accused; and if there be then cause to inflict any penalties, no others shall be pronounced except those incurred at the time the action was committed.

2. This is what is demanded by the public satisfaction of which a popular government is so jealous. The priests whose fate has to be pronounced on are connected with so large a number of citizens.

This vast number of Frenchmen—some of whom are bound to them by ties of blood, others by those of friendship, and many millions by the practice of the Catholic religion—perceptibly interests a government aiming at universal happiness. A proscription not preceded by a trial would cause too great a flow of tears. Alas! it will still be painful enough if, contrary to our expectation and the universal hope, some are found guilty after a trial.

Freedom of religion exists for all Frenchmen, not as a favor, but as an incontestable right. The religion practised by the great mass of citizens is not to be deprived of this freedom. Where would liberty be were it to remain without ministers?

We have to add that no one knows better the state, the condition of these unfortunate prisoners, than the population amid which they lived; their needs, their infirmities, their powerlessness to engage in manual labor in order to eke out a livelihood, owing to their age, their temperament, and their mode of life, greatly pain this numerous population, which owes them a debt of gratitude, and which has bemoaned their removal; it will ever consider itself robbed of an object essential to its happiness, so long as it shall be deprived of the sweet enjoyment of fulfilling with them a sacred duty which nothing can supersede, and the faithful observance of which constitutes throughout the world the security of empires.

3. Lastly, the honor of the Government is involved in granting a trial to the imprisoned priests; it is by this measure of equity that it will give additional proof to France that it holds in detestation all the revolutionary attempts of anarchy, and that henceforth every citizen without exception shall enjoy the safeguard of the laws.

Thus shall it win, even more than by victories and treaties of peace, the esteem and affection of neighboring peoples, who, attached to their religion, are ever distrustful of what might, if only by example, infringe on it.

Will prosperity bless the happiness that is in preparation for it if it owes it to proscriptions only? And in order to justify in its eyes a cruel transportation, is nothing to remain except a record of accusations unsifted in a court of law, and against which the accused have not been allowed to defend themselves?

Founders of the Republic, the law is the common bond of all. You will not except anybody from its protection. Conquerors of Europe, what have you to fear from a few hundred priests, weakened by the wretched life they have led for six years, and who have no desire to do any harm? Are they not moreover under the supervision of the municipalities? Do you not still possess the strength to repress them, and punish those who shall deviate from their duties as citizens?

All they ask is to live in peace, and not to be deprived of the sole resource left them of ending their days in the bosoms of their families. Were they guilty a thousand voices would have been raised against them, and the people who love them would, on the contrary, have become their enemies.

Ah, since they have constantly prayed during six years for those who have inflicted suffering on them, may the return of peace, instead of being sullied by their proscription, at last permit them to change their tears into thanksgiving for their deliverance!

We have set forth, in as precise a fashion as we could, a cause which is engaging the attention of all France. We still hope that the justice and humanity of the Directorate and of the *corps législatif* will receive our reflections with the interest which the subject itself inspires. How flattering it will be to the soul of every depositary of power to hear his fellow-citizens say: "There is no longer any arbitrary *régime* in France, and it is the lips of judges who, after mature investigation, have pronounced on the fate of every one of the imprisoned priests!"

(Signed)   F. F. NUSSE.

ROCHEFORT,
17th Prairial, in the Republican Year VII.

CHAPTER XIV

Masséna's inactivity—Latour-Foissac surrenders Mantua—Alessandria in the enemy's power—Defeat of Novi; Joubert's death—Bernadotte's grand proclamation—Fresh misfortunes—Bernadotte's genius—His views as to the conduct of the war—Sharp reproaches conveyed to Masséna; the Directorate dismisses him—Bernadotte opposed to his dismissal—Military firmness and political weakness of Bernadotte—Sieyès irritated against him—State of the *corps législatif*—The deputy Lemercier—M. Français de Nantes; his character; his intercourse with Lucien; his esteem for me—The deputy Briot—Augereau's amusing exclamation—Bonaparte at Cairo—Death of Pius VI.—Bonaparte's behavior towards him—Taxation for the Year VIII.—The state of the South—Anniversary of the 18th Fructidor—Semonville, the father-in-law of Joubert, turns the latter's death to account; his Spartan character and ability.

16th Thermidor, Year VIII.—The weaknesses of governments, especially those which are young, are unceasingly watched for by their enemies. No sooner has dissension invaded them than it immediately becomes known; while some believe that they can force their way into them and take possession of them, others see at least the means of enjoying immunity from the action of the law. From the divided centre relaxation spreads to the farthest limits. Armies as well as civil administrations seem to seek and profit by the enforced inattention of a weakened supervision. Thus in Helvetia Masséna continues to remain inactive, although in command of a fine and numerous army. Latour-Foissac, commandant of the garrison of Mantua, capitulates, and hands this important town to the Austrians. The troops of the coalition engaged in blockading it are to rejoin the main army. May they not reach their destination quickly enough to decide ulterior events in favor of the Russians! Alessandria falls into the power of the enemy.

Meanwhile comes the melancholy news of the battle of Novi, won by Suvaroff over Joubert. This intrepid general had said to us on leaving: "I shall either be killed or be victorious." He has kept his word, perishing on that fatal day with a large number of French officers and soldiers. It is fortunate to possess, at such a critical moment, a Minister of War who knows how to speak to the army and prevent it from giving itself up to despair. Bernadotte succeeds in holding our army together under the standards. The address he issues to the army is a splendid service rendered to the Fatherland.

To the Army of Italy.

Three years ago, hidden in the ranks, Joubert was hardly known; to-day his death attracts to him the gaze and esteem of all Europe. Wherein lies the secret of so great a reputation, soldiers of the Fatherland? This prodigy is one of those born of liberty, which raises to the skies its generous defenders. Joubert was one of its most ardent; he did not believe, even when in camp, that a soldier had the right to consider himself indifferent to the Republic. Uncertain, six months ago, as to whether he should again fight her battles in Italy, he had courageously renounced his own fame.

The Constitution resumes its sway. Joubert is again to go on active service. The time has come for him to rejoin his comrades in arms. Impatient to pursue his glorious career, he has hardly arrived when he perishes in your midst in the flower of his age!

On falling from his horse he cried out to you with his dying voice: "Comrades, march on the enemy!" You have heard his dying words; you have sworn on his grave to avenge him; your tears shall not be fruitless.

If in this fatal engagement, which is not a defeat, a mistake has been committed, it is that of excessive impetuosity. I have but one piece of advice to give you: show discretion in your valor.

Rally around the eternal principle of victories—discipline; it will give back to you all your successes, which are merely postponed. Numerous reinforcements of all arms are about to support you; let the old soldiers set the young conscripts an example of order and attention to duty.

Forward, brave friends! The Fatherland calls you. No, in spite of what the coalition may do, the fountain from which spring generals is not dried up. Formerly, under the kings, it could be said that Nature rests when she has produced a great man. I see among you more than one Bonaparte, more than one Joubert. Liberty has changed Nature. BERNADOTTE.

Simultaneously with our receiving the sad news of the loss of the battle of Novi we learn that the English have landed in the North of Holland, and that they succeed in intrenching themselves there; some days after, that the Dutch fleet commanded by Vice-Admiral Hory has mutinied and has passed over to the power of the English without engagement or capitulation. Following upon all these reverses, and when our position abroad is so difficult, Sieyès is compelled to recognize that it would not be sufficient, in order to weather the storms, to have a Minister of War who had never made war, and that there is needed no less than a man of spirit, sense, and talent, capable of understanding, conceiving, and directing a great *ensemble*, in order to set in motion intelligently all the operations which must at the present moment combine in order to obtain a common result. It is in times of unexpected danger that one can best judge resourceful men, and I had never been able better to judge Bernadotte than in this critical moment, when all calamities seemed to unite for the purpose of assailing the Republic. I had the opportunity of seeing at work the man of genius of whom I had until then just caught a glimpse, but whom I had not sufficiently appreciated in the course of our relations, particularly at the time of his appointment to the command of the Army of Italy, when he laid before me in so precise and eloquent a fashion his motives for declining it, with the unfortunate result that the appointment went to Schérer.

Far from being alarmed at all the sinister news swooping down upon us simultaneously, Bernadotte, rising and hastening towards the map of the scene of war which hung in our council-room, exclaimed: " Pray come and see with me where we stand at the present moment, and what our defence is to be on all points, the resources we have to oppose to the enemy, and how it is possible to increase them by means of courage and activity. First look at Italy: she would have been saved a first time if Macdonald, through self-love and the fear of being subordinate to Moreau, had not acted by himself, and had frankly co-operated with him; she would have been saved a second time had the offensive been resumed before the fall of the fortified towns, whose siege engaged a large part of the enemy's forces. Considering as a whole the movement of the allied forces—which need to come to an understanding, since the leaders as well as the nations are at variance—I am under the impression that several of their successes are due to the facility of communication they have enjoyed across the Alps, between Germany and Italy.

Believing that it was necessary to deprive them of these means of communication, I have ordered Masséna to extend the right of Lecourbe to the Saint-Gothard, to seize possession of this important point, and to retake the Grisons. I cannot praise too highly the ability and intrepidity with which Lecourbe has acted. I should have liked that, in thus depriving the hostile forces operating in Germany of their communications with those operating in Italy, Masséna had acted vigorously and at once against the forces opposed to his own. I believed that he had troops enough not only to act, but even to turn over to us some 20,000 men, whom I should have placed on the Rhine. I am at the same time fortunate enough to learn with certainty, through our agents in Switzerland and on the right bank of the Rhine, that Prince Charles has relieved Masséna of a portion of the troops opposed to him; that the Prince has taken away with him 25,000 picked men, who are marching in all haste towards the Lower Rhine. This is the result of my combinations, the object of which was to remove the Archduke by sending him a distance of over a hundred leagues from Masséna, to fight an army on paper, whose creation I had ostentatiously announced precisely in order to delay Prince Charles, as has happened. How is it that Masséna, who, placed as he is, must learn the movements of his enemy much earlier than ourselves, does not take advantage of this stroke of good luck to give battle? He can no longer pretend ignorance, since I have informed him of the state of affairs, and am sending him messenger upon messenger with orders to attack. If he does not make up his mind to do so, citizen

Directors, I am at a loss to explain his conduct. It is neither disobedience nor insubordination; I shall use severer words to qualify this behavior, and submit to you measures to put an end to it.

"You will readily perceive how fatal the loss of time is in war. If, when Prince Charles left Helvetia, Masséna had attacked at once, he would have come a conqueror out of his Helvetia, where he says it is so hard to live, and would have taken up his winter-quarters in a better country. Had Prince Charles, when half-way on his march, and even more, heard of Masséna's successes, I should have defied him to go a step farther. At the very least he would have been in the greatest perplexity, unable to communicate with Italy for want of the Saint-Gothard, and exposed to be cut off at several points, whether he attempted to march onward or retrace his steps. Instead of that, citizen Directors," Bernadotte went on to say with vehemence, "you see what is going on at the farther end of the Rhine. The English have landed in Holland. Brune, whose forces are insufficient, is clamoring for reinforcements. You know my actual resources: what have I to dispose of? And yet I must find some, for it is above all necessary to save Holland; the consequences attendant upon its loss would be too deplorable; everything must be sacrificed for this supreme interest. We shall save Holland, citizen Directors; I swear it to you. So far I have not been able to send Brune anything except cheering messages; I have made promises to him, and I will keep them. I am looking through my reserves, in order to do all that is possible; I have already despatched post-haste down the Rhine all the troops

I can lay my hands on. I will invent, create; I will not leave Brune in a strait; Holland must be saved."

We were all struck with admiration at the fecundity of views and means of Bernadotte, and the lucidity of his explanations on a subject which he succeeded in making plain even to Sieyès and Roger-Ducos, of whom no profound knowledge of the geography and topography of war could be expected. Sieyès, who did not readily bestow praise, and whose parsimony in this respect was akin to avarice, could not help saying: "General Bernadotte has thoroughly reasoned the matter out; all he says is golden; Holland must be saved." Sieyès adds that "General Masséna's conduct must be seriously investigated." Moulins, whose character is generally more inclined to indulgence than to violence, is on this occasion more severe than even Sieyès. "Masséna must be brought to trial," he says; "motives of interest and his complicity with army contractors are fettering his advance and causing the ruin of the Republic." Sieyès remarks that the sitting cannot close without some course being adopted. The Directorate enacts that "General Masséna is deprived of the command of the army, and that he is superseded by General Moreau, who is to command, under the name of 'Army of the Rhine,' the Army of Helvetia and all corps depending on it." Bernadotte, who has just been so outspoken about Masséna, asks us to suspend taking action against him; that for the present it be merely recorded secretly in the minute-book. As for himself, he is going to try and give the spur to Masséna once more, in order to compel him to act. "If he has by any chance obeyed my latest orders," remarks

Bernadotte, "how deeply should we not regret rewarding his success with a dismissal!" Bernadotte's request is granted; Masséna's dismissal shall remain secret until further orders.

While I saw Bernadotte behave so splendidly in military matters, and reveal so great a capacity, I asked myself whether this was the same man I had seen hesitating in so strange and almost childish a fashion, not to put it more strongly, in matters political—the man who, at the time of the 18th Fructidor, and even at that of the 30th Prairial, a milk-and-water revolution, if it can even be called a revolution, showed himself so timid and uncertain, screening himself in the first place behind Augereau, and in the next behind Joubert; and the answer I made to myself was as follows: To speak and act in military fashion was really in Bernadotte's province; he was thoroughly acquainted with all the resources of war; now nothing gives men greater courage than to be perfectly familiar with the weapons they handle; on the contrary, civil revolutions and politics were entirely new ground to the man who, having constantly been with the army, knew of the Revolution only the terrible inflictions with which it had on various occasions visited the generals themselves, who after a short-lived mutiny against her had ended in becoming her most humble and respectful servants. The most glorious exploits had indeed brought them closer to the Revolution, inasmuch as they had the honor of co-operating with it; but they had not given it any influence, any "grip." They were consequently held at arm's-length, and if they occasionally ventured to address it, it was only to bow to it respectfully, hat in hand

and in a state almost akin to prostration; still less would they have dared to measure themselves with it, even in a simple discussion. Thus it was that when the day came, owing to the necessities of the Fatherland, for military men to interfere once more, it had been for them an entirely new thing which made the bravest of them tremble, as indeed they should. Bonaparte himself, less of a novice than the others, owing to his revolutionary antecedents at Toulon and on the 13th Vendémiaire, did not tread the path of politics with as much audacity as he affected; he had said that " he would show himself on the 18th Fructidor," but he had not shown himself. He had got his agents to feel the ground, in particular the spy Lavalette, but he had not come forward in person, and had contented himself with sending others to the front. The man whom he had considered the most proper for the execution of his designs had been Augereau—a regular political dare-devil, a man of spirit and patriotism, but without intelligence, who, had he had more of it, would perhaps not have dared to second us even as much as he did, and to arrest with his own hand, on our mere oral order, inviolable deputies.

I had spoken in this sense in presence of my colleagues. It was greatly to be desired that Bernadotte, " so strong in military knowledge, might perhaps be a little stronger in politics." Sieyès heard me, treasured up the words that had escaped my lips, and gave their meaning a far greater extension than I had intended. " Yes, indeed," had remarked Sieyès, " it is greatly to be desired; for though I have listened with genuine satisfaction to his military exposition, I am far from according the same adhesion to all his political pretensions. Bernadotte himself does not know exactly what they are; he has hesitated a long while before becoming a patriot, at a time when it was not permissible for any one not to be one, since reason dictated that course. Now that it is allowable to think twice about patriotism—and especially Jacobinism, which seeks to palm itself off as patriotism—here is Bernadotte trying to be more of a Jacobin than all of us together. This shows a lack, first, of taste, and, next, of common-sense. The Jacobins were all very well when it was necessary to disorganize and overthrow. Now it is a question of reorganizing and reconstructing. Bernadotte appears not to understand this, and to look upon us as Chouans. He bawls of Fatherland and liberty at the top of his voice; he would fain scream like an eagle, while at the best he whistles like a blackbird—which he indeed resembles, for he is at heart too good to be a decided bird of prey. I am willing that he should direct and make war; that is his business, and he understands it; but as regards politics and revolution proper, he is a child, and a dangerous child."

Gohier and Moulins thought Sieyès's remarks about Bernadotte rather severe, and pointed out that more consideration should be shown to the indispensable man who was just now rendering such important services to the Fatherland. I indorsed what they said, adding that Bernadotte's frankness in his dealings with everybody, and the special confidence he had shown me both in his letters and his spoken words, gave me the hope that I could make myself understood by him, however severe might be the truths I should tell him; I therefore would undertake to arrange everything in this respect, and I entreated Sieyès not to show or retain any prejudice against Bernadotte. It was somewhat venturesome to expect that Sieyès could rid himself of spleen and resentment. Events will still further unmask characters.

It was more natural that Sieyès seemed to realize that France's military reverses should somewhat excite the man whose sole duty it was to repair them, and who was sufficiently cognizant of the extent of this duty and of the requirements of war to know that they could not be met, unless the nation once more displayed the energy which had supplied so many resources and given birth to so many miracles. Such were undoubtedly the noble sentiment and the sincere idea of Bernadotte, when confronting the lofty mission the burden of which he had undertaken. The military and the patriotic zeal of the Minister of War could not be separated under such grave circumstances. It was one and the same thing.

The recent composition of the *corps législatif* had constituted a kind of retaliation for the law of the 22d Floréal. Many deputies previously excluded by this law had been returned by the new election. They were doubtless inspired with the purest patriotic sentiments, coupled, however, with feelings of rancor which sought to be appeased. These feelings had already derived some satisfaction, on the 30th Prairial, from the expulsion of the Directors and the changes in the Ministry, but this was not sufficient for the ambition of some. This is a very common danger, especially in States where the frequent changes of officials and rulers present to all the chance of reaching the top of the ladder. Moreover, the various events happening beyond our frontiers furnished all public speakers with strong grounds for complaint, and consequently fine subjects for eloquence. In the Council of Ancients, it is the citizen Lemercier (since President of the Ancients, senator, and *pair de France;* in those days a rabid enemy of the Royalists) who causes to be referred to the Directorate a pamphlet on a confederation of the Royalists of the department of the Charente-Inférieure with those of the department of the Haute-Garonne. It is Briot who cannot find in Talleyrand's pamphlet the proof of his innocence, and who denounces him at all points as a "perverse being and a traitor of all times and to all *régimes.*" It is Français, so-called "de Nantes," although from the department of the Isère, the shrewdness and roughness of which he possesses, qualities in no wise connected with the land of Brittany, whose people are generally credited with being simple and open-hearted—Français, with whom I am extremely satisfied, and who so formally pronounced himself in my favor, and in mine alone, on the 28th Prairial, who presents to the Council of Five Hundred a report wherein he attributes the misfortunes of the Fatherland to the fact that instead of the spirit of the Revolution being regulated, it has been extinguished before the Revolution has been fully accomplished. He causes a resolution to be adopted establishing the celebration of the anniversary of the foundation of the Republic. All are agreed on this point; so far this is ostensibly and honorably Republican; but the citizen Français is not content with this. We are informed that he is constantly plotting with

Lucien Bonaparte; that he is urging forward those deputies less enlightened than himself, who place trust in his counsels. The citizen Français is one of those who most assiduously pay me court, and I would fain believe in his advances as sincerely as I respond to them. In his vehement harangue of the 3d Messidor he called my three expelled colleagues the "three tyrants," and I confess that this appellation is somewhat forcible. He added that one Director had fought the battle single-handed for the past eighteen months, but that his frank and kindly character could do nothing with narrow-minded creatures, whose petty souls instinctively devoted them to the vilest mischief-making. Français de Nantes further said that "Barras was the only Republican in the Government" whose primary duty it was to be Republican above all things. It will be perceived that, in the matter of caressing words and even flattery, I personally have all that I can expect from Français; but in his most obsequious caresses there seems something ironical and tricky, which does not inspire any sense of security in those who hold intercourse with him. It is certain that his intimacy with Lucien can neither be justified nor explained, and that beneath it lies concealed an intrigue, the development of which will appear later. Français was too prudent and wily to go solemnly and frequently to the *Manège*, which we had closed; but he had made others go thither, and, although he appeared to have nothing to do with it, from time to time he threw firebrands. He is truly one of the deputies who most urge on the others to defiance, and are desirous that the "dangers of the Fatherland" should be loudly proclaimed. With these magic words, taken in their literal sense by ardent minds, he kept the *corps législatif* in a perpetual state of ferment. Thereupon Briot ascends the steps of the tribune, and avers that a *coup d'état* is in preparation; that the *corps législatif* is being oppressed; that the people should come to its rescue; that when neither liberty nor independence is any longer enjoyed, it is time for the people to arise and work out their own salvation. Augereau, seeking to outdo Briot's speech, believes he is giving utterance to something more forcible when he exclaims: "Citizens, it is bruited abroad that the Directorate intends to make a *coup d'état* like that of the 18th Fructidor; now I know what I am about, and I maintain that it is impossible, because the Directorate has no right to do so!" An explosion of laughter greets the words of the speaker, who with a terrible and threatening mien repeats, while thumping on the tribune: "And I, I maintain that it has not the right to do so!" He is quickly asked by all "whether he was quite sure that he himself possessed this right when he so thoroughly operated in Paris on the 18th Fructidor." Poor Augereau was fated to furnish one more example, added to so many others, of the difference between military and oratorical capacity.

The veiled but more actively intriguing conduct of the brothers Bonaparte is a sustained revelation of the mission of which they have remained the instruments in France, for the carrying out of which Bonaparte has left them funds. It is likewise certain that the General of the Army of Egypt is paying no less attention to France than he did when in command of the Army of Italy, and that Cairo constitutes for him merely a stepping-stone to the position he intends to gain at home. Events will reveal all that lay concealed in the minds of those who had remained in France, as well as in that of the man who was away.

We learn officially that Pope Pius VI. has just died at Valence, in his eighty-second year and the twenty-fifth of his pontificate. Had these twenty-five years been accomplished, he would have had the right to sit in the apostolic see of St. Peter. The days he has lacked to enjoy this honor, which no Pope has so far reached, have been replete with misfortune, which he has endured with dignity and courage. The idea of his dethronement is one of those which the history of Bonaparte can claim. It was he who, during his command, after having petted and cajoled Pius VI., laying claim to the honor of "calling himself his son," had begun by despoiling him of his valuable pictures, his diamonds, and his money, and had ended in causing Berthier to be sent to him, for the purpose of carrying off the rest and tearing him from his throne.

A law is passed fixing the land taxation for the Year VIII. at two hundred and ten millions, and the personal property taxation at forty millions. The *décime* per franc on land-taxes is abolished, as well as the supplement to the taxes on personal property and the sumptuary taxes, as established by the law of the 6th Prairial last. This certainly constitutes some alleviation for the present, and resources for the future, which should instil peace into men's minds; but the evil is present. All military and civil services are in arrears; it is necessary to meet urgent needs, and the enemies of the Republic seem to combine for the purpose of refusing the State everything. The returned *émigrés* and their relatives are bestirring themselves actively, and again showing themselves as audaciously as they did previous to the 18th Fructidor. The Directorate believes it can restore quiet in the seventeen departments stirred up by them by applying to them the law on hostages. An idea may be conceived of the fearfully disturbed state of the departments of the South by reading one of the bulletins by which we were kept informed as to the state of those districts:

La Ciotat.   BULLETIN OF THE SOUTH.

17th Fructidor,
Year VII.   "Those who set the rulers against the ardent Republicans, and the ardent Republicans against the rulers, are not the true friends of the Republic and of the rulers."

Department of the Bouches-du-Rhône.

Scattered bands are stealing, plundering, and assassinating. Pronounced Republicans, especially those who are incorruptible, are on lists of proscription. Whoever devotes himself to the full carrying out of the orders of the Government is threatened with death.

It must be known in Paris that the citizen Gueymard, president of the canton of Saint-Zacharie, was butchered a while ago. The deed was perpetrated by thirty armed brigands; they shot him dead, then gouged out his eyes and mutilated him.

The brigands believed that among the persons arrested was a citizen named Châteauneuf, inspector of barriers in the Var, and were greatly annoyed at not finding him.

Last week two other Republicans were assassinated, after having been compelled to kiss a crucifix.

Quite recently the citizen Borresy, a master-mason, was butchered near Aubagne. His brother has fallen a victim to the powerful Jean.

The day before yesterday, near Cassis, a band of seven

stripped four persons, among whom was an artillery captain, to whom the brigands said: "Go and tell your commandant that we are Royalists and *émigrés*."

Lastly, a band of fifty brigands has been seen. It is said that it was recruiting secretly.

The above is an outline of what is taking place in our neighborhood. There is no doubt but that it is sought to "Vendée-ize" the whole of the department of the Bouches-du-Rhône and the borders of the Var; this will happen if a prompt remedy is not applied.

As to the Means of Preventing and Extirpating Brigandage in this Portion of the South.

Courts-martial composed of the right men should at once be set to work, and be made to proceed briskly.

The law on brigandage should be applied to all cantons where a single Republican has been assassinated.

Keep a strong garrison in Marseilles.

Let well-commanded patrols remain permanently on the roads leading from one commune to another; this throughout the South, and as far as Lyons.

No man should be suffered to carry a gun or pistols and other weapons while travelling or in the country districts without a special license, which he shall neither lend nor transfer.

The gendarmerie and soldiery shall demand the production of such licenses, and arrest whosoever shall be unprovided with one after the date indicated.

Guard-rooms shall be established at various points on the highways.

The troops shall, at a given signal, concentrate from all points at the spot whence the signal has been issued.

Military commissions shall try all the *émigrés* now in prison, and search shall be made by trusty persons to discover the *émigrés* of both sexes tolerated in the South, and in particular in Marseilles, where the *émigrés* of Toulon are keeping up a hot-bed of permanent conspiracy by their speeches, letters, etc.

As to the Principal Administrations of the Department and of Marseilles.

There can be no doubt that in order that the orders of the Government shall be punctually executed, it is necessary that the members of the administrations be true and pure Republicans.

Barbier and Crassis are pointed out as the only members of the central administration upon whom any reliance can be placed; the three other administrators are intriguers, or reputed as such.

Mauche, ex-commissary of the Directorate, is, so it is said, a libertine, a professional gambler, and an ambitious man. Previous to holding office he was a blustering patriot; since then he has been seen arm in arm with anti-Republicans; hence this department is in arrears in regard to the collection of taxes, in regard to the progress of public spirit, and has become the lair of the brigands.

Micoulin, a former commissary of the *bureau central* of Marseilles, is not a whit better than Mauche; he is a young man who was called out by *réquisition* (extraordinary and forced levy); he was formerly an ultra patriot, but now he is as gentle as a lamb towards the Royalists and *émigrés*.

The *bureau central* of Marseilles is very badly constituted; it makes a pretence of causing laws and enactments to be executed, but in the main its indolence is more than suspicious, or, to speak more truly, of the most guilty nature. In a district as fanatical and depraved as that of Marseilles, it has not even caused temples to be opened and put in readiness in every quarter for the celebration of marriages according to the law—marriages which are still being performed in the town-hall of each *arrondissement*.

The citizen Escalon, the new commissary of the Directorate in the department, is a tried Republican, a good father, a good friend, and a good Frenchman; by virtue of his fortune and sentiments he is inaccessible to corruption; he has set an example to conscripts, having sent three of his sons to the army.

It is important quickly to organize the central administration and the *bureau central*, to expel from them those undeserving of confidence, and to fill their places with men carefully selected. This measure is indispensable and most urgent.

The citizen Giraud, the commissary recently appointed by the Directorate in succession to Micoulin, is reputed to be a wise and firm Republican.

These two new selections meet with the approval of the mass

of Republicans; it is to be hoped that experience will show that they have not been mistaken in their opinion.

The municipality of Marseilles is fairly well composed.

The day of the anniversary of the 18th Fructidor is at hand. Boulay de la Meurthe, President of the Five Hundred, says in his speech: "The object of this *fête* is to celebrate one of the most signal triumphs of the Republic over royalism." He recalls the causes which led to the taking of the violent and even extra-constitutional measure, the great and useful results by which the Directorate was to have signalized the dictatorship with which it was invested, and the abuse it made of this immense power. "The 30th Prairial," he said, "was no less necessary than the 18th Fructidor, and the *corps législatif* itself needs all its wisdom to steer clear of the shoal on which the old Directorate was wrecked."

Were it in such serious times possible to be a little less serious than the events themselves, I should here record an anecdote which Bernadotte tells us in connection with the death of Joubert. The firm and vigorous conduct of the Minister on that occasion, which had been a cause of genuine alarm to many energetic Republicans, permitted him to notice with no little irony a trait which would prove somewhat amusing were it not connected with an intrigue which has not been without its influence on the destiny of Joubert, and consequently on the destiny of the Republic.

Semonville, in order to indulge, like so many others, in a speculation, had married his step-daughter to Joubert, and came post-haste to the Ministry of War to make sure "if his death, the news of which was circulating, was an assured fact." On Bernadotte's hesitating to confirm a piece of news which he thought would pain him deeply, Semonville, in a broken voice and Spartan tone, said to him: "But have we at least won the battle?" For the time being Bernadotte imagined he saw in Semonville a Roman. This Roman came on the following day, and subsequently, to assail the Minister with requests for money for his widow, for offices and promotions for his relations, always obtaining admission as "the father of General Joubert," and working the death of the unfortunate general as if it were a rich mine.

Thirty years ago Semonville was only at the outset of a life which had nevertheless had many antecedents; since then he has gone on developing himself with ever-increasing distinction under all successive *régimes*. His affairs have always continued to flourish. Talleyrand alone can stand comparison with him as a chameleon.

CHAPTER XV

Aristocratic sentiments of Sieyès; his *mot* in regard to the *canaille*—M. de Lubersac and his vicar-general; Sieyès attacked by the newspapers; his atrabilious speeches—His dread of the Jacobins and the *corps législatif*—List of the deputies who alarm him—Marbot; his noble character; he offends the sensitiveness of Sieyès and is dismissed—Lefebvre succeeds him—Lefebvre's circumspection; he takes counsel with Jourdan—My position in the Directorate—Calumnies spread against me—Mysterious visit of a few deputies to Bernadotte—They threaten to issue a warrant for my arrest—The King of Sweden and Walter Scott—A general at the head of the deputation to Bernadotte—Who was this general?—Anecdote giving rise to the calumny levelled at me—My relations with Louis XVIII.—Fauche-Borel—Subordinate intriguers—Fauche-Borel writes to me—I communicate his letter to the Directorate, which looks into the matter—Talleyrand undertakes to follow it up—M. Eyriès—Betrayed by too much wit—Fauche-Borel asks for another intermediary—My letter to him—M. Guérin—Official letter from Fauche-Borel—Letters-patent from the King—Infamous corruption; the whole intrigue revealed to the Directorate—Fouché informed—David Monnier—What it is sought to do with the correspondence—My opinion in the matter—Talleyrand's *mot* to Bonaparte against the Bourbons—His anti-Bourbonist hatred—The haul he would like to attempt.

EVER since his entrance into the Directorate, Sieyès, owing to his display of temper at several of our sittings and even at public audiences, had offended a good many people. The newspapers had got hold of the fact, and charged Sieyès with aristocracy. He had been reminded of the old, old anecdote of the days when he was the vicar-general of M. de Lubersac, Bishop of Chartres. Under the impression that he was on a certain occasion celebrating mass in the presence of "gentle-folk," he had turned round, and seeing that his congregation consisted of "common folk," had been unable to control his vexation, and had left off saying mass, exclaiming, "I do not say mass for the *canaille!*" The recollection of this anecdote and several other strictures passed on the atrabilious character of Sieyès, his spiteful priestly nature, his intimacy with the most corrupt men of his period, and in particular with Talleyrand—all this furnished daily food for conversation and for the public journals. Some of the editors of these sheets, when once they have entered upon polemics, seek to keep them going forever, to "have the last word," and believe it their duty to hunt a man down to the day of his death. Sieyès's irritation grew apace; he committed the mistake—an enormous one for a public man, who should always remain impassible—of giving way to all his impulses and to constant chatter, most extraordinary on the part of a man famed for his imperturbable silence. Sieyès unfortunately made for himself or for us, or rather against us all, a still more reprehensible use of his ill-temper. He emptied his bile into the speeches he had to pronounce as president of the Directorate, when his principal study should have been to forget his own personality. He might have done even better than forget it. He might have become reconciled with the popular party by ceasing to offend it; and it would have remembered with gratitude the early and immense services rendered to liberty by the author of *Essai sur les Priviléges, Qu'est-ce que le Tiers-État?* and other deservedly famed productions, which had shed a flood of enlightenment over France and determined his early triumphs. Woe to the statesman who gives way to his political resentments, and who unconsciously mixes them with the exercise of his office! The saddest fate awaits him, and it may be said that the Fatherland is truly in danger; for, the lawful course of justice not satisfying his passions, he must needs seek other means, and overstep the rights and the limits of duty. His adversaries, on their side, place themselves in a state of defence, and whatever the outcome it means disaster to the Fatherland. Sieyès, not only a witness of but a sincere participant in the 18th Fructidor, had been the first to proclaim that it was rather the work of Carnot than our own, since it was Carnot who had rendered the event necessary. So here he was provoking another crisis, since he was entering upon a fight which could end only in the violent victory of one of the two parties. Neither the example of Carnot, Treilhard, nor Merlin, who fell victims to their spleen and spite, nor any of the many recent and striking examples, serve as a warning to Sieyès, nor, while warning him, tone down his implacable disposition. All the anxieties and terrors successively displayed in our presence by Carnot, Treilhard, and especially Merlin, are now besetting Sieyès. He sees Jacobins everywhere. Bernadotte sends him the secretary-general of the War Department to confer with him, as president of the Directorate, about most grave and urgent interests, in particular about the landing of the English in Holland. Sieyès replies to him with an amount of alarm still greater than that so far caused by the event: " We are beset by greater dangers than this—those coming from the Jacobins, who wish to assassinate us." He sees the faces of these Jacobins who frighten him in all about us— Ministers, generals, civil agents, State messengers, and ushers of the Directorate.

Fouché, who daily makes him the most satisfactory reports, in no wise satisfies him. He sees in everything that this Minister promises to do against the two parties a basis of special protection granted to the Jacobins. In vain does Fouché tell him that this apparent protection granted to the Jacobins is nothing but a surer means of controlling them and of penetrating their ranks while pretending to be on their side; that, after all, were one to pronounce one's self against them, it might still further irritate them, and put an additional weapon into the hands of the Royalists, who were already rising in one part of France. "You do not believe, citizen Fouché," Sieyès would reply, "that the Royalists would find a defender in me; I abandon the Royalists to your tender mercies, but the anarchists with them. Pound them all up in the same mortar, and I will say that you understand your duty."

Sieyès was equally uneasy about the *corps législatif*, whose sittings were indeed characterized by violent discussions, which would not have presented any great danger had the Directorate, confining itself within its attributes and knowing how to maintain them, remained united, and had it not unfortunately been known that it was divided against itself.

In consequence of all these declamations of Sieyès, repetitions of those of Carnot, we asked him one day who were the deputies whom he was willing to except from his animadversion, and in whom some confidence might be placed. He promised to give us a list of them, but on the following day he said to us: "They are all good or bad, according to the way in which they are put to use;" and instead of furnishing us with a list of those deserving of some esteem, he handed us one, he remarked, "of men who should be distrusted." This list bore the names of Bergasse, Bertrand, Berlier, Lamarque, Quirot, Jacomin, Talot, Saliceti, and the brothers Bonaparte, both of whom he looked upon as good-for-nothing scoundrels, ever engaged in jobs and in machinations against the Government. "All these folks," he would repeat incessantly, "will not suffer being ruled; they are ungovernable." "And you," was our reply—"you are incapable of governing, for you are forever giving way to vague declamations; you never specify anything, nor do you propose any mode of execution."

One of the generals reinstated as the result of recent revolutions, and chief among those who caused Sieyès uneasiness, was the commander of the 17th division, Marbot, one of the most genuine patriots of the period, an honest and intrepid man, who had served us with all the resources he possessed on the 18th Fructidor. His fortune, as he had told me in friendly conversation, was so small that he actually needed the pay attached to his rank. Marbot lacked the political capacity which could make him judge with precision the degree of maturity reached by the Revolution, and the impossibility at this time of resorting to means or individuals obsolete, or harmful under certain conditions. Marbot, governed by a noble soul, would have liked to see all the friends of the Republic unite against its enemies, and he believed that its real enemies were the

Royalists. This opinion led him to incline towards those whom Sieyès called Jacobins; that is to say that, looking upon these Jacobins as the first soldiers of the Republican army, Marbot thought it advisable to use tact in dealing with them, to treat them with affectionate regard, to enlighten them, and at least not to fire upon one's own troops. I had several times spoken with Marbot on this point; I understood his political morality, the sincere expression of an upright heart which did not mix with any intrigue. Sieyès had sought to draw Marbot over to his side at once. Whether it was that he had spoken to him in too metaphysical language which Marbot did not understand, or whether he had offended him by his irritability, Marbot had not left on the mind of Sieyès the impression that he was altogether one with him in his opinion of men and things. This was enough for Sieyès not to forgive Marbot. "He must absolutely be superseded in the command of the 17th division," said Sieyès; "he must be sent to join the army if we are not all to perish." These utterances of Sieyès seemed to us the result of his usual exaggeration, begotten of the fears assailing him; but as he opened every session with them, we were worried, in order to enjoy peace, into granting him Marbot's dismissal. I succeeded in getting accepted as his successor General Lefebvre, one of the most distinguished soldiers of the Army of Sambre-et-Meuse, our chief general of the vanguard, who, so often wounded on the field of battle, had not yet recovered from the wounds received at Stockach. I had had opportunity to judge of Lefebvre's military merits, and to get him his due on several occasions. I had found him devoted to his country, both on the 18th Fructidor and under all circumstances. It was sufficient that my friendship for Lefebvre should be a matter of notoriety for Sieyès not to feel quite reassured about him. He could and should have been so nevertheless, for, however sincere a Republican Lefebvre might be, he did not enter seriously upon political discussions.

Immediately on his assuming his duties, the Directorate having ordered him to close the clubs which were agitating Paris, Lefebvre caused our orders to be punctually and promptly executed. But, far from seeking to push matters beyond his orders, Lefebvre would have liked that the patriots should not lose in the Republic the rank which was theirs by right of conquest and by the very necessity of the maintenance of the Republic. Was its defence to be handed over to its enemies? Lefebvre's conduct was rather the result of instinct and natural good sense than of subtlety. Hence it was that, owing to the political timidity which existed in him no less than in other military men, he felt the need of propping himself up with and leaning on those whom, in his military religion, he considered his superiors. General Jourdan, under whom Lefebvre had served, had remained the object of his deference. He listened to him with conviction, and conferred with him on what seemed to him difficult points. Lefebvre, who was wont to open his mind to me in this connection, inspired me with perfect security, and daily gave me personal guarantees of the loyal conduct which guided and would ever guide Jourdan in the Councils.

Meanwhile, in the midst of discussions which were daily becoming more ardent, Jourdan's *rôle* seemed to some persons if not equivocal, at least without unity or system. I was unable to refrain from mentioning the matter to Lefebvre with some uneasiness and even mistrust. Lefebvre at once suggested that he should bring General Jourdan to me, in order that we might have an explanation. Jourdan replied to General Lefebvre that, considering the feelings of dislike entertained by the patriot party for the Directorate, and for me personally to a greater degree perhaps than for others, he was compelled to be very circumspect in his relations; that " if he called upon me as usual, he ran the risk of becoming suspect to his party; that he must adopt some means of seeing me without his compromising himself."

It was with some astonishment that I heard Lefebvre tell me this. The affection I had shown General Jourdan had been publicly and solemnly expressed. When expressing his gratitude to me in person he was as a consequence expressing sentiments which he disowned elsewhere. To put it plainly, his position was false, if not his character. " So, so," I said to General Lefebvre, " here we have the two-faced Jourdan, just as some people have said. I had put down to his timidity a certain embarrassment in his looks, his difficulty in looking me in the face—a peculiarity I do not like in the case of men with whom I entertain relations I believe to be of mutual esteem. Moreover, if he is false towards me, or towards what he calls his party, which I thought was ours, I pity him. Frankness is ever the soul of great things. As, moreover, the sentiment of the public weal has so often made me overlook many personal considerations, since General Jourdan wishes to see me without danger to himself, I am willing. Tell him to choose his hour." Lefebvre, who left me at a very late hour, wrote to me at midnight the following letter :[1]

| 17ᵉ DIVISION MILITAIRE | *LIBERTÉ* | *ÉGALITÉ* |

PARIS HEADQUARTERS, 22d Fructidor, Year VII.
of the French Republic, one and indivisible.

General Lefebvre, commanding the Division, to the Director Barras.

I have the honor to inform you, my dear Director, that General Jourdant (*sic*) will have the honor of calling upon you to-morrow, the 23d inst., at six o'clock in the morning. Pending the pleasure of calling upon you myself, I beg you to be assured of my sincere attachment to the grave.

LEFEBVRE.

I received General Jourdan at the hour appointed. I anticipated his explanations with all the affection I had always shown him. I found him as embarrassed as his matutinal visit foreboded. He hung his head even more than was his wont. He could not look me in the face. "Well, general," I remarked, "now that we have not met by chance, we have something to say to each other." "Citizen Director, the Fatherland is in danger; great evils call for strong remedies; France is on the brink of the abyss; she must be saved." "I am quite willing, general representative of the people, to save her, but I know of only one means, and it is the one which I pointed out to you in reply to the letter you wrote to me in full confidence last Prairial. It is the union of the authorities to whom France has in-

---

[1] The autograph is inserted in the manuscript of Barras.—G. D.

trusted her destinies. I know the Revolution better than you do, general; permit me to declare to you that it is with this knowledge that I assert to you that, if the true friends of liberty will but come to an understanding, the question of the Royalists will cease to exist. In spite of their raising their heads in a few districts in La Vendée and in the South, I assure you that their power is not real. The Royalists and royalty itself have been things of the past ever since the victories of the Republic, beginning with Fleurus and ending to-day. The Royalists can in no wise be brought upon the stage again unless by our own fault, by coming in in the train of one triumphant faction or another. Now the whole contest, I repeat it, ever since the organization of the Republic, before and after the 9th Thermidor, merely lies between parties wrangling with one another for power; Royalism, which interferes occasionally, carries a certain personal strength, which, however, disappears immediately before the breath of the Republicans. It is the Republicans themselves, unfortunately divided among themselves, who make all the stir of which they complain. Without going to seek examples any further, just look how false or strange our position is in this talk we are now having. I have always received you with kindliness and consideration; you have given me, both by word of mouth and in your letters, proofs of an esteem which you have perhaps avowed before others. Look at the manner in which you now call to see me, and the hour you have chosen to come to the Luxembourg! What do you mean by the regard you feel compelled to show your party, and which you made our comrade Lefebvre mention to me?

He, you, and I, are we not of the same party—that of the Republic, that of the good and wise liberty for which we have fought, each one of us on different battle-fields? Do you take me for an aristocrat or a Chouan? Do you consider yourself a better patriot than I, since you fear to jeopardize your popularity if you let the public hear the sentiments you express to me in private? I am not a woman whom one seeks to meet clandestinely. I am a sincere and loyal defender of all Republicans. I am he whom all can avow, and although my name is not Bayard, I am bold to assume his motto: '*Sans peur et sans reproche.*' Frankness, general, in the tribune as well as in my drawing-room, at midnight as well as at six o'clock in the morning, union based on mutual esteem—this is what will allay the tempest, and once more launch the ship of State on a calm sea."

I told General Jourdan, in as delicate a fashion as possible, that his conduct lacked uprightness. I would have excused his having seemed not to understand me on this point; but what made me most regret not being understood by him was his lack of comprehension of the troublous times through which we were passing. The means of the Terror, proclamations of the Fatherland in danger, forced loans, the law on hostages — all that was at least worn out, and could no longer be productive of any results. Liberty could not longer pursue its course and defend itself except with the resources of its legal organization, by calling upon all citizens of course, but in a regular way and without any shock, to unite for the common defence, on the grounds of the safety of all and of general security. The aristocrats had been sufficiently drubbed by the Revolution to no longer dare to rebel; they were resigned to the Republic, and cowed by all the lessons they had received; all that was necessary was to maintain their obedience, and the taste for liberty would come to them as to everybody else. "We have," I further said to General Jourdan, "what we did not have at the outset of the Revolution, and in far more critical times, when the enemy, in possession of a part of the frontier, was midway between it and Paris. We have to-day an organization; we have great civil and military organizations; we should force all to join them. This is very easy if the malcontents have nothing to hope from our divisions. I assure you, general, that the sentiments I express are those of my colleagues; it is on behalf of them all as well as for myself that I accept the compliments you have seen fit to pay to me alone. The whole Directorate is one in sincerely desiring the Republic." "But Sieyès," remarked General Jourdan ironically, "is he what is called a good Republican? Has he not entered into certain engagements in Berlin?" "Make your mind easy on that score," I replied to Jourdan; "Sieyès has no more regard for the King of Prussia than for the other kings. Since he has returned from his embassy he is forever speaking to us with both contempt and hatred of the Prussians and their monarch. He says they are so many knaves and beggars, and that they are the Jews and the Italians of Germany. Moreover, Sieyès is as Republican as you and I; so do not be any more anxious on this point than on the others, my dear general."

I took leave of Jourdan after these words, and showed the delicacy of not inviting him to dinner, as usual, in order not to do violence to his position, which I had fully grasped. Such was my behavior towards the members of the *corps législatif* represented in a way by one of their chiefs. Such were my innermost thoughts in regard to my colleagues of the Directorate; this method of acting proceeded from my heart as well as from my conscience; it was painful to me to see that my conduct was not appreciated by some of them, and this from various points of view. Owing to my refusal to connive at Sieyès's fits of ill-temper, or rather of fury, against the Jacobins, he classed me with both Jacobins and anarchists. Moulins censured me for other reasons than those of Sieyès; because I would not incline favorably towards the threatening turbulence of the new clubs, Moulins considered me an aristocrat bound to the old *régime* by recollections of nobility and family interest.

While I was thinking and acting thus uprightly, calumny was relentlessly pursuing me, coupling my name the while with that of Sieyès himself. I was informed that Sieyès and myself were generally credited with the intention of changing the Constitution and the existing state of things. I also heard that a deputation of the *corps législatif* had called upon the Minister of War, Bernadotte, to communicate this suspicion to him. According to the idea thus promulgated, Sieyès was alleged to entertain the desire of having the Duke of Brunswick elected as king, while I was supposed to be paving the way for the return of the Bourbons. The deputation which made this communication to

Bernadotte even went so far as to say to him that it contemplated issuing warrants for the arrest of Sieyès and myself.

Bernadotte mentioned the incident at the time, and even since he has become a king he has communicated it in writing to historians (see the appendix to the *Life of Napoleon* by Walter Scott). Bernadotte is under the impression that on this occasion he inquired of the deputation denouncing us "what were the proofs in support of the allegations set forth." On being answered that there was nothing positive, the Minister is supposed to have replied that "he would in no wise participate in the proposed illegal act"; he adds that he said further, when taking leave of these gentlemen so hard to please in the matter of patriotism, "I require of you your word of honor that you will renounce this design; it is the only way in which you can secure my silence in the matter." A member of the deputation, with whom Bernadotte had served, answered him: "It was our intention to invest you with a high power, fully persuaded that you would not abuse it; since you do not view things from the same standpoint as ourselves, all is at an end: let all that has passed be buried in the deepest oblivion."

In his artless narrative Bernadotte has shown the delicacy of not naming General Jourdan; but unfortunately I cannot entertain any doubt that the last speaker could have been no other than the very general from whom I had, two months earlier, received such intimate written communications, who two days previously had come to renew them at the rendezvous he had asked of me for six o'clock in the morning, and at which I had spoken to him with so much effusion. I do not pretend that this behavior of Jourdan's constituted falseness. I will only say that military men little accustomed to patriotic frankness, and whose character has no natural decision, are often liable to go astray in the matters with which they are not familiar, especially when express orders have not traced for them the precise road they are to follow.

It is possible, moreover, that many of the unjust aspersions of which I was the object seemed well founded to those who spread them; they were perhaps connected also with alleged facts explained imperfectly or not at all, in particular with a somewhat strange affair known to my colleagues, and which, had it been possible to make the nation cognizant of it there and then, could but have secured to me in a greater degree the esteem which enemies themselves cannot refuse to faithful accomplishment of duty, to probity in the exercise of the functions with which the nation has intrusted us. I must here relate in all its simplicity this alleged affair, which constituted the beginning of the *rôle* it was then sought and has been since sought to pretend I was playing, with the object of re-establishing on the throne the dynasty of the Bourbons. This simple recital, corroborated by documents setting forth actual facts, will show what was the fixity of my principles in regard to our political question, the truth, the sincerity, and, I venture to say, the probity of my Republicanism.

Thrice retained in my position by chance, and maintained throughout every crisis we had passed through, I had received from most civil and military men, who worship power only, all the felicitations which they never failed to address to it. I was not overwhelmed by such flattery, and if I consented to retain power, I did not at any rate conceive the idea of increasing it. But whenever it so happens that, under any condition of things, a man seems to exercise a greater power than others, he naturally becomes the object of attempts and seductions of every kind. This will explain how it was that from afar Louis XVIII. looked upon me as the head of the Directorate, as indeed events made me appear. My position explains how the Pretender came to conceive or to accept the idea of causing me to be approached in my capacity of a member of the Government.

There was in those days, in the neighborhood of Hamburg, an intriguer styling himself the agent of the Pretender Louis XVIII. He pretended that for several years he had filled several missions to the governments and high civil and military functionaries of the Republic, boasting that he would reach them and even sound them in the interests of royalty's cause. It is true that this individual, Fauche-Borel by name, had on several occasions been commissioned by Louis XVIII., by the Prince de Condé, and by the English Government with various missions, which consisted in approaching directly or indirectly the men invested with the highest powers of the Republic, and corrupting them by liberal promises of positions, promises backed up with sums of money; but Fauche-Borel and his associates, when offering their services to the Royalist party as agents of corruption, had begun by corrupting themselves — that is, by pocketing the funds placed in their hands by the ingenuousness of their employers. This is how Fauche-Borel and Company, receiving considerable sums from Wickham, the Prince de Condé, and Louis XVIII., pretended they had remitted them now to Pichegru, now to others, to whom they never spoke; this is how, in the early years of the Revolution, they appropriated to themselves the wages of corruption. It was unavoidable that in order to keep up this species of speculation —since they could not prove the genuineness of the relations which were the pretext of their intrigues, inventing daily fresh stories in order to establish in the eyes of the dupes who paid them an appearance of the intercourse they were supposed to entertain with the eminent personages of the Republic— the impostors should be occasionally compromised. Their frequenting of the gambling-houses of the royal cause, which they were the first to betray while appearing to be proscribed for its sake, the apparent and even the actual persecutions to which double spies are sometimes exposed—all this nourished and sustained the credit of their manœuvres with the innocent or stupid Royalist plotters.

One of the intriguers assuming a many-sided *rôle* was Fauche-Borel, a former bookseller in Switzerland and in Paris, who had failed in business everywhere, but who had, nevertheless, in his very failures and their attending and dangerous embarrassments found resources for the development of the faculty of subordinate intrigue which he had received from an ignoble but active nature, still further excited by the stirring spectacle of a great revolution. Fauche-Borel, expelled from everywhere, ran hither and thither, presenting himself to the princes on the strength of the persecutions he pretended he had suffered on their behalf in the course of the first missions he had been intrusted with by the principal confidential agents of the Bourbons. Thus it was that Fauche-Borel secured the opportunity of soliciting and obtaining higher missions from the princes who might still possess the means, as they had the credulity to intrust to him the money which the foreign Powers placed at their disposal.

As I have just made clear, the important and decisive *rôle* I had already played on the stage of the Revolution gave me an altogether special importance, drawing upon me the attention of all intriguers. So it was that Fauche-Borel thought he could train his batteries on me. And yet the General-in-chief of the 9th Thermidor, of the 13th Vendémiaire, and of the 18th Fructidor could hardly appear accessible to the seductions of the lovers of royalty. Fauche-Borel thought it all the more clever to make the Pretender and the several Cabinets from whom he drew funds think that I was precisely the most vulnerable, since I was the man whom it was most necessary to win over. In consequence of this, Fauche-Borel wrote to me from Wesel under the name of Frédéric Borelly, and with his accustomed impudence stated that he had "important revelations to make to me, of interest both to France and the Directorate. He would like to have passports for Paris, or the despatch on my part of an agent enjoying my full confidence."

Fauche-Borel's letter, coming as it did from abroad, was handed to my porter at ten o'clock in the morning; it was immediately communicated by me to the Directorate on the same day at the opening of the sitting. The Directorate was of the unanimous opinion "not to neglect this proposition, and to send at once an agent who should gather all the information that could be procured." The mission should emanate from the Ministry of Foreign Affairs. Talleyrand, who was himself to confer it, was summoned. On the communication of the document and of the Directorate's intention, which he eagerly embraced, he said that the matter deserved the greatest attention, that "nothing should be neglected in politics, that although the Bourbons might be of little importance in themselves, the intriguers surrounding them might be of more, that they were indeed France's true enemies." It may be that the censure of his conduct by the Republicans, and the danger of his losing his portfolio, made him feel the need of displaying a greater luxury of patriotic sentiments, and of bringing all his guns to bear on the Bourbons, in order to defend himself against the accusations of which he was the object; he added that he was "just about to send to Cleves an agent named Eyriès, and he would commission him to see Borelly at Wesel."

The mission of Eyriès had no result; Borelly, who indeed saw him at Wesel, but who perceived that he was fathomed by this man of wit, thought it wiser to conceal himself in a cloud of mystery, and to ask me to despatch to him a more authentic agent, one truly invested with full power by me. The Directorate decided that another agent should be sent, provided with a letter from me. I gave the following letter, written under the eyes of the Directorate and annexed to its record-book:

I acknowledge the receipt, sir, of the letter you wrote to me, and which was sent to me by the citizen Eyriès; I have communicated it to the Directorate, which has ordered the Minister of Foreign Affairs to grant a passport to the citizen Guérin, the bearer of the present letter, to whom you can in all confidence give all and every information, and hand the documents you state are of paramount interest to the Republic, the Government, and to me in particular.

Pray receive my salutations.   P. BARRAS.

M. Guérin, who was entitled to our fullest confidence owing to his sentiments of devotion to the Republic, faithfully fulfilled his mission. He made sport of Fauche-Borel in the most serious tone, and mystified him so completely that he wrote, and M. Guérin brought to us, the following letter:

Fauche-Borel's Second Letter.

WESEL, 17*th Vendémiaire, Year VIII.*

CITIZEN DIRECTOR,

The citizen Guérin, invested with your special confidence, and bearer of the letter you deigned to address to me under date of the 2d inst., will have the honor of supplying you orally with the particulars, which it would take too long to place before you in a letter written in haste. I shall therefore content myself with transmitting the mere facts to you, and informing you without circumlocution of what I am commissioned to tell you. Nor shall I undertake to speak to you of the present situation of the French Republic; no one can better appreciate it than you and your colleagues, while the addresses which reach you from the various departments can leave no doubt in your minds as to the dangers that are foreseen.

His Majesty Louis XVIII., deeply moved at and bemoaning the evils in store for France should hostile armies come to invade her soil, and having everything to fear from the civil war which would follow thereupon, places in your hands all possible means and facilities wherewith to save France from an invasion and secure to you, in your position, the assurance of a complete success. You are French, citizen Director, and this is enough for you to seize eagerly the happy dispositions of two great Powers, who are, just at present, prepared to help you with their funds and strength.

Military events, which are daily occurring, might, were you to delay too long, cause them to alter their resolution, and you would have lost forever the opportunity of rescuing unhappy France from the calamities threatening her, and you would postpone the dawn of peace, so prayed for by all nations.

You will see by an extract from the memorandum laid before the Emperor of all the Russias, and which I hand somewhat hurriedly to the citizen Guérin, how kindly are his intentions, as well as those of the English Government; you may place full reliance on them.

The copy of letters-patent destined for you will convince you of the King's intentions, and leave you nothing to desire in this direction. The Court of Prussia would see with great satisfaction an operation of this nature, and you might reckon with certainty upon its mediation; I have positive assurances to this effect.

The citizens Botot and David are in a position to satisfy you in regard to all that preceded my journey and that of a friend to London and to St. Petersburg. It will suffice for me to tell you that, previous already to the 18th Fructidor, I had been commissioned to join you; but in those days we could not offer you the guarantees which we now possess, and which leave nothing to be desired on the part of the Emperor of all the Russias, as in regard to the intentions of the English Government and the mediation Prussia would grant in this negotiation.

The perusal of the letters-patent dispenses me from entering into verbose particulars. You will gather from them, citizen Director, that it is reserved for you to save France, to procure peace for Europe and tranquillity for the world. You can do it, you possess the means for doing it, and posterity will ever pronounce your name with a feeling of admiration and gratitude.

Deign, citizen Director, to grant the continuation of your confidence, when pursuing this matter further, to the citizens Guérin and David. Should the latter not be sufficiently known to you, I can recommend him as a person of merit and personally devoted to you.

We have come to an understanding with the citizen Guérin as to meeting again in order to proceed together to the place of deposit, where to receive the funds necessary for the operation, and where the letters-patent, duly signed and sealed, shall be delivered to him in exchange for your letter of acceptance.

Receive, citizen Director, the homage of my profound respect, with which I have the honor to be,
Citizen Director,
Your most humble and most obedient servant,
Louis Frédéric Borelly.

LETTERS-PATENT FROM THE KING,

APPOINTING A COMMISSARY FOR PROCLAIMING THE MONARCHY.

LOUIS, by the grace of God King of France and Navarre, to Our friend and liege Paul, Vicomte de Barras, greeting:

Called by Our birth and the ancient constitution of the State to take upon Ourselves the burden of the government of France, convinced as We are that the first and most essential duty commanded Us by virtue of it is to restore the happiness of Our people by putting an end to the succession of calamities which have not ceased overwhelming them since the commencement of the Revolution, informed that the good and faithful subjects who constitute almost the totality of the inhabitants of Our Kingdom await only the expression of Our firm and stable word in order to co-operate with Us in the important objects of the re-establishment of the holy religion which We profess and that of the Monarchy, We have resolved, in consequence of the knowledge We possess of your ability and personal disposition, to commit to you the execution of this laudable and important commission.

For these and other reasons dictating this course to Us, with and by the advice of Our Council, of Our certain knowledge, of Our full and legitimate power, and of Our Royal authority, We have said and ordained, and do say and ordain, what follows:

ARTICLE 1.—We have appointed and do appoint you, Vicomte de Barras, as Our special Commissary, for the purpose of preparing and executing the pure and simple re-establishment of the French Monarchy, by all proper means which are or shall be at your disposal, conferring upon you the necessary authority and power to that effect, reserving unto Ourselves to provide subsequently for the government of Our Kingdom in conformity with Our affection for Our subjects, and with Our invariable will to procure their advantage.

ARTICLE 2.—We have authorized and do authorize you to select such number of Commissaries as you shall deem necessary to take as coadjutors to co-operate with you in the accomplishment of Our views, conditionally upon their acceptance of their commission within three days, failing which their appointment shall be null and void.

ARTICLE 3.—It is in consequence Our will that, within six months reckoned from this date, the re-establishment of the Monarchy shall be proclaimed in Our name throughout the extent of Our Kingdom, and in all countries now occupied by French troops and governed by French authorities, without prejudice, however, to the agreements to be entered into with foreign Powers, as soon as Our re-establishment shall place Us in a position to labor towards the return of peace and public tranquillity.

ARTICLE 4.—We have moreover authorized and do authorize you by these presents to adopt all measures which may be necessary to re-establish and maintain public order until the time of Our return into Our dominions, or that of Our Brother Monsieur, Lieutenant-General of the Kingdom.

ARTICLE 5.—When the re-establishment and the proclamation of the Monarchy shall have been made by you throughout the extent of Our Kingdom, or in a part thereof, We forbid each and every judge, each and every court of justice, or any other authorities whatsoever, to take cognizance, under any pretext and under any circumstance, of facts which have preceded, since the origin of the Revolution, or which shall precede or accompany the re-establishment of the Monarchy, in so far as the said facts may directly or indirectly concern yourself or the other commissaries acting as your coadjutors. We declare any person or persons who shall take cognizance of them enemies of Our Sacred Person, and do ordain that, the case occurring, they shall be prosecuted as guilty of high-treason, reserving unto Ourselves, when We shall have re-entered Our Kingdom, to pronounce by means of an Ordinance of Amnesty as to the facts relating to those of Our subjects not herein specified.

ARTICLE 6.—We pledge Our Authority and Royal Word to maintain forever and in all places yielding obedience to Us your liberty and tranquillity, and those of the Commissaries you shall have taken as coadjutors, as well as to employ Our intervention, if needs be, for your and their security in foreign lands.

ARTICLE 7.—We likewise pledge Our Authority and Royal Word to guarantee to you, as well as to the Commissaries aforesaid, the full and entire enjoyment of all rights and properties possessed or acquired by you or by them throughout the extent of Our Kingdom, and in those countries now occupied by French armies or authorities; and this notwithstanding all laws bearing or to bear in this respect having derogated from them in so far as necessary by these presents in all that concerns you as well as the Commissaries whom you have selected as Coadjutors.

ARTICLE 8.—Should it happen, however, that the owners of such rights and properties should refuse to ratify the sale made of them, or that owing to important considerations We should see fit to re-enter into possession of such rights and properties as should form part of Our personal domain, We bind ourselves to compensate you by an equivalent value, such compensation being likewise granted for such of the aforesaid rights and properties as should form part of the Domains of Our Crown, which it is not in Our power to alienate.

ARTICLE 9.—Desirous, moreover, of giving to you and to your Deputy-Commissaries a special mark of Our satisfaction and good-will, We ordain that in a month, to be reckoned from the day when We shall have assumed the reins of government, there shall be paid to you, on presentation of the present Letters-Patent, against your simple receipt and without any other ordinance, control, or visa, by way of personal compensation, the sum of *twelve million livres tournois*—to wit, *ten millions* for yourself, and *two millions* to be divided by you among your co-operators as and in such a manner as you shall see fit.

ARTICLE 10.—The sum referred to in the preceding article shall be paid to you in specie and according to the present standard, and it shall be levied concurrently on all ordinary and extraordinary funds, taking precedence over all other payments.

ARTICLE 11.—The present Letters-Patent shall not be subject to any registration, and, notwithstanding this, shall stand good as a declaration and ordinance relating to the needs and service of Our Person.

Given at Mittau under Our private seal, the tenth day of May, in the year of grace one thousand seven hundred and ninety-nine, and the fourth of Our Reign.

LOUIS.

[L. S.]

By the King:
Le cte. de SAINT-PRIEZ.

REASONS FOR THE PRINCIPAL MODIFICATIONS MADE BY THE KING TO THE DRAFT OF LETTERS-PATENT SENT BY M. MONNIER.

1. The King, in lieu of addressing Letters-Patent "to all who shall see these presents," addresses them directly to the Vicomte de Baras (*sic*), because the address of Letters-Patent should be made to the persons who are the object of them, and hence do they derive their name of "letters." The formulary of which the draft makes use is consecrated to "edicts and declarations," which are general laws. It is even all the more necessary to employ the form of Letters-Patent in the present special case, inasmuch as according to the last article the deed is to be exempt from registration, and were the King to give it the form of an edict His Majesty could not dispense it from registration in the Courts.

2. Articles 1 and 2 of the project, having a common object, have been comprised in a single article; Article 3, on the contrary, which embodied two separate dispositions, has been divided into two. Lastly, the order of these three articles has been reversed, because it is natural first to confer the power of re-establishing the Monarchy, and next to ordain the proclamation of the re-establishment.

3. In Article 1 the King adds to the word "re-establishment" the words "pure and simple," in order to characterize more plainly the nature of the mission intrusted to M. de Baras. But he inserts at the end of the article the clause "reserving unto Ourselves to *provide*," etc., in order to remove all *suspicion* of despotism or even of an absolute Monarchy.

4. The draft states too positively (Articles 1 and 2) that the King wishes to confine himself to the ancient limits of his kingdom, which might cause displeasure to the army; it is preferable

simply to announce peace, and to declare that the treaty shall have reference merely to *conquered countries*. It is for this reason that in the last dispositions of Article 3 the King speaks of these countries with the clause "without prejudice," etc.

5. Article 4 added to the draft was necessary in order to authorize M. de Baras to govern until such times as the King or Monsieur might themselves govern.

6. The King suppresses Article 4 of the draft, and substitutes for it a separate act. And indeed His Majesty cannot indicate in the Interior any public coffer wherefrom his Commissary might take 1,500,000 francs for the expenses of the movement, and cannot, moreover, give an assignment on the public coffers of a foreign Power. Now it would not be proper for the King to insert in his Letters-Patent a clause the execution of which would notoriously be impossible to him.

7. The reason of the clause "reserving unto Ourselves," etc., which terminates Article 5, is that in the case, natural to foresee, of the Letters-Patent becoming known, it might be thought, were this clause omitted, that the King does not intend granting an amnesty.

8. In Article 7 the King has not added to the word "property" the word "immunity." This expression could signify only an exemption from taxes, which the King cannot guarantee, because he would be unable to grant it.

9. The King has suppressed the end of Article 7 of the draft, and has added the article which stands eighth in the Letters-Patent. The following are the reasons for this alteration: His Majesty has not the power of confirming the sale of the properties of the Crown Domain, considering that their inalienability is pronounced by a fundamental law. His Majesty might, if absolutely necessary, renounce the properties forming part of his private domain; but it may likewise happen that important considerations may compel him again to enter into his own. With regard to the properties formerly belonging to private individuals, the Letters-Patent assuming that the proprietors be authorized by the laws to claim them, "the King, if he did not wish to ratify the sale," could not compel them to it except by an act of tyranny which would tarnish the beginnings of his reign; and this act of tyranny would not even be practicable in regard to properties situated in countries which, in consequence of the event and subsequent treaties, should no longer belong to France.

It is therefore just, or rather it is a necessity, that the Commissaries should remain content with an indemnity in the case foreseen by Article 8.

10. Article 10 of the draft embodies the following clause: "At latest in a month's time dating from the re-establishment of the Monarchy proclaimed in Our City of Paris." This clause requires modification. *First*, did M. de Baras cause the Monarchy to be proclaimed in Paris without causing a large portion of the troops or of the provinces to return to their duty, he would be only giving civil war to the King. *Secondly*, the King will have no means of paying the twelve millions so long as he shall not have again entered upon the exercise of his authority. *Thirdly*—and such is the meaning of Article 9 of the draft, according to which the promised sum "is to be paid by the principal Treasurer of His Majesty and from the funds destined to his *personnel*, etc."—since the King will not have a principal Treasurer, funds destined to his personal use, ordinary and extraordinary coffers, except when he shall be on the throne, it is therefore necessary to say: "Dating from the day when We shall have assumed the reins of government."

11. This clause of Article 9 of the draft in regard to the "funds destined for our *personnel*" applies the King's privy purse to this payment; and truly the King would prefer to pay them from his privy purse were he able to provide them. But this special application—a matter of indifference to M. de Baras, since it little matters to him whence the money comes so long as he is paid—would be detrimental to the King's interest, since it would give rise to the belief that the King proposed to have an enormous privy purse, and to make it serve clandestinely the extravagances of which the public complained previous to 1789. As it is necessary to forestall this opinion, which would be false in itself and fatal to the King, the payment must be made in a general fashion from all the coffers ordinary and extraordinary, as stated in the course of Article 9 of the draft.

The whole of the correspondence brought by M. Guérin was at once laid before the Directorate; it unfolded, in lieu of an attempt to save the Republic, a plan to destroy it by the most infamous of all corruptions. The Directorate summoned my secretary

Botot, whose name had been used. Botot denied all connection with the matter. Fouché caused the arrest of Monnier, the correspondent of Wesel. Documents incriminating him were found at his residence; an official report was drawn up. After keeping Monnier in close confinement and subjecting him to several interrogatories, Fouché laid before the Directorate a detailed report of the procedure, adding: "All I have been able to obtain from the wretch is a flood of tears and a confession of having taken part in a negotiation which he did not think was criminal, and from which, without hoping for its success, he expected pecuniary help which would rescue himself and his family from poverty." Fouché proposed in conclusion that David Monnier should be set free and placed under the supervision of the high police. Fouché stated also that he had personally ascertained that the dwelling of Monnier as well as its tenants presented an appearance of most genuine distress. The Directorate adopted the deductions of the Minister of Police. The whole of the foregoing was recorded in the secret register of the Directorate.

Such is the exact truth in regard to my relations with the Court of Mittau in those days, and in regard to my alleged relations with Louis XVIII. I shall have occasion to speak of the matter more fully when I come to the portion of my Memoirs corresponding with the year 1819. What may be stated at this point is that every Power of Europe which had trusted Fauche-Borel was shamefully and foolishly deceived by the credulity of the adventurer, equalled only by his knavery. The Powers associated with this machination were fooled and thwarted by the unanimity of the members of the Directorate, whose political probity was in no wise accessible to the advances of kings. As regards myself, could they for a moment believe that as pledged a Republican as I was, conqueror at the siege of Toulon, on the 9th Thermidor, on the 13th Vendémiaire, and on the 18th Fructidor—that the man raised to the dignity of member of the Government of the Republic would also belie the character and the honor he had always professed and maintained in so many combats?

The result of this first mission of M. Guérin was the beginning of a great success. It could not be ignored that it was due to the primary instructions so carefully laid down by Talleyrand. M. Guérin had brought to us the Letters-Patent of Louis XVIII., which revealed the thoughts and hopes of the Pretender. He had repeated to us all the effusive utterances of Fauche-Borel, revealing the development of the Bourbonist combination. The Directorate could thus at once lay hands upon the whole affair, the money, and the persons themselves; for the thoughts resulting from the step taken and the discussion of the affair proved that nothing was so easy of accomplishment as to induce, or rather to allow, to come into the net of this deception the most august personages. They would have come as far as the frontier, and even crossed it.

As for myself, however determined might be my patriotism and the fixity of my Republican principles, I confess that they did not go as far as to push things to so horrible a piece of treachery. The first part, which consisted in accepting the money of the corrupting Cabinets, and of putting it to a use the publication of which might, as a consequence, have left corrupters and corrupted less reassured—this first part seemed to me fair game. The result would do nobody any harm, and it was certainly a way of doubly assuring the incorruptibility necessary to the functionaries of all grades to whom were intrusted the guarding and defending of the Republic. As to the idea of seizing upon the persons of the Bourbons themselves drawn into the trap, there were only priests coldly vindictive and implacable, such as Sieyès, Fouché, and Talleyrand, to whom such an infamy might seem amusing.

It has been said, on several occasions subsequent to this, that Talleyrand had shown himself the avowed enemy of the Bourbons; that he had advised Bonaparte "to place between them and himself a river of blood"; that when Bonaparte had followed this advice, and had revealed his intention of sending the Duc d'Enghien to his death, Talleyrand had not only participated in the deed, but that he had been the first instigator, its decisive and ironical counsellor. I have in this respect nothing but the assertions of contemporary historians, to whom Talleyrand has thought it beneath his dignity to reply. What I know personally is that in the present affair concerning the Bourbons, when some wished to draw the principals across the frontier, in order perhaps to send them to their death, or at the very least to hold them as hostages, Talleyrand considered nothing too audacious, nothing too revolutionary against those he called the irreconcilable enemies of France. I have already pointed out the possible reason, but not the excuse, for Talleyrand's conduct; when stating that all his actions had for their object his remaining a Minister. Ever since he had been one, and previous to the present provocation, Talleyrand had offered and given to the Directorate statistics of the Bourbons in and beyond Europe. The d'Orléans branch was in no wise excepted, but it was not in Europe; it will be remembered that it had gone to America. Already in several anterior reports had Talleyrand informed us as to the exact situation of the princes of the House of Bourbon, from one end to the other. He was indeed in those days the Minister who pronounced himself most openly against the Bourbons. He had suggested, as the simplest matter and as "a Republican epigram upon royalty," the idea of laying hands on these unfortunate wanderers from town to town, and at the time outcasts from everywhere. "On the present occasion, if they could be drawn to Wesel with their agents, there would be," according to Talleyrand, "nothing easier than to seize upon them and convey them to France, where they should be dealt with according to what the Directorate might decide." He called this "a splendid haul, one by which all the fish would be caught at once." It is not to me that it will be given to follow, or even to see the sequel to this affair, which will again return to Talleyrand when he shall himself return to the Ministry, and about which he will take good care not to give any explanations, which explanations I shall be compelled to furnish myself as a result of the injustice of the wicked supported by the ignorance of the crowd. It will soon be seen how important it has been to plant here the first landmarks of truth.

END OF VOL. III